THINKING ABOUT GOD IN AN AGE
OF TECHNOLOGY

Thinking About God in an Age of Technology

GEORGE PATTISON

OXFORD
UNIVERSITY PRESS

OXFORD
UNIVERSITY PRESS

Great Clarendon Street, Oxford OX2 6DP
Oxford University Press is a department of the University of Oxford.
It furthers the University's objective of excellence in research, scholarship,
and education by publishing worldwide in

Oxford New York

Auckland Cape Town Dar es Salaam Hong Kong Karachi
Kuala Lumpur Madrid Melbourne Mexico City Nairobi
New Delhi Shanghai Taipei Toronto

With offices in

Argentina Austria Brazil Chile Czech Republic France Greece
Guatemala Hungary Italy Japan Poland Portugal Singapore
South Korea Switzerland Thailand Turkey Ukraine Vietnam

Oxford is a registered trade mark of Oxford University Press
in the UK and in certain other countries

Published in the United States
by Oxford University Press Inc., New York

© George Pattison, 2005

The moral rights of the author have been asserted
Database right Oxford University Press (maker)

First published 2005

British Library Cataloguing in Publication Data

Data available

Library of Congress Cataloging in Publication Data

Data available

Typeset by SPI Publisher Services, Pondicherry, India
Printed in Great Britain
on acid-free paper by Biddles Ltd., King's Lynn

ISBN 0-19-927977-2   978-0-19-927977-7

1 3 5 7 9 10 8 6 4 2

Acknowledgements

The ideas that now find expression in this book first took shape in a lecture reworked through several presentations in the De Montfort University Chaplaincy Centre (Leicester), University College Dublin, and the Theological Society of Aarhus University. I am grateful to those who organized those events and those whose questions helped clarify my own thinking. Other parts of the book had outings at the 2003 Art and Christianity Enquiry conference in St Petersburg and at the 2004 conference on Theological Aesthetics at St Bonaventure's University, New York. Again, I am grateful to the organizers and participants in those events for their constructive involvement. Various parts of the book have been read over or discussed with colleagues, chiefly in the Department of Systematic Theology in Aarhus University, and I am especially grateful for the help I received from Niels-Henrik Gregersen, Niels Grønkjaer, Kies van Kooten Niekerk, Troels Nørager, and Peter Widmann. Anne Runehov helped me with the references to Persinger's mystic helmet. A first draft of the whole manuscript was read by Jessica Frazier, whose student's-eye view has, I hope, contributed to the final work being more reader-friendly than it might otherwise have been. Oxford University Press's readers made useful comments, and I am especially grateful to the positive input given by John D. Caputo. My editor, Lucy Qureshi, has been constantly supportive and helpful. Thank you to Jennifer Smith for photocopying.

Edwin Muir's poem, 'The Transfiguration', is reproduced by permission of Faber and Faber Ltd. and of Oxford University Press New York.

George Pattison
Oxford
March 2005

Contents

Introduction: Technology's Question to Theology

Why and in what way could or should theology be concerned with technology? Surely technology does not challenge the truth of theology in the manner of Darwinism or Marxism or Freudianism or postmodernism? Surely a religious believer can drive a car, fly in a plane, or use the internet without any of these things being seen as inconsistent with the life of faith? Isn't technology simply an ensemble of tools and instruments that is morally, ideologically, and religiously neutral? And if, from time to time, a particular form of technology threatens to get out of control or to diminish rather than to enhance the quality of life, isn't that something to be dealt with on a case by case basis, using the resources of ethical reflection, democracy and science itself to bring the situation back under control?

This is certainly how things have been understood. To be sure, there have been any number of popular and academic theologies dealing with the relationship between religion and science, between religion and politics, and between religion and ethics. These debates have often involved issues centred on particular technical applications (nuclear weapons, stem cell research, etc.), but technology as such has rarely been thematized as the matter of theological reflection. There are some exceptions, which will be discussed in Chapter 2, but for the most part theologians' comments about technology (when not focused on particular concrete problems) have assumed rather than argued for the positions they take—as in Matthew Fox's comment that, since the seventeenth century, 'religion has become privatized and science a violent employee of technology'.[1] This is presented as a self-evident fact—which, of course, it isn't. As we shall see, this neglect of thinking around the question of technology reflects a deep-seated element in theology's own self-understanding, but, whatever the reasons, it has left a gaping hole in theological literature—and precisely at a point where, as seems more and more certain, the future of humanity itself is at stake.

In saying this, I do not mean to invoke one or other nightmare apocalyptic scenario in which we collectively self-destruct through nuclear, biological, or some as yet unimagined form of warfare, or that we render our planet uninhabitable before we are ready to colonize other worlds. Such scenarios are by no means impossible, indeed they are real possibilities, but (at the time of writing at least) not immediately probable.[2] More elusive, but no less thought-provoking,

---

[1] M. Fox, *Original Blessing: A Primer in Creation Spirituality* (Santa Fe: Bear, 1983), 10.

[2] Even though an eminent scientist such as Sir Martin Rees can confidently predict a one-million-death catastrophe within the next twenty years as the result of 'bioterror or bioerror'. The reader is able to place bets on this prediction at *http://www.longbets.org/rules*!

is the sense that, catastrophes apart, humanity is already being changed by the impact of technologies it has itself devised. This change may or may not go so far as to bring about a biological mutation in the species *homo sapiens,* but it has already penetrated deeply into our social and psychological sensibilities, making us feel differently about who we are and, therewith, influencing the way in which we act upon our environment and ourselves. For what is perhaps most striking about contemporary technology is not simply the marvel (or horror) of one or other technical achievement—space travel, the internet, the cultivation on animals of organs for human transplants—but simply the sheer pervasiveness of technology in everyday life. Television, the mobile phone, and the internet—the 'information bomb'[3]—coupled with the seemingly irresistible expansion and sophistication of travel (above all, the car and the plane, with space tourism apparently just round the corner) make technology the omnipresent medium and condition of contemporary living. As an advertisement for one mobile phone company put it, 'I have my world in the palm of my hand and I take it with me wherever I go.' Although (as I recall) the image accompanying these words was one of waves crashing onto the rocky shore of a desert island, the message was clearly not that we should escape technology for the sake of life on such an island but that there is now nowhere we can or would want to be that is outside the global communications network. There is enough truth in this message to make it virtually impossible for us to take seriously any idea that we can or should simply want to get rid of technology. Of course, I want the computer systems that manage my bank and credit-card accounts to be sophisticated enough to resist criminal hackers; when I fly on a plane, I am reassured by the thought that those who have designed and made it and those who maintain and operate it all do so to the best possible technical standards; when I am taken into hospital, I certainly do not want malfunctioning equipment to be deployed in mending, replacing, or restoring this or that bodily part or function. Technology is with us wherever we go and we simply cannot escape it. If by some fantastic sequence of events all the governments of the world were to unite in renouncing technology (whatever that might involve), the enacting of that renunciation would call for careful technical management over many generations—even in a world without terrorism a nuclear-power station or a chemical factory cannot just be abandoned to the elements without entailing risks at least as serious as having them in operation. De-technologizing would paradoxically confront us with one of the greatest technological challenges of all.

It must be stressed that the issue is not simply that technology has become the all-encompassing environment of human living. Technology is not merely a cultural fact with which we have to reckon, it permeates the way in which we experience and understand both the world and ourselves. When it is said 'I have my world in the palm of my hand and I take it with me wherever I go' this is not

---

[3] See, e.g. P. Virilio, *The Information Bomb* (London: Verso, 2000).

only a statement about technology, it is a statement about the self-image and the identity of the person using it: as the originators, the users, and the objects of technology, we can no longer push the question of technology to the periphery of our thinking, as if it were a mere supplement to the 'real' questions of science, questions one used to see in book-titles along the lines of 'Man's Place in the Universe'. 'Man's place in the universe' is no longer something we can realistically conceive of as some kind of fact, waiting out there to be described and evaluated: it is something we ourselves are constructing and transforming through a technology that can no longer be regarded as 'merely' an instrument intervening between ourselves and our environment. Precisely with reference to an understanding of the present age as an age of technology, the Catholic philosopher Romano Guardini wrote in his *Letters from Lake Como* (subtitled 'Explorations in Technology and the Human Race') that 'Our age is not just an external path we tread; it is ourselves.'[4] In other words, technology is not just something that mediates between our mental intentions and the physical world about us, technology gets inside our heads and affects the very way in which we conceive our reality. It has become inseparable from the way we ourselves are, a thought reflected in such technological myths as *The Matrix* or in Teilhard de Chardin's image of the planetization of consciousness as the 'noosphere', which he described as a global membrane of consciousness brought into being by the processes of human evolution and which, he thought, was finding its 'eye', that is, its capacity for self-vision and self-direction, through the most recent development of technology.[5]

The positive possibilities of such developments inspire utopian advocates (Teilhard himself was one such) as well as attracting the serious money of the corporations and governments that are investing in it. Equally there are those who see in it a danger to the very concept and existence of humanity. These critics do not see technological planetization as consciousness finding its all-illuminating eye but rather as an event whose magnitude has cast an impenetrable shadow over human reason itself. It is arguable that it is also changing the nature of science. Paul Virilio, who has drawn attention to the perils of technology in a long string of books and articles, writes of 'the fatal confusion between the operational instrument and explanatory research',[6] which, as he sees it, result in the situation that 'Science, which was once a rigorous field thriving on intellectual adventure, is today bogged down in a technological adventurism that denatures it.'[7] Scientists may or may not recognize in this a fair comment on the state of their collective undertaking (and it would probably play differently in different branches and contexts of science), but whatever the underlying implications

[4] R. Guardini, *Letters from Lake Como: Explorations in Technology and the Human Race,* tr. G. W. Bromiley (Grand Rapids: Eerdmans, 1994), 81.
[5] See P. T. de Chardin, *The Phenomenon of Man* (London: Collins, 1959), 200 ff.
[6] Ibid. 1.
[7] Ibid. 3.

of the technological mindset for serious science it is clear that in the last fifteen to twenty years all previous conceptions of knowledge acquisition and knowledge transmission have been called into question, not least with regard to the way in which the daily life of universities has been transformed in almost incalculable ways by IT.

By raising such far-reaching questions about the nature of human being itself and the nature of our knowledge of the world and of ourselves, technology has become a field of ultimate and thus of religious concern: to know or not to know in the manner promoted by technology, to be or not to be the being that technology is making of us: this is now a real and urgent question for thinking as well as for political, economic, and environmental policy-making. Yet if one asks, how then can these questions *not* demand the most serious attention of Christian thinkers, one is confronted by the surprising fact that, as I have noted, they have largely been passed over by theology. What is doubly surprising in the failure of technology to establish itself as an item on the theological agenda, is that there have been a succession of theologies over the last fifty years that have urged the religious and theological community to involve itself in, and even to define itself in terms of the questions and realities of contemporary life, to become fully and unashamedly secular. In Chapter 1 we shall be examining a number of these secular theologies. Philosophy, politics, the economic order, theoretical science, gender, and culture have all been given their due by such theologies but, typically, technology features only marginally, if at all, in their account of the contemporary questions and realities that theology needs to embrace. This, I suggest, has proved to be a fatal flaw. Precisely because such theologies have sought to redefine religion and theology in terms of an analysis of contemporary or 'modern' life, the omission of what is proving itself to be the central and most dynamic element of contemporary reality—technology— means that their project is unfulfillable in its own terms. And there are further implications.

We do not need to trade in the kind of dystopic visions of the technological future brilliantly depicted in Aldous Huxley's pioneering *Brave New World* to see that if the question of technology confronts us with both a question and the need for a decision about human identity itself, then any simplistic embrace of the technological solution is immediately excluded. In other words, the kind of enthusiasm for 'modern thought' or 'the secular' that has characterized radical modern theology becomes much more problematic when repeated in the context of the question concerning technology. It is one thing to say that theology needs to get itself out of the ecclesiastical ghetto and to shed medieval or other pre-modern cosmologies and metaphysical systems in favour of a scientific and secular self-understanding, but something else again to assent to the view that there is no alternative to the future according to technology. In the former case, one could still imagine the human subject as passing relatively unchanged through the different world views it adopted in different periods of history.

'Medieval man' and 'modern man' did not differ essentially but only in the way in which they pictured the world about them. Today, however, it is a question as to the very viability of the human as we have known it hitherto—and whatever our final view or decision concerning this, it must at least give us pause for thought and challenge us to weigh the dystopic possibilities against the utopic possibilities, and to be sure of our own mind before we plunge into irreversible decisions. If it is indeed time for *homo sapiens* to lay down the bloody trophies of its historic and prehistoric past (and, let's face it, we haven't always been a very *nice* species), then let it be done with an appropriate thoughtfulness, with dignity and an acknowledgement of the enormity of what is happening. Theology needs to listen to, to understand and to articulate itself in relation to the contemporary world as never before, but this does not necessarily mean merely adapting itself to whatever it perceives to be the dominant trend of the times. Rather, it is a matter of learning to think about essential religious concerns in relation to the fact that the theologian too cannot but participate as much as anyone else in the realities and intellectual currents of his or her age.

At this point a word should be said about the relationship between this present study and the large and ever-growing field of studies, debates, and even institutions devoted to the relationship between religion and science. I have already noted that the current phase of technologization can be seen as calling into question familiar views of the relationship between theoretical science and technological application. Later we shall be examining the view of technology developed by Martin Heidegger for whom technology was by no means merely 'applied science' but the goal and, ultimately, the rationale and truth of science. Yet even if we accept that science today is inconceivable without technology, it would still seem that one cannot simply bypass the questions that theoretical science continues to pose to religion. In other words, whatever is to be said for or against technology, don't scientific views as to the origin of the universe and of the species that inhabit our small planet, along with increasingly fine-tuned scientific accounts of the relationship between the brain and the mind—don't these scientific *truths* pose questions that theology must face *before* it turns to technology? How can theology even begin to hold forth on the subject of technology when it has not yet proved its credentials as a member of the intellectual community in which and in which alone matters of science and its technological application hold sway? At the very least, it would seem necessary to at least sketch the view as to the relationship between religion and science that is presupposed in the critique of technology, if only so as to address the doubt that this critique might be a veiled rejection of the scientific world view as such. The question, I think, is fair and I shall, briefly, attempt to address it. A full answer would, of course, demand a whole other study, and what follows is no more than the merest thumbnail sketch, an indication of the direction I would take were I to attempt such a thing.

It is clear that, as previously stated, the relationship between religion and science is the focus of a large and ever-growing field of studies. Within this field a number of fairly well-trodden paths have established themselves. There are, perhaps most vociferously, those who see science as having demonstrated the theoretical poverty of religion and who therefore look forward with some eagerness to religion disappearing from the human scene. From Freud through Watson and Crick to Richard Dawkins religion has been denounced as an illusion from which humanity should rid itself as quickly and as wholeheartedly as possible. Others who largely share the basic principles of such a critique might nevertheless allow some residual function to religious practices, symbols, and texts, perhaps seeing them as operating on a par with aesthetic experience—although these nevertheless remain ultimately explicable in biological terms (something like this seems occasionally to be the view of Daniel C. Dennett). It is also possible that one can see religion as thoroughly explicable in scientific terms yet also as being, in some sense, 'a good thing'. Such could be the view of those who seek to identify the brain functions 'responsible' for mystical experiences so as to be able to stimulate them artificially.[8] Historical religions would then be seen as false accounts of what was nevertheless an important and valuable dimension of human life. A more positive role for the resources of historical religions would be found amongst those who in various ways attempt some kind of synthesis between religion and science, an attempt one sees in such well-known scientist-theologians as John Polkinghorne and Arthur Peacocke and which can, indeed, be traced back at least to early natural theologians such as Robert Boyle, John Ray, and others. Here one encounters talk of levels, kinds or dimensions of experience and explanation, and the search for interpretative structures that allow each—science and religion/theology—to have their own legitimate place within the complex pattern of cosmic and biological development. Theology, on this view, is no less 'about' reality than is science, only its concern with reality is, for now, of a different kind.[9] With different nuances, such approaches reflect the strategies identified by Ian G. Barbour as 'dialogue' and 'integration'.[10] A somewhat different model of co-existence would be found amongst those who stretch the talk of levels and dimensions to the point where there is little or no common theoretical or experiential ground between the

---

[8] See especially the work of M. Persinger. See M. A. Persinger, *The Neuropsychological Bases of God Beliefs* (New York: Praeger, 1987) and idem, 'Experimental Stimulation of the God Experience', in R. Joseph (ed.), *NeuroTheology: Brain, Science, Spirituality, Religious Experiences* (Berkeley: California University Press, 2002), 279–93.

[9] Polkinghorne, for example, writes of theology and natural science that 'both are responses to the way things are and both proceed by conjoining logical analysis with intuitive acts of judgement...they are complementary, rather than antithetic disciplines' (J. Polkinghorne, *Science and Creation: The Search for Understanding* (London: SPCK, 1988), p. xii). Peacocke similarly writes that 'A critical-realist science and theology cannot but regard themselves as mutually interacting approaches to reality' (A. Peacocke, *Theology for a Scientific Age: Being and Becoming—Natural, Divine and Human* (Oxford: Basil Blackwell, 1990), 21), though he also lays special emphasis on the increasingly complex and multilevelled nature of the 'reality' to be approached.

[10] See I. G. Barbour, *Religion and Science: Historical and Contemporary Issues* (London: SCM Press, 1998).

practice of religion and the practice of science. From the side of religion, science may then be regarded with complete equanimity as an autonomous function within the overall economy of human life that does not impinge upon the equally autonomous religious practice and experience of, e.g. worship and prayer. Barbour notes that this approach (which he calls 'independence') is characteristic of neo-orthodoxy and existentialism.[11] One could go further back and identify something similar in Schleiermacher's concern for the proper autonomy of theology, although the scientific environment in which Schleiermacher operated was very different from that which the twentieth-century theologian had to confront. Wittgenstein's idea of diverse language games that are simply incommensurable, without any of them having to be 'wrong', has also influenced recent versions of this independence strategy. Barbour cites Lindbeck's renowned 'cultural-linguistic' approach to theology as one example of this, but something similar can be seen in the otherwise very different approach to the philosophy of religion by a Wittgensteinian philosopher such as D. Z. Phillips.[12] However, as both Lindbeck and Phillips show, such an approach is likely to lead to disengagement from the dialogue with natural science, let alone any programme of integration.

Like many other Anglo-Saxon philosophers of religion I find myself strongly attracted by this last strategy, 'separate but equal' as we might call it. However, it is, I think, precisely the question concerning technology that, finally, makes it as untenable as the judicial decision that supported the segregation of whites and coloureds in the United States on the grounds that treating the races as 'separate' did not mean treating them unequally. In practice, when it came to transport, housing welfare, etc., 'separate' always meant 'inferior' as far as coloureds (to use the language of the time) were concerned. So too in the case of the relationship between science and religion. The advance of bio-technology, of pharmo-psychology, and of IT make it increasingly hard to identify or to hold on to areas of social, cultural, and experiential life that are not vulnerable to colonization by science-based technology. Art dissolves into fractal geometry and even human identity becomes programmable. Even if it is characteristic for our hyper-complex society that social and intellectual life are continually being differentiated into an endless multiplicity of self-generating and self-contained systems (so that each system—technology, for example, or religious belief—can effectively be treated as incommensurable with other systems), some kind of reckoning with the boundaries and relations between such systems would seem to be essential if we are not to succumb to some kind of collective and individual schizophrenia. In our current situation a dualism that simply holds itself aloof from dialogue cannot offer anything more than a very provisional tactic for preserving a threatened intellectual species. In these terms, dualism may have been necessary and may even be necessary where the distinctiveness of religious

---

[11] Ibid. 84 ff.
[12] See, e.g. D. Z. Phillips, *Religion Without Explanation* (Oxford: Basil Blackwell, 1976).

life, experience, and understanding are threatened by a reductionist wipe-out, but it can only offer a respite, nothing more. We cannot in the long term co-inhabit a finite planetary, social, and psychological space without talking about where our diverse activities begin and end, trusting to luck that one system won't end by consuming all the rest.

If at this point one begins to talk about thinking about God as a form of thinking that is 'other' than the thinking involved in such technology, a way of thinking that in its incommensurability with technology was both able to be resistant to it and to provide a basis for rehumanizing our self-experience and self-understanding, would this mean the rejection of the science from which—historically at least—the technology we have today sprang? I think not. In examining Heidegger's view that technology reveals the truth of science, I shall emphasize that he also insisted that science and technology were only possible because they are based on a particular revelation of truth. As indicated, Heidegger himself seems to see a direct line from classical science to contemporary technology. However, even if such early representatives of the scientific spirit as the founders of the Royal Society made clear their interest in the technological applications of science, it does not follow that 'planetary technology' exhausts all the motivations and intellectual investments of theoretical science. This leaves open the possibility that a thinking that is other than the thinking of technology is open to a dialogue with science that can be sustained at a relative distance from the parallel critical dialogue with science-based technology. In any case, it is not even the case that to attempt to think otherwise than thinking technologically would have to be hostile to technology, even if the tension implied in the phrase 'other than' is, in this instance, likely to be even greater than the tension involved in the dialogue with theoretical science. For whereas those working in the more theoretical branches of science are often ready to accept the possibility of discourses other than their own, our experience of technology is that its agents seem to feel no such limitations. What can be done will be done, and technological innovation constantly outstrips the efforts of philosophers, moralizers, and law-makers to keep up with it. This not only heightens the tension in any attempted dialogue, it also increases the urgency of making a beginning. Therefore, whilst one can conceive of a theological critique of technology that *first* established its relation to theoretical science and *from there* moved on to draw up its accounting of technology, all I shall undertake here is a more modest 'thought experiment' in which I attempt to see what a thinking about God that is other than the thinking that comes to fruition in technology might be *like*.

At this point, a word should also be said about the term 'theology'. Several years ago I wrote a book called *The End of Theology and the Task of Thinking about God*.[13] In some senses the present work is a sequel to that book, going

[13] G. Pattison, *The End of Theology—And the Task of Thinking about God* (London: SCM Press, 1998).

further into the situation in which we are today to think about God. Although I have already used the word 'theology' and will, from time to time, continue to do so in this present book, I remain troubled by it, sensing that it already sets thinking about God on a wrong track. This is partly because it implicitly sets the direction of thinking about God in terms of a set of coordinates drawn from the specific history that makes 'theology' what it is. Certainly I do not wish to dismiss the past or to deny that we can learn from it, but precisely in its relation to science and technology 'theology' as we have known it in the past has too often functioned as a constraining and deadening force, blinding us to issues, perspectives and methods that are of much greater urgency than what sometimes become merely antiquarian glass-bead games. 'Theology' today has need of a freedom that the very connotations of 'theology' seem to deny. If there is to be anything like theology at all in our time and in the future, then it cannot be the mere defence or revivification of some ancient paradigm of thought, but a living, thinking attempt to think through and articulate what God (or Christ, or prayer, or any other 'theological' topic) could possibly mean for beings living through the new axial age we are currently experiencing. The past can become available to us as a resource in confronting the question of technology and we can benefit from being open to the concrete life of tradition, but we need not go to meet it as those who are concerned to defend or promote a given 'theology', Catholic, Protestant, traditionalist, or modernist.

No less importantly, it may be that the underlying idea of a field of expert discourse that the term 'theology' implies, already points to a submerged congruence between the idea of theology and the agenda of technology. Theologians would, on this view, take the role of experts or knowledge-managers in relation to humanity's religious life, adjudicators of what can or can't be believed or said about God. Whether theology is or needs to be experienced as some sort of scientific expertise is a question to which I shall return in Chapter 8. For the present, I simply add that the question of what 'theology' is or has become is, for us, inseparable from the question as to the nature, style, and purpose of the contemporary technological university and, I suggest, it is an open question whether a kind of thinking about God that allows for the role of existential questions of salvation, worship, and obedience can realistically retain a place in a community where knowledge is constructed in accordance with the technological paradigm and therefore in such a way as precisely to exclude the existential concern for such things from counting as 'knowledge'.

None of this, it should be added, is to imply that all of those who are currently happy to profess themselves to be 'theologians' are either rigid traditionalists or covert technologists or that they are incapable of or uninterested in 'thinking about God' (my preferred expression). It is simply to flag the danger of allowing usage and familiarity to conceal assumptions and directives that we may wish to hold open in the face of certain decisive questions. What it means to think about God in the light and shadow of an age of technology, we do not yet know.

We are only just beginning to face the question. How can we *know* where it will lead?

The development of my argument is divided into three parts. In the first (Chapters 1–3), I begin in Chapter 1 by offering a survey of the secular theologies of the 1960s–1980s. Here I note that despite their proclaimed intention of coordinating theology with the secular world there was a striking absence of any significant concern for the question of technology, one of the most salient features of the secular world itself. Chapter 2 also has the character of a survey, only this time it is a survey of a number of twentieth-century theologies that explicitly addressed the question concerning technology. These are mostly seen to argue either for a kind of subordinationism, in which technology is acceptable as long as it can be subordinated to the theoretical or moral perspectives of doctrine, or else for outright opposition (a position chiefly represented by Jacques Ellul, also—interestingly—the most prolific theological writer on the subject). However, the kind of critique of traditional theology found amongst the thinkers surveyed in Chapter 1 makes subordinationism problematic: where theology itself is in crisis it is scarcely in a position to give direction to such a large and complex human undertaking as technology. On the other hand, the kind of rejection of technology seen in Ellul offers virtually nothing for us to think about or do that might contribute to a creative response to the problems posed by technology. The enquiry therefore turns in Chapter 3 to Heidegger's formulation of the question concerning technology, one of the main themes of the second half of his philosophical career. Although there is a negative tone to much that Heidegger says about technology, he is unlike Ellul in that he does offer us some possibilities of responding creatively to the technological challenge. These are chiefly centred on his strategy of pursuing a kind of truth-oriented thinking that can complement the ideas that have led western philosophy and science to find their fulfilment in technology. Poets such as Hölderlin are given a key role in opening our minds to what such thinking might be like. This may seem rather a weak response to the colossal force of contemporary technology and it is clear that thinking of the kind Heidegger proposes can have no direct impact on our management of technology (of course, we should not immediately assume that, in this context, 'weak' equals 'bad' or 'mistaken').

Nevertheless, I suggest that Heidegger highlights how technology itself is intertwined with forms of intellectual culture in which these kinds of issues have a legitimate and even an important place. Could thinking about God find a foothold at this point? Heidegger's own reading of the history of ideas suggests that classical theism is deeply compromised in the culture of technology and, in line with some of the theologians discussed in Chapter 1, he asserts that the God of classical theism must die. Yet he does not claim that all possibilities of thinking about God are thereby exhausted. In the three chapters of Part II, therefore, I take up the question of whether there is a kind of thinking about God that does not fall prey to the critique of philosophy and technology we have heard from Heidegger and, if so, what this might be like. Key themes that emerge in Chapters 4, 5, and 6 are the freedom, patience, and joy required for such thinking (Chapter 4), the subjunctive, paratactic, and equivocal characteristics of the language in which it finds expression (Chapter 5), and (in Chapter 6) the need of a vision that does not fix its object in the manner described by Heidegger as 'enframing', in which he locates the essence of the technological mindset. In Part III, I pursue the question as to how such thinking might relate to concrete problems of the technological society as these are refracted in the ethical challenges of the new biology, the technological orientation of the contemporary university, and the possibilities for art of what Walter Benjamin called 'the age of mechanical reproducibility'. After a short summary and conclusion, the epilogue sketches an essayistic response to the city as the most complex three-dimensional realization of the essence of technology.

The general shape of the enquiry might thus seem to correspond to Tillich's call for a 'theology of correlation', in which the questions of the day are reformulated and answered according to the perspectives of theology. There are echoes of this in the method I am pursuing here and I would certainly be happy to acknowledge a kinship with Tillich's looser formulation of an 'answering theology', in the sense of a theology that listens to and addresses the questions of the non-theological world. However, I do not offer thinking about God as 'the answer' to 'the question' of the age of technology. There is a correlation, to be sure, but not of such a kind that theology is presumed to supply an 'answer' to the practical problems generated by the negative aspects of technology. And I should reiterate that my aim is not to oppose technology but, precisely, to offer a theological response that is properly critical. I certainly do not want to indulge in the pseudo-Heideggerian jargon of 'overcoming' technology which, apart from its unhelpful polemical tone, can only obscure the issue as to how, in reality, we are actually to go on living good human lives in an age that is and that will for a long time to come continue to be an age of technology. As such, my aim is more to open dimensions of thought and reflection that might help sustain the rich diversity and aspirations towards wholeness of human life in this technological age that, to use again the words of Guardini, 'is ourselves'.

PART I

THE QUESTION

1

The Long Goodbye

In the last hundred or more years, one of the most prevalent assumptions about the changing relationship between religion and society has been summed up in the word: 'secularization'. As seen in the lens of the secularizing thesis, the West has been undergoing a centuries-long transition from a situation in which religion provided the unifying force connecting all social, cultural, intellectual, and metaphysical pursuits to one in which religion is, at most, only one among many forms of life in a pluralistic world—or, as some versions of the thesis would have it, in which religion has altogether 'withered away', leaving human beings to manage their world and themselves without the assistance of other-worldly beings of any kind. This period, in other words, has been a 'long goodbye' to God or, as the writer A. N. Wilson put it, 'God's funeral'.

There have, inevitably, been various versions of the secularization thesis, and it has been propounded in very different tones. In its early formulations, as in one reading of Hegel's philosophy of history, secularization was merely a transitional period that would lead to a reintegration of humanity's manifold practical and theoretical commitments in a form appropriate to the modern world, with religion itself being an essential part of the final picture. That aspiration was badly battered by the critical generations following Hegel who interpreted secularization as a historical or moral end in its own right, to be embraced and promoted as a matter of the highest urgency. Such was the passionate atheistic humanism of a Feuerbach, a Marx, a Freud, and many a scientific humanist of the Anglo-Saxon establishment. Others, notably Catholic apologists for the medieval Ages of Faith, accepted the secularization thesis as a *de facto* reality, but denied both its legitimacy and its necessity. Far from seeing it as a sign of progress, they regarded secularization as responsible for the fragmentation of life and the proliferation of all manner of social and psychological woes. We cannot hope immediately to recreate the medieval synthesis of religion and culture, but we can and should work towards turning the tide of the secular, they declared. Yet each decade that passes seems to make any thought of turning the tide that much harder, and many for whom the advent of a thoroughly secular world is accompanied by a sense of disenchantment and of a certain moral and cultural loss can no longer re-animate the old beliefs. Perhaps, it has been thought, art might partially restore life's fading aura, but art itself seems somehow caught up in the same inexorable process that has been robbing religion of its erstwhile power to bind heart, mind, and hand. The vision of a unified religious culture may haunt the margins of modernity, but cannot, it seems, be more for us than a matter of bittersweet nostalgia.

If one turns from generalizations to concrete historical analysis, the application of the secularization thesis is by no means straightforward, and at many points the reality of modern history has been downright ambiguous. Was the Holocaust a revelation of the reality of a world without God, of a scientific-technical mechanization of life that reduced human beings to the status of products on a conveyor belt of death? Or was it the fruit of centuries of religion itself, a hatred fostered by both Catholic and Protestant Churches in their depiction of Jews as God-murderers? Was Hitler's seduction of the German people made possible by his appropriation of the religious imagery and vocabulary of Messiahship and salvation? Or was his success down to the fact that, as the film director Hans Jürgen Syberberg put it, he was 'the greatest film star of the twentieth century', i.e. the first major political leader to have an intuitive understanding of the effectiveness of modern mass media? Similar questions could be asked about Soviet Communism or about the role of so-called fundamentalist Islam—is this latter an expression of an essentially conservative religious opposition to the secularization of life (as its own rhetoric suggests), or is it itself a product of inappropriate forms of modernization driven by the exigencies of a global capitalism that have systematically failed to take account of the non-economic dimensions of human flourishing (and, in this case, 'fundamentalism' may not really have very much to do with traditional Islam, least of all with the Islam of Al-Ghazzali, 'Ibn Rushd, or other great Muslim thinkers, scientists, and poets)?

Secularization is not, of course, a simple fact. Rather, the secularization thesis is essentially a contribution to theory, a way of viewing and explaining a multiplicity of facts, events, movements, and counter-movements, as well as a way of organizing our ideas and making them available for social and political judgements. Nevertheless, simply as a theory, it has itself been a powerful element in modern culture and, as we shall see, modern theology. In taking this thesis as my point of departure, then, I am not accepting it as true, but simply acknowledging its importance and, especially, its importance for a powerful current of modern thinking about God. Although this current—we might call it 'radical theology'—has by no means been universally accepted it does highlight a set of problems with which other forms of theology have also had to reckon. In particular it brings into focus the way in which modern theology lives with the peculiar tensions inherent in the fact that, on the one hand, it belongs to the 'secular' world of the contemporary university, whilst, on the other, it belongs (or, until very recently, has belonged) to the 'religious' world of the Church or other religious communities (such as the Synagogue). I shall later argue that this double contextualization is itself fruitful and even a requirement for serious thinking about God, reflecting both the truth claims of such thinking and its personal religious importance for individuals and communities. But whilst this can be read as an argument against what might be seen as the reduction of theology to religious studies or to just one more humanistic discipline, it is by no means an argument for the status quo of twenty years ago. Instead, a recognition of the necessary double-contextualization of thinking about God will, I shall suggest, oblige us to do some creative rethinking about the institutionalization of such thinking, which, in turn, has further implications for its social, cultural and, even, ecclesiastical profile.[1]

But this is to run on ahead of my own argument. I begin, then, with a brief review of a very particular strand within the larger movement of 'radical theology'. Although I emphasize that this is only one part of a highly diversified field, it has had a very significant influence in theology generally and even on the wider public debate about religion. At several points the issues it has raised have become matters of considerable public interest and debate, perhaps most famously in the 1966 *Time* magazine cover whose dramatic graphics posed the question 'Is God Dead?' Forty years on, the debate continues. It is, of course, by no means the case that radical theology has swept aside all opposition in the Church and the academy, and its opponents in a variety of traditions and schools are by no means all intransigent conservatives, let alone theological or philosophical lightweights. Nevertheless, the phenomenon of radical theology tells us a lot about the fate of religion and theology in the twentieth century and, therefore, about where we stand now, at the beginning of the twenty-first. To readers who can scarcely control their impulse to stop reading the moment they hear that radical theology is being taken seriously I have to say that although I *do* regard some of the claims of radical theology as having become part of our common intellectual horizon, I *do not* believe that, as a movement in ideas, it was finally able to deliver what, once, it seemed to promise. This, I shall claim, is, in large part, due to its inadequate treatment of the question concerning technology. For, surprisingly, although technology is an inescapable feature of the modern world that the radicals urged their readers to embrace, it is only rarely and fitfully discussed in the canon of modern secular theology.

It should be clear that my focus is very much on theology and on what theologians have had to say about thinking about God. Even if in some cases they seem merely to be repeating what secularizing critics have already said more brutally, it is important, for good or ill, that theology itself has internalized the secular argument. And it is important not only for those who have the task of teaching religion in our universities but, because of the singular role and status of the modern university, it is important for the view of religion in society as a whole. My survey is intended to be characteristic rather than exhaustive; that is, it will focus on a selection of examples that may stand for the whole, with a particular emphasis on the British debate in the post-war period, an emphasis

---

[1] See Chapter 8, 'Cyberversity or University?', below.

that inevitably reflects my own intellectual and cultural background. Precisely at this point, however, British theology has proved itself (for once) to be far from insular: in its early stages, the discussion drew heavily on modern German theology; in the mid-1960s the discussion took on a more transatlantic hue, whilst in the 1980s and 1990s it was the French connection that came to the fore. This may be said to reflect something about the secularization debate itself: that whilst it relates to large-scale developments across the industrialized world (and now, in the age of globalization, that means simply: across the world), the balance of forces in society at large and in the academic discussion is always configured very specifically in each country. Even within a region such as Europe, with a high level of social and cultural (not to mention economic and political) convergence, there can be significant variations on the central theme.

The longer-term background to the debate that found a *cause célèbre* in John Robinson's *Honest to God*, published in March 1963, could be said to stretch back to the early modern period and the beginnings of the Anglican Latitudinarian tradition, which sought to hold together the ideas of the early scientific revolution with classical Christian belief. But although it is mildly appealing to see Robinson in a tradition of 'liberal' Cambridge theologians already recognizable in the seventeenth century, his more immediate inspiration was in such radical modern German theologians as Rudolf Bultmann, Dietrich Bonhoeffer, and Paul Tillich. These in turn are partly to be understood against the background of a nineteenth- and twentieth-century German discussion in which the radical critique of religion found in Feuerbach, Marx, Nietzsche, and Freud powerfully interacted with the broad stream of liberal theology that, following F. D. E. Schleiermacher, the greatest theologian of the romantic period, was itself concerned to emphasize the human meaning and value of religion. From the radically humanist standpoint of a Feuerbach, writing in the 1840s, religion was nothing but the projection into an imaginary other world of what human beings believed to be the highest values. To say 'God is love', according to Feuerbach, is merely to say that love is the highest of all human values. The rituals of baptism and communion are merely affirmations of the central importance in human life of washing, eating, and drinking. Once this is known, all we need to do is shed the theological superstructure and reclaim these truths and values as our own. Feuerbach's thought was given a more revolutionary twist by Marx, translated both linguistically and intellectually into English by George Eliot, and also taken up into the militant nihilism of early Russian revolutionary thought. Even though Nietzsche was to offer a far more sophisticated and ultimately more damaging (because more sensitive) critique of religion, Feuerbach's basic principle was one of the central pillars on which subsequent modern Continental atheism was constructed. The cry that 'God is dead!' that Nietzsche was to make his own, was to all intents and purposes a leitmotif of modernist thought from the first half of the nineteenth century onwards.

None of the thinkers who so influenced Robinson—Bultmann, Tillich, and Bonhoeffer—would have accepted that God was dead, but they were attuned to the pathos and the force of Nietzsche's declaration. Even if they were rooted in the nineteenth-century tradition of liberal theology, with its characteristic conflation of the human and the divine (often under the designation of 'Spirit'), they realized (as the nineteenth-century liberals did not) that there was an urgent need to distinguish between the human elements of religion and its transcendent referent if religion (or faith) was to have anything significant to say.

Tillich, picking up the mantle of nineteenth-century idealism, declared that the only non-symbolic statement that could be made about God was that God was Being-Itself. Everything else, he argued, was symbolic and all symbols, even the most treasured, live and die and, once dead, cannot be artificially re-animated. The modern age has to accept that the symbolism of God as a personal individual being, supreme ruler of the universe, belongs to a hierarchical view of the world that we no longer inhabit. If God is to become real for modern human beings it cannot be on the basis of a merely rational theism and still less on the basis of ecclesiastical or social authority. God can only be existentially real for us on the basis of our own experience of the depth of existence that rationalism cannot explain and symbolism cannot exhaust. It is a paradoxical precondition of experiencing the power of God that we accept that all ideas and images of God are culturally variable. God is no longer Lord or King but the Ground of our Being and the issue of religion is not whether we 'believe' in God but whether we can find the 'courage to be' in our own lives, despite the threat of meaninglessness that especially afflicts us in our time.

Bultmann, writing primarily as a New Testament scholar, was more specifically concerned with the problems clustered around the challenge of preaching the gospel message of salvation in Christ to modern ears. He argued that the act of proclamation could be separated from its historically conditioned casing in the thought-world of the first century. We no longer live in a mythical three-decker universe in which heaven is situated above us and hell below. Nor do we live in a world in which magic or miracles can be appealed to as the causes of events. In one of his most condensed formulations he asserted that we cannot use the electric light and believe in the New Testament world of demons and miracles. Nevertheless, it remains possible for us to translate the world view of the New Testament into modern terms. Instead of talking about the flesh and the spirit as two realms under the authority of hostile cosmic powers we can understand them as pointing to two possibilities of human existence, in one of which (the flesh) we are alienated from our own possibilities (lost to ourselves, so to speak) whilst in the other we become capable of authentic self-commitment. The redemption of which the Gospel speaks is not to be understood as redemption from the evil one or from an evil cosmos but as redemption from the dead weight of a past that inhibits us from existing in the present and being open to the future. This is a redemption whose possibility is ever again awakened in Christian preaching, and

it is this that the Church's message should be aimed at rather than the perpetu-
ation of a redundant mythology.

For Bonhoeffer, whose writings have acquired an added authority in the light
of his martyr-like execution at the hands of Germany's Nazi regime, the key issue
seems to be the nature of Christian existence in the world. Bonhoeffer wants to
affirm that 'Man' has 'come of age' and that secularity is an ineluctable attribute
of this coming of age. The Church should not be trying to make people religious
but should itself be prepared to promote a model of living in the world 'as if God
did not exist'. Critical of theologians like Tillich who wanted to use contemporary Europeans' anxiety about the meaning of their lives as a point of contact for
Christian apologetic, Bonhoeffer wanted us to be able to affirm the meaningfulness of modern life in its own terms. The challenge was not flight from the world
but the practice of a radical discipleship in the world in which we responsibly
take upon ourselves the commitment of Jesus Christ's way of living as the man-
for-others.

Although experienced by many as strange and shocking at the time, such
themes were taken up into and made accessible for popular debate in Britain by
Bishop John A. T. Robinson's *Honest to God*, a book whose success (even if it was
a *succès de scandale*) is indicated by its sales of well over a million copies and the
fact that it has remained almost constantly in print since 1963. The core of
Robinson's argument (and the core issue in the debate his book generated) was
probably in his assertion that although Christianity no longer thinks of God as
'up there' in a geographical or cosmic sense it still speaks about God as if he is in
some metaphysical sense 'out there', i.e. not a part of the world we really live in.
'But,' Robinson asks bluntly,

suppose such a super-Being 'out there' is really only a sophisticated version of the Old
Man in the sky? . . . Suppose that the atheists are right—but that is no more the end or
denial of Christianity than the discrediting of the God 'up there' . . . Suppose that all such
atheism does is destroy an idol, and that we can and must get on without a God 'out there'
at all? . . . Perhaps after all the Freudians are right, that such a God—the God of
traditional popular theology—*is* a projection, and perhaps we are being called to live
without that projection in any form.[2]

The only kind of holiness that has any purchase today, Robinson insists, is a
'worldly holiness' that does not seek to separate itself from the world but to live in
it with a radical commitment to others.

Many of Robinson's readers did not like what they read. That a self-confessed
atheist such as Feuerbach could speak of our image of God as a projection of
human ideals was one thing, and that German theologians whom no one outside
university circles read could say similar things was also to be reluctantly endured,
but that a very publicly committed Christian theologian could say essentially the

² J. A. T. Robinson, *Honest to God* (London: SCM Press, 1963), 19–20.

same thing seemed incomprehensible. As one colonel wrote to Robinson: 'This book does little more than to quote from the heretical outpourings of Bonhoeffer, Tillich, and other alien agnostics. What little more it contains serves only to express in arrogant and often incomprehensible language your own pitiful lack of Faith and to undermine the Christian Ethics and belief of those who are unfortunate enough to read it and ignorant enough to be impressed by it.'[3] But it was not only irate colonels who found *Honest to God* too much to stomach. Not a few commentators from within the academy expressed an essentially similar view. Alasdair MacIntyre, for example, responded with an article beginning 'What is most striking about Dr Robinson's book is first and foremost that he is an atheist.' MacIntyre poses the following dilemma for modern theology: either it can be seen to turn itself into 'a closed circle, in which believer speaks only to believer' or else theologians translate their thought 'into the atheism of their hearers'.[4] Such religious language as we have left serves only 'to mask an atheistic vacuum', he rules.[5] As both popular and academic comments indicated, what was central to the whole debate was the question as to how far Christian theology itself was constrained by the process of secularization: whether this was merely an external force with which theology had to reckon (and which, according to some Catholic thinkers like Jacques Maritain, it had a fighting chance of reversing), or whether it was a movement so compelling, so in tune with the real order of things, that the only future for theology was to take the secular into itself.

In Britain many of Robinson's themes were developed with somewhat greater theological depth and more complex nuances by the Scottish theologian Ronald Gregor Smith, who as translator of Buber's *I and Thou*, of J. G. Hamann, and of Kierkegaard, came to the questions with a well-informed sense for the historical background of radical theology. Like Robinson, Smith was steeped in Bonhoeffer's motifs of 'man come of age' and 'secular Christianity'. But, Smith said, it was not the image of Bonhoeffer himself who best epitomized the worldliness to which Christianity was now being called. Instead it was another victim of Nazism, the aristocratic landowner and lawyer, Helmut James Graf von Moltke, executed in January 1945. Of von Moltke, Smith writes (in phrases modelled on Moltke's own letters from prison), 'He is a man of faith, and at the same time he is a man fully in this world. He does not feel at all other-worldly, and he is quite happy writing to his wife instead of turning consciously to God. He does not need to go to God, for God in his inexpressible grace has come to him. So he lives in the world, acts and joins in the responsibilities of the world, and yet he is sovereign over the world.'[6] It is, perhaps, significant that Smith chose as his

[3] J. A. T. Robinson and D. L. Edwards (eds.), *The Honest to God Debate* (London: SCM Press, 1963), 49–50.

[4] Ibid. 222–3.   [5] Ibid. 226.

[6] R. G. Smith, *Secular Christianity* (London: Collins, 1966), 17.

representative of secular faith someone who was not himself a theologian in any formal sense.[7]

A rather more spectacular development of the themes simmering in *Honest to God* was the movement that came to be known as 'the theology of the death of God'. It was this movement that provided the occasion for the above-mentioned *Time* magazine cover, and its leading representatives are generally reckoned as Thomas J. J. Altizer and William Hamilton, co-authors of *Radical Theology and the Death of God* and Paul van Buren, chiefly known through his *The Secular Meaning of the Gospel*. In many ways Altizer and Hamilton set out from the same theological landscape that formed the background of Robinson's work—Tillich, Bultmann, and Bonhoeffer are all important figures, indeed *Radical Theology and the Death of God* is dedicated to the memory of Paul Tillich. In the introductory section of the book Altizer notes that 'Tillich, in his early writing, formulated the theological criterion of contemporaneity with his thesis that a Christ who is not contemporary is not the true Christ; that a revelation which demands a leap out of history is not true revelation.'[8] However, he continues, Tillich's mature method of seeking to correlate contemporary questions with the 'answers' given by revelation, such that 'Christ is the "answer" to the *Angst* of the human condition',[9] seems to involve a retreat away from the radical historical immanentism that is intrinsic to our time's view of life and the reassertion of a more traditional theological focus on transcendence—what Robinson would call the God 'out there'. The same could be said of Bultmann. Against such mediating positions, Altizer insists that 'It is precisely the acceptance of Nietzsche's proclamation of the death of God that is the real test of a contemporary form of faith.'[10] With Dostoevsky, Blake, and tragic literature extending the hinterground of their reflections beyond the conventionally theological, the theologians of the death of God don't quite accept that they are nothing but secular humanists, using a theological language to mask an atheistic vacuum, as MacIntyre would put it. Why not?

For a start, Hamilton says, they are still, in some sense, 'waiting' on God. He is, of course, fully aware of the paradox involved in such a remark coming from one who, at the same time, proclaims the death of God. On the one hand, Hamilton writes that:

[7] Subsequent works in the British tradition of radical theology have included Alastair Kee's *The Way of Transcendence: Christian Faith without Belief in God* (Harmondsworth: Penguin, 1971) and John Kent's *The End of the Line: The Development of Christian Theology in the Last Two Centuries* (London: SCM Press, 1982). A powerful work coming out of Catholic thought and experience is Jacques Pohier's *God—in Fragments*, tr. J. Bowden (New York: Crossroad, 1986). It would, of course, be open to debate how far such recent Catholic theologians as Edward Schillebeeckx might be understood as treading a parallel path to that of the Protestant radicals.

[8] In T. J. J. Altizer and W. Hamilton, *Radical Theology and the Death of God* (Harmondsworth: Penguin, 1968), 26.

[9] Ibid.   [10] Ibid.

We have insisted all along that 'death of God' must not be taken as symbolic rhetoric for something else. There really is a sense of not-having, of not-believing, of having lost, not just the idols or the gods of religion, but God himself. And this is an experience that is not peculiar to a neurotic few, nor is it private or inward. Death of God is a public event in our history.[11]

On the other hand, Hamilton continues, 'we pray for God to return, and we seem to be willing to descend into the darkness of unfaith and doubt that something may emerge on the other side.'[12] This 'waiting', however, does not take the form of some kind of actual or metaphorical retreat up the seven-storied mountain of contemplation but 'We move to our neighbour, to the city and to the world out of a sense of the loss of God . . . And, for the time of our waiting we place ourselves with our neighbour and enemy in the world.'[13] Here, in contrast to 'sheer atheist humanism' the death of God theologians find a very positive point of contact with Christian faith which is still to be construed as 'an obedience to Jesus himself'. Even more vividly, Hamilton declares that 'Jesus is in the world as masked, and the work of the Christian is to strip off the masks of the world to find him, and, finding him, to stay with him and do his work.'[14] This programme, Hamilton admits, may be seen as 'a too simplistic marriage between Christology and ethics'—but that, he insists, is the form 'our' deprivation of God takes.

This focus on Jesus is, as the title of his book hints, also characteristic for Paul van Buren's *Secular Meaning of the Gospel*. Van Buren takes his point of departure in the largely British debate about religious language and the ability (or inability) of traditional religious language to measure up to the scientific requirement of falsifiability. Will a believer ever own up to there being a state of affairs that would render his belief false? asked Anthony Flew in such a way as to suggest the answer 'No'. On the contrary, no matter how grim the world is, whether we cite the Lisbon earthquake or the Holocaust, the believer will stick to his view that God is, nevertheless, a loving Father to all. R. M. Hare responded to this attack by suggesting that religious statements were never meant to embody cognitive claims but were expressions for precognitive assumptions about the world that guided our choice of facts and values and that could not themselves be argued for or against. For no apparent reason Hare called these assumptions 'bliks' and, perhaps unfortunately, used as an example a student who believes that all Oxford dons are out to kill him, an assumption that the student is then able to use to explain any aspect of their actual behaviour. Even their agreeable sociability is only designed to lure him into a false sense of security, it may be.

Despite its obvious drawbacks, van Buren takes Hare's idea of the 'blik' as a way of showing how the Easter event functions as the pivotal point of the New Testament's theology. Of Easter he writes that although the historian can say no more than that 'something happened' but has no reason to invoke the

---

[11] Ibid. 58.   [12] Ibid. 58.   [13] Ibid. 59–60.   [14] Ibid. 60.

supernatural, the theologian will speak of Easter faith as 'a new perspective upon life arising out of a situation of discernment focused on the history of Jesus . . . This was an experience of seeing Jesus in a *new* way and sharing in the freedom which had been his . . . we can say that Jesus' freedom from himself and freedom to be for others became contagious on Easter.'[15] There is, therefore, nothing to argue about with regard to empty tombs, bones, or the reliability of supernatural sightings. As van Buren puts it later on 'When an ordinary situation becomes an occasion of discernment for a man the change lies in the viewing, in what now becomes clear, in the light breaking; it is not an empirical change in the situation. All the physical facts remain the same, even if they can never seem quite the same to him again. This is not a metaphysical paradox; it is the expression of a change in a way of seeing.'[16] When the Christian creeds assert that Jesus Christ is true God and true man this means no more (van Buren would probably say no less) than the Christian's 'conviction that their criterion of human existence (which they have seen concretely in Jesus of Nazareth) was always the norm of human existence'—it is, in other words, simply to say that this is their most fundamental 'blik' and 'Of course a man may be converted out of one perspective into another, but as long as he has a particular "blik", the world he sees through it is for him the world as it "really" is.'[17]

From the perspective of the secularization thesis, then, the theology of the death of God suggests and illuminates the tensions, complexities and paradoxes of a transitional process. For all the radical rhetoric of unreservedly jettisoning the last remainders of ancient cosmology and fully affirming contemporary humanity's thoroughgoing secularism, for all the Nietzsche, Blake, and Ivan Karamazov, there is, after all, a point beyond which even the death of God theologians will not go. They remain, after all, *theologians*, and one way or another they want to go on speaking of God, waiting on God, doing the Christian thing. Just where the line is to be drawn, just where such a complex position separates itself from secularism and just where it must take a stand and can 'do no other' than witness to the Gospel are questions to which there are no easy answers. The only thing that is really clear is that this theology (if it could still be called that) went much too far for many conservative Christian thinkers but not nearly far enough for those humanists who felt no need to hang on to the last vestiges of loyalty to historic Christianity and who did not seem to feel the need to pass their time waiting on God.

Was it possible to go any further within theology itself without crossing the line and simply embracing Feuerbach and Nietzsche? It seems hard to think so, yet that would seem to be what happened in the series of books by Don Cupitt beginning with *Taking Leave of God* (1980).

---

[15] P. van Buren, *The Secular Meaning of the Gospel* (Harmondsworth: Penguin, 1968), 136–7.
[16] Ibid. 169.   [17] Ibid. 164.

Cupitt, another Cambridge theologian, had earlier contributed to a collection of essays entitled *The Myth of God Incarnate* that gave many of the issues connected with Bultmann's programme of demythologizing a fresh airing.[18] Although in some ways less radical than either Robinson or the death of God theologians, *The Myth of God Incarnate* did highlight the difficulties glossed over by the kind of recourse to Jesus and the gospels seen in some death of God theologies as a way of avoiding the crisis in the idea of God. Thus it played a part in bending the question back to what, philosophically speaking, is the more fundamental issue. For the historical record concerning Jesus and the life of the early Church may well point to a human historical possibility very different from that of contemporary conformism, and it may well be that such a possibility might reward existential commitment and ethical imitation and assist us in constructing a meaningful and worthwhile life—as may Stoicism or Epicureanism or Confucianism or many other possibilities to which history bears witness. But the religious claims of Christianity would seem to entail that in addition to any such secular recommendations, the Gospel must also be understood as saying something about God, and whatever 'God' means this would seem to imply something *not* reducible to the horizons of secular thought.

At this point, then, Cupitt took up the issue with a brisk confidence and a decisive, almost black-and-white clarity, looking to brush away the residual ambivalence of Robinson and the theologians of the death of God. The task to which Cupitt summoned his readers was not to wait for God to reappear or mysteriously to regenerate but simply to take leave of God. Once and for all. There is, he said,

An analogy between the residual presence of traditional religion in our modern autonomous psyches and the residual presence of the former colonial power in a newly independent country. It is true that there is a good deal of residual heteronomous religion about still in people's psyches. We may like to have it around, rather as many people find antique furnishings and décor comfortable in their homes and hostelries, but the fact remains that we are not going to be recolonized.[19]

As this quotation implies, a central element in Cupitt's approach was fully to embrace the principle of autonomy so clearly enunciated two hundred years previously by Kant. This principle, Cupitt remarks, has been accepted by morality but not, yet, by religion. What does this mean? Basically, that the truly modern person is someone concerned to construct a life in which they themselves choose their values, their aims, their beliefs and all the life commitments that flow from these, including (as neither Kant nor the early Cupitt mentioned but as has become very important in contemporary cultural debate) sexuality and gender.

---

[18] J. Hick (ed.), *The Myth of God Incarnate* (London: SCM Press, 1977).
[19] D. Cupitt, *Taking Leave of God* (London: SCM Press, 1980), p. xi.

Interestingly—and in this respect striking out in a quite different direction from that taken by the secularizing theologies of the 1960s—Cupitt does not declare himself to be against *religion*. On the contrary, he believes that religion can be humanly valuable—as long as it is understood to be a human product serving human ends, something we invent for ourselves to improve human flourishing. He is prepared to speak of his own position as 'Christian Buddhism'. And if there is occasionally just a hint of a mystical element in Cupitt that seems to hint at an experientially revealed dimension that is more than a simple social and linguistic construct (and which he sometimes equates with a Heideggerian conception of Being), it never really threatens this fundamental commitment to autonomy.

In the introductory section of *Taking Leave of God* Cupitt set out his pro-gramme in bold terms from which he has never subsequently retreated. To begin with, he says, 'It seems doubtful whether there is any immense cosmic or supracosmic Creator-Mind.' Therefore, and secondly, 'Objective theism does not matter so much as people think. What matters is spirituality; and a modern spirituality must be a spirituality for a fully unified autonomous consciousness, for that is the kind of consciousness that modern people have.' Thirdly, the highest principle of spirituality is that we 'become spirit, that is, precisely to attain the highest degree of autonomous self-knowledge and self-transcendence'. As a fourth principle Cupitt asserts that in relation to this task God is reconceived as 'a unifying symbol that eloquently personifies and represents to us everything that spirituality requires of us'. Fifthly, to require there to be any extra-religious reality of God—i.e. to think of God apart from his role in our autonomous self-development—is a sign of 'spiritual vulgarity and immaturity'. God is quite strictly a *focus imaginarius* and neither a person nor, as Tillich would have it, the transcendence of Being-Itself in its absoluteness over and above all human aspirations and commitments. Sixthly, and finally, 'It is spiritually important that one should not believe in life after death but should instead strive to attain the goal of spiritual life in history.'[20] Cupitt names this position 'non-realism', which means that the central concepts of religion have no reality outside their human, subjective function in the development of spirituality.

If Cupitt has never retreated from the venture of *Taking Leave of God*, he has, very consciously, shifted, developed, and transformed the original Kierkegaardian and Kantian rigour of his project in manifold ways. Already in his book *Life-Lines* he drew the conclusion that a religion modelled on non-realist principles would not be a static life-view, since a spiritually alive individual will necessarily pass through a number of different forms of belief and will have a different 'religion' at different stages of life.[21] But, given the centrality of religion-as-spirituality in our own personality formation, this means that it is not even a matter of a stable and

---

[20] D. Cupitt, *Taking Leave of God* (London: SCM Press, 1980), 8–10.
[21] D. Cupitt, *Life-Lines* (London: SCM Press, 1986).

constant self which experiences and adopts a succession of religious views but of a self that is itself caught up in an endless process of self-transformation. Following the movement of modern French philosophy, Cupitt's own version of the death of God was followed by his own version of the death of the self.

Wittgenstein had always been a major figure in Cupitt's curriculum, but in the mid-1980s a Wittgensteinian view of language was supplemented by Derrida's ideas of dissemination and deconstruction, transforming the rather rigid forms of Wittgensteinian language games into a dynamic play of ever-shifting linguistic constructs and happenings. No longer was there any 'depth' to which the religious thinker could or should appeal: everything was to be reconstrued as endless surface, like modern abstract art.[22] As the title of one of Cupitt's more recent books has it, everything is 'emptiness and brightness' and we inhabit a world in which 'nothing is hidden'. The task of the self is not to manage or to direct the complex, gentle flow of phenomena but to commune and go with it: 'just out of the play of forces, just out of secondariness—astonishing innovations and very complex systems can develop purely "naturally" without there being any sovereign, substantial Self in charge.'[23] Religion is no longer, as for van Buren, a 'blik' one holds on to through all changes and chances and that predetermines the view one has of the world. Religion is as changing and as infinitely variable as life itself. There is no elite knowledge any more, but only the endless flow of global communication. Religion is—perhaps literally—more alive than ever, because the age of theology is over and Life, not God, is what matters.

Like Cupitt, the American philosopher of religion Mark C. Taylor was early on influenced by Kierkegaard and the latter's proclamation that 'subjectivity is truth'. Yet Taylor became convinced that the Kierkegaardian individual was a symptom of modern humanity's estrangement and that Hegel remained a more 'trustworthy guide' in the quest for 'the way from fragmentation and disintegration among and within individuals to an intra- and interpersonal unification or integration'.[24] What Hegel offered was a vision of 'Unity *within* plurality; being *within* becoming; constancy *within* change; peace *within* flux; identity *within* difference: the union of union and non-union—reconciliation *in the midst of* estrangement. The end of the journey to selfhood.'[25]

The relevance of Taylor at this point is that, as for the other thinkers we have been considering, the problem of modern life and of the break up of the original unity of life's manifold functions within a single religious-cultural whole is not just a problem about the human self but a problem about that self and its God. The more specifically *theological* implications of Taylor's thought came to

---

[22] See, e.g. D. Cupitt, *The Long-Legged Fly: A Theology of Language and Desire* (London: SCM Press, 1987).

[23] D. Cupitt, *Emptiness and Brightness* (Santa Rosa, Calif.: Polebridge Press, 2001), 63.

[24] Mark C. Taylor, *Journeys to Selfhood: Hegel and Kierkegaard* (Berkeley: University of California Press, 1980), 276.

[25] Ibid.

expression in his 1984 book *Erring: A Postmodern A/theology*, a book that embodied the first major impact on Anglo-Saxon religious thought of the radical philosophy of deconstruction emanating from France and chiefly associated with Jacques Derrida. Like Cupitt, Taylor did not see deconstruction as simply one more phase of secular atheism, but as a movement in ideas that could fruitfully dissolve or reconfigure some of the questions that had been bedevilling modern theology, including—not least—whether it was at all possible to talk about God and, if so, how to do it.

Noting the importance Derrida himself assigns to 'the reading of Hegel' and to the influence of such familiar names in the radical theology canon as Kierkegaard and Nietzsche on Derrida's thought, Taylor suggests that *'deconstruction is the "hermeneutic" of the death of God'* and, as such, 'a possible point of departure for a postmodern a/theology'.[26] His reading of Derrida will itself disclose the precise force of his formulation 'a/theology' rather than simply 'atheology' (an expression already found in George Bataille's *Somme Athéologique*). In preparation for this, Taylor begins by claiming that the Western, Christian theological tradition has been built up through a sequence of binary or dyadic terms of which Taylor lists forty-one examples, beginning with God/World, Eternity/Time, Being/Becoming and running through to Speech/Writing and Seriousness/Play, though not, surprisingly, including Male/Female. Theology, like philosophy, has consistently privileged one half of the picture, thus: God, Eternity, Being...Speech, Seriousness—to the exclusion of the other half—World, Time, Becoming, Writing, Play, etc. This strategy finds its expression in the hegemonic ideas of God, self, history, and book.

It has been typical of modernism, including the theological versions of modernism found in radical and secular theologies, that having once rumbled the game plan of such dualism it has more or less loudly set out to reverse the valuations attached to the table of polarities and to promote the worth of the world, of time, and of becoming at the expense of God, eternity, Being, etc.—a programme that is clearly exemplified in the radical theologies we have been considering. But, Taylor notes, simply reversing the signs outside the brackets locks the would-be rebel into a cycle of mutual dependence in which the assertion of worldliness provokes a new supernaturalism, and so on. Such crude rebellion cannot finally subvert the underlying structure on which the hegemony of the hitherto dominant values is based. Dominant fathers and rebellious sons beget each other endlessly. 'What is needed,' comments Taylor, 'is a critical lever with which the entire inherited order can be creatively disorganized.'[27] This lever is deconstruction. How so? Because deconstruction shows that the polarities are always already inherent in each other in such a way that the concept of God is

---

[26] Mark C. Taylor, *Erring: A Postmodern A/theology* (Chicago: University of Chicago Press, 1984), 6.
[27] Ibid. 11.

meaningless without the concept 'world', eternity is meaningless without time, speech is meaningless without its hidden supplement of writing. Deconstruction therefore reads the 'scriptural network' of Western thought in such a way as to bring to light the internal limit, boundary or margin within the hierarchy of ideas itself. This renders the whole system permanently unstable, however, since it becomes impossible to establish any 'highest' idea or value that does not contain within it its own limit or negation.

Hence deconstructive writing is always paradoxical, double, duplicitous, excentric, improper... errant. Calling into question the very notion of propriety, the language of deconstruction can possess no final or proper meaning... Forever wavering and wandering, deconstruction is (re)inscribed betwixt 'n' between the opposites it inverts, perverts, and subverts... While not reducible to or expressible in a traditional oppositional logic of extremes, this mileu is the 'nonoriginal origin' of everything that is—and that is not.[28]

In keeping with the spirit of these remarks, the title *Erring* (of which the first 'R' is printed in reverse on the title-page) and the '/' that, as Taylor notes, can only be written, not said, point to the fact that 'a/theology' is something different from a simple atheology or, we might say, from a theology of the death of God or the radical humanistic theology of Cupitt's *Taking Leave of God*. A/theology is not 'theology' but neither is it the simple denial of theology. It is a negating of theology that is also a keeping open of theology's own question (even when, as it must, it denies traditional theology's 'answer' to this question). Consistently enough, *Erring* is thereafter almost impossible to summarize, being a sparkling and virtuoso ramble around many of the familiar tropes of theology that are reread by Taylor through the bifocal lens of deconstruction and so dissolved into ecstatic outpourings of wordplays and paradoxes. This passage from the concluding 'Interlude' is typical:

Conclusions, however, always remain inconclusive. Every text is an unconcluding postscript that is a pretext to/for another postscript. This infinite play of (the) word(s) marks the death of God, which is the end of The End. In the absence of The End, there is no ultimate conclusion. Thus there can be neither definite conclusions nor Final Solution. Instead of a conclusion, we are left with an Interlude, which, it appears, is always already playing. Inscribed between an Origin that never was and an End that never is, the Interlude is the *Inter Ludus* of scripture itself.[29]

This kind of writing is, of course, likely to arouse very different reactions in different readers, yet even if one had a certain sympathy with Taylor's project it would surely be hard to resist a degree of ennui in the face of such an endless stream of self-consciously excessive puns and interminable reversals or subversions of conventional meanings. The never-endingness of it all almost inevitably cancels out its own initial excitement, leaving the reader with a bewildered sense that none of it seems to be leading anywhere—as one might feel after

---

[28] Ibid. 10–11.   [29] Ibid. 183.

half-an-hour in the labyrinth depicted on the book's cover. And, Taylor might justifiably retort, why should it lead anywhere? We are only erring, not purposively striving towards anything.

Is this then the final (or should we say: non-final!) outcome of the internal secularization of theology, that the Queen of the Sciences has given herself over to endlessly unravelling the woof and warp of the received textual tradition? Is there any reason to see in this more than a deliberate trivialization of what could once, in the not too distant past, still be hailed as 'ultimate concerns', questions for which one would stake a life (as many, in situations of tyranny, did)? It seems that, however apt many of the complaints brought against theology, from without and within, something has gone missing or, to put it more precisely, that the original diagnosis for which a/theology offers itself as a lifelong cure was itself not quite complete. Or, as if the cure itself revealed the sickness: going round and round in circles. One senses that something is missing, something has been overlooked, something possibly rather crucial.

The problem, I suspect, is by no means Taylor's alone but has to do with an assumption underlying nearly all the questions that his (and my) theological generation inherited. It is the problem that up to and including early Taylor the task of modern theology was almost exclusively construed as a problem in the history of ideas, that is, as a problem of words, concepts and texts. For Robinson, the death of God theologians, Cupitt, early Taylor and many others (including their critics) the issue has been trying to find the concepts, images and ideas that would enable a renewal of truly radical and truly liberating Christian thinking to take place. But it seems as if each time theology comes to the boundary of its own possibilities, it falls back again into an internal self-critique, for which Taylor's deconstructive project provides one of the most consistent expressions. His description of the endlessly winding ways of his own errancy make as good a picture of many a would-be conservative theology as it does of his own a/theology—'words, words, words' going nowhere and not really 'about' anything much at all.

There is no doubt that many found Taylor's work a disequilibrating potion, whether chillingly or gloriously so. But, largely overlooked in the first flush of deconstructing enthusiasm, there were other intriguing possibilities for religious thinking in this new way of looking at texts and traditions. If, for example, Nonbeing is not simply the opposite of Being but its necessary supplement—what 'Being' always already implicitly is or brings forth—then a philosophical system that insists on the priority of Being will always carry within it the seeds of its own destruction. This much was already known from Hegel. But it could further be said that philosophies of Being had themselves been implicitly nihilistic. How so? Because the way in which they had interpreted the world—from the standpoint of absolute and immutable Being—meant judging the sublunary world of time and change and chance as 'nothing'. But, then, the opposite is also true: a nihilism that consistently negates the principles and values that belong to a philosophy of Being is itself only relative to what it negates. As Heidegger had argued with respect to Nietzsche, simply to overturn or to reject the values of the metaphysical systems that had governed Western thought since Socrates was misleading. All Nietzsche had done was, so to speak, to flip the coin. Nietzschean nihilism—the insistence that the world is nothing but flux, change, and becoming—is simply the obverse of the Platonic claim that 'reality' resides in eternal, unchanging, timeless truths. For Heidegger, then, Nietzsche did no more than reveal the nihilism implicit in metaphysics itself, that is, the nihilism implicit in the judgement that *if* there are no eternal truths or values, *then* the world is a meaningless flux. On the more general cultural plane this means that the secular revolt against religion may similarly prove to be merely a matter of changing the signs outside the brackets or flipping the coin. It is not the start of a genuinely new phase of thinking or history, but a reaction against a particular way of construing the world. But this raises the interesting possibility that there might be a way of thinking about reality that is neither metaphysical nor nihilistic, that is beyond metaphysics or that has 'overcome' metaphysics in the sense that it has simply left behind the shared paradigm undergirding both metaphysics and nihilism, both ecclesiastical theology and the secular negation of theology. Such a possibility would allow us once more to think about God, but to do so in a way that was neither metaphysical nor secular. The very acceptance of nihilism could, paradoxically, free us from the incessant and mutually destructive cycle of the conflict of Being versus Non-being. Not surprisingly, then, the 1990s witnessed rumours of a 'return of God to philosophy', rumours which involved some of the leading philosophers of contemporary Europe—Gianni Vattimo, Michael Theunissen, and, not least, Derrida himself.[30] Equally unsurprising was the interest of theologians and philosophers of religion in such a development, as seen in John D. Caputo's sustained wrestling with Derridean themes against the background of his own long-term programme of a radical hermeneutics in which themes from Kierkegaard, Heidegger, and Christian mysticism all played important parts.[31]

The question, however, was whether the kind of return of God that philosophers were prepared to allow for was really anything that religious believers could recognize as answering to their own sensed need for a 'living' God. Vattimo spoke explicitly of a 'weak' sense of faith, a faith that, inspired by the Incarnation, nevertheless (or, rather, just for that reason) held itself free from any kind of absolutists claims. Perhaps this was, after all, just another, less aggressive form of

---

[30] See, for example, the contributions to N. Grønkjær (ed.), *The Return of God: Theological Perspectives in Contemporary Philosophy* (Odense: Odense University Press, 1998) and to J. Derrida and G. Vattimo (eds.), *Religion* (Cambridge: Polity Press, 1998). See also J.-L. Marion, *God without Being: Hors-texte*, trs. T. A. Carlson (Chicago: University of Chicago Press, 1991) or the collection of Derrida's various writings relating to religion published as J. Derrida, *Acts of Religion* (London: Routledge, 2001).

[31] See, e.g. J. D. Caputo, *The Prayers and Tears of Jacques Derrida: Religion without Religion* (Bloomington: Indiana University Press, 1997); idem, *On Religion* (Routledge: London, 2001).

secular theology? As Vattimo put it in unscripted remarks at the American Academy of Religion in 1997, 'if my parish priest says he no longer believes in God, why should I go on calling myself an atheist?'[32]

In Britain, however, the movement known as 'Radical Orthodoxy' was making a strong bid for a very different kind of post-secular theology. The philosophers would be left wandering in the wilderness since, for the radically orthodox, 'only theology overcomes metaphysics', as John Milbank put it. This movement seemed to accept a considerable part of the postmodern critique of metaphysics and the Western tradition. However, the claim was that Christian theology had been seriously misdescribed in the process. If the postmodern critique holds good against the mainline of (non-Christian) idealist philosophy and its nihilistic opposite, Christian theology itself—supremely in Augustine and Thomas Aquinas—is not about 'Being' in the same way that philosophical idealism is. Christian theology has possibilities of thinking God otherwise than any merely philosophical venture of thought, possibilities in which it is not Being as an abstract category that is at issue but Being as the expression of the divine gift. If philosophy will not acknowledge this, Milbank claims, it is merely 'malicious'.[33] As Philip Blond somewhat shrilly declared:

To say that we should now bring an end to the secular is to say that we should reverse the dreadful consequences of the liberal erasure of God and take myth back from out of the hands of the fascists where it has all too often fallen ... For Christ binds together in his own body the invisible and the visible, and as a result He incarnates the transcendent in the flesh and prevents any subsequent account of human materiality divorcing itself from theology. And if it was the desire to give an account of this materiality before giving an account of God that initiated the whole despicable idolatry of the modern, then it is only an account of matter's absolute and utter dependence upon God that can overcome the dreadful vacuity and despair that this age has fallen into. For the celebration of this vacuity and its endless self-serving acts of negation and denial has become the new weak mysticism of the age.[34]

This, I take it, is aimed not only at the older liberalism of the 1960s but also at the kind of theological development we have seen in Cupitt, Taylor, and in Vattimo's avowedly 'weak' faith, not to mention the 'prayers and tears of Jacques Derrida' as interpreted by Caputo.[35] But can the problems bequeathed to the last quarter of the twentieth century by secular theology be got rid of that easily? Even Radical Orthodoxy is permeated by its context in the contemporary philosophy from which it takes so much of its *Fragestellung* and vocabulary, not to mention

[32] The quotation is from memory. It has been reported back to Vattimo, who did not recall it but, equally, did not disown it.

[33] J. Milbank, *The World Made Strange: Theology, Language, Culture* (Oxford: Blackwell, 1997), 50.

[34] P. Blond, *Post-Secular Philosophy: Between Philosophy and Theology* (London: Routledge, 1998), 54–5.

[35] On the 'pseudo-postmodernity' of Cupitt and Taylor, see, for example, G. Ward, 'Introduction' to idem (ed.), *The Postmodern God: A Theological Reader* (Oxford: Blackwell, 1997), p. xl.

its disdain for clarity.[36] To believe that we can recreate some kind of unfallen 'liturgical world' free from the ambiguities of the whole modern experience is simply naive. But, most importantly of all, secularity is not just a set of ideas.

The problem, it seems, is that 'theology' has been carved out of its natural environment and treated as if it were a thing in itself, contextless or, at best, with a context derived from such academic neighbours as philosophy, literary theory, social theory, or the philosophy of science. The modernity in whose image radical theology sought to reform theology was construed by the radicals themselves and is now construed by their radically orthodox opponents as a system of ideas and cognitive and moral commitments. Society is important, it is true, but only in so far as it reveals itself to be in the power of one or other social theory. Political commitments do indeed flicker back and forth across the pages of virtually all the figures discussed, yet even politics is construed primarily as a matter of theory. Socialism becomes an eschatological construct rather than a working political programme. To be sure, modernity includes theoretical perspectives, but are they the real driving force in the modern revolution?

Perhaps an important hint in the direction of a rather different approach is to be found in Bultmann's assertion that we cannot use the electric light and believe in the New Testament world of spirits and demons. To what does this hint point? Quite simply, to the point that modernity is not primarily a theological problem on account of its belief in autonomy or the scientific world view, but because it has taken shape as a technological civilization in which miraculous interventions *are no longer looked for or required even if they are allowed as theoretically possible.* Secularization may be only a theory, but the secularity that the theory addresses is not a theory of modernity nor even modernity's own theoretical assumptions, but the reality of the modernity's experiences of and experiences with technology in its complex and manifold forms.

Some radicals did recognize this and accepted the challenge. Arend van Leeuwen, for example, saw science and technology as a fruit of the specifically Christian contribution to human self-understanding and of Christianity's contention that our relation to God is not determined by our participation in any cult but by our capacity for responsible historical action. Technocracy marks the end of ontocracy, i.e. the sense that human life and fate is circumscribed and determined by a divine cosmic order. 'The spell of a divine universe is broken; upon every temple there falls the devastating judgement that it has been "made by man". Even modern science has to do simply with a "man-made" universe. It moves among the stars and probes the inmost secrets of the atom; and in all this

---

[36] See, for example, the incisive but respectful criticism of Milbank in G. Hyman, *The Predicament of Postmodern Theology: Radical Orthodoxy or Textual Nihilism?* (Louisville: Westminster John Knox Press, 2002). However, Hyman is himself a little too intoxicated by the rhetorical effects of the style of theology he criticizes. My suspicion is that the reificatory tendencies of this rhetoric signal an unacknowledged desire to endow philosophical and religious reflection with the intellectual status of scientific/technical thought.

man comes face to face with himself.'[37] In this context, he states, 'The technological revolution is the evident and inescapable form in which the whole world is
now confronted with the most recent phase of Christian history. In and through
this form Christian history becomes world history.'[38] Secularity and technology
are thus the marks of a world to which only Christianity, with its radical
understanding of human responsibility, can hope to respond. Harvey Cox's
best-selling *The Secular City: Secularization and Urbanization in Theological
Perspective* also involved a specific thematization of technology, since, as Cox
put it, the secular city itself is a 'technopolis'. Its 'citizen' is 'technopolitan man',
who 'sits at a vast and immensely complicated switchboard. He is *homo symbo-
licus*, man the communicator, and the metropolis is a massive network of
communications.'[39] The subtitle found on the book's cover (though not on its
title-page) reads that it is 'A celebration of [the city's] liberties and an invitation to
its discipline.' If we follow the pointer provided by Cox, then, the radical
theologies we have been considering and the affirmation of the secular they
recommend amount to a call to acknowledge, to embrace and to affirm this
communications network that technology makes possible and sustains. Their
message is to become in our theology the 'technopolitan' human beings that, by
virtue of our unavoidable participation in the life of the city, we existentially
already are. The task of radical theology is therefore *not* simply to reflect on, to
retrieve or to transform the historical expressions of Christian faith in response to
the theoretical criticisms offered by one or other current of contemporary
thought, but to consider how faith might be thinkable in an environment
determined by and as technopolis. This technopolis is not to be construed as
some sort of inert fact 'out there' that theology has to think about. As Cox's
references to communication already imply, the characteristic feature of contemporary technopolis is not simply that it is an ensemble of machines, industry,
highways and urban conglomerations, but that it is a concrete system of communicative practices. But the university itself and the other institutions that
make theology possible (such as publishing) are themselves both actively and
reactively caught up in the communicative network. That is to say that theological reflection is in its most simple expression pervaded, mediated, and
transmitted under the conditions of technology—a truth which may take as
banal a form as the fact that I am writing this now on a computer connecting me
to the total global network of electronic information. The very media in which

[37] A. Th. van Leeuwen, *Christianity in World History* (London: Edinburgh House, 1964), 417.
[38] Ibid. 408. As van Leeuwen sees it, this has important implications for inter-religious dialogue.
Because it is through the Christian West that technology has become a global reality, and other
religions such as Buddhism, Hinduism encounter it only at second hand, their responses are 'no
more than a misguided attempt to cure the ills of the technocratic era with the medicines of the
Neolithic one' (408).
[39] H. Cox, *The Secular City: A Celebration of its Liberties and an Invitation to its Discipline*
(New York: Macmillan, 1965), 41. However, a more critical approach to modern mass media is to
be found in the same author's *The Seduction of Spirit: The Use and Misuse of People's Religion*
(New York: Simon and Schuster, 1973).

thought becomes part of the public world are technological through-and-through. There are important themes here to which we shall return at a number of points, but, it should be repeated that, clear as Cox's celebration of the specifically technological element in modern secular society was, it was something of an exception in the radical theology of the 1960s and 1970s.

Mark C. Taylor too came to make the question of technology central to his thinking, first in *About Religion: Economies of Faith in Virtual Culture* and, most recently, in *The Moment of Complexity: Emerging Network Culture*. However, it is perhaps significant that this latter ends not with an attempt to think about God but an apologia for the for-profit e-Ed Global Education Network.[40] Restraining the smile with which a travelling ironist might have greeted this move on the part of one once known as a Kierkegaard specialist, I note only that Taylor's analysis, whatever the strengths and weaknesses of its details, provides a consistent and upbeat, state-of-the-art view of where we are now—in the midst of a communicative network whose complexity surpasses the 'secular city' of the 1960s by at least as high a factor as that city itself surpassed the great industrial cities of what Lewis Mumford called the 'pæleotechnological' nineteenth century. That this move on Taylor's part comes as the next step beyond *Erring*, and the deconstruction of metaphysics advertised there, indicates that he, like Heidegger, sees technology as the ultimate aim, purpose, and meaning of metaphysics. This—technology—is what the whole history of metaphysics has been leading up to. We shall be exploring in greater depth what this claim means in Heidegger's hands, but, in a preliminary way, we can note several consequences that seem to follow from it. Firstly, if metaphysics does indeed finally mean technology, then all talk of some theoretical 'overcoming' of metaphysics becomes, simply, ridiculous (and it is important to note that Heidegger himself was chary of the idea). For we cannot 'overcome' technology in the sense of being able to put it behind us, as Blond wants to do with all non-Christian philosophies. As I stated in the Introduction, we simply cannot pretend that in any realistically conceivable future we could simply leave technology behind. In any case, very few people seriously want such an 'overcoming'. But even if we were to think of 'overcoming' technology in terms of theology somehow coming to be in a position from which it could guide the future development of technology, the actual capabilities of the theological community seem to fall so far short of what would be required for such a task that it is almost as risible as the idea of abandoning technology. The realities of the political, industrial, and commercial development and management of technology are, on the one hand, too power intensive and, on the other, too pluralistic, to imagine any one form of Christian theology setting the agenda for the whole process.[41]

If recognizing that the question of metaphysics is, at bottom, also the question concerning technology puts a stop to the louder claims of some forms of

---

[40] For further discussion see Chapter 8, below.
[41] I shall return to the problem of such 'subordinationism' in the following chapter.

neo-conservative theology, it also presents a no less serious problem for the secular theologians. For the reality of the technological society is by no means obviously congenial to the kind of democratic secular humanism espoused by most of the radicals. If Bonhoeffer and others spoke in the name of 'man come of age', that selfsame 'man' has himself become more than a little relativized in the 'virtual', 'post-human' world of 'simulacra' that technology is shaping for us. It is one thing to call for the remaking of God in the image of humanity, it is something else to call for the remaking of God in the image of the technology that, today, gives shape to the human image itself. To put it another way, one cannot realistically buy into secularity without simultaneously buying into technology. The two are interdependent in almost infinite ways. Some of the radicals, as we have just seen, accepted the consequences of this identification, though Cox has subsequently pulled back from the almost unqualified admiration for 'technopolis' expressed in *The Secular City*. But whether they confronted the question of technology or not, the way in which they allowed an ideology of the secular to sweep the board of theological discourse meant that the radicals effectively left theology powerless in face of the yet more axial question concerning technology and its meaning for the fate and future of human beings.

It does not follow that the acceptance of the secular must now be answered by the rejection of the technological. Since, if we once take on board the enormity of the question concerning technology, the issue cannot be how theology might 'overcome' technology in any crude sense. It is, rather, this: in a situation in which technology is both the external and the internal environment of contemporary thinking, is it at all possible to think otherwise than in the manner of technology and can such thinking have the form of thinking about God? Can we go on thinking about God in this situation? And if it turns out that thinking about God is a gift we have lost or that has become atrophied in us, can we begin again? And how might we do so? What such thinking, were it possible, would then mean for our concrete existence in a technologically determined world would, of course, be a still further question. As a preliminary step, however, it would seem sensible to think for a little about technology itself and about what exactly it is that confronts, surrounds us, and permeates us in this age of technology. But though it seems that theology has said very little about this, not even when it has declared itself to be secular and thus a part of the contemporary technological world, it has not been completely silent. In the next chapter, therefore, and by way of preparation for gathering my own reflections on thinking about God in the age of technology, I shall briefly survey some of the twentieth century's more important *theological* contributions to thinking about the nature and meaning of technology. Even if this was never more than a marginal issue in the work of the great modern theologians, that it was in some small measure recognized and addressed by them cannot but be of significance for our own thinking, which, as always, is that of dwarves struggling to get onto the shoulders of giants.

2

Theologies of Technology

For all their avowed readiness to embrace the secular, the radical theologies we have been examining mostly dealt with the question of God in an essentially traditional way, as a question in the history of ideas, and they did not address the question as to the possible influence on these ideas of the technologies of the culture in which they were being formulated. Even where the Marxist critique of religion was taken seriously, as it was by many of them, the element in Marxism that could have opened up a serious discussion of technology was glossed over in favour of an emphasis on the intellectual, cultural, and political implications of the Marxist critique. Admittedly, one could cull an extensive crop of throwaway remarks that point to the presence of certain technologies as integral to the background of the matter at issue, as in Bultmann's remark about the electric light, but these generally fell far short of making technology as such a topic of sustained reflection. This is in striking contrast to the extensive attention given in the same period to science in its various forms. The big debates about cosmic and human evolution, about the psychological reality of soul and spirit, or the social meaning of belief were, essentially, theoretical debates framed in more or less the same terms as the early Church's debates with the various forms of classical philosophy or the defence or promotion of Christianity in relation to one or other world religion. Nor is this surprising, since the most obvious implications of a whole series of scientific discoveries—heliocentrism, the geological record, evolution—was precisely to challenge what the Church held to be truths guaranteed by revelation. It therefore seemed natural to defend these truths at the theoretical level at which they were being attacked.

Theologians largely shared the popular assumption that science was primarily a theoretical undertaking, an attempt to find out about the way things are, or about the way in which the universe was made, hangs together and continues to develop—whether in the macrocosmic perspectives of cosmology or the microcosmic issues of brain and consciousness. This assumption was, in part, a reflection of the scientific community's self-presentation as a community of those seeking the objective truth of things, an ideal embodied in such scientific 'heroes' as Kepler, Galileo, Newton, and Darwin. This quest was portrayed as being of an other and a superior order to the mere 'application' of science—a view that was frequently glimpsed in the background of assertions concerning the supposed 'misuse' of science in the hands of politicians and the military. It is not the science itself that is to blame, it was said, since science itself is neutral. Science can give us the key that enables us to make nuclear weapons, but whether nuclear weapons are in fact made and whether they are in fact used are matters that lie outside the orbit of science in the strict sense. This way of presenting science corresponded to theology's view of its own task as being about the presentation of a truth that is independent of and sovereign over all immediately practical human interests. Jacques Maritain, a Catholic philosopher in the Thomist tradition, saw it as a matter of reproach that what is now called 'science' represents a defection from the original, contemplative ideal of science as wisdom. In the aftermath of the dissolution of the medieval synthesis, he argued, philosophy 'became, as Descartes said, "practical", and its goal was to make us "masters or owners of nature"... so as to found physics, science and the mathematical possession of nature. In this way everything is at once turned upside down and pulled to pieces'.[1] For Maritain and others in the Catholic tradition the reversal of the 'proper' order of the theoretical and the practical that occurs in modern technology is already a blow to the possibility of theology. Putting it crudely, it is below theology's theoretical dignity to engage with the question of technology. In this spirit modern theology and modern religious sensibility in general can be seen as endorsing Spengler's remark that 'Ever and ever again, true belief has regarded the machine as of the devil.'[2] Religious belief and practice has instinctively and repeatedly taken its stand with romanticism in either rejecting modernity and its sustaining technologies outright or else taking an attitude of extreme reserve towards them. These technologies, technology as such, is acceptable, even unavoidable—but only as long as it is kept in its place as subordinate to the theoretical, spiritual, and moral directives of theology and belief.[3]

In this respect, theology has shared extensive common ground with a line of cultural analysis and critique that was classically formulated in Schiller's *Letters on the Aesthetic Education of Man* (1795), in which the inner fragmentation, divisions, and self-alienation resulting from the predominance of rationality in modern life are described with paradigmatic clarity. For Schiller himself the key to restoring our lost unity is to be found in poetry and art. Many of his themes are taken up in romanticism and are familiar to English-language readers through, e.g. Coleridge, Wordsworth, Ruskin, Arnold, and Emerson in the nineteenth century and Eliot, Auden, and even Tolkien and his many imitators

---

[1] J. Maritain, *The Degrees of Knowledge*, tr. B. Wall and M. Anderson (London: Geoffrey Bles, 1937), 29.

[2] O. Spengler, *The Decline of the West*, tr. C. F. Atkinson (London: Allen and Unwin), ii. 502.

[3] In this respect, Maritain's attitude to technology is an extension of the distinction he draws between fine art, directed towards contemplation, and mere craft, something which is honourable enough in its place but only so long as it accepts its subordination to the higher spiritual orders.

in the twentieth.[4] In another development of Schiller's ideas, in the tradition mediated through Hegel, we find something similar in the quasi-Marxist movement in ideas generally known as critical theory. In Theodor Adorno and Max Horkheimer's influential 'dialectic of Enlightenment', the social and technical products of modern rationality help human society to liberate itself from subjugation to immediate natural demands but, in so doing, they come to constitute a second nature that constrains and oppresses its own maker, like a Frankenstein's monster or a golem let loose.[5] The affirmation of the progressive and critical Enlightenment, they argue, must be accompanied by a refusal of Enlightenment as ideology or as the expression for bourgeois society's self-satisfied achievements. A similar approach is reflected in Herbert Marcuse's view of civilization as a man-made complex of power relations that represses and frustrates human beings' own instinctual self-expression and fulfilment.[6] Although technology itself contains many possibilities for good, technology as we know it exists in capitalist society as 'terrorist technocracy'.[7] Less confrontational in tone, the Schillerian echoes, mediated through Hegel, Marx, and modern sociology and psychology, continue to be heard in the thought of Jürgen Habermas, where technology is by no means rejected but is nevertheless seen as threatening to suborn humanity's moral and expressive needs and aspirations. Only if the scientific and technical agenda is brought into the orbit of ethical reflection will it truly serve human good.

Critical theory itself was largely a child of the interwar years, a period when questions of technology were especially prominent in many areas of culture and society. This owed much to the impact of the First World War itself, the first major international war that was experienced as 'technological' warfare, with the simultaneous transformation of 'traditional' warfare by the machine-gun, chemical weapons, the tank, air power, and the submarine. The traumatic impact of that event on those who lived through it can scarcely be underestimated. Yet this was also followed by the further challenge of the Soviet Union, in whose ideology technologization played a central role (so much so that Lenin could define Communism as 'electrification plus the soviets'). In this regard, theologians too shared the concerns of their times. Strangely, however, the period after the Second World War—no less 'technological' than the First!—saw the question of technology dissipated into questions of particular technologies that emerged as

---

[4] I am not saying that all of these were directly influenced by Schiller, though many were, but simply that the kind of diagnosis and the kind of prescription they offer is essentially congruent with his.

[5] It is fitting, but not surprising, that the title of a recent popular book about technology referred to the Jewish legend of a man-made living creature, the golem—see H. Collins and T. Pinch, *The Golem at Large or What you Should Know about Technology* (Cambridge: Cambridge University Press, 1998).

[6] H. Marcuse, *Eros and Civilization: A Philosophical Enquiry into Freud* (London: Routledge and Kegan Paul, 1956).

[7] H. Marcuse, *Technology, War and Fascism* in *Collected Papers of Herbert Marcuse*, ed. D. Kellner (London: Routledge, 1998), i. 63.

especially troubling at one or other time. As noted in the Introduction, this situation has largely prevailed until today, when it is probably the combined impact of the information revolution and the technologies associated with contemporary genetics that have brought the question concerning technology back into the theological arena.

II

If the First World War was indeed a spur to thinking about technology, it is perhaps no coincidence that several of those who contributed most to the first round of theological thinking about technology had direct, literally 'front-line', experience of that war. This is certainly true of Teilhard de Chardin, who had served as a stretcher-bearer in the battle of Verdun and whose dazzling vision of cosmic evolution combined perspectives from his own work as a scientist with insights and aspirations from his devotional life as a Catholic priest. Yet Teilhard is atypical in the fundamentally positive view he takes of modern technology. For not only did he blend the scientific idea of cosmic and human evolution with the religious idea of matter being transformed into the body of Christ in a kind of ultimate transfiguration he called the Omega Point, he also affirmed the development of planetary technology as a key element in this process. Human evolution, Teilhard believed, marked a turning point in the process of evolution as such. Why? Because with the emergence of human beings there also emerged the phenomenon of consciousness and consciousness, he claimed, involved a reversal in the preceding movement of evolution. 'Until the coming of man,' he wrote, 'the pattern of the Tree of Life was always that of a fan, a spread of morphological radiations diverging more and more, each radiation culminating in a new "knot" and breaking into a fan of its own.'[8] At the point at which consciousness becomes self-consciousness a curious reversal occurs. The outward-moving 'fan' of ever-expanding variations turns in upon itself. If this is, at first, an individual event (such that the role of the individual remains crucial for Teilhard), the interaction of a whole multitude of individual self-consciousnesses (human beings!) constitutes a new evolutionary event characterized by a previously unparalleled complexity. This event is the emergence of what Teilhard calls the 'noosphere', a sphere of thinking consciousness that, in his words, is 'the thinking envelope of the earth'.[9] Teilhard did not, of course, know the term 'memes', i.e. encoded transmitters of cultural values and forms analogous in function to genes only operative at the social, not the individual level, but he

---

[8] P. T. de Chardin, *The Future of Man*, tr. N. Denny (London: Collins, 1964), 158.
[9] Ibid. 132. The term 'noosphere' seems to have been coined by Edouard LeRoy but is also associated with the Russian geochemist, V. I. Vernadsky, who, under the ideological conditions of the Soviet Union, articulated something very close to what his contemporary, the Jesuit Teilhard de Chardin, was also struggling to describe.

seems to have had a rather similar idea. Culture, he believed, has taken over from heredity: 'heredity, hitherto primarily chromosomic (that is to say carried by the genes) becomes primarily "Noospheric"—transmitted, that is to say, by the surrounding environment.' And, he asks rhetorically, 'what system of chromosomes would be as capable as our immense educational system of indefinitely storing and infallibly preserving the huge array of truths and systematised technical knowledge which, steadily accumulating, represents the patrimony of mankind?'[10] As seen by Teilhard, globalization is not primarily an economic or a political phenomenon (as it is usually seen today) but the self-realization of the biosphere as a single, complex consciousness-event. Crucially, this is not simply a matter of human consciousnesses interacting, but their interaction is both facilitated by and takes form as technology: 'For a long time past there have been neither isolated inventors nor machines. To an increasing extent every machine comes into being as a function of every other machine; and again to an increasing extent, all the machines on earth, taken together, tend to form a single, vast organised mechanism.'[11] With reference to radio, television, and computers (Teilhard died in 1955) he greets the advent of 'a vault above our heads, a domain of interwoven consciousness, the site, support and instrument of super-vision and super-ideas'.[12] This state of affairs is a springboard for a new and unpredictable evolutionary leap, but one that, though unpredictable, can be anticipated eagerly by faith as pointing towards the coming of the cosmic Christ, the discovery, as Teilhard put it, 'not merely of Something but of *Someone* at the peak created by the convergence of the evolving universe upon itself'.[13] Having evolved—in and through its science and technology—a collective super-brain, humanity will now go on to discover its heart. A brief summary such as this cannot, of course, do justice to a visionary thinker who, in one and the same passage, can combine science fiction with devotion to the blessed sacrament. There is undoubtedly much in Teilhard that, today, seems over-optimistic, even naïve, yet he is at the very least an important reminder that in the encounter with technology, religious thought always has a choice: that a stance of critical opposition is by no means forced upon it and that it is possible—if rare—for theology to take one of the greatest of all leaps of faith and to see in planetary technology an event that is not merely part of some divine plan but a turning point in God's continuing incarnation in the world. Yet, for the most part, Teilhard remains the exception who proves the rule.

The conclusion of the Catholic philosopher Romano Guardini's *Letters from Lake Como: Explorations in Technology and the Human Race* is also one of optimism. However, Guardini shows more of the Schillerian reserve vis-à-vis the modern technologized world than does Teilhard. In these letters, originally published between 1923 and 1925, Guardini contrasts the kind of human invention manifested in the architecture and agriculture of the Lake Como

---

[10] Ibid. 162.   [11] Ibid. 165–6.   [12] Ibid. 169.   [13] Ibid. 179.

region with the products of modern technology. The former are not, of course, 'natural'. They are 'man-made', yet they cohere with the landscape, the rhythm of the seasons and the encompassing world of nature. This, Guardini says, is how it is with genuine 'culture' and in such works of culture as a sailing ship, the open hearth of an old Italian country house, the hand plough, the candle. But the world of steam ships, coal-fired stoves, tractors and electric light is something different again. A particular kind of desire has united with a particular understanding of nature to create a situation in which

Something new comes into being...a whole world of works, goals, institutions, and orders that are no longer determined by our living constitution but by unleashed natural force, by the rational autonomy of this force which goes its own way and no longer worries about any organic standard. This new force is governed by a human attitude that no longer feels itself tied by living human unity and its organic compass and that regards as petty and narrow the limitation in which the earlier time found supreme fulfilment, wisdom, beauty, a well-rounded fullness of life.[14]

Although it is produced by human beings, what technology itself produces is neither human nor natural. 'What takes place here is not human, at least if we measure the human by the human beings who lived before us. It is not natural if we measure the natural by nature as it once was.'[15] Yet if what has happened with the advent of modern technology is destructive of one way of being human, Guardini is not prepared simply to succumb to nostalgia and cultural pessimism. We must match the new possibilities unleashed by technology with 'a new human attitude that is a match for them. We must put mind, spirit, and freedom to work afresh,' he writes.[16] 'Our age has been given to us as the soil on which to stand and the task to master. At bottom we would not wish it otherwise. Our age is not just an external path that we tread; it is ourselves.'[17] In this situation the common human task—and, he says, the specifically Christian task—is resolutely to take on responsibility for these, our own most awesome works. Although he regards what he calls the event of 'the Germanic essence entering history' as a harbinger of such a new step he also emphasizes that he is not conceiving of this in terms of some new Aryan religion or racial ideology, but as a new way of engaging with historical reality. 'After Jesus Christ all new religions are literary fantasies,' he remarks,[18] suggesting that the point is not so much a new idea of the human but a way of releasing the energies found in the Christian revelation itself.

Like Teilhard, Nicholas Berdyaev and Paul Tillich also had first-hand experience of the traumatic events of 1914–1919, and they too expressed themselves positively, sometimes almost rhapsodically, about humanity's technical capabilities. Also like Teilhard, they exerted a significant influence on mid-twentieth century theology and, not least, on the theological radicals. Yet whilst emphasizing the positive possibilities of technology and the essential novelty of the

---

[14] Guardini, *Letters from Lake Como*, 72.   [15] Ibid. 73.   [16] Ibid. 80
[17] Ibid. 81.   [18] Ibid. 86.

question that technology posed for Christian thought, it was characteristic of both of them that they sounded a note of significant reserve and, in the last resort, opted for something more akin to Maritain's call to subordinate technological thinking to a higher 'wisdom' to which theology or religious thinking has some kind of privileged access.

Berdyaev's thought can seem to advocate an extreme dualism in which the creativity of freedom and spirit are consistently threatened from the side of the material world. He appears to see almost every human social and cultural phenomenon as a potential form of slavery, a lure to drown the demands of spirit in sensuality, art, collectivism, nationalism, money, or in the objectifying habits of philosophical thought represented by the great systems and ontologies of the nineteenth century. It might be expected that on this basis he would have taken an essentially negative stance towards technology. That seems to be the line in his book *The Fate of Man in the Modern World,* where he writes that

... the chief cosmic force which is now at work to change the whole face of the earth and dehumanize and depersonalize man is not capitalism as an economic system, but technics, the wonder of our age. Man has become a slave to his own marvellous invention, the machine. We may well call our epoch the epoch of technics. Technics is man's latest and greatest love. At a time when he has ceased to believe in miracles, man still believes in the miracle of technics. Dehumanization is, first of all, the machinization of human life, turning man into a machine. The power of the machine shatters the integrity of the human image.[19]

Yet Berdyaev refuses the option of rejecting technology outright. As he writes in *The Destiny of Man*

Our moral attitude to technical inventions is bound to be ambiguous and contradictory. Those inventions are a manifestation of man's power, of his kingly place in the world; they bear witness to his creativeness and must be recognized as good and valuable. Man is the inventor of tools which he puts between himself and the natural elements; the invention of the simplest tool is the beginning of civilization. The justification of technical progress in the wide sense of the term is the justification of human culture and a negative attitude to it means a desire to return from civilized to primitive life. The romantic rejection of technical progress does not stand criticism.[20]

Technology is neither good nor bad nor yet morally neutral but essentially *ambiguous.* 'On the one hand it lessens spirituality and makes man's life more material and mechanical. On the other hand it stands for dematerialization and disincarnation, opening up greater possibilities of freedom for the spirit ... And

---

[19] N. Berdyaev, *The Fate of Man in the Modern Age,* tr. D. Lowrie (London: SCM Press, 1935), 80–1.

[20] N. Berdyaev, *The Destiny of Man,* tr. N. Duddington (London: Geoffrey Bles, 1937), 225. Berdyaev is not, of course, a 'theologian' in any strict sense. However, his writings were dominated by religious questions and, as mentioned in the main text, he exercised a very significant influence on many European theologians in the middle third of the twentieth century.

the human spirit must find the inner strength to endure this change and not to be enslaved by this new reality...'[21] Technical achievements are neutral, Berdyaev adds—but only up to a point. The kind of power that contemporary technology gives to humanity (he is writing at the threshold of what was then called the 'atomic age') calls for a new heightening of our moral sense—although, as he concedes, these problems have as yet scarcely occupied philosophers at all.

A similar ambiguity and a similar sense for challenges yet to be faced are found in Tillich's writings about technology, now gathered in one volume as *The Spiritual Situation in Our Technical Society*.[22] In many respects Tillich's view of technology is deducible from the general structures of his fundamental ontology. The whole sphere of human being, as he sees it, is articulated in and through a series of polarized categories such as individual and society, self and other, freedom and destiny and, at the most abstract level, Being and Non-Being. According to the original purpose of creation these mutually support and enable one another: society provides a context in which the individual can survive physically and develop culturally and personally; the individual in turn brings his or her own creative gift to society. In the actual, fallen situation of human beings these structures lose their created balance and positive reciprocity: the individual feels oppressed by society and society regards individualism as a suspect, antisocial force. The structures that should serve to hold the world in being become structures of destruction. Original harmony cannot be restored simply by invoking a lost status quo, or by imposing an impossible heteronomy on individuals who have learnt to think and act for themselves, autonomously. It can only be found by breaking through to the position Tillich describes as theonomy, where the divided powers are freely re-united in a 'New Being'.

In the essay 'The Logos and Mythos of Technology', Tillich traces the possibility of technology back to nature itself. 'Where something is successful through the use of suitable means, there is technology,' he writes, commenting that

... no area of reality can be named where there would be nothing technical to find. $T\epsilon\chi\nu\acute{\alpha}\zeta\epsilon\iota\ \acute{\eta}\ \phi\acute{\upsilon}\sigma\iota\varsigma$—one could say, nature acts technically; more precisely translated, it acts cunningly... Nature acts technically when the carnivorous plant, comparable to the jaws of an excavating machine, closes itself at the slightest pressure of an insect, when the eye is the model for a photographic camera, when a bird is the model for an airplane, and when a dolphin is the model for a submarine... The riches of nature are not possible without the technical element.[23]

---

[21] N. Berdyaev, *The Destiny of Man*, 227.

[22] It is, of course, very useful for the contemporary reader to have such a collection, but we should not be misled into thinking that Tillich focused on technology in the way that the volume might suggest. The essays and articles it contains come from a wide variety of periods and contexts.

[23] In P. Tillich, *The Spiritual Situation in our Technical Society*, ed. M. J. Thomas (Macon, Ga.: Mercer University Press, 1988), 52.

The emergence of the human brain and its potential for acting technically is itself an example of such 'natural' technology. In human beings, however, this kind of technical dimension is subordinated to a preconceived and specified end. This is not necessarily negative and may creatively preserve and nurture one or other aspect of nature as, Tillich suggests, it does in psychotherapy and pedagogy, where technical intervention serves to promote the flourishing of its object (in this case the human being). He calls this 'developmental technology'. But there are also forms he names 'actualizing technology' and 'transforming technology'. The former of these is the technology involved in such activities as artistic creation, bringing something new into existence through the invented machinery of, e.g., a violin or a paintbrush. The latter, 'transforming technology', is what is generally meant by the simple term 'technology'. Here the end is in some sense fundamentally alien to the means. Such technology 'does not develop, rather it destroys living nexuses. It fells a tree and transforms it into a technical material: wood. It blasts rock formations and transforms them into a technical material: stone.' Once the purpose that the material is to serve is fulfilled, the material itself is cast aside. 'A worn-out machine still exists, to be sure, but only as scrap . . .'[24]

Technology as we know it in its developed form has a threefold rationality: the rationality of the technical element itself, i.e. that the machine really is 'well-designed' for the purpose it is to fulfil; that it is constructed in accordance with scientific knowledge of the relevant materials; and, not least, that it serves a rational economic and societal purpose. Again, the fundamental dynamics of Tillich's ontology imply that this essential rationality makes it impossible for us simply to dismiss technology. Technology draws its strength from powers that belong to the basic structures of Being. However, like all the other manifestations of the basic structures of Being, technology as we know it exists in a situation in which these structures are distorted and separated. Like other forms of rationality that have broken loose from their ground in pre-rational Being (humanly experienced, for example, as tradition or feeling), a technologized world is one that is experienced as empty and lacking the fullness of spontaneous life. It is the manifestation of a power that has broken away from Eros (the realm of human longing and desire), and goes on to subject Eros to alien restraints. It speaks to human beings only in and as rational beings, neglecting or subjecting the other dimensions of their being. Such tendencies provoke the negative revolt against technology. This, however, is a mistake. Technology can be liberat*ing*—if it itself is first liberat*ed*.

Technology has transformed the world, and this transformed world is our world, and no other. Upon it we must build; and more than hitherto we must incorporate technology into the ultimate meaning of life, knowing well that if technology is godlike, if it is creative, if it is liberating, it is still also demonic, enslaving, and destructive. It is

[24] Both quotes, ibid. 54.

ambiguous, as is everything that is; not more ambiguous than pure spirit, not more ambiguous than nature, but as ambiguous as they are.[25]

It may be worth noting that in the period of this essay, Tillich counted himself as a Marxist and had close personal and scholarly links with the early critical theorists. This shows itself in important aspects of his assessment of technology. Technology cannot be separated from the specific historical context in which it has been developed, namely modern bourgeois society, and the ambiguity of technology is clearly related to the ambiguity of this society itself. It is to be affirmed as an advance on the preceding social condition and, as against political romanticism, there can be no regression to a pre-modern, pre-bourgeois, pre-industrial world. On the other hand, as we encounter it today, bourgeois society and its concomitant technology works oppressively on the human beings whom it affects.

In subsequent work Tillich picks up on a number of specific manifestations of the problem of technology. In a late lecture at the Harvard Divinity School he crystallizes a topic that can be glimpsed on many pages of his work: the problem of the self that loses its sense of self and feels itself to be reduced to a thing, reified, not by the workings of an alien power but in relation to its own freely produced object-world, i.e. the sphere of human technical production. Such a process culminates in what he called the 'negative utopias' of *Brave New World* and *1984*. Already in the 1920s, however, in 'The Technical City as Symbol' he explores the phenomenon of the modern city as an answer to humanity's quest to make itself at home in the world, a quest that, according to Tillich, is itself a counter-movement to the quintessentially human experience of the 'uncanniness' of existence revealed in the existential analysis of anxiety. Like other forms of technology, he says, the modern technical city is an attempt to overcome uncanniness. Unfortunately the technical intervention involved in constructing the city exemplifies the negative aspects of what he has called 'transforming technology': 'The soil, the bond with the living earth, is taken away. Hewn or artificial stone separates us from it. Reinforced concrete buildings separate us more than loam, wood, and bricks from the cosmic flow. Water is in pipes; fire is confined to wires.'[26] Thus the technical city itself is experienced as uncanny, an alien power in which we feel ourselves strangers, a fate especially vivid in the modern urban phenomenon of the proletariat, living in a perpetual situation of insecurity, impoverishment, and disintegration (Tillich's essay, it may be noted, was written the year after the release of the movie *Metropolis*, with its archetypal images of the city as a new Moloch, a voracious idol that demands the incessant sacrifice of its own dehumanized children).

In 1963 Tillich discerns a similar ambiguity in relation to the beginnings of manned flights into space. On the one hand he acknowledges the natural astonishment, admiration and pride that such achievements evoke. But as at

---

[25] In P. Tillich, *The Spiritual Situation in our Technical Society*, 60.   [26] Ibid. 183.

every creative intellectual step forward, the essential ambiguity of the human situation is all the more thrown into relief.

One of the results of the flight into space and the possibility of looking down at earth is a kind of estrangement between man and earth, an 'objectification' of the earth for man, the depriving 'her' of her 'motherly' character, her power of giving birth, of nourishing, of embracing, of keeping for herself, of calling back to herself. She becomes a large material body to be looked at and considered as totally calculable.[27]

It is, he adds, the most radical step in demythologizing human beings' place in the cosmos. At the same time he notes the problems associated with the conjunction of space and military technology and the difficult question of justifying costly technical research of unproven human worth whilst important issues of economic justice remain un- or at least under-addressed.

The underlying thrust of Tillich's view of technology, therefore, is that despite its many negative effects, we should not be seeking to escape from technology, but to recontextualize it in a different kind of society, in which technical values are once more made to serve all-round human flourishing. To this extent—and despite his very different assessment of progress and the phenomenon of modernity—Tillich's project is not entirely alien to that of, e.g. Maritain. Each of the trio Maritain, Berdyaev, and Tillich (circa 1950 amongst the three most influential religious writers in the Western world) can be seen as sharing the analysis that technology as we know it has, in a sense, run wild and is working as an anti-human power. The task, however, is to reintegrate it in a larger, more inclusive humanism than has yet been achieved and to subordinate it to the ultimate perspectives of religion.[28]

An influential and optimistic version of such subordinationism can be found in W. Norris Clarke's essay 'Technology and Man: A Christian Vision'. Clarke takes his orientation from the official Catholic teaching expressed in such documents as Pius XII's 1953 address 'Modern Technology and Peace', in the course of which the Pope declared that

Very far, then, from any thought of disavowing the marvels of technology and its lawful use, the believer may find himself more eager to bow his knee before the celestial Babe of the manger, more conscious of his debt of gratitude to Him Who gives all things, and the intelligence to understand them, more disposed to find a place for those same works of technology with the chorus of angels in the hymn of Bethlehem: 'Glory to God in the

---

[27] Ibid. 190.
[28] Another example from this period would be Gabriel Marcel, a Catholic philosopher and writer, often loosely referred to as a Christian 'existentialist'. See especially G. Marcel, *Men Against Humanity*, tr. G. S. Fraser (London: Harvill Press, 1952). The question of technology is addressed in chapters 3 and 4, 'Techniques of Degradation' and 'Technical Progress and Sin'. For Marcel the spread of the technological attitude is accompanied by a shift from the existential mode of 'Being' to that of 'Having'. From our perspective it is perhaps startling to read Marcel's challenging question: 'How shall we be able to grasp the fact that radio is one of the palpable factors making for our present spiritual degradation?' (*Men Against Humanity*, 39).

highest' (Luke 2:14). He will even find it natural to place beside the gold, frankincense and myrrh, offered by the Magi to the Infant God, also the modern conquests of technology: machines and numbers, laboratories and inventions, power and resources.[29]

Whilst admitting that there are more pessimistic strands within Catholic opinion,[30] Clarke affirms the idea that all human activities can be coordinated within and subordinated to the service of a common good that is defined in humanistic terms and backed up by the biblical teaching of man's having been made in God's image. God Himself being both contemplative and active, man should both seek to understand the laws of nature and also to act upon it:

He must also try his hand as a worker, not to create some totally new world out of nothing, which only God can do, but to recreate the world that has been given him, malleable and plastic under his fingers, to be transformed by his own initiative and artistic inventiveness, so that it will express in a new way both the divine image of its Creator and the human image of its recreator.[31]

Acknowledging the 'radical ambivalence' of technology that results from its being the work of a being marred by sin, the possibilities of its misuse are balanced both by humanity's persisting natural goodness and by the fact of redemption through Christ. In the case of the latter not only does God himself give an example of 'using matter as an efficacious instrument or medium' both in the Incarnation and in the sacraments of the Church that is Christ's continuing body in the world, but 'the labor of the young Jesus as a carpenter in Nazareth already lends, in principle, a divine sanction to the whole technological activity of man throughout history.'[32] Under these conditions, it seems technology can be embraced as a tool serving the purposes of the human spirit. However, Clarke is not without a sense for the risks attendant on the present situation and, he suggests, it is only in obedience to God and only under God, not as 'lonely gods of a purposeless universe we did not make', that we can see the technological project through to a good end.

This 'subordinationist' approach to the relationship between technology and religion was more or less standard for Christian theology thirty years either side

[29] Quoted in W. Norris Clarke, 'Technology and Man: A Christian View' in C. Mitcham and R. Mackey (eds.), *Philosophy and Technology: Readings in the Philosophical Problems of Technology* (New York: The Free Press, 1983), 254.

[30] More sombre Catholic views to which Clarke refers are those of Marcel and Mounier. Eric Gill would be another case in point (Gill was strongly dependent on Maritain in his theoretical writings) as would Bernanos. Kees van Kooten Niekerk suggests that positive appraisals of technology are characteristic of Catholicism, due largely to the influence of Thomas Aquinas' harmonizing approach to the relationship between nature and grace. Niekerk quotes Wilhelm E. Fudpucker (another Jesuit to whom Niekerk refers as a disciple of Teilhard) to the following effect: 'Technology not only comes forth from Christianity, it takes us into Christianity in a new and fuller sense.' Guardini could also—with appropriate reservations—be enrolled amongst the Catholic 'optimists'. See K. van K. Niekerk in S. Andersen, T. E. Andreasen, K. van K. Niekerk, *Bioetik som Teknologivurdering* (Århus: Center for Bioetik, Århus Universitet, 1997), 195–7.

[31] Mitcham and Mackey, op. cit., 251.   [32] Ibid. 251, 252.

of the middle of the twentieth century. However, the picture is reproduced with many differences of focus and nuance. One late example of this is in Rustum Roy's 1980 Hibberd Lectures, published as *Experimenting with Truth: The Fusion of Religion with Technology, Needed for Humanity's Survival*. Here Roy argued that, on the one hand, the incredible advances in what he calls science-based technology (which he abbreviates as SbT) have rendered the world's religious traditions basically moribund and useless. 'We cannot look to any presently constituted world religion for the slightest help in containing or taming the activities of SbT,' he asserts, thus dismissing the kind of hopes expressed by Clarke that technology might allow theology to exercise a guiding hand.[33] On the other hand, Roy is not an uncritical fan of SbT. 'SbT', he says, 'has delivered about as much as the human system can absorb.'[34] Left to itself 'Technology is absolutely and inexorably collective. It demands and gets regimentation, standardization, planning and order.'[35] The totalitarian system of the then Soviet Union was an attempt to manage this situation, but its programme was, in Roy's judgement, unfulfillable, if only because of the distortion introduced into the system by the preponderance of its military functions. The only way to manage technology was, he argued, for a 'Religious Hegemony' over technology. How, given the redundancy of historical religious traditions was this possible? Two factors seem central in Roy's recommendations. The first is that ' . . . the major changes caused by SbT are all finished.'[36] This might seem like an extraordinarily naïve remark in face of the extent of technological innovations since 1980, though I don't think Roy would have been perturbed by this. He could argue that these changes are essentially within existing paradigms of technical transformation and that the information revolution and gene technology are simply developments of technologies already operative at that time, even if their exponential growth in the intervening period might seem to some to mark a qualitative leap. The other part of his argument is that although no current religious traditions can immediately 'master' technology, a suitably transformed kind of religion has the potential to do so. His personal commitment is, as he makes clear, to the kind of radical theologies discussed in the previous chapter, with special emphasis on Tillich, Bonhoeffer, Bultmann, and Robinson. Religion, thus recast, can articulate the framework of ultimate concern within—and within which alone—SbT can be made to make human sense.

Roy forcefully rejects the kind of approach to the relationship between science and religion seen in such popular works as Frithiof Capra's *The Tao of Physics*, not simply because he disagrees with the specific argument of the book, but because he does not regard the issue of world views or the truthful representation of the nature of things as the ground on which science and religion should be meeting.

---

[33] R. Roy, *Experimenting with Truth: The Fusion of Religion with Technology, Needed for Humanity's Survival* (Oxford: Pergamon Press, 1981), 44.
[34] Ibid. 20   [35] Ibid. 33.   [36] Ibid. 19.

On this ground science wins every time. Rather, he insists, 'Science policy is the point at which the contact with our religious insights must be made.'[37] In other words, it is in the actual social, cultural, and political debate about values and aspirations that religion works to set the goals and parameters for SbT. In very different registers this theme recurs both in studies that are orientated towards the Churches' practical responsibilities in relation to technology[38] and those that take a more theoretical approach.[39]

A complex and nuanced approach to the question that might also be mentioned here is that of Philip Hefner. Hefner's view of the question of technology is embedded in a grand narrative that seeks to incorporate the modern scientific world view into a coherent theological picture. The scientific view of cosmic and human origins is accepted without reserve. However, within the evolution of human life, biological development is seen as reaching a level of complexification at which the biological being *homo sapiens* becomes a 'co-creator'. At this point culture supervenes on biology and a space for free action opens within the continuum of merely causal development. Science itself is only possible as a cultural activity and, therefore, science and its products are culturally dependent on free human decisions. This situation reaches a peak in a highly technicized society such as our own. Hefner writes: 'In technological civilization, decision-making is universal and unavoidable; it is the foundation for that civilization.'[40] This is not just a matter of governments needing to have a policy for the management of technology, since the issue that comes to a head at this level of technologization is more than merely social, it is also evolutionary, so that human beings really do become co-creators of what the future will be. In our technological civilization 'human decision has conditioned virtually all of the planetary physico-biogenetic systems, so that the human decision is the critical factor in the

    [37] R. Roy, *Experimenting with Truth*, 16.
    [38] See, e.g. C. Birch, *et al.* (eds.), *Faith, Science and the Future: Preparatory Readings for the 1979 Conference of the WCC* (Geneva: World Council of Churches, 1978); F. Ferguson, *Technology at the Crossroads: The Story of the Society, Religion and Technology Project* (Edinburgh: St. Andrew's Press, 1994). See also I. Barbour, *Ethics in an Age of Technology* (London: SCM Press, 1992), where Barbour sets out a practical programme by which Church members and other concerned citizens can take steps to 'redirect' technology. Like Roy, he implicitly seems to identify science policy as the decisive meeting ground for theology and science with regard to the question of technology.
    [39] e.g. David J. Hawkin, *Christ and Modernity: Christian Self-Understanding in a Technological Age*, SR Supplements, vol. 17 (Ontario: Wilfred Laurier University Press, 1985). Hawkin too invokes the Tillichian idea of a 'theonomy' that would reintegrate the threat to human autonomy presented by technology. In a very different key and in a blaze of funky neologisms, Erik Davis argues in his book *Techgnosis: Myth, Magic and Mysticism in an Age of Information* (New York: Harmony, 1998) that it is no accident that new technologies are themselves fertile in the production of myths and mystical ideas but that, finally, technology cannot itself produce the spiritual horizon needed for its own creative possibilities to be maximized. Technological possibilities, he insists, should not be mistaken for social or spiritual ones as 'netaphysicians' [sic!] characteristically assume.
    [40] P. Hefner, *The Human Factor: Evolution, Culture, and Religion* (Minneapolis: Fortress Press, 1993), 38.

continued functioning of the planet's systems.'[41] What religion specifically adds to this is a body of myths and rituals that shape the cultural perception and reception of scientific and technological activity. In this way—as opposed, say, to the approaches of Polkinghorne and Peacocke—theology (which rests upon the deliverances of myth and ritual) is not directly concerned to represent reality in a manner complementary to that of science. Rather, it is involved in shaping the cultural parameters within which we take the co-creating decisions that our technological civilization is demanding of us. Locating theology here, rather than in the attempt critically-realistically to construct a persuasive account of how the world is, is an important step, and one to which we shall return in thinking about the contribution that Heidegger's reflections on technology can make to our own theological interest in the question. Nevertheless, it should be stressed that Hefner's basic approach to technology (in seeming opposition to Heidegger) is optimistic: technology, like ourselves, is a part of nature, and what it will be is dependent on our own co-creating activity. At the same time, technology is not one sphere of human co-creating activity alongside others. Technology today both stimulates that activity and reflects it as nothing else. Who we are is so inseparable from our technological cultural practice that we can already speak of ourselves as cyborgs, as no longer defined by 'humanity' alone, but by our human technological practice. The implications of this view are concisely summarized in the concluding proposals of a series of addresses published as *Technology and Human Becoming:*

Technology is itself a sacred space.
Technology is itself a medium of divine action, because technology is about the freedom of imagination that constitutes our self-transcendence.
Technology is one of the major places today where religion happens.
Technology is the shape of religion, the shape of the cyborg's engagement with God.
Since we are cyborgs, technology is also the place where, like Jacob, we wrestle with the God who comes to engage us.[42]

III

But is the 'subordinationism' for which so many theological writers called really achievable, whether in the name of the Catholic Church or of the theological radicals? Isn't technology too assured in its own forward- and outward- and inward-expansion to worry about what religionists have to say? Can Church or theological representation on science policy panels do more than contribute to applying an occasional slight brake on the rate at which the whole process is inexorably accelerating? Doesn't such representation itself finally contribute to

---

[41] Ibid. 152.
[42] P. Hefner, *Technology and Human Becoming* (Minneapolis: Fortress Press, 2003), 88.

the ideological legitimation of technological progress which always wins through in the end, suitably rubber-stamped by ethicists and theologians? Hasn't the whole thing gone too far? Isn't the reality of the situation that we face apocalypse rather than integration?

That, at least, seems to have been the view of the French thinker Jacques Ellul, described on the Jacques Ellul home page (!) as, in one line, 'technology critic, historian, sociologist' and, in the next, as 'theologian of hope, ethicist, activist' (this last being a rather dull translation of the French *penseur engagé*). This double-description in some way pinpoints the difficulty of interpreting Ellul's dramatic and extensive work on technology. He devoted three major works to the question of technology: *The Technological Society*, *The Technological System* and *The Technological Bluff.* In the introduction to the first, he says, guardedly, that he deliberately keeps within the limits of description. Whether or not this is the case (one could be forgiven for believing that every line is palpably saturated with implicit evaluations), this is a signal that we are not going to find any explicit theological verdict on the technological society. What Ellul is attempting or claiming to offer is a description and analysis of a society and system written in purely historical and sociological terms: a human description of the human condition as found in the technological world. On the other hand, the outcome of this 'description', 'that there was nothing to say to a person of my society beyond a stoic exhortation to keep going in God's abandonment'[43] might be seen as the negative image of a preliminary theological judgement that humanity is constitutionally incapable of self-salvation and, apart from grace, is condemned to hopelessness—a judgement that fits well with Ellul's acknowledgement that his own theological thinking was constantly inspired by Karl Barth and Søren Kierkegaard.[44] If Christianity is to proclaim hope, Ellul says, it can do so convincingly if and only if it bears the impress of a thoroughly realistic assessment of the world's actual historical situation and possibilities. And that, as Ellul remarks about his own sociological and historical work, means the acknowledgement that we are in a blind alley. With specific regard to technology, we are now so gripped by the technological system that 'Man in our society has no intellectual, moral, or spiritual reference point for judging and criticizing technology.'[45] Ellul may be overstating his own case here—a question to which we shall return—but how does he arrive at this dark conclusion?

Our 'technological society', Ellul argues (in this respect striking out in a very different direction from those, like Tillich, who see technology as in some sense rooted in humanity's natural and prehistoric life), represents a new development within history. It is not a matter of the machine alone, though the machine is

---

[43] J. Ellul, *Hope in Time of Abandonment*, tr. C. E. Hopkins (New York: Seabury Press, 1973), p. vii.

[44] See idem, *Living Faith: Belief and Doubt in a Perilous World*, tr. P. Heinegg (New York: Harper and Row, 1983), p. ix.

[45] J. Ellul, *The Technological System*, tr. J. Neugroschel (New York: Continuum, 1980), 318.

'deeply symptomatic' of the nature of technique, being 'solely, exclusively, technique; it is pure technique, one might say'.[46] What technique (or 'technology') in the strong sense of the term does is to integrate the machine into society or to remake society in the image of the machine. Thus, Ellul says, 'the industrial revolution was merely one aspect of the technical revolution . . . [that] resulted not from the exploitation of coal but rather from a change of attitude on the part of the whole civilization . . .' (*TS*, 42, 44). This change is towards the priority of means over ends, since 'technique is nothing more than *means* and the *ensemble of means*' (*TS*, 19). If a technical innovation is possible, then it is necessary.

None of our wise men ever pose the question of the end of all their marvels. The 'wherefore' is resolutely passed by . . . But what good is it to pose questions of motives? Of Why? All that must be the work of some miserable intellectual who balks at technical progress. The attitude of scientists, at any rate, is clear. Technique exists because it is technique. The golden age will be because it will be. Any other answer is superfluous (*TS*, 436).

But to see technology merely in terms of the application of science, as if 'scientists' alone were responsible for it, is to see only the tip of the iceberg. The mindset of technology is no less represented by what Ellul calls 'managerial action'—'technique applied to social, economic or administrative life' (*TS*, 11).[47] It is consistent with Ellul's starting point that when he later comes to take account of the information revolution he does not find anything surprising in it. 'Information theory is not a new science, nor a technology among technologies. It has developed because the technological system exists as a system by dint of the relationships of information.'[48] That society is being remade according to the imperatives of technology means that 'technique . . . ceases to be external to man and becomes his very substance, and it progressively absorbs him' (*TS*, 6).

The results of the technological revolution are stated in now familiar terms: the destruction of tradition; the acceleration of change to a rate human beings cannot bear; rationalization; standardization; automatism; the subordination of the individual to the mass; the suppression of freedom and, indeed, of nature. The negative aspect of all this is not merely that rationalization, for example, invariably means redundancies for thousands of workers. Because technology works on human beings themselves, in their 'very substance', human beings themselves are transformed by it. This transformation can be seen in the genesis of new neuroses (Ellul mentions the disease of 'urbanitis'![49]) as human beings experience the stress of the self-transformation required of them by the technological society.

---

[46] Idem, *The Technological Society*, tr. J. Wilkinson (London: Jonathan Cape, 1965), 4. Hereafter references are given in the text as *TS* followed by page number.

[47] Cf. S. Pattison, *The Faith of the Managers* (London: Cassell, 1997).

[48] Ellul, *The Technological System*, 91.

[49] The Danish cultural historian Martin Zerlang has also written of the coincidence of the birth of the modern city and the diagnosis of a new range of diseases such as neurasthenia, vertigo, agoraphobia, and claustrophobia. See M. Zerlang, *The City Spectacular of the Nineteenth Century* (Copenhagen: Center for Urbanitet og Æstetik, Arbejdspair 9, 1995), 9.

Every sphere of human life, including thought and culture, are caught up in this transformative process with analogous results. Thus, the replacement of the theatre by the cinema means that the spectator's scope for free reaction and judgement is significantly curtailed: 'The motion picture by means of its "reality" integrates the spectator so completely that an uncommon spiritual force or psychological education is necessary to resist its pressures' (*TS*, 377). In cinema, even dreams become a mass phenomenon (although it would be very much to the point, Ellul does not cite the now common designation of Hollywood as 'the dream *factory*'). Later, in *The Technological Bluff* it is to be Euro-Disney and Michael Jackson that pre-eminently represent the evacuation of genuine freedom and profound humanity from our cultural world. Already in the nineteenth century Kierkegaard saw and unmasked the key features of technology, but his protest was not heeded. It was, Ellul guesses, 'too close to the truth' (*TS*, 55).[50]

The problem is not simply that technology brings with it a sequence of negative effects that could be dealt with on a piecemeal basis. What Ellul perceives as the dishonesty of the view that one can enjoy the positive aspects of technology while dealing with its 'problems' on a one-by-one basis, lies behind the harshness of the words he deals out both to the papacy and to the World Council of Churches, whose attitude to technology is said to be essentially one of deference. What is crucial is that technology functions as a whole, as a system, and indeed as a system that totalizes every phenomenon absorbed into it. There is no neutral ground. 'If we make use of a technique, we must accept the specificity and autonomy of its ends, and the totality of its rules. Our own desires and aspirations can change nothing' (*TS*, 141), says Ellul. The technological world that is coming to birth is essentially and profoundly monolithic. Seeing the whole picture, he asks, 'Who is too blind to see that a profound mutation is being advocated here? A new dismembering and a complete reconstitution of the human being so that he can at last become the objective (and also the total object) of technique' (*TS*, 431).

This totalizing, omnivorous power is the technological system. However, even Ellul seems to acknowledge that it has not yet completely permeated society as a whole. The world has not yet been reduced to a megamachine. 'A technological society is one in which a technological system has been installed. But it is not itself that system, and there is a tension between the two of them.'[51] There remain possibilities for resistance, although they are being steadily and, it would seem, inexorably eroded. But even these possibilities may be alarming: modern art, Ellul says, had to go so far as to resort to madness in its resistance to technology, since 'only madness is inaccessible to the machine' (*TS*, 404).

---

[50] It is striking that Kierkegaard is also seen as a (critical) prophet of the internet by the philosopher Hubert Dreyfus: see H. L. Dreyfus, *On the Internet* (London: Routledge, 2001).
[51] Ellul, *The Technological System*, 18.

As it presents itself today, the technological system is, as the title of Ellul's third technology book suggests, a bluff, or even a downright deceit. Its promise is that of utopia, of a freedom in which human beings will be able to develop and to enjoy their powers to the maximum. But its reality is the reduction of human freedom to a functional element within a depersonalizing totality. Is it too bold to see in this portrait a 'type' of a familiar theological adversary, one who is a liar and the father of lies? Perhaps. In any case, the technological system proves, finally, to be imperfect. It makes mistakes and 'leaves a margin of chaos'.[52] It is here that the possibility of critique is to be found.

We must be prepared to reveal the fracture lines and to discover that everything depends on the qualities of individuals. Finally, not really, if we know how little room there is to maneuver and therefore, not by one's high position or by power, but always alter the model of development from a source and by the sole aptitude for astonishment, we profit from the existence of little cracks of freedom, and install them in a trembling freedom which is not attributed to or mediated by machines or politics, but which is truly effective, so that we may truly invent the new thing for which humanity is waiting.[53]

However, though Ellul speaks of being 'truly effective' and 'truly inventing the new thing for which humanity is waiting', it is hard to see that he leaves us with very much to hope for other than hope itself. As he stated the case in *Hope in Time of Abandonment*, the human basis of hope is limited to the three 'decisions' of 'indolence' (i.e. the refusal of the values of a civilization of work), prayer, and realism. But does such 'realism' leave scope for anything other than simply transposing the task into another dimension, an eschatology that, from the point of the world's situation, is either altogether inward or altogether transcend-ent? Can Ellul offer more on the plane of human action and value than a kind of negative dialectic, a critique of the present in the name of an impossible and humanly unattainable freedom? If technology is charged with a totalizing ten-dency that sucks all phenomena into its infernal machinery, is this not a projection of Ellul's own Barthian method, namely, the reduction of the phe-nomena in their entirety to a single category (in this case 'technology') that is then used as a name for the kingdom of this world, for everything that is not and is intrinsically and essentially opposed to the Kingdom of God? Is there anything here one could lay hold of as a concrete strategy of resistance or transformation?[54]

These questions are formulated with an eye to the theological dimensions of Ellul's work, but they are essentially analogous to the questions that lie at the

---

[52] Idem, *The Technological Bluff*, tr. G. W. Bromiley (Grand Rapids: Eerdmans, 1990), 412.
[53] Ibid.
[54] For view of Ellul that takes up such questions see D. J. Fasching, 'The Dialectic of Apocalypse and Utopia in the Theological Ethics of Jacques Ellul', in F. Ferré (ed.), *Technology and Religion: Research in Philosophy and Technology*, (Greenwich, Conn.: JAI Press, 1990), x. 149–65; see also Hawkin, *Christ and Modernity*, 85 ff.

heart of the failure of the counterculture of the 1960s in its secular as well as its more mystical forms. Here too was a critique of modern technological society in which many of the complaints articulated by Ellul were to be heard again and again. The problem is that if society is so totally in the grip of a dehumanizing technology that there are no lines of creative development leading from the present to a better future state, then it becomes impossible to give human meaning, worth, and value to any envisaged utopia 'beyond the wasteland'. The rupture between what is and what will be is so complete that it is impossible to find criteria for distinguishing between fantasy and terror. Nor, indeed, can we even say for what or for whom the utopia beyond the apocalypse is being conceived. Would humans who had become so utterly absorbed into the machine as to be indistinguishable from it deserve—would they even desire or welcome—any such new world? We might say that for Ellul himself the Christian doctrine of creation serves to provide a possible context for answering such questions, since that doctrine names the being and the relationships that are to find fulfilment in any possible eschaton. Even so, the illegibility of the divine signature to the work of humanity as we now find it seems to be so great that it is no easy task to say whom the transformation we are to hope for will actually benefit. Versions of the critique that lack any such background in a doctrine of creation are, of course, even more badly placed with regard to this question. Humanity, technologized through and through, becomes something to be overcome in the name of a post-human entity for which there is no name and whose values cannot be justified within the horizons of the mere present. Liberation and terror are indistinguishable.

IV

The realization that there were limits to economic and technological growth, the oil crisis of the early 1970s, debates about nuclear energy and an increasing awareness of humanity's manifold abuse of the environment made the kind of optimistic subordinationism of Clarke and others considerably less persuasive. This period has consequently seen a succession of radical, green or eco-, and feminist theologies that more or less take for granted the kind of understanding of technology seen in Ellul, whether or not he is the direct source for the various authors' critical perspectives. For the liberation theology of Ruben Alves it was Marcuse rather than Ellul who provided the theoretical framework for rejecting technologism as an inherently oppressive and hopeless power. In the technological society humanity itself is simply absorbed into and made a part of the technological system. In a riposte to Van Leeuwen, Alves comments that 'If we agree with van Leeuwen that technology was, in a certain sense, the mother of a new freedom for history, we must add now: like Saturn it devoured its own child.'[55] For feminists, technology is all that Ellul says it is, but its shadows are made even darker by the way in which it is, ultimately, an expression of patriarchy, 'boys with toys' as the 1980s slogan had it. Technocracy's dominion over the planet reflects and expresses patriarchy's dominion over women. Mary Daly gives a characteristically forceful statement. 'Phallic myth and language', she says, 'generate, legitimate, and mask the material pollution that threatens to terminate all sentient life on this planet.'[56] With reference to Rachel Carson's ground-breaking ecological study *Silent Spring*, Daly writes that 'the springs are becoming more silent, as the necrophilic leaders of phallotechnic society are carrying out their programs of planned poisoning for all life on the planet.'[57] As the title of Daly's book indicates, she is largely preoccupied with gynaecology, a medical practice whose 'purpose and *intent*', in her words 'was/is not healing in a deep sense but violent enforcement of the sexual caste system'.[58] On this basis she sees no essential difference between witch trials, vivisection by Nazi doctors, and modern mainstream gynaecology. All are different manifestations of the same underlying phallotechnic spirit. As with Ellul, the condemnation of the techno-logical system goes so deep that there can be no talk of amelioration. But whereas Ellul clings to a hope in an impossible eschatological future, Daly looks to separatism, i.e. the voluntary withdrawal of women from the man-made world.

Few feminist theologians have followed Daly in this withdrawal, though many share her sense of a deep symbiosis between patriarchy and technology. It is in this vein that Rosemary Radford Ruether pictures the modern world view inaugurated by Newtonian physics:

All innate spiritual elements having been eliminated from nature, human spirit need no longer interact with nature as a fellow being, but could see itself, like the clock-maker God, as transcendent to it and ruling it from outside. Soon this presupposition of God could itself be discarded, leaving the scientists, together with the rulers of state and industry, in charge of passive matter, infinitely reconstructible to serve their inter-ests.[59]

Amongst the tangled roots of this situation, she claims, must be counted

... patterns of domination, whereby male elites in power deny their interdependency with women, exploiting human labor and the biotic community around them. They seek to exalt their own power infinitely, by draining the lives of those other humans and nonhuman sources of life on which they depend ... The system of domination has grown increasingly global; at the same time the links of interdependence between the human and biotic parts of the chain have grown increasingly remote from each other. It becomes

---

[55] R. M. Alves, *A Theology of Human Hope* (Washington: Corpus, 1969), 27.
[56] M. Daly, *Gyn/Ecology: The Metaethics of Radical Feminism* (Boston: Beacon Press, 1978), 9.
[57] Ibid. 21.   [58] Ibid. 227.
[59] R. R. Ruether, *Gaia and God: An Ecofeminist Theology of Earth Healing* (London: SCM Press, 1992), 196.

increasingly difficult for elites in modern cities even to recognize these links or to imagine the ripple effects of destruction unleashed by the operations of their daily lives.[60]

Although observant of the patriarchal structures of the biblical creation story, Ruether rejects Lynn White's view that the 'dominion' over creatures which God gives to Adam in Genesis 2 is to be understood in terms of a carte blanche for planetary exploitation.[61] Rather, she says, 'Humans are not given ownership or possession of the earth . . . [but] usufruct of it. Their rule is the secondary one of care for it as a royal steward, not as an owner who can do with it what he wills.'[62] Here, as generally, she is resistant to glib simplifications. Her aim is not to endorse the one-dimensional black-and-white scenarios of Daly's vision but to work for the actual reversal of the damage human beings are wreaking on the planet. Her final recommendations are basically those of involvement in locally based green action groups and personal lifestyle change. In contrast to the view that will be explored below in Chapter 7, she does however see a direct line from a repentant change of consciousness at a religious level to transforming action in the world.

Other green or ecological theologies likewise tend to spend relatively little time on analysing technology. Taking for granted that the devastating effects of current technology are there for all to see (recall Matthew Fox's jibe of 'evil technology'[63]), and likewise assuming that even if historically influential the idea of 'man' having 'dominion over the earth' is (at the very least) unhelpfully one-sided, these theologies have typically been more interested in constructing alternative frames of reference that could help us to think and act otherwise than in the manner of technology. What is at stake is a reconceptualizing or even a remythologizing of the relationship between humans, nature, and God that can help us to break habits and patterns of dominance and exploitation. These may have more or less Christianized versions of the Gaia hypothesis (or something akin to it) hovering in the background, i.e. a view of the earth that sees it as itself a living, sentient whole within which and through which alone we become what we are and not simply the indifferent stage on which the drama of humanity's creation, fall and redemption gets worked out. Examples would be Paul Samtire's vision of 'Brother Earth', the works of Matthew Fox and his 'creation spirituality', and Sallie McFague's image of the world as God's Body.[64] It may be added that

---

[60] R. R. Ruether, *Gaia and God: An Ecofeminist Theology of Earth Healing* (London: SCM Press, 1992), 200–1. Not all feminists necessarily share such techno-scepticism, viz. Donna Haraway's remark that 'I would rather be a cyborg than an earth mother.' See Donna J. Haraway, *Simians, Cyborgs and Women: The Reinvention of Nature* (London: Free Association Press, 1991).

[61] White's essay 'The Historical Roots of Our Ecologic Crisis' originally appeared in *Science* 155, 10 March 1967. It is anthologized in Mitcham and Mackey (eds.), op. cit. Norris Clarke's theology of technology could, of course, be read as giving a rather strong endorsement to White's view (which, in the essay itself, he says is that of a 'churchman', i.e. it is an appeal for theological rethinking rather than simply an attack on Christianity from the outside).

[62] Ibid. 21.   [63] See Introduction, above, n. 1.

[64] See P. T. de Chardin, *The Phenomenon of Man* (London: Collins, 1959; H. Paul Samtire, *Brother Earth: Nature, God and Ecology in the Time of Crisis* (New York: Camden, 1979); M. Fox, *Original* Blessing; idem, *The Coming of the Cosmic Christ: The Healing of Mother Earth and the Birth*

despite Teilhard's positive take on technology, there are important elements of his vision of evolution as a process of continuing incarnation that make him an important precursor of some of these newer theologies and spiritualities. Jürgen Moltmann characteristically links the ecological crisis with the need of a more Trinitarian theology. Such a theology, he says, overcomes the false conception of God as a subject/creator for whom the world is the mere object of his activity, a conception that lies at the root of humanity's self-image as a subject confronting a world that is simply there to be used for its benefit. Instead of the kind of knowledge that serves the interests of domination, he claims, Trinitarian thinking leads us to a knowledge characterized as and by participation.[65] More recently, Moltmann too has appealed to the 'wisdom' motif that we encountered already in Maritain, although in Moltmann's case this is worked out with more specific reference to a biblical idea of wisdom.[66]

V

An interesting and interestingly different recent study, *Habits of the Hi-Tech Heart: Living Virtuously in an Information Age* by Quentin J. Schultze, brings the kind of moral and theological critique of technology we have seen in Ellul into the world found this side of the information revolution. Unlike Ellul, however (and, in this respect, more like Ruether), Schulze is more interested in devising specific tactics for ameliorating the negative pressures of cyber culture than in simply consigning it wholesale to perdition. He sees such an ameliorative approach as stemming from a perspective congruent with de Tocqueville's observations that 'moral responsibility is a prerequisite to democratic life' and that this involves a concern for the concrete task of preserving and furthering the actual possibilities of democratic life here and now. Schulze's complaint against cyber culture is precisely that it systematically erodes these moral capacities. Like Ellul, he sees technology as tending to totalize itself and its world and as being as pervasive in a manifold of cultural activities as it is in science or industry. It is precisely the informationism of the present that reveals and actualizes technology's total character. The virtual world of electronic communication is a continuum along which serious science meets, blends into and is confused with processes of relentless trivialization. Very much in the spirit of Paul Virilio, whom he cites, Schulze sees the world of cyber culture as a moral vacuum: 'As a quasi-religion, informationism preaches the *is* over the *ought*, *observation* over

of a Global Renaissance (San Francisco: Harper and Row, 1989); S. McFague, *The Body of God: An Ecological Theology* (London: SCM Press, 1993).

   [65] See J. Moltmann, *God in Creation: An Ecological Doctrine of Creation*, tr. M. Kohl (London: SCM Press, 1985).

   [66] J. Moltmann, *Science and Wisdom*, tr. M. Kohl (London: SCM Press, 2003).

intimacy, and *measurement* over *meaning.'*[67] In line with this a whole stream of
negative evaluations is set in motion: knowing becomes reduced to mere jour-
nalism, and institutions of knowledge such as the public library that fostered
communal values of citizenship yield to informational databases that are entirely
user-oriented; religious affiliation can be chosen to suit one's personal preferences
and the personality itself can be redefined according to arbitrary choices—
'"Building" a persona', Schulze comments, 'is one of the chief rhetorical strategies of the information age'[68]; but, paradoxically, the increase of information
and the endless exchange of information between such constructed personae is
matched by an increase in the individual's sense of isolation and the loss of
intimacy; cyber communities define themselves not by shared public life but by
specialized interests; somewhat echoing the vocabulary of Maritain, he sees a
decline from wisdom to knowledge to information; instead of truthfulness what
matters are the images produced by the cyber world's 'symbol brokers'.

Schulze does not attempt to claim the apocalyptic high ground of Ellul's
ultimate hope, although he makes clear that his suggestions for a succession of
counter strategies to the enveloping cloud of cyber confusion is rooted in a
religious starting point. Revealed religions, he comments early on, are a 'rich
source of moral wisdom that can virtuously shape our informational practices'.[69]
We can learn from such religions that we are dependent on 'language, story and
image to understand who we are and what our purpose is on earth'[70] and that
messages belong to contexts that belong to 'practices passed along from generation to generation'.[71] To enter into the kind of communal relationships within
which such learning can occur we need to reverse the tempo induced by the fever
of 'bandwidth envy' and to slow down, to be willing to listen, to be silent, to
remember, to care about what it is we are hearing and to be accountable. If this all
sounds a bit dull, we also need a sense for the comic in face of the 'foolishness
masquerading as progress' that is typical of hi-tech endeavours.[72] Along with such
a 'comedic perspective' we also need to rediscover friendship. A condition of all
such forms of re-learning of community is orality: 'We are creatures of the
spoken word, our native medium, and no humanly devised communication
technology can improve on it... Human speech is the primary means for
incarnating human community.'[73] Such communities as we might build, however, are not envisaged in terms of some old-world rooted agrarian community
with a history of a thousand or more years of settled habitation. Invoking a term

---

[67] Q. J. Schulze, *Habits of the Hi-Tech Heart: Living Virtuously in an Information Age* (Grand
Rapids: Baker Academic Press, 2002), 26.
[68] Ibid. 144.   [69] Ibid. 22.   [70] Ibid. 71.   [71] Ibid. 74.
[72] Ibid. 95
[73] Ibid. 174, 177. The whole question of orality as a key category of ecclesial practice has, in
recent years, been associated with Walter J. Ong and has become a major theme in contemporary
homiletics where it would typically be presented in such a way as to give support to Schulze's
position. See, e.g. W. Ong, *Orality and Literacy: The Technologizing of the Word* (London: Methuen,
1982).

that has strong biblical and distinctively American resonances, Schulze sees us as people ineluctably on the move: the question is whether we construct our passage through the world according to the manner of thieves and tourists or as 'sojourners'.

Although Schulze's account of cyber culture is drawn in the sharp polarities characteristic of Ellul, with little or no trace of the celebration of technology's intrinsic creative element found in Berdyaev and Tillich, his response is not simply to counsel us to hope for an eschatological fulfilment coming from the far side of every possible utopia. Neither does he anticipate a simple 'subordination' of technological values and lifestyles to the higher wisdom of revealed religion. Instead he offers a more immediate, more pragmatic, more limited set of responses. Having criticized Ellul for dismissing out of hand the attempt to make a real difference in our day-to-day dealings with technology and having questioned the feasibility of the grander versions of the subordinationist approach, it would therefore seem inconsistent to criticize Schulze for trying to be practical without being too grand. Nevertheless, although I happen to think that there is some practical wisdom in much of what he says, the way in which he poses the question reveals a residual dualism that, on the one hand, inhibits a full acceptance of the legitimacy of technology in its proper sphere and, on the other, unhelpfully limits the scope of faith and theology. Why is this?

To answer this question we need to look more closely at what is involved in the idea of a narrative tradition that lies at the heart of Schulze's strategy. This reflects the widespread turn of contemporary theology towards communitarian and narrative-based theologies. Such theologies have characteristically stepped away from any direct contest with science or philosophy over the nature of truth or the way things are and argue that religious beliefs, symbols, values, and practices can only be understood from within, by playing the language game and inhabiting the form of life to which they belong. In their own terms, such theologies must and generally do resist asking about the status of the narrative's basic terms. These are simply the bedrock behind which one cannot go and which it is simply fruitless to attempt to overturn. All one does in such an attempt is to demonstrate that one is playing a different language game from those attempting to inhabit the rich land built up, layer upon layer, on this bedrock. The truths of religion cannot be assessed from outside the orbit of religion itself. If, for many practitioners of such theologies, this involves accepting the self-limiting ordinance that religion for its part must similarly keep to its own turf and not try interfering with (for example) the processes of science, the boundaries between what is and what is not properly internal to any given discourse may nevertheless be variously interpreted.

From the point of view of the present enquiry it would seem hard, given such a starting point, really to raise the question as to *whether God can be thought in a godly way* for one living in the conditions of the contemporary technologized world. Why not? Firstly, because our enquiry accepts the technological world and its institutions as the given landscape within which our own thought moves. This does not mean that, with Mark C. Taylor, we simply embrace the e-world with utopian fervour. The negative tendencies highlighted by the critical voices we have been considering are to be listened to, although (obviously) a mere survey of the kind offered in this chapter cannot provide a basis for deciding which elements of technology are to be accepted or rejected or whether it is at all possible to enter the domain of technology without buying into the whole programme (as Ellul claimed we would have to do). What then does this 'acceptance' of technology mean? To answer this question we will need a more adequate view of the relationship between technology, knowledge, and thinking than we have yet achieved, although we have gathered especially helpful pointers from, e.g. Guardini. Provisionally, however, it can be said that the point is not to counter technology on its own terms, to propose more or less of it, but rather (1) given the saturation of contemporary institutions and processes of knowledge by technology, and (2) accepting with the radical theologians that this signals a kind of 'death of God' within those institutions and processes, going on to ask whether—*nevertheless*—a kind of thinking about God is still available to us and what such thinking might be or be like, seen within the perspective of a technologized world. But, secondly, this means entering on a kind of questioning of the foundations of religious thinking that narrative theologies characteristic-ally and designedly avoid. That is to say there is a real question, a real 'whether', at play in this enquiry that would be excluded in principle by the narrativists. Schulze's case, for instance (at least in the text under consideration), is premised on the acceptance of the legitimacy of religious communities and of their basic theological narratives that justifies taking them as a base from which to counter the depredations of cyber culture. The line of questioning of the present enquiry, however, requires us to suspend the privileged discourse of any particular religious community *in the first instance*.

Although I accept that *total* abstraction from concrete traditions and commit-ments is neither possible nor desirable, and although my enquiry is consciously and deliberately framed in the light of concerns that belong specifically to the crisis of Christian thought in our time and aims to serve the renewal of Christian thought, I do not see why this should preclude our critically reflecting on the foundations of our own commitments, traditions and narratives. On the con-trary, such reflection is constantly and urgently demanded, if only because the kind of self-contained community that the narrativists describe or assume just doesn't exist. Gavin Hyman has summarized the narrativist perspective in speak-ing of the theological need 'to locate oneself, groundlessly, within a story, a narrative, a tradition that is all-embracing and outsideless',[74] but this, as I see it, is just the problem. There is in fact no one anywhere in the developed world (i.e. the world shaped by and as technology) who actually inhabits an all-

---

[74] G. Hyman, review of G. Pattison, *Agnosis: Theology in the Void*, in *Journal of Literature and Theology*, 12 (1998), 423.

embracing, outsideless story, narrative or tradition. No one now thinking has or could develop their thought to anything beyond the most rudimentary form without that thought being filtered, structured, and shaped by a *plurality* of stories, narratives, and traditions and therefore without having at some point to engage in a comparison and evaluation of their own starting point with various possible 'outsides' (such as the narratives of science and technology). Putting it at its simplest, no one grows up simply and merely enclosed in the Christian story—not least because, as users of technology, we cannot but participate in the intellectual, social, and cultural structures that originated technology and that sustain it and make us competent to use it. These structures necessarily include the structures of the much-maligned Enlightenment rationality, although I shall argue that they are not limited to such rationality. Indeed, we also come to thinking as participants in a culture in which the technological structuring of thought and imagination (the book as well as the cinema and the internet is, after all, already a product of technology) has for centuries been interwoven with romantic counter-technological currents and the complex and shifting presence of many diverse cultural traditions (as, for example, in modernism's 'discovery' of African art and Russian ballet). In such processes religious and antireligious elements have played back and forth across borders that are constantly being redefined. There is no way in which we can think seriously about anything except in so far as we think it in relation to the conflict of possible interpretations to which every phenomenon within the contemporary world is exposed. This may sound like relativism, but it is simply the condition of being able to argue about and for the truth of any particular interpretation: that this truth is proved in a complex, multisided and developing exchange of ideas and perspectives.

This means that if thinking about God is to be a genuine possibility for our time it can only be so if we are able to give an account of its relation to the truth of our time, a truth that (I suggest) is not found in science alone but, more particularly, in technology and in the refraction of human consciousness in the lens of technology. And this remains the case even if—perhaps especially if—the thinking we are aiming at is a thinking that is radically distinct from anything that is or could be the object of technological framing and manipulation. If it does not reckon with the truth of technology then it is simply fantasy. In this respect one might say that although radical theology was justified in embracing modern thought and in taking a sober view of the actual alienation of ecclesiastical theology from the patterns of both academic and popular contemporary thought, it stopped halfway. It is part of the radicals' achievement that, like many others, I have no embarrassment or guilt in saying that a Christian believer can in general terms accept the theoretical perspectives of Darwinism. However, the radicals seemed largely to overlook that modern scientific thought is not merely a theoretical enterprise but is also shaped in and as technology. If, however, it is allowed that secular thought is only the tip of the iceberg of technological thinking, if secular thought is in its essence technological thought, then it comes to seem possible that secular theology had scarcely begun its real work when it ground to a halt. Essentially it preoccupied itself with the view from the deck of modernity and, for the most part, did not care to penetrate the techno-logical engine room that was driving the whole enterprise. That step can no longer be postponed.

These comments lead to a further observation. If radical theology were to move beyond its purely theoretical concerns and broach questions of technology, its strategy of assimilation would need to be seriously reviewed. For technological thinking—at least as understood by its critics—is a continuous challenge to the personalist values and paradoxical transcendence affirmed by many of the radicals themselves. No one today can seriously argue—I don't think anyone does argue—that we could or should simply embrace technology as the all-determining horizon of thinking about God in a manner analogous to that in which the radical theologians urged us to make secular thought the defining environment of theological reflection. This is partly because technology itself is by no means a settled horizon, but a complex of decisions and operations that are constantly under way. But it is also because no one doubts that although technology may make big and even convincing promises, it also holds even bigger dangers. A thoroughly secular human being remains, after all, a human being. It is not clear, however, whether after several generations of genetic engineering we would be able to recognize our genetic descendants as human beings, although whether the species as a whole or some super-privileged or underprivileged group within it would be the main recipients (beneficiaries?) of such technological manipulation remains to be seen. I am happy to be Darwin-ian, but this by no means decides the response that I am challenged to make to the technology made possible by Darwinian science.

These remarks vis-à-vis the project of radical theology may also be applied to the so-called post-secular current of theology of the last decade. Like the radical theologians, these 'refutations' of secular thought remains essentially an essay in ideas, a match of like with like, even if the 'other' against whom the match is played is viewed as strictly unauthorized to play. Even the extension of the debate into the field of social science leaves unasked the relation of such 'science' to the larger framework of technological thinking in which (it could be argued) it belongs and in which alone its ultimate significance for human self-representation can be seen. However, the interest of post-secular theology in such issues as the meaning of the city or the relation of theology to the general economy of knowledge within the contemporary university points towards the question concerning technology, even if this is not clearly thematized as such.

A final perspective on the ultimate failure of radical theology is simply this: that the philosophy of the modern period was always more than the ideological reflection of the period's objective forces. In some of its expressions, at least, it was also the practice of critical self-reflection on the part of those fated to inhabit the modern age. Here, however, radical theology was too often not modern enough. It transposed the given social and cultural material (modern thought, the secular world) into a theological dress without engaging in the kind of critical reflection on that material that is characteristic of the genuinely modern, thoroughly self-critical spirit. But how could one incorporate the modern into theology without simultaneously incorporating the need to reflect critically on the nature and destiny of the modern?

But although we have surveyed a range of theological interpretations of technology, of the technological society and the technological system, and have heard a number of views as to the way in which contemporary technology is getting under our intellectual skin and into our very minds, we are still far from really seeing the necessity for Christian thinking really to draw the question of technology into the question of its own inner identity. In other words, we have not taken the step from conceiving of technology as a problem *for* theology to seeing it as part of the problem *of* theology, namely the problem as to whether and how it is at all possible for us to go on thinking about God in this age of technology. To help us take that step, we turn now to the thought of Martin Heidegger, a philosopher for whom the question of technology became the central question of philosophy and its fate in the modern world.

3

Heidegger and the Question Concerning Technology

I

Although the question concerning technology played a role in the thought of Martin Heidegger that is scarcely paralleled in the case of any other major philosopher of the twentieth century, many might nevertheless regard Heidegger as an unfortunate choice of a partner-in-dialogue with whom to reflect on the meaning of technology for thinking about God. For it is easy to read Heidegger's view of technology as no more than the singularly obscure philosophical expression of a reactionary rejection of the modern world in favour of the traditional peasant world of Black Forest farmers and, as such, both obtuse and unhelpful. And even if that charge turns out to be misplaced, isn't Heidegger so notoriously difficult and so over-discussed that we would have to make a lengthy detour through the tortuous route of specialist debates that can, in any case, only ever reach an uncertain and revisable outcome? And, finally, isn't the whole thrust of his critique of technology indissociable from the least creditable aspect of his life and work, namely, his joining the Nazi Party in the spring of 1933, a biographical and intellectual event that makes it almost impossible for us to reach any kind of balanced view as to what Heidegger's view of technology really was? These doubts can be focused in just one question: was Heidegger's critique of technology to be understood as one aspect of his break with Nazism, when he came to recognize that the Third Reich was no less locked into the military-industrial complex than was what he called Americanism and Communism, or was it some kind of spiritualization of the Nazi celebration of a mythical Germanic past? Whichever way we answer the question—and there is evidence for both views—Heidegger's concern for technology seems to be tied to a set of cultural and political questions that would lead us far from the main track of this enquiry.

Such reservations have real force and, from the outset, it should be made clear that I am not intending to enter into the narrower scholarly debate about the meaning of Heidegger's philosophy, still less to defend him where he is indefensible.[1] Instead, I am aiming merely to take a lead from aspects of Heidegger's thought that, I believe, can prove helpful in formulating the guiding question as to what it might mean to think about God in an age of technology. Naturally, I hope that what I shall say will reflect a credible reading of a challenging and controversial thinker, but the chief point is not to contribute to the ever-growing mountain of Heidegger literature but simply to sharpen the focus on the matter under consideration.

We should immediately note that although the presence of a strong anti-technological current in Heidegger cannot be denied it is not the whole story. Heidegger did not simply fulminate against technology, he acknowledged both its necessity and the fact that it was here to stay. His analysis was not offered as a way of getting rid of technology but of understanding it. Only when we understand it, he insisted, can we decide whether or how we wish it to contribute to our common future. Let us therefore begin by looking at some of the positive reasons for channelling our enquiry through Heidegger at just this point.

The first, which might seem somewhat odd after what has just been said about the problems associated with his account of technology, is that much of what Heidegger has to say about the question of technology is very close to what has become a kind of popular wisdom. For Heidegger clearly belongs to a tradition of critical thinking about science and technology that can be traced back to Schiller and that we have seen reflected in Tillich and Berdyaev and, more radically, in Ellul. Of course, these kinds of diagnoses of the ills of technological society have become so widely diffused in popular discussion as no longer to seem distinctive or original and a hostile critic could use this as evidence of the essential banality of Heidegger's views. I prefer to take this 'populism' as indicating that, whether or not Heidegger's account is finally acceptable, it reflects and articulates in a philosophically coherent way an attitude that is widespread in our contemporary world.

It is in keeping with this 'representative' aspect of Heidegger's thought that, although the tone of what he has to say about technology is often negative, many of his key ideas are also found in theorists who basically take a far more positive approach. This is especially true of the proponents of critical theory. Clearly, the essentially left-wing orientation of critical theory has meant that its representatives are likely to feel uncomfortable about acknowledging kinship with a thinker whose own politics were so distasteful to them. Yet the continuities between Heidegger and such critical theorists as Marcuse, Adorno, and, more recently, Habermas cannot entirely be denied—least of all with regard to their common awareness of the negative effects of a one-sided development of technology. Habermas, for example, does not see either technology or the science underlying technology as needing to be got rid of. Nevertheless, he does regard the tendency

---

[1] See, however, my study, G. Pattison, *The Routledge Guide Book to the Later Heidegger* (London: Routledge, 2000).

to give a special and unargued privilege to technological discourse as needing to be checked and balanced by the complementary discourses of ethics and of humanity's expressive (i.e. artistic) life. Science and technology, in other words, should not be allowed to dictate the agenda of ethics, an agenda that, Habermas believes, must also be integral to the political life of society. Equally it should not be developed at the cost of our capacity for self-expression, our 'dramaturgic' possibilities as Habermas sometimes refers to them. The relationship between Habermas's thought on technology and religion is not a question that will detain us at present, although it is an issue to which we shall return in a subsequent chapter.[2] At the same time as articulating themes shared with critical theory, however, Heidegger is at the same time close to such contemporaries as the Catholic Guardini, whose call for resolute decision and responsibility vis-à-vis technology anticipates key elements in Heidegger's thought.

In fact, the complaint that Heidegger's view of technology is merely a philosophically polished expression of a basically Luddite attitude towards technology is misconceived, as we shall see. It is clear that, even if his personal preferences ran in the direction of traditional rural life, *as a thinker* Heidegger acknowledged that there was no escape from technology. Technology is a dimension of contemporary reality that has its own justification and its own inner dynamic, a dynamic that, for us, is far from exhausted. Heidegger's friend Ernst Jünger imagined humanity as moving historically towards an equatorial line that, once crossed, would see a reversal in the nihilistic values underpinning technological 'progress'. Heidegger himself, however, explicitly rejected this view. The problem was not how to move beyond technology in a historical sense, but the kind of understanding we have of technology here and now and the attitude we take towards it.[3]

A second reason for making Heidegger the particular focus of this discussion of technology is to do with the way in which he connects the question of technology to the institutionalization of knowledge and thinking in the contemporary university. Of course, people who don't go to university are just as capable of thinking as those who do, a point that Heidegger, who insisted (not entirely convincingly) that his philosophical work was 'of the same kind' as the work of Black Forest farmers, would have been the first to acknowledge. The importance of the university at this point is not because that is the only place where thinking happens but because the university as we know it embodies the concrete interface between technological rationality and thinking in the strong Heideggerian sense of the word. As such the question concerning the university is unavoidable by

[2] See Chapter 7 below. It can for now be said that it is fairly clear that whatever value religious thinking might have for contemporary human beings, it would on Habermas's account be by virtue of some kind of relation to the ethical and the expressive rather than to the technological dimensions of life.

[3] See M. Heidegger, *The Question of Being*, tr. W. Kluback and J. T. Wilde, Dual language edition (London: Vision, 1974).

virtue of its role in the construction of what counts as public knowledge. In conjunction with political, legal, and other scientific institutions, the university remains one of our society's chief forums for the testing and, so to speak, 'quality assurance' of the opinions and speculations of public discourse. Even if those teaching and researching in universities feel that their insights are neglected in favour of the thoughtless populism of the mass media, the mass media themselves are assiduous in seeking interviewees, writers, or commentators from within the university to stand guarantor for one or other opinion, whether this concerns the wives of Henry the Eighth, a new theory of sexuality, or a discovery of previously unknown subatomic particles.

It is because it must engage with the public knowledge of our time that the question of theology too, with regard to its possibility, its nature, and its benefits, unavoidably involves the question of the university. If the university sets the 'gold standard' of public knowledge, any kind of religious thought that refuses to undergo the particular discipline of contemporary academic life will inevitably fail to make good any claims to truth it might wish to make.[4] However, if the university itself is now deeply symbiotic with the technological system, then the question as to the thinking about God in an age of technology is also a question as to the relationship between thoughtful religion and the university. This question itself becomes altogether concrete in the phenomenon of theology (Christian or otherwise), and of religious studies as university disciplines.

A third reason for turning to Heidegger at this point is to do with the way in which he brings the question concerning technology into conjunction with the question of art. This latter question has, of course, been central to many modern responses to technology from the very dawn of the industrial revolution. Many versions of romanticism—arguably the leading paradigm of artistic production and experience in the modern period—have shown a clear hostility or, at least, reserve towards technology. But, often, they have also offered an alternative to both philosophy and religion as a means of shaping a mental or spiritual framework within which to articulate this reserve. Yet, sometimes, art and religion (and art and philosophy) have sought each other out, often with explicit reference to a common interest in resisting the onward march of technology. And, we should not forget, from Wedgwood to computer graphics, the practice of art has frequently made use of the best technological innovations in its own cause. This makes for multiple possibilities of convergence and divergence between art and thinking about God in relation to the world of technology. Again, Heidegger can help us to identify some of the key moments in this complex story. As we shall see both in this chapter and in Chapter 9, his own thoughts on the relationship between art, philosophy, and technology (and,

---

[4] I am essentially in agreement here with the kind of stance taken towards theology's necessary 'publicness' made by David Tracy. See D. Tracy, *The Analogical Imagination: Christian Theology and the Culture of Pluralism* (London: SCM Press, 1981), ch. 1 and 2.

indeed, religion) are focused in his reflections on the German poet Hölderlin. These are amongst the most important elements of his later philosophy, though often overlooked in English language commentary. What he says about Hölderlin, however, invites interpretation in relation to many other artists, art movements and views of art (as when, in Chapter 8, I attempt to read Heidegger's Hölderlin interpretation alongside some thoughts about the cinematic vision of Andrei Tarkovsky).

A further important theme that comes to play a crucial role in Heidegger's account of technology is what he called 'planetary homelessness'. This theme is perhaps less prominent than that of poetry and art, although it is closely connected with them. After sketching what Heidegger means by this expression in the present chapter, I shall return to it in my closing reflections on 'the city of the homeless'.

II

In starting to explore how Heidegger understood the question concerning technology, let us begin not with anything technological in the modern sense but with a material object made by human beings that provides a striking contrast to the way in which modern technology relates to things and to its materials. This is part of Heidegger's renowned description of the 'work of art' that is a Greek temple. The temple, he writes,

First fits together and at the same time gathers around itself the unity of those paths and relations in which birth and death, disaster and blessing, victory and disgrace, endurance and decline acquire the shape of destiny for a human being ... Standing there the building rests on the rocky ground. This resting of the work draws up out of the rock the mystery of that rock's clumsy yet spontaneous support. Standing there, the building holds its ground against the storm raging above it and so first makes the storm itself manifest in its violence. The luster and gleam of the stone, though itself apparently glowing only by the grace of the sun, yet first brings to light the light of the day, the breadth of the sky, the darkness of the night. The temple's firm towering makes visible the invisible space of air. The steadfastness of the work contrasts with the surge of the surf, and its own repose brings out the raging of the sea. Tree and grass, eagle and bull, snake and cricket first enter into their distinctive shapes and thus come to appear as what they are.[5]

In this kind of work, as Heidegger comments a few pages later, 'metals come to glimmer and shimmer, colors to glow, tones to sing, the word to speak' (*PLT*, 46

---

[5] From the essay 'On the Origin of the Work of Art' in M. Heidegger, *Poetry, Language, Thought*, tr. A. Hofstadter (New York: Harper and Row, 1971), 42 [*GA*, 5, 27–8]. Further references to this collection are given in the text as '*PLT*'. I have given the German source of all Heidegger citations as found in the *Gesamtausgabe* published by Vittorio Klostermann in square brackets following the English translation reference. The *Gesamtausgabe* references are given as *GA* followed by volume and page number. Where these alone are given it is because I do not know of an English translation.

[*GA*, 5, 32]). If—as Heidegger himself so often does—we go back to the Greek language, the temple itself is a work of *techné*, but this is a *techné* that does not impose itself upon what we might loosely call nature. Rather, it allows nature to reveal itself, to be seen as nature. It opens up to human beings the wonder of their world and environment and gives to them a sense of their own distinct yet fragile being as mortals dwelling on earth, beneath heaven. Whereas some versions of early Greek civilization or of poetry and art might interpret this in terms of a human idea imposing itself on or coming to shine through the material form of mere nature, Heidegger's emphasis is on what we would call the material element itself. What we see in the temple is not the realization of an idea (let's say the architect's vision of what it should look like), but what the temple's own material being gives us to see. It is this way of working matter itself, and not any 'idea' that first opens the world up to human habitation.

That is one way of relating to matter. But there is another way that is also exemplified already in the remote human past. This is the use of matter as an instrument (as material, we might say) for achieving certain predetermined ends. Heidegger also refers to this as seeing matter in terms of equipment. As opposed to the way in which matter is 'used' in temple-building, 'In fabricating equipment—e.g. an ax—stone is used, and used up. It disappears into usefulness' (*PLT*, 46 [*GA*, 5, 32]). Matter used in this way ultimately becomes 'mere' matter, an ensemble of 'mere things'. This 'equipmental' way of using or relating to matter is characteristic for technology and, in the modern era, it has become the dominant and virtually the exclusive way in which we understand matter, nature, and things. Instead of 'bringing forth' the natural in nature, as the kind of art exemplified in the temple does, technology 'challenges forth' (*herausfordert*) whatever it is in nature we happen to need. Instead of allowing nature to reveal itself out of itself, technological man sets up a frame (*Gestell*) that sets out the parameters within which alone a now objectified nature is to be known and used (and, like the stone in the axe, even 'used up'). Whereas a traditional watermill relies on the flow of water that it uses but which it does not control, the modern hydroelectric turbine transforms water into electricity in such a way that it can be stored and used at will as a 'resource'. Moreover, this 'resource' or product has lost any exclusive relation to its source—coal, gas, wind, or uranium are just as serviceable for producing electricity as is water. It is this approach to nature as a repository of resources that provides the 'frame' set up in advance of any particular experience or set of experiences of nature that ultimately sets the stage for the advent of modern technology, though it itself pre-dates technology. Such 'enframing' and not this or that form of technology constitutes the real danger threatening humanity—a view that encompasses even the atom or hydrogen bomb. 'Man stares at what the explosion of the atom bomb could bring with it. He does not see that the atom bomb and its explosion are merely the final emission of what has long since taken place, has already happened' (*PLT*, 166 [*GA*, 79, 4]).

A further aspect of enframing is that what is 'set up' in this way becomes a 'picture'. The distinctiveness of the modern 'world picture' (*Weltbild*), Heidegger remarks, is not that it is in one way or another superior to the medieval world picture or the Greek world picture. What is truly distinctive about it is precisely that in the modern age the world is seen *as* a picture: 'The world picture does not change from an earlier medieval one into a modern one, but rather the fact that the world becomes a picture at all is what distinguishes the essence of the modern age.'[6] Whereas in other ages humans experienced themselves as belonging *within* a world, they have now come to understand themselves as subjects confronting the world as an object positioned over against them. This situation applies to the world as a whole and to the entities that make up the world or that are found within it—including the human subject's own experiences. 'Hence world picture, when understood essentially, does not mean a picture of the world but the world conceived and grasped as picture.'[7] This 'picture', however, is not understood by Heidegger as something that we moderns simply contemplate in a detached kind of way. Once more the connection with technology is decisive: what having the world before us as a pictured object enables us to do is to project into that world a way of knowing, appropriating, and organizing the 'reality' thus depicted.

Although I have thus far used the possibly misleading terms 'humanity' and 'nature', the real danger that concerns Heidegger is not the human exploitation of nature, but that humanity itself is reduced to being a mere 'resource' in the fulfilment of technologically determined goals (a concern, we may note once more, which finds an echo in Habermas's critique of instrumental rationality's tendency to subvert human ethical and expressive needs and requirements). Implicit in all of this, of course, is the view that modern science has not developed as a result of some disinterested concern for truth, but as an essential accompaniment of a fundamentally instrumental approach to the world. As Heidegger puts it, 'Within the complex of machinery that is necessary to physics in order to carry out the smashing of the atom lies hidden the whole of physics up to now.'[8]

As his comments about the atom bomb make clear, Heidegger does not see technology as something that suddenly appeared with the industrial revolution, and much of his later philosophy is taken up with tracing the long and often convoluted path leading to where we are now. Amongst the important milestones on this way to which Heidegger gives his attention are: the change in Greek philosophy that can, broadly, be identified with Plato; the translation of Greek philosophy into Latin and its subsequent Christianization; Newton's revolution in the understanding of motion; and Friedrich Nietzsche's doctrine of eternal recurrence. I shall, therefore, briefly run through these points. It is, however,

---

[6] M. Heidegger, 'The Age of the World Picture' in idem, *The Question Concerning Technology,* tr. W. Lovitt (New York: Harper and Row, 1977), 130 [*GA*, 5, 90].
[7] Ibid. 129 [*GA*, 5, 89].   [8] Ibid. 124 [*GA*, 5, 84].

important as we do so to remember that Heidegger himself spurned the idea that real philosophical thinking could be acquired through lists of 'results' and the chief thing for him was always for the student really to engage with the ideas at issue. The kind of summarizing approach being adopted here cannot but oversimplify lines of thought that are precisely intended to resist being summarized!

The detail of Heidegger's understanding of Greek philosophy is extremely complex, not least because it is largely worked out in a sequence of lecture courses each focused on particular texts. The interpretation of these texts often involves Heidegger in new and sometimes controversial translations, and, indeed, the question of translation, language, and understanding is a continuous and vital thread throughout his thought. There are also significant shifts in his position with regard to particular thinkers (such as his view concerning the usefulness of Aristotle's account of earlier Greek philosophy), so it is inevitably a simplification to speak of 'Heidegger's view' of Greek thought in general and of Plato in particular.

With this reservation in mind, we may nevertheless broadly say that Heidegger sees Plato as marking an epochal shift in ancient consciousness. Of course, Plato was not the founder of the philosophical tradition and, using Socrates as a mouthpiece, many of the positions for which he argues are developed in dialogue with such predecessors as Heraclitus and Parmenides. But, Heidegger suggests, something has happened between the original experience of truth that comes to articulation in the works of these so-called Presocratic writers (though, of course, Heidegger himself points out that this term already imposes a particular interpretation of the history of ideas on them—they did not see themselves as 'Presocratic' any more than Kant thought of himself as a Pre-Hegelian!). To see what that 'something' is we might pause to consider Heidegger's own idea of truth.

Heidegger takes his bearings from the original Greek word for truth, *alétheia*. Understanding the initial '*a-*' as a negative prefix, and tracing the central part of the word back to the root *lath* 'to be concealed', *alétheia* is shown to mean 'unconcealment', the world as shining forth in its own natural luminosity. The original Greek experience of this luminosity, however, was not in the manner of spectators viewing an illuminated object 'out there'. The primary medium of truth was, for them, language, *logos*, itself. Language was not then experienced as an instrument, an ensemble of purely conventional signs that could be 'used' to describe things or express thoughts. Language was itself the illuminating power—something we can still partially glimpse by going back to the root meanings of the Greek words themselves. The Presocratics thought within the light of this original revelation of truth. In Plato we find a still vivid recollection of this illumination. Nevertheless, truth is now linked in an exclusive manner to the idea, εἶδοσ, which, in its meaning of aspect or view, establishes the presupposition upon which the eventual construction of a 'world picture' will build. In

Aristotle *logos* has become the object of logic, a formalized and conventionalized system that was no longer 'heard' in its own right but only as a means of articulating formal relations and judgements. It becomes possible to distinguish between matter and form, a distinction that paves the way to reducing the experienced world to being a mere equipment. It is no longer the truth that speaks out of the word itself that is decisive but the representation of the thing, what it appears 'as'. This shift is, for Heidegger, perhaps the most decisive change in all of recorded history, since it opens the way for the development that culminates in modern technology. But several other steps are necessary before this can occur.

The first is what Heidegger calls the translation of Greek philosophy into Latin. Inevitably such a translation carries with it the risk (a risk to which he believes philosophy succumbed) of losing the guiding light of the meanings embedded in the original vocabulary of philosophy. In Latin, Heidegger believes, the central concepts of philosophy became legalized and objectified, transformed into a system of concepts and categories with which to classify and manage the world, rather than letting the world's own luminosity come to expression. Truth, in the famous medieval definition becomes the correspondence (*adequatio*) of the thing known (*res*) and the idea (*intellectus*) in which the thing is represented. The combination of such representational thinking with the matter-form distinction tightens the grip of a way of thinking governed by the imperatives of enframing. Via the Latin *representatio* the modern idea of representation— *Vorstellung* in German, literally 'placing before'—'means to bring what is present at hand before oneself as something standing over against it, to relate it to oneself, to the one representing it, and to force it back into this relationship to oneself as the normative realm.'[9]

In the course of this development, Christianity takes over the field of Western philosophy, adding its own distinctive idea of God the Creator to the inherited philosophical world view. How does this affect things? Against the background of the Aristotelian distinction between matter and form and despite the fact that it 'assure[s] us that all of God's creative work is to be thought of as different from the action of a craftsman' (*PLT*, 29 [*GA*, 5, 14]), the Christian philosophy of the Middle Ages reduces the world as never before to being a mere instrument or resource for human purposes. But this is not only bad news for the world. It is also, Heidegger hints (though he doesn't go into this very extensively), bad news for faith, reducing God to the level of the world that He has in turn reduced to being a mere instrument of his purposes.

Thus where everything that presences exhibits itself in the light of a cause-effect coherence, even God can, for representational thinking, lose all that is exalted and holy, the mysteriousness of his distance. In the light of causality, God can sink to the level of a cause, of *causa efficiens*. He then becomes, even in theology, the god of the philosophers,

---

[9] M. Heidegger, 'The Age of the World Picture', 131 [*GA*, 5, 91].

namely, of those who define the unconcealed and the concealed in terms of the causality of making, without ever considering the essential origin of this causality.[10]

This view of Christian philosophy is, of course, far from acceptable to many theologians,[11] and it is by no means fanciful to suggest that Heidegger's own early absorption in medieval philosophy as an aspiring Catholic philosopher—indeed his early vocation to the priesthood—provoked a negative intellectual reaction that made it difficult for him to see other currents and possibilities within the mainstream of Christian thought.[12]

However, Heidegger does not simply spurn the philosophical tradition (including medieval theology). Although the transformation of *logos* into logic obscures much of the primordial openness of Being disclosed in the original Greek experience of truth, even this logic (along with the science and technology that subsequently build upon it) would not be possible if it did not embody one aspect of that experience, i.e. one aspect of truth. The 'error' of science is not to be understood simply as a mistake but as one way of articulating the truth that early philosophy brought to light—yet, ultimately, it is *only one* way. If, as he often does, Heidegger presents the story of Western civilization as the story of a forgetting of Being, it is nevertheless an important part of his overall philosophical position that some trace of the original Being, of the original vision of truth, remains in even the most distorted texts of later philosophy. These thus remain capable of being prized open, as it were, to reveal the truth within. In other words, Heidegger's aim is not to persuade us to reject the tradition (nor the technology to which it has led), but to interpret it in another and broader perspective. Another way of putting this would be to say that if the term 'Being' is a symbol for the whole of truth, what philosophy, science, and technology offer is always and necessarily only a partial view of truth. This only becomes dangerous if we once confuse the part with the whole. Nevertheless what is illegitimate in its claim to be the whole, may have a perfectly justifiable role within the economy of truth once it is seen as only a part. Again there is an analogy with Habermas, and the latter's attempt to moderate the hegemony of technological reason by contextualizing it in relation to the other discourses that belong to human flourishing.

The final link in the intellectual chain leading from Plato to technology is Newton and, especially, the revolution Newton brought about in the understanding of motion.[13] Newton's first law of motion is the law of inertia, that

---

[10] Ibid. 26 also M. Heidegger, *Vorträge und Aufsätze* (Pfullingen: Neske, 1954), 34. Compare the views of Norris Clarke and Lynn White cited in the previous chapter.

[11] A particularly forceful criticism of it can be found in various of the writings of theologians of the 'radical orthodoxy' tendency.

[12] In the following chapters of the present book, we shall seek to explore several ways in which the religious tradition itself might open up paths for thinking about God that do not stand in the service of instrumental reason.

[13] Although Hans Jonas is very hostile to Heidegger on many counts, he also gives an account of the seventeenth-century revolution in science and natural philosophy that is very much in the line of Heidegger's comments on Newton, but also with discussions of Newton's forerunners that are not

'Every body continues in its state of rest, or uniform motion in a straight line, unless it is compelled to change that state by force impressed upon it.'[14] In the older, Aristotelian theory of motion, every body had its own peculiar form of motion, with the highest form being the circular motion of the celestial bodies. Thus, whereas on the Aristotelian view the moon has its own form of motion, a form that belongs to its nature and 'naturally' keeps it in its orbit, Newton shows that if the moon were not constrained by the earth's gravitational field it would simply fly off into space. Newton's postulation of a uniform theory of motion applicable to all possible bodies thus opens the universe up to explanation in terms of a single set of laws and relations, namely those of mathematics. Nature, writes Heidegger, 'is now the realm of the uniform space-time content of motion.'[15] Bodies no longer have 'concealed qualities, powers and capacities' but 'are only what they show themselves *as*'.[16] The way is cleared for positivism's view of the world, summarized in Wittgenstein's saying that 'The world is the sum of facts, not of things.' So we enter the scientific-technological landscape that, since Newton's time, has expanded so as to fill virtually the entire horizon of contemporary humanity.

The thinker in whom the ultimate, metaphysical truth of this situation came to its purest expression, according to Heidegger, was Nietzsche. Nietzsche is not just any thinker in the history of ideas but the one who brought the whole Western tradition to completion. The key elements of Nietzsche's thought in which this completion is most clearly visible are his ideas of the will to power and eternal recurrence. Particularly with regard to the latter, Heidegger is keen that we should not dismiss it as merely a poetic or mythical fantasy or see in it an attempt to propose an alternative cosmology. Both will to power and eternal recurrence are, according to Heidegger, essentially metaphysical ideas. This means that they articulate an attitude towards Being as a whole. And what is this attitude? It is, he says, one in which beings—the entities that make up humanity's world of experience—are understood as existing in a process of endless becoming which, nevertheless, is subject to a law of repeatability, i.e. that it is an eternal becoming whose character is the endless repetition of the same. But what brings about this 'sameness'? It is, precisely, will to power understood as the subjective will of human beings taken as the criterion for everything that shows itself in being. The original *alétheia* or uncovering of beings in their Being that first awoke the wonder of early Greek thinkers is now altogether covered over. 'Now the last reverberations of any intimation of

paralleled in Heidegger. See 'The Seventeenth Century and After: The Meaning of the Scientific and Technological Revolution', in H. Jonas, *Philosophical Essays: From Ancient Creed to Technological Man* (Chicago: University of Chicago Press, 1974).

[14] M. Heidegger, *What is a Thing?*, tr. W. B. Barton and V. Deutsch (Chicago: Henry Regnery, 1967), 78 [*GA*, 41, 86].

[15] Ibid. 92 [*GA*, 41, 93].   [16] Ibid. 93 [*GA*, 41, 93].

alétheia fade,' Heidegger says.[17] What manifests itself in will to power and eternal recurrence is a will to what Heidegger's translator calls the 'permanentizing' of chaos, i.e. the refusal to see the world as anything other than an intrinsically meaningless succession of chaotic powers that man must, so to speak, call to order. Things have no meaning in themselves but 'mean' only whatever we take them to mean as being serviceable to our will and our power. This, in turn, corresponds entirely to the essence of machine technology, which is the concrete embodiment of this will to instantiate the eternal recurrence of the same in historical humanity. The 'permanence' of objects is not owing to the fact that they can be assigned to various eternal essences, as in Aristotelianism, but their regularity and predictability as objects of scientific observation and technological manipulation.

However, this is not just a matter of a particular attitude towards the world 'out there' but a transformation of human beings' own self-understanding and self-experience. Jünger's concept of 'total mobilization', though coined in the context of the aftermath of the First World War and the rise of totalitarianism, can also be extended to the character of the modern world as a whole: that human beings are no longer defined by the traditional bonds of family, kinship, ancestral faith, soil, or place but are functional units in a global market. Jünger writes that

It suffices simply to consider our daily life with its inexorability and merciless discipline, its smoking, glowing districts, the physics and metaphysics of its commerce, its motors, airplanes, and burgeoning cities. With pleasure-tinged horror, we sense that here, not a single atom is not in motion—that we are profoundly inscribed in this raging process.[18]

Anthropologically, this process found its epitome in what Jünger called the *Gestalt* of 'the worker': it is the rootless, religionless (or, at any rate, post-Christian), worker who is both the expression of total mobilization and its agent, the one for whom and through whom and in whom total mobilization is or is becoming real. If Heidegger riposted that this *Gestalt* was itself to be seen as determined by the enframing of reality that can ultimately be traced back to Plato's εἶδος, he largely agreed with Jünger's description of the contemporary world as one of total mobilization. The picture is, of course, very much of a piece with the kind of dystopias common in the interwar period and familiar from films such as *Metropolis* or novels such as Zamyatin's *We*, technological nightmares in which human beings are reduced to the status of mindless robots in the service of an impersonal collectivity. However, it is important to stress that Jünger, at least in the 1920s and early 1930s, was essentially enthusiastic about the prospect of such total mobilization. Nor is the resonance of the idea limited to that particular era, much as Jünger's own illustrations naturally focus on

[17] M. Heidegger, *Nietzsche: The Will to Power as Knowledge and as Metaphysics*, ed. D. F. Krell, various translators (New York: Harper & Row, 1987), 173 [*GA*, 6.2, 12].

[18] From the anthologized version in R. Wolin, *The Heidegger Controversy: A Critical Reader* (Cambridge, Mass.: MIT Press, 1993), 128.

topical examples. On the contrary, the image of total mobilization opens up a perspective on contemporary existence that is not exhausted by such apocalyptic visions. In his genial essay *Heidegger, Habermas and the Mobile Phone*, George Myerson pinpoints the way in which contemporary user-friendly technology can facilitate a kind of banalization of communication, and a reduction of language to the transmission of fragmented bits of knowledge, for which the phonetic sign systems of texting are an apt medium.[19] This is a long cry from the nightmare factories of *Metropolis*, but no less susceptible to interpretation in terms of total mobilization (and perhaps it is no coincidence that it is precisely the *mobile* phone that has become such a powerful agent and symbol of this phase of technologization).

Heidegger draws attention to another aspect of the way in which the dynamics of technology work upon human beings in the phenomenon he calls 'planetary homelessness', something that might also be seen as an aspect of total mobilization. This may take a dramatic and even an apocalyptic form. The following lines from Tillich's sermon 'Love is Stronger than Death', written in the aftermath of the Second World War, are still as applicable as when they were written:

We have seen millions die in war, hundreds of thousands in revolutions, tens of thousands in persecutions and systematic purges of minorities. Multitudes as numerous as whole nations still wander over the face of the earth or perish when artifical walls put an end to their wanderings. All those who are called refugees or immigrants belong to this wandering; in them is embodied a part of those tremendous events in which Death has again grasped the rein which we believed it had relinquished forever.[20]

Fifty years after these words were written, the refugee and the immigrant remain a powerful figure of contemporary reality. The surface of the planet is criss-crossed by the tracks of people fleeing persecution or repression or seeking economic and material improvement for themselves and their families or, often, both together. Even within the confines of nations and except for the last residues of the aristocracy and the lingering 'peasant' communities work is now rarely hereditary and each generation must relocate to maximize its opportunities for success. My grandfather, born in the nineteenth century, lived in a remote village in and around which his family had lived for many hundreds of years. His descendants since then have shifted the geographical location of the family at least once in every generation. The intensity of the political pressures generated by such movements are, as we all know, reported daily in the media and give rise to some of the most controversial elements in the contemporary political map.

But 'planetary homelessness' need not take such dramatic forms as 'illegal immigrants' or 'asylum seekers' fleeing war or torture. In 1969 Heidegger

---

[19] G. Myerson, *Heidegger, Habermas and the Mobile Phone* (London: Icon Books, 2000). This would be very much in line with the view of Schulze discussed in the previous chapter.
[20] P. Tillich, *The New Being* (New York: Charles Scribner, 1955), 171.

returned to his native village of Meßkirch to help celebrate its 700th anniversary. It was very much the kind of community where tradition still retained a powerful presence at the start of the twentieth century, yet Heidegger commented that the first thing that struck him on returning was that every house sported a television antenna. What does this mean? It means, he said, that even when sitting at home, people are no longer sitting at home round the family hearth—thanks to the television they are 'in' the studio, the stadium, watching yet another stream of refugees fleeing conflict, or escaping into the fantasy world of a costume drama. Television (at least prior to the mobile phone!) is perhaps the most visible sign of technology's dominant role in contemporary culture, but also a sign of the dwindling of local community and culture. Heidegger comments:

Spellbound and pulled onward by all this, humanity is, as it were, in a process of emigration. It is emigrating from what is homely [*Heimisch*] to what is unhomely [*Unheimisch*]. There is a danger that what was once called home will dissolve and disappear. The power of the unhomely seems to have so overpowered humanity that it can no longer pit itself against it. How can we defend ourselves against the pressure of the unhomely? Only by this: that we continually enable the bestowing and healing and preserving strength of what is homely to flow, to create proper channels in which they can flow and so exert their influence.[21]

If in these many ways the power of technology and its economic and political impact is continually transforming every detail of our daily life, this is no less so, perhaps more intensively so, in the context of university life as elsewhere. On this point, Heidegger is absolutely clear that the issue is not between science and the humanities. It is not a matter of traditional academics in the humanities holding back the barbarism of science. On the contrary, he believes that the model of scientific work that has come to the fore in the natural sciences has basically set the paradigm for all university work:

. . . a science today, whether physical or humanistic, attains to the respect due to a science only when it has become capable of being institutionalized. However, research is not ongoing activity [*Betrieb*] because its work is accomplished in institutions, but rather institutions are necessary because science, intrinsically as research, has the character of ongoing activity. . .[22]

He spells out a further implication of this in words it would be tempting to describe as prophetic:

[T]he decisive development of the modern character of science as ongoing activity also forms men of a different stamp. The scholar disappears. He is succeeded by the research man who is engaged in research projects. These, rather than the cultivating of erudition, lend to his work its atmosphere of incisiveness. The research man no longer needs a

---

[21] M. Heidegger, *Reden und Andere Zeugnisse eines Lebensweges, Gesamtausgabe* (Frankfurt am Main: Vittorio Klostermann, 2000), xvi. 575–6.
[22] Heidegger, *The Question Concerning Technology and Other Essays*, 125 [*GA*, 5, 83–4].

library at home. Moreover, he is constantly on the move. He negotiates at meetings and collects information at congresses. He contracts for commissions with publishers. The latter now determine along with him which books must be written. The research worker necessarily presses forward of himself into the sphere characteristic of the technologist in the essential sense. Only in this way is he capable of acting effectively, and only thus, after the manner of his age, is he real.[23]

In contrast to such a 'research man' old-fashioned scholarship will, Heidegger says, appear 'thin' and 'romantic'. We could complete Heidegger's picture by adding what may, in fact, be already implicit in it: that our 'research man' is no loner, but first and foremost is what he is as a member of a research team or 'project'. If the old-style scholar, alone in his study, imagined himself to be in pursuit of the truth of things, the researcher has no such ambitions. He is more concerned with the management, operation, and success of his project, and this is as true of those working in the field of religion as in any other.

If Heidegger sees it as characteristic for research that the outcome of such a project is set up in advance, this does not mean that he is accusing researchers of falsifying their data to prove predetermined answers. Rather, he is saying that the investment of personnel and equipment in any serious research project can only be justified if it is clear from the beginning what kind of outcome and application can be expected from it. And this is clearly true of most contemporary research institutions: that those proposing one or other project must be able to specify how their project will relate to its given field and what sort of shift it will bring about in the field if it is successful. Research is, in this sense, always strategic. It is not and cannot be a matter of just browsing through the shelves and seeing what turns up.

As so often, it is hard not to sense that there was something about this that Heidegger personally disliked. Whereas the one he calls an 'essential thinker' needs only one single thought, a thought which concerns 'beings as a whole' 'the researcher needs constantly new discoveries and inspirations, else science will bog down and fall into error.'[24] Yet Heidegger clearly accepts that the tendencies condensed into the figure of the 'research man' are irresistible. Not to go the way of the research man is to expose science to 'bog down and fall into error'. The research man is inseparable from the character of the knowledge of our time, which is in turn both inseparable from technology and the globalization of the knowledge industry. Only by doing its business in this way can the academy make its way in the world. At the organizational and institutional level at least, Heidegger—the post-war Heidegger, that is—accepted that we cannot turn back the clock.

---

[23] Heidegger, *The Question Concerning Technology and Other Essays*, 125 [*GA*, 5, 85].
[24] M. Heidegger, *What is Called Thinking?*, tr. F. D. Wieck and J. Glenn Gray (New York: Harper and Row, 1968), 50 [*GA*, 8, 53].

The figure of the research man condenses both the essential profanity and the essential autonomy of the modern culture of knowledge. Modern science—like modern art—aspires to set its own targets and only to follow those imperatives that it imposes upon itself. If it is constantly threatened by one or other external claim or pressure (heteronomous religion, the state or big business) this is experienced as a threat to its proper integrity. In this connection, however, we have to note that the brief period, 1933–4, when Heidegger was Rector of Freiburg University, he himself actively promoted the Nazi's policy of *Gleichschaltung* ('coordination') according to which university policy and the complex pluralism of the modern university was to be subordinated to the destiny of the German people as embodied in the will of its leader Adolf Hitler. This, he then claimed, was a higher or more fundamental truth than the 'truths' pursued by specialist academics.[25] Not every heteronomous model of truth will draw such horrendous consequences in its wake, but the case should make us pause before too simplistically scorning the value-free amorality of the contemporary technological university. Heidegger, at any rate, seems not only to have made a rapid retreat from administration but also to have accepted that this way of 'coordinating' university studies with the life of society was simply not possible. If the university was to be something more than the institutionalization required by an ensemble of research projects that 'something more' would not come from political target-setting. This too is in the last resort just another variety of enframing.

But does that mean we can dispense with the question as to the nature of the knowledge that it is the university's task to manage or of our responsibility towards this knowledge? Can we, should we, give up asking 'Why? For what—and for whose—good?' But is it at all possible to conceive of any kind of thinking that is so 'other' than the thinking embodied in technology as to be able to resist being absorbed by it and yet, in this resistance, constituting a creative and not merely a critical response to technology?

For Heidegger, the answer is very simple in principle, though infinitely difficult in execution. There *are* forms of thinking that lie outside the orbit of technology and we have two ways of access to them. One is the simple leap into the unmediated givenness of experience, as when Heidegger counsels his students simply to look out of the window at the tree blooming outside. 'The tree faces us. The tree and we meet one another, as the tree stands there and we stand face to face with it. As we are in this relation of one to the other and before the other, the tree and we *Are*.'[26] Another way (and one to which Heidegger devotes the largest part of his lecturing and writing) is through certain key texts bequeathed to us by the tradition. The difficulty is that these texts require interpretation, and that

[25] For a further discussion of this see Chapter 8 below.
[26] Heidegger, *What is Called Thinking?* 41 [*GA*, 8, 44]. For a discussion of the relationship between this passage and the no less renowned role played by tree-epiphanies in Buber and Sartre, see A. Rudd, *Expressing the World: Skepticisim, Wittgenstein, and Heidegger* (Chicago: Open Court, 2003), ch. 12.

interpretation is of a singularly laborious kind, requiring an assault on many of our most habitual presuppositions about what it is to read.

In Heidegger's own work two main groups of texts stand out: the writings of the so-called Presocratics and the work of certain modern poets, most notably Hölderlin. These give us access to models of thinking 'otherwise' than in the mode of the metaphysics that has saturated even our everyday ways of thinking and speaking about the world. At one point Heidegger showed an interest in East Asian thought, and, although he did not follow this through, we can see, once more, how his idiosyncratic formulations also express something that is very much a part of the more general cultural sensibility of our time, namely that poetry and Eastern philosophy might prove to be sources of an alternative reality, pointers to a way out of the all-consuming embrace of the modern wasteland. As Heidegger himself puts it, if Nietzsche marks the culmination of Western metaphysics and, in his ideas of will to power and eternal recurrence, gives expression to the reality of the Western view of the world, Hölderlin (two generations before Nietzsche) is already thinking towards a new beginning, a return of the gods from 'beyond the wasteland'.

Heidegger did not immediately conflate such poetic thinking with 'thinking' in the strong sense. Rather, he spoke of the 'proximity' of poetry to thinking. Through his intercourse with the poet, the thinker is given something important to think about, although he must think it as thought and not as poetic vision. Are we, then, thanks to our poets, poised to move 'beyond the wasteland'?

Heidegger seems not to endorse any too precipitate expectations of this kind. In his lecture series published as *What is Called Thinking?* he remarks that the most thought-provoking thing about the present age is that we are not yet thinking, even though the wasteland is growing all around us. Yet, paradoxically, this very failure to think is itself thought-provoking. But, as the lectures (and, indeed, the whole body of his work) make clear, if we do once start on the path of truly thinking, we have no ready-made model to give us guidance as to methods and goals. Thinking is not like a lost technique that could be revived by the rediscovery of some ancient textbook (like, for example, the revival of stained glass manufacture in the nineteenth century). We can only learn about thinking by accepting the provocation to think that is to be found in our present thoughtlessness. The poets and the Presocratics (or, for that matter, the Daoists) cannot think for us. At best they can bring us to the point where we can begin to think for ourselves. For thinking is never something we can pick up off the peg, it is always what we still have to learn. If, as Heidegger puts it, 'science does not think' and if science, nevertheless, is the universal measure of what can count as truth in a technological society, thinking—its aim, its value, its very possibility— exists for us only as a question, the question of whether there is any other way for us to relate to Beings-as-a-whole (including, of course, ourselves) than the way of science. But, Heidegger would say, this is just the point. Science doesn't think because research, as we have noted, must (according to Heidegger) set up its outcomes in advance and must operate according to the parameters set by its strategic goals. *Thinking*, however, is essentially concerned with what withdraws from thought, with what cannot be thought or with what we have not yet been able to think.

As usual, Heidegger is being provocative. How can we think what we cannot think? The idea seems absurd. But if we just think about it for a moment the point is not, after all, so very odd. Is it not an everyday experience that we are moved to think about something precisely when we don't immediately understand it or are puzzled by it? There's something in a landscape, a newspaper article, a human situation, or an academic paper that doesn't seem to fit, something that niggles and teases and resists explanation—and it's just this kind of 'something' that really gets us *thinking* in an active sense, rather than just throughputting the information with which the landscape, the article, the situation, the paper feeds us. Philosophical thinking, of course, is not quite the same as the thinking that is set in motion by the kind of examples I have just given. Philosophical thinking is not thinking about this or that but, according to Heidegger, thinking that is aroused by the question of being-as-a-whole, a question focused in such subsidiary questions as: why is there something rather than nothing? or: what does it mean for me to be at all? or: what does it mean for consciousness that it cannot exist without some relation or other to a given world? Such questions come into view when we are awoken out of our ordinary everyday immersion in the flow of life by a sudden sense of uncanniness, a sense that the world is no longer as solid as it seemed, as if it had been invaded by an aura of nothingness, as if it might just as well not be as be. In such moments the world seems to withdraw, and this withdrawing, Heidegger says, leaves a vacuum, into which our thinking is sucked like a current of air being sucked into an atmospheric vacuum. And, he comments, this is precisely the significance of Socrates for Western thought:

All through his life Socrates did nothing else than place himself in this draft, this current, and maintain himself in it. This is why he is the purest thinker of the West. This is why he wrote nothing. For anyone who begins to write out of thoughtfulness must inevitably be like those people who run to seek refuge from any draft too strong for them. An as yet hidden history still keeps the secret why all great Western thinkers after Socrates, with all their greatness, had to be such fugitives.[27]

Why technology calls for thinking, then, is not that it confronts us with this or that set of problems or challenges with regard to our stewardship of planetary resources or social arrangements, but that it calls into question the very meaning of our being here, the kind of responsibility we have for the world and for ourselves, for 'Being', as Heidegger would put it. And it does so because, as dwellers in the world shaped by technology, we cannot, it seems, escape the sense

---

[27] Heidegger, *What is Called Thinking?*, 17 [*GA*, 8, 20].

that for every great leap forward there not only remains something missing but, in the phrase that provides a kind of *leitmotif* to the early lectures of *What is Called Thinking?*, 'the wasteland grows'. Something, it seems, is withdrawing from our grasp and the more we try to hold it fast the greater the sense of its absence. Which may seem rather flimsy, or even fanciful. But Heidegger at least believes that in a very real sense the whole future of humanity is involved in this question. Do we simply commit ourselves to the scientific-technological under-standing of reality, or, hopeless as it may seem, do we still dare argue for other conceptions and other evaluations, aware as we do so that there is inevitably a 'scientific' explanation for our conduct? Do we dare to say that there is something that technology not only has not been able to get a grip on but something that necessarily eludes it, a source of human meaning and value that can never emerge within the horizons of technology? If we dare to say this, then (it may be) we are ready to start thinking, to ask not only the question concerning what we *are*, but also the question concerning what we are *to be*.

III

I have attempted to expound Heidegger largely in his own terms. In choosing to do this I may well have stretched some readers' patience. Especially those from an Anglo-Saxon background will be likely to object that the whole thing is simply too general, an over-inflated grand narrative that culminates in empty assertions that cannot be the basis for any kind of coherent, practical response to the real problems of technology that confront us today. However, I believe that without falsifying Heidegger's own philosophical agenda we can qualify the picture I have presented in a number of ways that help show its relevance to those who are not convinced Heideggerians and, not least, to those concerned specifically with thinking about God in an age of technology.

The first of these qualifications concerns Heidegger's understanding of phil-osophy and what might be called the grand narrative aspect of his account of the relationship between metaphysics and technology. As I have suggested elsewhere, it is very easy to be misled by Heidegger's rhetoric into thinking that he is in fact making grander claims than he really is.[28] Heidegger himself alluded to the tone or voice of philosophical reflection, and if his own philosophizing sometimes sounds not a little over-pompous, there is also another much more cautious, much more questioning note that, in the end (I believe), is the more important. If we learn to listen to what is being said by Heidegger when he is speaking in this quieter tone then we begin to realize that he is doing more than indulging in sweeping assertions. Using the rhetoric of the grand narrative that he has inherited from his own literary and philosophical tradition he is in fact calling

[28] See my *The Later Heidegger*, 210–15.

into question some of the basic assumptions underlying that selfsame tradition, assumptions which it cannot, in its own terms, question. This Heidegger, I have claimed, is closer to deconstruction than to a simplistic kind of Heideggerianism. The narrative he creates is one that at many points undercuts itself. What the quieter Heidegger is trying to draw our attention to is not the big picture but, precisely, what the big picture leaves out. Attention to this 'something missing' is precisely the task that thinking alone is capable of addressing. In non-Heideggerian terms this means that the task of philosophy in relation to technology is not simply to develop, to defend or to criticize particular models of scientific knowledge or particular claims regarding the justification of such knowledge. These may or may not have their proper place in the overall configuration of philosophy, but they do not exhaust philosophy's agenda or responsibilities. Philosophy may also—and, if it is truly thoughtful *should* also—ask about the meaning of science and technology for human life as a whole, and this means going beyond narrowly defined questions of epistemology and, even, ontology. The task of philosophy is not merely to give rules for determining what is the case nor even how we may come to know what is the case. It is also to ask about what it means that we should be asking such questions in the first place.

A second qualification concerns Heidegger's view of the nature of scientific and technological rationality. It is clear that he broadly sees this as embedded in the mental operation he called enframing. It may well be that this is ultimately inadequate as an account of everything that goes on in the name of science and technology. Are there not a multitude of other forms of thought and action involved in any serious science? Will not many scientists say of their work that far from imposing a preconceived frame on reality they are responding to what reality itself imposes on them as unprejudiced observers? And, more generally, isn't the whole history of science and technology in the last five hundred years too rich, too varied to be brought under the rubric of any single overarching formula? In his study *Against Method* Paul Feyerabend, in discussing the development of modern science and quoting Herbert Butterfield, put it nicely when he wrote that

History is full of 'accidents and conjunctures and curious juxtapositions of events and it demonstrates to us the complexity of human change and the unpredictable character of the ultimate consequences of any given act or decision of men'. Are we really to believe that the naïve and simple-minded rules which methodologists take as their guide are capable of accounting for such a 'maze of interactions'? And is it not clear that successful *participation* in a process of this kind is possible only for a ruthless opportunist who is not tied to any particular philosophy and who adopts whatever procedure seems to fit the occasion?[29]

And, as Feyerabend adds a couple of pages later, it is no surprise that 'the history of science will be as complex, chaotic, full of mistakes, and entertaining as the ideas it contains, and these ideas in turn will be as complex, chaotic, full of

[29] P. Feyerabend, *Against Method* (London: Verso, 1988), 9–10.

mistakes, and entertaining as are the minds of those who invented them.'[30] All of which might be taken as putting the kind of unifying history of ideas pro-pounded by Heidegger out of contention for serious consideration. Yet even if we were in entire agreement with Feyerabend, I do not think that the use or value of Heidegger's account of technology actually stands and falls with (his) strong claim that it is the sole and adequate account. All that is necessary for us to take it seriously (and seriously enough to use in orientating our own enquiry) is the claim that it identifies *one* actual and important conjunction of ideas and practices within the complex philosophy-science-technology, and, that this con-junction is effective in concrete and important ways in the current phase of technologization. Heidegger, in other words, doesn't have to answer all our questions about technology, all he has to do—from the point of view of the present study—is to make us aware of one current, one tendency, one rhythm in the development of technology as we know it. If he does this successfully (which, I believe, he does), then, given the importance of just this particular tendency for our contemporary reality, it becomes worth using as a starting point for further enquiries.

Yet Feyerabend's comments do seem to undermine the kind of thematization of technology that we find in Heidegger. What, after all, do the philosophies of Plato and Aquinas, a nuclear power station, a cluster bomb, a computer game, and radiotherapy really have in common? Hasn't the very concept of technology been stretched to and beyond breaking point in such all-encompassing usage, so all-encompassing indeed that it could be taken to mean simply the entire history of Western consciousness?

A first counter-argument to this would be that, indeed, Heidegger's use of the term 'technology' is broad and makes connections between apparently uncon-nected fields of theory and practice. But then, it could be added, isn't this precisely its philosophical virtue, namely, to practise philosophy as, in its own way, a response to the injunction 'Only connect!'? For if one part of philosophy is about analysing discourse down to its atomic constituents—'What *exactly* does this statement say?'—another part (and these parts may not, finally, be separable) is about showing that single propositions actually occur as embedded in larger and many-levelled contexts of meaning to which we also need to attend if we really want to understand what's being said in just this one sentence.[31]

In this regard one might compare Heidegger's use of the term 'technology' to the way in which we use words like 'art' or 'law'. After all, what have the following in common: applying pigment to canvas, taking a photograph, pretending to be someone you're not (acting), constructing a sentence with peculiar rhythms and rhymes, scraping horse-hairs on cat-gut? These are, of course, all practices

---

[30] P. Feyerabend, *Against Method*, 11.
[31] See the section 'Philosophy and World-view' in my *Short Course in the Philosophy of Religion* (London: SCM Press, 2001), esp. 130–4.

regularly subsumed under the word 'art', and although theorists continue to wrangle over what exactly art is most people don't find it hard to sense a kind of family resemblance between these activities that would not stretch so far as to cover certain technological practices, such as monitoring the coolant systems of a power plant. And although the term 'art' would be an eminent case of a general term that can be used in utterly vacuous ways, it could also be that having such a word is, in certain contexts, a real benefit. But what exactly is the benefit of gathering all the different things that Heidegger ascribes to technology under one heading?

Whether we are speaking about creative innovation or daily use, different kinds of technologies obviously call for different kinds of expertise. I simply cannot switch from designing aircraft tyres to being a research biologist or vice versa, nor, whether I am an aircraft tyre designer or a research biologist, do I use the same sorts of skills as I do when I ring home or drive my car. These are all technologically determined activities yet they seem to call for different aptitudes, different bodies of knowledge and know-how. Nevertheless, it is not entirely vacuous to say that in order for any of these activities to be possible certain mental disciplines are called for and that these disciplines are not just a matter of individual personality but need to be institutionalized in formal structures of education and training that produce citizens capable of making career choices between biology and engineering, and capable of using phones and driving cars. Although some individuals may not get far beyond the minimal levels of literacy and numeracy required for this, it is also necessary that a significant number of others proceed through further and higher education for the system to function at all. Now we do not need to subscribe to the view that all Western education is 'thought control' (Pink Floyd) to see that it does, nevertheless, require and instruct in certain ways of representing and analysing problems—the kinds of 'transferable skills' that ministries of education are eager to see propagated. Nor are these limited to purely technical functions but, importantly, include the management skills of organizing time and resources, deciding on goals and programming for their achievement.

That there are nuclear power plants or that the genome campus exists thus depends on much more than the correctness of the science specifically related to these particular projects and the competence of those directly involved in their scientific work. It also depends on cultures of learning, systems of political decision-making, economic infrastructure, etc. That these interlock and function as effectively as they do may be simply down to the fact that the knowledge they incorporate is knowledge as to how things really are in the world and, being basically realistic creatures, humans are guided by a sound instinct in giving effect to them. Heidegger wouldn't deny this since he accepts that science and technology stand within a particular revelation of truth. But their actual constitution as the dominant forms of public knowledge and resource management is dependent on our also internalizing and enculturating that truth in our collective habits of mind. Technology, in other words, is a cultural, political, economic reality as well as being, simply, a technical reality. By means of the links he establishes between the history of philosophy and contemporary science and technology, Heidegger enables us to raise questions about these background dimensions of technical practice itself. The point is not immediately to be able to affirm or to condemn this or that particular technical application, but to ask about the extent to which and the manner in which the requirements of technical practice are both embedded in and setting the agenda of other, non-technical dimensions of education and, indeed, of life.

These comments touch on what is perhaps the most problematic aspect of Heidegger's critique of technology, namely its implicit political agenda. For if we once start talking about the relationship between science and technology on the one hand and society and culture on the other, aren't we then in the arena where political decisions about science policy become unavoidable? But isn't Heidegger's own political history as good a warning as any against allowing the non-technical sphere to interfere with science, be these religious, political or whatever? Isn't it vital to preserve the autonomy of science, both for science's own good and for the good of society as a whole? And, lest we think this was just the error of a single individual, isn't Heidegger's case paralleled by examples from other times and places where we have seen the dreadful outcomes of Soviet, fundamentalist or, it could be argued, neo-liberal interference in the development and use of technology? Yet neither the catastrophe of Heidegger's own attempt to subordinate science and technology to a heteronomous political agenda nor the accumulation of parallel instances means that science and technology can safely be left to scientists and technologists. In the measure that their work has an impact—often a massive impact—on others, then they surely must be answerable to those whose lives they affect. Ian Barbour for one has forcefully argued that it is precisely the pervasive influence of technology in society today that calls for active citizenship at every level of the political process and that the non-expert has every right to be fully involved in the debate.[32] To call for a deeper contextualizing of the processes of science and technology is not of itself to call for some counter-Enlightenment crackdown on progress, but to put down a marker concerning the need for progress to be balanced against 'large, important good'. Critically, however, we may say of Heidegger at this point that precisely the absence of any significant ethical dimension in his thought makes him prone to configure the relationship between technology and society in a somewhat heteronomous way. A more ethically nuanced approach, I suggest, would help us to secure a form of contextualization that is not imposed on science and technology in the manner of an alien power but relates them in a more internal way.

---

[32] See I. Barbour, *Ethics in an Age of Technology* (London: SCM Press, 1992).

We shall return to the question of the ethical in a later chapter, but there is one further qualification of Heidegger's philosophical project to be made at this point. For Heidegger, as for so many twentieth-century philosophers, questions of language are decisive. The importance of the poet is precisely that he is the one who speaks the poetic word, the meaningful word that is to open horizons of truth obscured by the language of science and technology. This may seem sheer romanticism. However, we might again appeal to Hefner's insights concerning the contextualization of science and technology in human culture, noting that language is, of course, one of the primary bearers of all levels of cultural reality and practice and thus one of the chief ways in which we can be co-creators. On this point, Heidegger's point can also be elucidated by Lewis Mumford's comments about the relationship between language and technology. Mumford, approaching the question of technology from a far more empirical and human-istic standpoint than Heidegger, asserts that language is the necessary condition of any kind of technical development and that we simply cannot imagine anything more than the most rudimentary development of tools amongst early hominids without also imagining the tool-makers and tool-users as gifted with language. Language provides an ordering of the world and of social relationships that is integral to the possibility of serious technical development. Language, he says, was the first product of human culture. And the most important and complex: 'No modern technological device surpasses in the articulation of its parts or its functional fitness the qualities of the least important language.'[33]

In its ideal structure and its daily performance [language] still stands as a model, though an unnoticed one, for all other kinds of effective fabrication, standardization, and mass consumption... Language is the most transportable and storable, the most easily diffu-sible, of all social artefacts: the most ethereal of all cultural agents, and for that reason the only one capable of indefinite multiplication and storage of meanings without over-crowding the living space of the planet... But though the parts of language are stand-ardized and in a sense mass-produced, they achieve the maximum of variety, individuality and autonomy.[34]

Like Heidegger, Mumford sees language today as being under threat of debase-ment and as tending to lose the grammatical and metaphorical complexity of earlier languages, chiefly as the result of political and commercial abuses. Our capacity for dialogue, he comments, is 'being undermined by a new system of control and one-way communication that has now found an electronic mode of operation.'[35] Whether or not we share Mumford's dark prognoses, his point, I think, helpfully illuminates Heidegger's own concern with language: that even if we cannot speak of a direct causal relationship between language and technology (and certainly not of any simple, single line of causality), the way in which we use

[33] L. Mumford, *The Myth of the Machine: Technics and Human Development* (New York: Harcourt, Brace and World, 1966), 89.
[34] Ibid. 96–7.   [35] Ibid. 97.

and understand ourselves in language is both influenced by but also—at least potentially—significant for the way in which we experience, use and direct our technological abilities. The philosophical reflection on language should not, perhaps, hope to exhaust our common concern with the words we speak, write, sing, or otherwise transmit, but as the discipline concerned with thinking about the truth in and of language it must be integral to the family of intellectual and cultural forms in which we think about what we say.

In the course of his sustained philosophical meditation on language, Heidegger encourages us to think about whether there can be any kind of thinking that deserves the name of truth other than the thinking that comes to expression in science and technology. Of course, many scientists and philosophers of science will have no difficulty in conceding that there are many other things going on in language and in culture than science itself. There is no reason why even the hardest of hard-nosed scientific empiricists cannot say, 'Sure! We're not totalitarians. Let there be lights, music, song, dance, poetry, drama, let's work hard and party hard, and we don't even mind if in some smoky corner a couple of especially earnest characters are drunkenly disputing the meaning of life: it's all fine—just as long as we remember that all these things belong to party-time and not work-time.' In other words—it's all fine as long as other discourses limit themselves to expressive or aesthetic functions, and don't start claiming to be true or normative. But is it that obvious that the question about the meaning of it all is merely a question for the more melancholic party-goers? Isn't it—couldn't it be—also a question concerning the *truth* of it all? And, if so, isn't that a question that essentially concerns members of the academy as a whole since it is then a question about what is to count as the proper shape and matter of public knowledge?

If we allow this to serve as a reformulation of Heidegger's question, what happens if we now imagine that one of our melancholic party philosophers goes one step further than simply saying 'There must be more to life than all this knowledge and know-how' and adds 'Perhaps this "more" is a hint that we should be thinking about God, because I've heard that whatever else we may think or say about God, *Deus semper maior: God is always greater*—greater than any actual realization of intellectual, linguistic or cultural possibilities, greater than any of the horizons that separately or in unison constitute our contemporary reality.' In the light of this claim, then, the philosophical question concerning technology would evolve into a question more specifically for the philosophy of religion, the question as to what it would mean to think about God in an age of technology.

I indicated in the previous chapter that I regard it as one of the successes of modernist or radical theology that it has demonstrated that belief in God does not require us to oppose the progress of science and that genuine thinking about God has little or nothing to do with opposing the account of creation in Genesis to the biological or cosmic theorizing of a Darwin or a Hawking. The questions of religion and the questions of science are different kinds of questions that can, nevertheless, co-exist and need to co-exist in a single human breast. That, at least, is a rough statement of the consensus prevailing in large reaches of university-based theology. Heidegger's position may also lead us to some form of concordat along the lines of 'separate but equal', but it does so on the basis of a far more thoroughgoing recognition of the demise of the old way of doing theology than most theologians are able easily to accept. If Nietzsche's declaration concerning the death of God is itself the obverse of his metaphysical vindication of technology, then Heidegger agrees that we must accept the death of the God of the Aristotelian-Thomist mainstream of Christian thinking as a precondition for thinking further about God now, in our time. But Heidegger's acceptance of the death of God is significantly different from that of the secularizing theologians considered in the first chapter, since he does not try to speak in the name of scientific secularity itself. On the contrary, the move whereby he accepts the death of God and the move whereby he registers a question against the hegemony of science and technology are essentially one and the same. God must die because the God who has governed Western thought for so long is himself essentially a cipher for what was to emerge in Nietzsche as technologically oriented will to power. If there is to be talk of thinking about God otherwise than in the mode of technology it must be thinking of a very different kind and maybe even a God (or gods) of a very different kind.

Yet in turning the question in the direction of thinking about God we are possibly moving in a direction in which Heidegger himself would have been reluctant to go. Much has been written about the religious element in Heidegger's later thought, and it is hard to deny that thinking itself acquires a quasi-religious aura in some of his formulations, as when he speaks of the 'piety of thinking', identifies thinking with thanking or introduces Eckhart's idea of *Gelassenheit* (very approximately, 'detachment') as indicating the mood best suited to philosophizing. From Hölderlin too he takes the motif that we live in an age following the flight of the old gods and that, as Westerners (dwellers in the *Abendland*, the evening-land), we are fated to live at a distance from the time of mythical origins in which mortals and gods walked and talked together. But this does not exclude the possibility of a possible future return of the gods, or even of 'the' God.

Heidegger, as stated, is reluctant to commit himself at this point. It is clear that his preferred option for speaking of 'the gods' (lower-case, plural) rather than 'God' indicates his persistent wish to keep any 'theology' his way of thinking might lead to at a firm distance from Jewish or Christian ideas of God.[36] Again, it

---

[36] Crucial questions as to the kind of religiosity in play in the later Heidegger (and his misrepresentation of biblical faith) were already raised by Martin Buber in 'Religion and Modern Thinking' in M. Buber, *The Eclipse of God: Studies in the Relation between Religion and Philosophy* (London: Victor Gollancz, 1953). For a more recent comment one might mention J. D. Caputo, *Demythologizing Heidegger* (Bloomington: Indiana University Press, 1993), esp. ch. 9, 'Heidegger's Gods'.

is important to note that what is to be attempted in the following chapters is not being done in the name of Heidegger but as an independent thought experiment that claims no more than an analogy to Heidegger's own programme of 'thinking' as a counter-movement to planetary technology.[37] In offering this analogy I note simply that Christians are not obliged to accept Heidegger's judgement that their tradition is, in its totality, without alternatives to the scientific-technological vision of God-as-Supreme-Being. Even so, if we are preparing to commit ourselves to the risk of thinking about God we would do well to listen to Heidegger's own caution. On the one hand, possibilities of false dawns and self-deception abound. Nothing would be easier than to exploit a sense of crisis in the present juncture of human self-questioning as a way of uncritically reintroducing this or that version of the Christian tradition as 'the' Christian answer to modernity's (or postmodernity's) need. On the other hand, we should never underestimate the power of the scientific approach to reabsorb whatever alternatives may be proposed and thus to demonstrate that these 'alternatives' were, after all, subordinate themes within the larger picture of contemporary knowledge. This power is due not simply to the brutality of the technological will-to-power but to the fact that (if Heidegger is correct) it is truth itself that has made both science and technology possible. They are only powerful because, however distortedly or opaquely, they are nevertheless 'true'. That is why, finally, the problem or crisis of technology cannot be solved merely reactively, by going back to some archaic form or model of thought.

Let me at this point reformulate my previous comments about what I take to be the essential modesty of Heidegger's own claims for non-technological thinking. In the same way that Heidegger can be understood as limiting himself to the question as to whether philosophy can allow for forms of truth other than those that fit the frame of technology, so too the question of thinking about God can be understood as limited to a pre-theological reflection on the kind of thinking that a non-technological thinking about God might be. In other words, I am not setting out to produce a programme for the academy, for the Church, or for

---

[37] There is already a long tradition of attempting to find in Heideggerian 'thinking' a way through some of the difficulties in which theology has become enmeshed as a result of the collective experience of modern atheism. In the 1960s the question tended to be framed in terms of the possibility of a 'non-objectifying' thinking about God. Heidegger himself responded to this question in connection with a colloquium held at Drew University, Madison, NJ, in April 1964. See M. Heidegger, 'Einige Hinweise auf Hauptgesichtspunkte für das theologische Gespräch: Das Problem eines nichtobjektivierenden Denken und Sprechen in der heutigen Theologie', in idem, *Phänomenologie und Theologie* (Frankfurt am Main: Vittorio Klostermann, 1970). Perhaps especially interesting was the work of Heinrich Ott; see, e.g. H. Ott, *Denken und Sein: Der Weg Martin Heideggers und der Weg der Theologie* (Basel: Zollikon, 1959), esp. 158–75; and *Wirklichkeit und Glaube* (Göttingen and Zürich: Vandenhoeck und Ruprecht, 1969), esp. ii. 31–66. On the one hand, there was no special emphasis in the debates of the 1960s and 1970s on the question of technology. On the other, Ott himself uses an essentially Heideggerian model of thinking to argue, against secular theology, for the obligation of theology to hold to a discourse concerning the *personal* nature of God.

society, but merely to address or to focus a set of reflections, a question, a thought. Yet it would also be disingenuous to disclaim anything but a detached philosophical interest in this thought and, as opposed to Heidegger, I do not wish to separate thinking from the concrete personal and existential contexts to which it belongs. My reflections are thus *pre*-theological in the sense that they neither presuppose nor constitute an argument for any particular doctrine or practice, yet they are also guided by an existential and human interest. If it is possible to think about God in a manner that both belongs to the public domain of contemporary intellectual culture and that nevertheless resists being incorporated into the frame of technology, then certain decisions are already being made concerning ideas of what counts as human flourishing and certain practical questions are being weighted in a particular way. In Chapters 7, 8, 9 and the Postscript I shall therefore, though briefly, sketch some of the points where thinking about God touches the realities of contemporary life, although here too the emphasis concerns more the formal conditions of such points of contact than any detailed doctrinal 'answer'.

What, then, could it mean to think about God in, with and under the conditions of an age of technology and to do so in such a way that our thinking would not be immediately reabsorbed into the domain of knowledge management? How could we put such thinking into words without it being overtaken by the cultural prejudices that occupy the language available to us? And even if we thought we were succeeding, could we reasonably expect to get any kind of hearing for a form of thinking that refused to be put into the picture framed by the research man's panoply of projects, conferences, and publications? But before we can talk about succeeding, how can we even begin to think about God, if such thinking is to be defined in terms of what no eye has seen, no ear heard, no heart conceived—a condition that not only marks the distinction of this kind of thinking from the massive achievements of science and technology but also indicates that we are not in a position to rely on this or that given theological tradition for guidance or for assurance that we are on the right track? Can we even imagine such a thing?

PART II

A RESPONSE

4

We are Free to Think about God

I

In the preceding chapters, I began by considering the ban imposed by a line of theological radicals on thinking about God, a line stretching from Altizer to Cupitt and beyond. I then went on to claim that thinking of our present age in terms of technology rather than secularity both underlined the difficulty of thinking about God, but also gave rise to a need to try to think otherwise than in the mode of technology. But can we in fact think about God in a manner that is both other than the thinking institutionalized in what Rustum Roy called science-based technology yet also meaningful? Heidegger offered some hope of a form of thinking that would be other than the thinking encountered in the world of technology, though he himself was, to say the least, extremely reserved concerning its possible value vis-à-vis the questions of theology. However, as was stressed at the end of the previous chapter, I am not claiming loyally to apply Heidegger to theology. Whether the content of Heideggerian thinking is essentially or potentially compatible with the thought of God is not a question I intend to address directly. The point is rather to take the example provided by Heidegger as the basis for a parallel move within the internal discourse of Christianity. In this connection it should be emphasized that for most of the next three chapters I am not concerned with elaborating an idea or concept of God that might somehow be claimed to be immune from the assaults of technological rationality. My thought experiment is of a far more limited nature than that: it is merely to try to pick out some of the formal traits of a thinking about God that would be other than the thinking that finds expression in planetary technology. It is not so much a matter of what such thinking would find itself *saying*, but merely what it would be *like*. What form or kind of thinking could it possibly be? Although I shall offer some reflections in Chapter 10 as to what might be said about God that would be compatible with these formal requirements, it is not my aim to set out anything like a full doctrine of God. For no matter how majestic the doctrine of God we might construct, it would not have met the challenge of my question if it was formulated within the patterns of thinking that belong essentially to technological enframing.[1]

[1] For this reason, therefore, I am methodologically suspicious of the kind of claim made by Philip Clayton in his admirable and important book *The Problem of God in Modern Thought* (Grand

A preliminary comment about the possibility of such an attempt is simply to note that, whatever the more specific content of our thoughts about God (and without considering whether these were worthy of their subject matter), we are free to think about God in just the same way that we are free to think about whatever we are in fact free to think about. This might seem to be an empty and even arbitrary starting point for such a serious enquiry as 'how to think about God in an age of technology', but it draws attention to something that is of the utmost importance for this particular act of thought. From the outset, it removes the question of thinking about God from the debate between authority and autonomy that has been raging ever since the Enlightenment. It has been typical of religious apologetics to draw attention to the limits of autonomy and to introduce God (or faith, or the Church) as the basis and guarantor of these limits. Secular theology, as we have seen, broke this mould by arguing for the acceptance that 'man' had 'come of age' and no longer needed the external authority of Church or revelation to guide his moral and religious thoughts, sentiments, and decisions. However, as we also saw, this typically involved a move that ultimately made it hard to distinguish faith and its content from the general horizon of secular humanity's thoughts and activities. A religion without God, without redemption, and with only the guiding star of human autonomy seems only tenuously linked to the historical reality of religion. Nevertheless, in emphasizing the freedom of thought as integral to the possibility of thinking about God, I am going with the insight of the theological modernizers that a religious perspective that is to work for the ultimate flourishing of human beings can no longer take its primary orientation from the 'miracle, mystery and authority' of Dostoevsky's Grand Inquisitor. Thinking about God becomes actual for us to the degree that we know ourselves to be thinking it freely, and not under any kind of duress or necessity. On the other hand, that this freedom is understood to include the freedom to think about God also indicates a critical reserve in face of secular theologies. For such theologies themselves paradoxically adopted a powerfully authoritarian rhetoric that made manifesto-like declarations concerning what 'we' can 'no longer' think or say. Bultmann insisted we *cannot* use the electric light and believe in the New Testament world view, while Bonhoeffer, in a quotation that van Buren for one takes as the starting point of his secular reading of the Gospels, says that 'we *must* live in the world as if there were no God.'[2] Cupitt too says 'A modern person *must not* any more surrender the apex of his self-consciousness to a god. It *must* remain his own.'[3] What lies behind such injunctions that run through the literature of secular theology like a

Rapids: Eerdmans, 2000), where he suggests that a research programme—defined in almost Heideggerian terms as 'an ongoing and definable program of enquiry'—might be capable of making genuine progress with regard to the metaphysical problem of God (43 f.).

  [2] van Buren, *The Secular Meaning of the Gospel*, 15.
  [3] Cupitt, *Taking Leave of God*, 9.

ground bass? Whence all these 'musts' and 'cannots'?[4] It is certainly odd that the very move that is intended to underline and affirm the autonomy of the human subject is constantly accompanied by such strong assertions of what that very same subject cannot and must not do or think. In insisting here on the freedom to think about God, I suggest at one and the same time that this thinking need not be understood as dependent on some heteronomous power, human or divine, but, equally, that we have the freedom, if we choose to avail ourselves of it, to think about God. God, in other words, is not 'off limits' to thought's essential freedom.

I have just asked, teasingly, where secular theology got all its 'musts' and 'cannots' from. In fact, the answer is candidly stated by the secular theologians themselves as an integral element in their argument. These 'musts' and 'cannots' are rooted in the necessity that characterizes the propositions, arguments, and procedures of scientific and technological rationality. Bultmann's electric light will only work if its design, construction, and operation are in accord with the known laws of electricity and of the materials of which it is made. Even if in the twentieth century this 'necessity' was widely redefined by science itself more in terms of probability and non-linear complexity than of the mechanistic relations posited by Enlightenment and nineteenth-century science, this was really a closer definition of the web of statistical probability than an abandonment of necessity as such. The very randomness observable in certain processes was itself integral to the seamlessness of the cosmic order. 'Chaotic' processes were not really chaotic but just processes that called for a new level of complexity in their mathematical mapping. So, the argument ran, reality and theology *must* accept the world described by science as the sole environment of truly modern thinking because this world itself allows no exceptions. Even the thought that thinks about God is as dependent on the biological status of the human being and on the chemical processes of the human brain as any other thought and, ultimately, must be analysable in terms of those processes. As biology and information science converge, surely (it seems) the gap between such law-bound spheres and what we experience as our freedom to think about this or that will be progressively whittled away until it vanishes altogether. Given a fine enough map of the brain and a powerful enough computer (suitably adapted to interact in determinate ways with its environment), thinking about God will itself be shown to be no 'transcendent' mystery but a predictable and technologically manipulable brain function, like any other.[5] Theology, it is claimed, *must* accept the force of such

---

[4] In putting the question like this I am deliberately echoing Chestov's challenge to Kierkegaard's insistence that a Christian *must* suffer and that one *cannot* be a Christian without suffering. See L. Chestov, *Kierkegaard et la philosophie existentielle* (Paris: Vrin, 1972 [1936]), e.g. 258–9.

[5] See, e.g. A. Newbury, E. D'Aquili, and V. Rause, *Why God Won't Go Away: Brain Science and the Biology of Belief* (New York: Ballantine Books, 2001, 2002). It should be emphasized that this is not an *anti*-religious study, but nevertheless argues for a view of religious experience as essentially translatable into scientific terms. See also Introduction above, n. 8.

developments if it is to have any right to be taken seriously. Moreover, it must also accept the political, social, educational, and cultural conditions that sustain this science and its technological expression. Of course, the actual political conditions of the world today make it possible for a fundamentalist religious state to possess weaponry and hospitals based upon the most advanced technology, but the essential incoherence of the ideology that allows for such a parasitic phenomenon has long been known.[6] With that warning in mind, surely theology cannot wish to lock itself into an analogous inconsistency? Even to dwell on the possibility of thinking otherwise than in the mode of technology is not only to step outside the logic of biological function and economic exchange in which talk of 'need' and 'necessity' have their *sitz-im-leben*, it might also be seen as renouncing any claim to either usefulness or objectivity. Such renunciation can scarcely be anything other than folly, or so the more serious of the secularizers would have it.

Yet to insist on thought's freedom to wander outwith the known limits of science and technology *need not* be construed as useless or foolish. We have seen from Heidegger how his conception of 'thinking' is indeed postulated as a counter-movement to technology but not necessarily as anti-technological. Precisely as a counter-movement to technology it offers a balance to an over-rationalized, over-managed form of life that becomes distorted and oppressive precisely to the extent that it is unable to allow any other 'take' on reality than its own. In this spirit, the work of original thinking is to keep open the possibility of a whole in relation to which all that is known and all modes of knowing that history has developed up to and including the present are only parts, only provisional and anticipatory sketches (though this 'only' should not by any means be taken to imply contempt or belittlement). In the concise phrase of George Grant (reflecting, I think, his reading of Heidegger), 'Thought is steadfast attention to the whole'.[7] Even if non-technological thinking cannot presume simply to deliver the 'whole' that has eluded the best efforts of scientists, philosophers, and artists in many centuries of intellectual endeavour, even if that 'whole' remains intrinsically resistant to comprehension, and even if it proves, finally, to be a symbol rather than a state of affairs, the idea of the whole holds out a kind of promise to human existence that merits thinking about. Non-technological thinking—whatever that may turn out to be!—may have no specific 'use' and no 'objective basis' but may nevertheless be justified by the hope of learning something about ourselves that we have not yet got within our sights, even if it cannot be 'justified' in the sense in which philosophers of

[6] See, for example, V. S. Naipaul, *Among the Believers: An Islamic Journey* (London: Deutsch, 1981).

[7] G. Grant, *The George Grant Reader*, ed. W. Christensen and S. Grant (Toronto: University of Toronto Press, 1998), 120.

science talk about the justification of scientific theories. Possibly it is indeed something for which there is no *need*, in the sense that it does not serve this or that predetermined intellectual, cultural, or psychological lack. However, if folly, justification, and need are defined in such a way as to limit what can be thought and said to what can be fitted within the concepts and categories of a given map of mental and social reality then the game is up before it has started, since we shall already have accepted the limits of technological enframing and foreclosed on the possibility of any truly significant alternative.

The idea that the freedom of thought itself provides the best clue to the possibility of thinking about God not only puts this enquiry on a different footing from heteronomous ecclesiastical responses to modernity and from the radical theologians' insistence on the impossibility of thinking about God, it also establishes my argument on very different ground from that occupied by much previous philosophy of religion, where the attempt to secure God as the proper object of philosophical reflection or religious faith has been precisely to empha-size the compelling nature of the arguments offered for the existence of God, and even to speak of God himself as a 'necessary being' and a necessity of thought. Thus the necessity for thought of the idea of God continued to be asserted even when God's existence itself was left undecided. We *have to* think the idea of God, Kant claimed, even when we cannot say of Him that He exists. Only the idea of the universe as governed by a Supreme Being can underwrite our own scientific and practical faith in the unity, rationality, and purposefulness of the world. Conversely, Nietzsche's hypothesis concerning the death of God is intertwined with his 'discovery' that there is no unity, rationality, or purposefulness under-lying the world order and that these are merely human projections imposed on a chaotic universe that is in itself indifferent to our view of it. Once we have freed ourselves from the prejudice of having to think about the universe as rationally ordered, Nietzsche argued, there will be no further need of God. By linking the possibility of thinking about God with the essential freedom of thought, how-ever, we are (against Kant) marking our fundamental lack of interest in associ-ating God with any kind of necessity whilst at the same time (against Nietzsche) refusing to see the freedom of thought and the thought of God as being mutually exclusive. The thought of God does not exist for us otherwise than as a thought freely willed.

Some might object that this is to give such weight to creaturely freedom as to impinge upon the freedom that is God's prerogative. Here, however, Schelling's argument that if freedom is indeed a fundamental attribute of God then a creature made in God's image must also be understood in the light of *its* freedom remains powerful. On such a view, the recognition of creaturely freedom is itself precisely the best argument for attributing freedom to God. There is therefore no competition between God and creatures for a finite quantum of freedom, but the freedom in one corresponds to and calls for the freedom of the other.[8] In each case freedom is in its essence infinite, even though it must also accept the limitations of finite existence whenever it comes to actual expression. I am free to reach out my hand and take the glass of water from the table, but, being the kind of finite being I am, I am not free to reach out and take a glass of water from a table five miles away.[9] This restriction does not make the freedom of the act of taking the glass that I am able to take any less free. The limitation is quantitative not qualitative. But the qualitative act of freedom can in no way be seen as an encroachment on God's freedom, as if God could only expand His freedom at my expense. The relationship of two free beings is not such that the freedom of one limits the freedom of the other qualitatively, even if one has the power to place a quantitative limit on the other, as when the law incarcerates a criminal: but precisely in thus holding him responsible for his actions it acknowledges the criminal as a free agent, whilst the criminal, except in the most extreme circumstances, retains the freedom to refuse the justice or the sentence of the law.[10]

The kind of useless, unjustifiable, and foolish possibility of thinking that is being played with here does not simply spurn the realm of necessity. It is integral to what I am proposing here that, unlike fundamentalism, it involves understanding and accepting the limits placed on the discourse it wishes to set in motion, and it acknowledges the requirements of justification and necessity that hold for any discourse that gives itself out to be 'scientific'. In other words, the exercise of attempting to think about God in the terms being broached here will have fully internalized the critical principles of Kantian philosophy and have accepted the stipulation that in venturing beyond the boundaries of epistemology and ontology it surrenders the right to claim for its 'results' the status of knowledge as defined by the enterprise of science. We cannot and should not expect thinking about God to yield invincible evidences or arguments that would enable us to transform the understanding or practice of science or the structures of society. If at the same time we nevertheless trace possible lines of relationship between such thinking and the domains in which reason, justification and necessity hold sway these will never be such as to constitute a higher justification or another kind of necessity, and if this seems to limit the 'usefulness' of such

---

[8] See F. W. J. Schelling, *Philosophische Untersuchungen über das Wesen der menschlichen Freiheit und die damit zusammenhängenden Gegenstände* (Frankfurt am Main: Suhrkamp, 1975 [1809]), 42. The idea was revived by Berdyaev and indeed lies at the very heart of his philosophy. See, e.g. N. A. Berdyaev, *The Meaning of the Creative Act* (London: Gollancz, 1955 [1912]).

[9] The limitations on the exercise of freedom in the space-time world we actually inhabit also, of course, apply to God. Even if we allow for the possibility of miraculous interventions by God, these interventions can only acquire concrete form under certain limitations. The sun can stand still and the waters part only if there is a concrete constellation of circumstances in which the entities concerned relate to each other as finite and conditioned beings.

[10] The demand of accountability is central to much of Dostoevsky's literary/theological discussion of issues of crime and punishment and has recently been powerfully raised in Lars von Trier's film *Dogville*. The freedom from law claimed by the criminal is, of course, one of the key issues in Camus' novel *L'Étranger*.

thinking then it should be remembered that it also offers a check against *mis-using* it in the service of some new heteronomy.

Abjuring any predetermined use for or application of thinking about God, it is nevertheless important that we recall another element in Heidegger's plea for any nontechnological thinking: that the most challenging challenge of technology today is not how to solve this or that complex of technological problems (how to develop genetic engineering or a manned mission to Mars), but to accept and to understand our responsibility for technology as a total phenomenon and our freedom in the exercise of that responsibility. In other words, whatever technology *is*, whether it is the product of a deliberate strategy or whether it has, so to speak, sprung up like a thicket by a series of incalculable historical chances, it is a phenomenon that, if we knew how to choose, we are free to reject, to direct, or to redirect. As a human activity it cannot entirely escape the possibilities of human action and decision, even if for the present its accelerating progress outstrips the capacities of moral, religious, and political traditions and institutions to cope with it. Heidegger offers his own thinking as a step towards the possibility of human beings becoming capable of making a decision with regard to their responsibility for planetary technology. If we say that the attempt to think about God may prove to be a deepening of that possibility, then this is not to say that it could ever simply be applied to the 'problem' of technology, as if it were itself a technique to manage the unmanageable. It is important to note the modesty both of Heidegger's own proposals and what is being ventured here. In the first place this is only a step or, even less, only preparation for taking a step. To succeed would only be to have *begun* on a way of thinking, to have become engaged in a process, to have made a commitment. It would not be to give us a solution to a problem, and to think of it as being directed towards solving a problem would already be to subordinate the freedom of thinking to the 'need' that had summoned it forth and to be once more back in the domain of instrumental thinking. We do not think or think about God *in order to* be able to deal with technology, but, keeping our thinking about God in a conscious relation to a world shaped by and as technology, we look to a recontextualizing of our relation to that world. That we do think about God makes a difference, if only in the weak sense that a technological being who (perhaps without noticing it) has given up on thinking about God will come to have a different relation to his technology from an equally technological being who, in spite of the folly and trouble of the thing, keeps open the possibility of such thinking. That difference may not itself be calculable in technological terms (as if we could ever find out whether those who think about God make worse or better technologists), but it would still be a humanly real difference.[11]

---

[11] A further discussion of the way in which the practice of thinking about God might relate to concrete decision-making with regard to technology is to be found in Chapter 7 below, where the question is linked to the much-discussed role of ethics in setting parameters for technological development.

But how are we to give any distinctive content to this freely chosen path of thinking about God? Isn't all that has been said so far merely a statement of intent or, perhaps, the celebration of a freedom without qualification, constraints, or limits, thinking that has left the realm of quantifiable results, compelling arguments, and manageable applications far behind? Isn't freedom meaningful only in a structure of meaning? Wouldn't an absolute freedom without constraints or limits, a freedom that could think or do anything at any time, be something to fear rather than to honour or to love? We would wish such a freedom neither for God nor for ourselves. Our folly does not extend that far! Can we then say anything more about the kind of freedom we are thinking of here? Let us go back a step.

So far, we have not reached the point of actually thinking about God. We have been thinking of such thinking only as a possibility or as a question of the form: can we, might we, *may* we turn our thinking to God? Even in saying that, yes, we *are* free to think about God, we have only uttered an abstract and empty formula. Before we could begin to know what it might mean, before we could *do it*, we would have to be capable of thought: only a thinking being can think about God. 'Before', however, does not necessarily mean 'previously', as if we first of all had to learn thinking 'before' we could graduate to thinking about God. It is possible that the opposite is in fact the case: that both in our collective history and in our individual development the thought of God accompanies the first steps of thinking in the atmosphere of myth and fantasy in which thinking moves before it acquires clarity, distinctness, and application. Many would add that to be able to move away from this initial mythical state of thinking and to abandon the thought of God is precisely the mark of maturity in thinking. But the issue here is not one of sequencing, as if it mattered whether the thought of God belonged to the childhood or the old age of the individual or the species. It is more a matter of the analytical or structural priority of 'thinking' in thinking about God, and my suggestion is that it is in the character of thinking itself that we find the possibility of thinking about God. To put it another way: the possibility of thinking about God is a possibility that is given with or co-present in the possibility of simply being able to think. For thinking can think anything that can be thought, and it is as free to think what does not exist as what does exist. It can think of theorems and unicorns, of facts and dreams. As the condition of being able to produce thoughts that have more than a casual or arbitrary interest particular forms of thought—thought schooled in one discipline or mode, science, logic, or even the art of poetry—will limit this boundless freedom in various ways. Reporting the stream of consciousness may occasionally make for an interesting literary experiment, but rarely for an interesting conversation. Conversely, even the most disciplined logician cannot, as a thinker, renounce thought's astonishing freedom, and is as entitled as anyone else to lean back after the rigours of the day and dream. And even the chaos of a mind broken by illness, in which thought exists only as the bringing forth of fearful or absurd monstrosities that overwhelm the struggling personality with terror and anxiety—even such thoughts nevertheless testify to the sheer power and scope of thought. Thought can think anything that can be thought. It is even free to try thinking about God.

II

We are attempting to think through the crisis of technology, and already this freedom of thought indicates one possibility of thinking beyond technology. 'Facts, figures and logic,' sang Donovan many years ago, 'people are much more given to magic.' And it is true that, since we can think whatever can be thought and therefore think what we like about whatever we like, we may well choose to think about magic in preference to thinking about machines. Nor can it be any surprise that magical worlds have re-entered our world as potent 'alternatives' to the age of technology (if, indeed, they ever left: it is striking that the great age of fairy-tales coincided with the high point of the industrial revolution). Narnia and Middle Earth and other imaginary worlds of that kind picture a life in which the values of courage, friendship, truthfulness, honour, loyalty, etc. are inexplicably blessed with a magic that invariably prevails over that of the dark powers. That these dark powers usually have a close affinity with 'science' is clear not only from the texts themselves but also from Lewis's science fiction (especially *That Hideous Strength*, a crude and ugly satire on the scientific attitude) and essays such as *The Abolition of Man*.[12] Such imaginary worlds are incontrovertible evidence of the power of the human imagination, however we understand the detailed workings of that power. But Narnia and Middle Earth do not, of course, 'exist', or they 'exist' only in the imagination, by the same power of thought with which a four-year old transforms a chair into a pirate ship. Even though the four-year old may insist that the chair 'really' *is* a ship, most readers of Tolkien and Lewis know even as they read that what they are reading about is not 'real', that it is only a fantasy. Is this, then, the use and value of our freedom of thought in relation to the crisis of technology: that it can compensate for the over-rationalized 'reality' of public life by giving us a fantasy world in which to spend our spare time, i.e. our non-useful time (with or without the aid of heavy-metal concerts, computer games, or movies)?[13]

Religious believers, at least, would be reluctant to think that their beliefs could only offer this kind of alternative. They might be willing to concede some

---

[12] C. S. Lewis, *That Hideous Strength: A Modern Fairy-Tale for Grown-ups* (London: Pan, 1955); idem, *The Abolition of Man, or, Reflections on Education with Special Reference to the Teaching of English in the Upper Forms of Schools* (London: G. Bles, 1946).

[13] Of course, Narnia and Middle Earth are only two of the more respectable alternative realities available. Drugs and porno point both to the prevalence of the most bizarre fantasy in the technologized world and to its endless, if essentially tedious, variety.

analogy: that imaginatively transposing ourselves into the world of Abraham, of Isaac and of Jacob, or meditatively visualizing Jesus's ministry in Galilee are pedagogical exercises that draw on the same powers that are in play in fantasy fiction. They might even (against Hegel, for example) want to argue that such imaginative narratives are proper to religion and an element that not only cannot but should not be overcome or left behind in personal and communal religious life: that Judea *can* become 'the Teuton's fatherland' when the growing mind is moulded by the biblical narratives.[14] The stories told by the religions are not just recreational (in the usual sense), but stories to live by and, both historically and today, not without effect in shaping our collective moral sensibility: that is, they are *really* re-creational. However, my point here is not to add my voice to the theological promotion of the category of narrative,[15] but is simply and primarily to draw attention to the freedom of thought, a freedom to invent, and even to dwell on what is altogether unreal if it so chooses. No matter how vigorous or, in its own terms, persuasive the re-emphasizing of 'story' may be, it cannot hide the fact that story-telling is in one respect dependent on our capacity for thinking what is not real. The proximity of the popular senses of 'story' and 'fiction' is important and not accidental. Story-telling is both a measure of thought's freedom, but also a warning that this freedom does not of itself guarantee the truth of what it is able to summon into thought.

Thinking about God, then, is a possibility of thought, 'God' is something we are free to think, whether or not God exists and whether or not we can even attain a clear and distinct idea of God. But is such thinking only one more evidence of our propensity for magic as a compensatory alternative to reason, truth, and logic? To answer this question fully we must look more closely at the starting point of our question concerning thinking about God. In doing so we shall see how such thinking sets out on a very different course from that reflected in fantasy, myth, or the great narratives of historical religions. This does not preclude the possibility of possible analogies to these nor, on a psychological or cultural level, to deny their value. I offer no argument here for or against their place within the overall compass of a religious world view. But such imaginative and narrative visions do not of themselves reveal what makes thinking about God genuinely thoughtful.

We have seen that Heideggerian 'thinking' is thinking that holds itself open to a whole that is never immediately given in intuition and which has not, as yet, been brought into being by any actual social or scientific construction of reality. Thinking of this kind is guided by the passion to think what has not yet been thought, what resists or escapes thought. It can be described as negative in so far as it is nagged by the thought that Heidegger himself so often repeats: that 'we are

[14] The reference is to a remark by Hegel in his early essay on *The Positivity of the Christian Religion*. See G. W. F. Hegel, *Frühe Schriften* (Frankfurt am Main: Suhrkamp, 1971), i. 200.
[15] See the critical comments regarding Schulze in Chapter 2.

not yet thinking' and that something essential to our self-understanding continues to elude us. Or, it can be described as positive in so far as it finds itself, in thought, seeking to become open to the whole. Each of these aspects conditions the other. Thinking is not merely a negative reaction to the insufficiency of existing knowledge, since it is also in the spell of an (as yet) undisclosed horizon of wholeness. It is the promise of this horizon that makes possible the elevation of thought above the immediate contexts of predetermined experience. As has often been remarked, it is not when he is overwhelmed by his misery, but when he first believes in the promise of a better world that the slave begins to rattle his chains. On the other hand, this 'whole' itself, this horizon of promise, precisely because it is '(as yet) undisclosed', because it is neither given in immediate intuition nor available as something we can construct out of our currently existing resources, is 'present' only as a possibility that we have not yet managed to conceive or realize and so it makes its appearance as a negative or critical movement in relation to the present. Serious thinking does not indulge in criticism for its own sake but is aroused to criticism by its experience of the failure of existing paradigms, world views, and futurological visions to fulfil their own claims to represent the whole or to provide a perspective that would make sense of the whole. At first this may have a merely negative form, as when someone complains about the hollowness, the emptiness or the mere superficiality of what the world calls life. Such complaints may, in fact, spring from wounded pride or, in Dostoevsky's sense, from 'spite'.[16] But they may have a more profound root. An aversion to mobile phones expressed in a stream of polemical remarks about the rudeness of mobile phone users in public spaces *may* prove to be the obverse of a deeper and more important concern to preserve the richness and nuance of human conversation. Equally, it may 'just' be a negative reaction occasioned by one especially obnoxious fellow-commuter, and nothing more. Similarly, and even when it 'looks like' a merely negative reaction, the expression of reserve towards some new technological innovation or towards the phenomenon of technological innovation as such may in fact turn out to be an indirect statement concerning an as yet inarticulate apprehension of a depth of reality that technology threatens to conceal or even destroy. Behind the focus on the particular object that is the immediate target of hostility may be a systemic concern for some larger, important good. However, only thoughtful and thought-provoking questioning will, in any particular case, enable us to decide.

At the level of everyday life, it may well be the negative moment that comes to expression first—the child's persistent refusal to accept an answer, the adolescent's rejection of the way things are, parental grumblings about mobile phones, the eco-activist's spurning of technology. This is the moment of disequilibrium in the beginning of any enquiry, the moment in which we discover that we don't

---

[16] See F. Dostoevsky, tr. R. Pevear and L. Volkhonsky, *Notes from Underground* (London: Vintage, 1993). Pevear and Volkhonsky, however, translate the term familiar as 'spite' as 'wickedness'.

actually know what we thought we knew, that we are not or don't have to be what we thought we were, that we are free to think otherwise than is expected of us. And it is, of course, possible for thinking to become fixed in this negative moment, to question for questioning's sake, to lose itself in irony and criticism. The pathos of the negative has been a powerful rhetorical tool in the hands of much recent philosophy and theology, and there has perhaps been no greater philosophical sin in modern times than that of making light of the moment of negation. Thought first gets to be taken seriously when it marks its negation of whatever has gone before. To stress the 'de-' or the 'non-' or the 'post-' of one's thinking is to offer a guarantee that it is free of any covert dogmatism. Hegel perhaps prepared the way, by insisting that his own 'way of despair' was deeper and more thoroughgoing than Descartes' 'way of doubt'[17]—but, since Feuerbach and Kierkegaard, Hegel has also been the chief target of the inexorable out-flanking movements of post(!)-Hegelian thought. A constant stream of graduate humanities students bid for their philosophical spurs by 'overcoming' Hegel or some subsequent 'master' philosopher, deconstructing Derrida, perhaps—or going even further and negating the negation by *con*structing a post-postmodern paradigm of thinking. Rebellion without a cause, however, is not a sustainable option, nor does it necessarily betoken thoughtfulness. If thought's first awakening takes form as the voice of rebellion, rebellion only becomes interesting when it thinks about what it is doing. Is the negative moment, then, simply to be treated as a passing phase, something one goes through in order to get from one paradigm to another, as one passes through adolescence on the way from childhood to adulthood?[18] Something like that seems to have been the ultimate vision of Hegel's system, in which the story of mind or spirit is told as a story in which the negation of the initial, immediate stage of being is itself negated and, with this second negation, a new synthesis of the disrupted elements is achieved and a new level of knowledge attained. As others have pointed out, Hegelian philosophy thereby makes itself a narrative, a kind of *Bildungsroman* or coming-of-age novel. It is a story of how the adolescent, having lost faith in the myths of the ancestors and passed through all-consuming doubt and even despair at last finds peace in the exercise of insight and judgement matured by experience. In this perspective, the negative moment is a kind of precursory reflection of a whole that does not yet exist and for which an image and a name has not yet been found and perhaps never will be.

---

[17] The contrast Hegel draws here makes use of a wordplay on the German terms *Zweifel* (doubt) and *Verzweifelung* (despair, i.e. the intensification of *Zweifel*/doubt).

[18] The analogy is, perhaps, a dangerous one, and it is clear that there is also a profound disanalogy between the adolescent's questioning of parental authority and a thoughtful questioning of the limits of technology. The point of the analogy is simply that in each case we can and must distinguish between the kind of questioning that is focused on some particular, isolated issue and questioning that is directed at a whole system of knowledge, experience, and understanding. Only the latter will prove to be not merely critical, but creatively critical.

How do these comments relate to thinking about God in an age of technology? In choosing to think about God are we merely cocking a snook at the all-powerful myth of phallotechnics, at the self-satisfied complacency of the media scientist's contempt for religion, or are we already moving in the slipstream of a longing for a whole that technology alone can never give us? Again, we must beware of jumping to conclusions. Of course, there are examples of how the breakdown of one paradigm marks the transition to another. Whether in the life of the individual, in the history of nations or in the progress of science there are important instances of how the agonies of doubt and loss of faith in one system are merely the birth pangs to something new and better. The decline of Rome is intertwined with the rise of Christendom. The unravelling of Aristotelian cosmology was both a spur to and a consequence of new knowledge about the universe and of a new theory in which to contain that knowledge. But is such a model so easily transferable to the question of thinking beyond the possibilities of the age of technology? Even though we may already question the right of science and technology totally to determine what is to count as reality, it would be gravely to underestimate the power *and the truth* of science and technology if we fancied that some new paradigm was lying ready for us, just over the horizon. Even if the defining constituents of the field of possibilities within which science and technology operate can already be seen in their essential outlines, the actual realization of those possibilities promises to provide almost unlimited scope for human activity. Within the essential field of scientific activity there are still enough new facts about the outer and inner universe to discover, enough new technical applications to develop and enough need for social rationalization to provide a collective agenda stretching far into the future. At that level we cannot presume on any kind of futurological prognosis that the age of technology will sooner or later give way to a new age of faith. There is, therefore, no necessary transition from negative to positive.

But that is not the issue, for 'the whole' that serious thinking finds missing in the scientifically and technologically shaped present, a lack that may first rise to consciousness in the 'merely' negative protest against technology, is nothing to do with the undoubted fact that science and technology have not yet exhausted their historic possibilities and that all we have before us now are only the first rough sketches of a future scientific civilization stretching into an illimitable future. Nor would the kind of thinking 'beyond' technology being thought about here be vindicated if this nascent civilization were to crash-land in the next twenty years, taking us all down into some horrific post-technological state of anarchy. Whether the other worlds of futurology and fantasy have a positive or a negative hue, there is a fundamental difference between thinking of the kind we are considering and such imaginative visions. Because it accepts the truth of science and technology, thinking about God is bound to accept that its own achievements, such as they might be, cannot count as some kind of alternative or supplementary 'knowledge'. Indeed, to see some kind of God-consciousness as the goal of a purposive negation of the present world order—the blueprint for a future beyond the future of scientific-technological progress—would once more be to reduce God to an event within the world, a new theory or a new form of society, a 'spirituality' we need in order to live humanely with the new discoveries that have moulded our horizons, the 'inner world' of technology's 'third wave', perhaps. All such speculation fails theologically because it claims to make sense of a whole that must necessarily elude it. In reality the visions of futurology can only be approximate, preliminary, or partial solutions to a question that has only been grasped in an approximate, preliminary, and partial way. When we tap them with the hammer of thinking, do they not begin to sound just a little hollow? And even if they proved to be genuine metal, wouldn't that very success bring with it the risk that we had strayed back into the reach of 'enframing' and its planned outcomes? Like the imaginary worlds of fantasy fiction, such futurology offers thinking a content, when we scarcely know if we have even begun really to think. Let us then go back, once more, to the difficult moment of beginning to think.

If we are to think about God at all then the thinking that this will require of us (whatever else it may be) will be thinking into and out of what most concerns us now, in our present. 'Our present', of course, is not simply what the media are commenting on today, but the present of thinking itself, what actually engages us in the effort to think. But if in our thinking we have only got as far as critically raising the question as to the totality claims of science and technology; if, as beginners in thinking, we have only succeeded in calling into doubt some current frame of conceptual reference and, in this way, have registered our thinking under the sign of negation, then it would seem as if the freedom that belongs to thinking about God must also be the negative freedom of criticism and denial. Are we finally limited to saying that God is whatever is not the world, whatever is unknowable by science, whatever cannot become the object of technological manipulation, fantasy or speculation; the wholly other, infinitely, and qualitatively different unknown and unknowable one?

But, to repeat, seeking to move beyond the dominant horizon need not be merely a response to the perceived limitations of that horizon and nothing more. There may also be a sense of anticipation driving forward the act of seeking, a movement of hope in the very moment of criticism. Would we dare to begin negating if we really thought that nothing would come of it? Even if psychologically, historically, or biographically the moment of negation comes first, may it not be that this is for the sake of and in the power of an openness to a whole that we cannot yet name? Might it not be just such an unspoken, unimagined apprehension that first stirs us to criticize whatever offers itself as an impossible substitute for, or a too preliminary realization of this whole? Might it not be that we already have a sign pointing to possibilities that are not simply negative within the act of negation itself? And might not the meaning of this sign prove to be the real meaning of criticism? Indeed, if the movement of negation is not to remain stuck in rebellion or not to collapse into nihilism, does it not require such an inner orientation, however secret, towards the whole? But this orientation and openness to the whole are not adequately describable in terms of simple 'positivity', as if they were the good news following on the bad news. Orientation and openness are not states in which we can presume that an answer has been given or a new order has taken shape. They indicate a sense of direction and signal readiness: they represent a forward movement but not necessarily arrival at a determinate destination or the achievement of a determinate result. If the moment of negation can be read as a sign pointing to a concealed fullness, it is so only to the extent that we acknowledge the distance from its object implicit in the term 'sign' itself, that the sign is never what it signifies, that 'every representation is a depresentation' (Derrida), and that the very existence of this sign is a sign that the fulfilment to which it points is wanting.

Let us not be in too much of a rush. That Derrida has spoken (or, at least written) does not prove anything, least of all if we are prepared to take Derrida seriously. So, let us ask again: given that 'God' is not available to us as a new paradigm, as a possible future or an alternative reality, as a closer or more distant positivity, is there anything within the critical movement of thought itself that allows for the possibility of thinking about God in a way that is more than or other than negative? Not in the manner of some kind of intellectual conjuring trick whereby the plus and minus signs outside the brackets are reversed by sleight of hand, so that negative becomes positive, as if our human need were itself evidence of divine response.[19] We are not talking about denying our abandonment or our need but of exploring more deeply just what this abandonment and this need mean.

Up until this point, the most we have managed to say is that the questioning of the present allows for questioning about what lies beyond the present, about what is not present to us but, in our questioning of the present, can become of present concern to us. The negative freedom of thought—the freedom not to be bound by the horizons of the present—is a freedom to think according to whatever possibilities thought itself gives us. In learning to become free from predetermined answers concerning 'what is' or 'what can be known', we are simultaneously free to think of 'what might' or 'may' be, to think (in short) of whatever comes to mind. To discover possibilities that have not yet been realized and possibilities that perhaps can never be realized. To be led by an apprehension of a whole we have no immediate way of articulating. But, as long as we are not forgetting the starting point that all of this involves accepting the principle of

---

[19] Something like this was, for example, an argument often used by Tillich—that the courage to acknowledge despair testified to the truth that the despairer was already gripped or moved by a power greater than that of despair. See, for example, the discussion of 'Absolute Faith and the Courage to Be' in *The Courage to Be* where Tillich writes 'No actual negation can be without an implicit affirmation . . . Even in the despair about meaning being affirms itself through us. The act of accepting meaninglessness is in itself a meaningful act.' P. Tillich, *The Courage to Be* (London: Fontana, 1971), 170–1.

criticism and self-criticism, the vigilance of negation is on hand to prevent us from transposing 'what may be' into 'what is' or allowing the openness of thought to congeal into fantasy or futurology.

III

The freedom of thinking itself sets us free to think about God, if we so choose (with the corollary that we can only think about God if we do indeed *choose* to do so)—but is it possible to discover further features of what such thinking might involve solely on the basis of what we have considered thus far and without presupposing some finished concept of God that has not yet been established?

If the simple fact that even in a situation from which God is excluded from the dominant paradigms of thought and knowledge we are free to think about God has provided us with a starting point of sorts, we might also note the no less simple fact that in thinking about God *we* must think it, or, more precisely, *I* must think it, *you* must think it, *each of us* must think it for ourselves. Precisely as a free, unforced thought, this is not a thought that will think itself (if any thought ever is). Even if, as I shall argue below, it is also proper for us to learn to think this thought as the matter of concerned and caring dialogue, it is nevertheless equally true that all participants in that dialogue must think it for themselves. We can even say that it is a condition of real dialogue, for there can be no dialogue where the participants are not really thinking, for themselves, about what they are saying.

Thinking in general is always experienced by me as *my thinking*, as *what I am thinking*. So too thinking about God will not appear to the one who is thinking as a kind of accidental occurrence within a flux of random musings but a determination and a resolution to think about God or, at least, to try. It is, something we *do*, or, to use a term associated with phenomenology, something *intended*. For phenomenology's founder, Edmund Husserl, the starting point of the notion of intentionality is precisely its 'act-character', although Husserl did not think of this in terms of an unchanging subject which expresses itself in a succession of mental acts.[20] Rather, the subject itself is what and as it is only in and through its concrete intentional acts. Imagine that I decide to go to the local gallery and look at some paintings for the sake of enjoying an aesthetic experience. In the moment in which I stand in front of a painting and see it as a work of art, I myself undergo a subtle change of consciousness and, whatever else is going on in my life, whatever else may be more or less unconsciously going on in my mind, in that moment I exist mentally as the subject of an aesthetic experience. In seeing the work as a work of art my thoughts are shaped by the logic of an aesthetic

---

[20] See E. Husserl, *Logische Untersuchungen*, II/1, p. v, 'Über intentionale Erlebnisse und ihre "Inhalt"' (Tübingen: Max Niemeyer, 1993).

intention that has a distinctive structure that separates it from, for example, thinking about art as a commodity or, if the work in question is a statue and I am running from my enemies, as something to hide behind. Yet, Husserl would claim, that I see it this way is my mental act. I, and only I, can enact the aesthetic intention in this particular moment. In phenomenological terms, thinking about God, then, will (minimally) be thought turned intentionally to God with the desire to think of God in a manner appropriate to this particular kind of thinking.

Of course, the mere fact that I am thinking of something does not mean that that something exists or is as I imagine it to be and the question of fulfilled and unfulfilled intentions would come to be an important question in phenomenological research. Nevertheless, that thought is intentional means that it is always *directed* towards some determinate content, even if that content is not made clear in the first moment in which the thought dawns on me. Thinking about God is both thinking in which I have to be active, as the thinker, and thought that seeks to think *about* God. What it means to be the 'subject' of any given intentional thought cannot, therefore, be known in advance of the process of analysing that thought itself. The subject 'exists' only as the thinker of the thought or of the comprehensive body of thoughts to which the thought belongs. What it means to be the sort of person who likes looking at paintings is not a matter of saying 'I am an artistic sort of person, therefore I like looking at paintings', but rather the intentional activity of looking at paintings, probably quite spontaneous in the circumstances of a person's actual life, is the best evidence both for the meaning of art itself and for the meaning of being a person who likes art. Intentionality embraces both subject and object. So too with thinking about God. If thinking about God as an intentional act means that I have to think it, I cannot presume that that 'I' concerned will prove to be the same as the 'I' I imagine myself to be at the outset. In intending the thought of God, I lay myself open to all that the thought of God might bring with it.

I have noted that even the most cursory overview of the conditions under which thinking about God would have to occur today shows that God cannot be presupposed as a part of the world in such a way that all the theologian has to do is to explain or to interpret what this 'God' *means*. Whatever else may be said for or against them, the secular theologians were entirely correct in their assertion that God is no longer a part of the common sense furniture of the world, a part of universal consensus concerning how things are. Thinking about God, then, must be capable of reaching or of being drawn beyond the horizons of the given, of what can be assumed or presupposed. The intentionality involved in thinking about God leads the thinker beyond every provisional objectification or positivity that might seem to fulfil it. As the thought of God, it is the thought of what in itself transcends thought and, in this transcendence, is the ultimate lure of thought. Sustaining the intention to think about God, then, will demand a singular discipline of courage, patience, and humility before the impossibility of the task and the thinker must be open to learn things about her own self that might challenge every single element of her self-image. In the light of what has just been said, however, we cannot claim any kind of superior moral courage, patience or humility for the thinker, since we are only talking about the thinker as the thinker of this one single thought. What sort of person the thinker may be in the rest of her life we do not know and will not be attempting to find out, but, as thinker, she has freely to choose the thought of God, has to keep on thinking it, has to mean it, has to intend it. The role of such intentionality as a condition of thinking about God—a willed, sustained, humbly courageous, and open intentionality—is rarely commented on in the literature of the philosophy of religion nor even in that of dogmatic theology. It is always so easy to overlook the most obvious and crucial step! If it has been more or less bypassed by the academy, however, it is something to which the literature of the religious life copiously testifies, seeing it not just as the beginning but as the continuing medium of serious religious thought.

The anonymous mystical text *The Cloud of Unknowing* (late fourteenth century) articulates the point with the author's characteristic frankness and clarity. Readers are advised to lift their hearts to God 'with humble love. And really mean God himself who created you, and bought you, and graciously called you to this state of life. And think no other thought of him. It all depends on your desire. A naked intention directed to God and himself alone, is wholly sufficient.'[21] It might seem as if this passage assumes more than at first appears and that the reference to God as creator, as redeemer, and as the giver of a specific grace implies acceptance of a particular—i.e. Christian and Trinitarian—conception of God. The 'naked intention' then would not be the way in which one first got to think about God but the way in which one activated a belief in God that was already accepted at the theoretical level. Clearly the author did write from within a particular cultural horizon and could presume upon his reader's willingness to believe that God was there to be thought about and adored. Yet it is equally clear that he does not regard holding to the teaching of the Church in an external way as sufficient for truly thinking about God. In the moment of religious realization, even the fullness of doctrine becomes dispensable, as the next paragraph makes clear, where it advises reducing this naked intention to a single word 'preferably of one syllable . . . The shorter the better, being more like the working of the Spirit! A word like "GOD" or "LOVE".'[22] The lower part of meditation may occupy itself with what usually counts as religious activity— 'spiritual meditation, an awareness of one's own wretched state, sorrow and contrition, a sympathetic and understanding consideration of Christ's passion and that of his servants, a gratitude which praises God for his wonderful gifts, his kindness in all parts of his creation, physical and spiritual'. This, however, falls

---

[21] Anon. *The Cloud of Unknowing*, tr. C. Wolters (Harmondsworth: Penguin, 1961), 61.
[22] Ibid.

away as the soul proceeds to 'the higher part of contemplation—at least as we know it in this life' which 'is wholly caught up in darkness, and in this cloud of unknowing, with an outreaching love and a blind groping for the naked being of God, himself and him only'.[23] The division of 'higher' and 'lower' belongs, of course, to the author's world. If we seem here to be leaping over what he would say are essential preconditions of thinking about God, this is not simply the reflection of our hubris. It is, firstly, because the situation in which we are attempting to think about God is no longer that of Christendom, in which such beliefs and practices can be assumed unproblematically; and, secondly, it is because the logic of *The Cloud* is that although the 'naked intention' is described as 'higher' (and thus, seemingly, resting on the foundation of the 'lower') it is in fact itself the necessary condition of any actual thought of God. The 'higher' is, in this case, the more basic category. None of the practices belonging even to the 'lower' part of contemplation make sense if there is not active within them a deliberate but simple will directed towards God. As another anonymous text, possibly by the same author, puts it, this will is 'a blind shot with the sharp dart of longing love'.[24]

The Cloud of Unknowing is rare in the pith and force of its expressions, but it both reflects and transmits a constant theme in Christian spirituality—we might think of Augustine's emphasis on allowing ourselves to be led towards God by the restless longing of a heart that can seek God even when not knowing what he is, provoking the repeated question 'What do I love when I love my God?'[25] In Post-Reformation traditions of Catholic spirituality a similar motif appears in the idea of 'the prayer of simple regard' or in de Caussade's theme of self-abandonment to divine providence while, in a Protestant context, Kierkegaard would speak of a simple 'urge' that drives the self towards God, asserting that 'the urge towards God is a human being's highest perfection' even though the urge has no content other than its own sense of needing God. For Kierkegaard, sensing the twilight of Christendom drawing close, this 'urge' begins to break free from a dogmatic or ecclesiastical context, and the distinction between the kind of relation to God into which it brings us and the kind of relation that is supposedly reflected in theoretical truths about God is sharply drawn. To want God in the double sense of the English 'want' (to be in need of and to wish for) is, Kierkegaard says, the only and necessary condition of being in relationship with Him.[26] And there might be analogies from other religious traditions, the *kawannah* or

[23] Ibid. 64.

[24] Quoted in E. Underhill, *Mysticism* (London: Methuen, 1967), 85.

[25] Cf. J. D. Caputo, *On Religion* (London: Routledge, 2001), especially ch. 1.

[26] See, e.g. the discourse 'To Need God is a Human Being's Highest Perfection', in S. Kierke-gaard, tr. H.V. and E. H. Hong, *Eighteen Upbuilding Discourses* (Princeton: Princeton University Press, 1990 [1844]).

concentration of Jewish mysticism,[27] the movement of love of Hindu bhakti devotion.[28]

The issue is not one of simply stirring up the will as if we could think about God just by willing ourselves to do so. Will or an analogue of will may belong here, reflecting the role of freedom in freely thinking about God that I have sought continually to emphasize. *The Cloud* is not simply testimony to a certain kind of willing, however, since the *thought* that is intended is always comprised within the wilfulness of the 'naked intention' of the heart. Indeed, 'will' is positively misleading if we imagine it to be some kind of act over which we have deliberate and fully conscious control or something that exists apart from the act of thinking. It is rather the kind of 'will' that is revealed in Augustine's 'restless heart', i.e. a heart that is moved before it moves itself, yet whose restless movement is shaped as thought, a thought—or a way of thinking—articulated in the driving force of the questions that are the ever-moving argument of *The Confessions*.[29] In relation both to *The Cloud* and to Augustine it is perhaps relevant that in discussing the place of medieval mysticism in the history of philosophy, Hegel remarks in his idiosyncratic way that the standpoint of the Middle Ages is, in one respect 'that the idea is apprehended by the heart'. However, he does not understand this in terms of 'mere' emotion or affectivity. What the heart experiences in medieval mysticism is its identity with God, that the individual qua individual is what it is 'with God and in God' and that this contains a necessarily speculative element that is a 'summons to thinking'.[30] And it is not clear that this is entirely different from what Kierkegaard means when he speaks of the 'urge' that knows its need of God, since he makes clear that this urge is not something wordless or unconscious but occurs as a very concrete and specific movement in the development of the self that, tearing itself out of its absorption in the world, has been brought into the orbit of self-concern and self-questioning. Heart and thinking, desire and self-knowledge, will and intentionality are separable only on the basis of retrospective analysis. The primary phenomenon is simply that of the 'thinking, feeling heart', Kierkegaard's 'urge',

[27] See, e.g. M. Buber, tr. M. Friedman, *The Tales of Rabbi Nachman* (New York: Humanity Books, 1974), 14.

[28] See F. Hardy, *Viraha-Bhakti: The Early History of Kṛṣṇa Devotion in South India* (New Delhi: Oxford University Press, 1983). Hardy emphasizes the emotional quality of *bhakti*, as opposed to the more intellectual picture given by many commentators on the *Bhagavad-Gita*. In Buber, however, the point is more precisely the possibility of what might variously be called concentration, devotion or intention as a fluid moment in which both heart and head are involved and may each play a part in directing and shaping the other.

[29] And therewith, as John D. Caputo has pointed out, throwing a bridge of sorts towards another kind of inconclusively circling thinking, the 'religion' broached in Derrida's *Circumfession*—which, in turn, relates itself questioningly back to Augustine and his *Confessions*. See Caputo, *On Religion*.

[30] G. W. F. Hegel, *Vorlesungen über die Geschichte der Philosophie*, in *Werke 19* (Frankfurt am Main: Suhrkamp, 1971), ii. 542–3. It is worth commenting that one of the crucial transitional periods in Heidegger's early philosophical development was concurrent with an intensive reading both of Augustine and of the medieval and post-medieval mystical tradition.

in which we might hear both an echo of the 'touching' or 'stirring' that Kant speaks of in connection with the sublime and an anticipation of the 'passivity before passivity' with which Lévinas indicates the 'decreating' (to use S. Weil's term) of every gesture of mere self-assertion or transparent subjectivity that might offer itself as the first or foundational moment of consciousness.[31]

To speak of the freedom that is involved in thinking about God as primarily a matter of *the heart* is also to say—tautologically—that such thinking will require *courage* on the part of the thinker. The thinker must put himself into his thought and go with that thought beyond what the conventions of his time have previously allowed him to think. This is especially true when, as here, the question is how to think about God in the age of technology. For it is a very different thing to think about God in a context where God is generally regarded as the keystone of the whole edifice of knowledge from venturing to think about God where this thought is excluded by the dominant paradigms of knowledge. This is not to belittle those who raised their thoughts to God in the ages of faith and attempted to think in its purity the idea of God that was held in only a rough and inconsistent way by the multitude. Whether in a Thomas in the Catholic world, or a Hegel in Protestantism, the desire to know God as a proper object of intellectual activity committed the thinker to the most demanding efforts of thought and, it should be added, these thinkers were often able to achieve more than any contemporary effort of thinking about God can hope for. Furthermore, even though they could take advantage of a prevailing assumption in favour of belief in God, their philosophy was not simply a straightforward translation of popular faith into intellectual form. The record shows that at each step they had to struggle against alternative views and misunderstandings and, at many points, to appear to be going against the tide. Such grand systematic efforts also demanded courage. It is not to diminish their achievements in any way to say that the possibility of presuming upon a basic contemporary assumption in favour of religious belief gave a certain hope of success in their philosophical and theological work that we simply do not have. And, as we know, it is one thing to commit all one's strength to a task in which success, if not promised, is nevertheless possible, and another to make the same commitment to a task where not merely the outcome but the very point of the exercise is generally regarded as, at best, doubtful and, very probably, madness. For us, the task of thinking about God—a task that has always been daunting in itself—becomes all the more demanding by virtue of the fact that we do so in a situation where the prevailing assumption is that the task is unachievable in principle because there is no God and that *there is nothing to think about*. Thinking about God, in our time, therefore demands of us the courage to step out into the void, to abandon the

---

[31] E. Lévinas, *Autrement qu'être ou au-delà de l'essence* (Paris: Livre de Poche/Kluwer Academic, 2001), 81. For S. Weil, see S. Weil, *La Pesanteur et la Grâce* (Paris: Plon, 1948), 36 ff. See also J. P. Little, 'Simone Weil's Concept of Decreation', in R. Bell (ed.), *Simone Weil's Philosophy of Culture: Readings Towards a Divine Humanity* (Cambridge: Cambridge University Press, 1993).

certainties, assurances, and assumptions that normally accompany our thinking, and to recognize that since we are seeking to think about what is designated as 'nothing' by the dominant system of knowledge there is nothing in that system itself nor in the social world that it underpins that is not open to question. Such a radical reversal of perspective means that to make God the matter of our thinking would be to illuminate the whole field of thought in a new and unfamiliar light, so that we find ourselves as if journeying in a strange and alien landscape—even in thinking the most ordinary and everyday thoughts. Everything seems different from what we had imagined. There's nothing familiar any more. We have become strangers and pilgrims, awakened in a more immediate and intimate way to the planetary homelessness that belongs to our contemporary intellectual, social, political, and cultural environments. Courage is needed, then, not because we will be laughed at for the quixotic gesture of thinking about something that's not there (though that may also happen), but because thinking about God will bring our whole world into question—and, until the question of God itself is resolved, that question itself must remain open and unresolved. Abandon certainty all who enter here.

This courage is nothing flash or showy, or shouldn't be. Philosophy rightly fears that invocations of courage or resolution may merely be for the sake of cutting short difficult passages of thought. One now reads in embarrassment those passages in *Being and Time* where Heidegger summons his readers to the philosophical courage to take upon themselves the burden of their finitude, mortality, and nothingness and through this act of intellectual heroism to lay the only possible basis for thinking the question of Being. Such rhetoric is too close for comfort to the then contemporary rhetoric of fascist demagoguery, in which the fate of a people, otherwise doomed to annihilation, rested in the 'triumph of the will' of the strong leader—a rhetoric to which, as we know, Heidegger himself succumbed. Something of that same rhetoric lives on in the endless mantra-like intoning (this time against the express thought of Heidegger) of 'overcoming' metaphysics, as if metaphysics or technology were some kind of primordial chaos monster that only the most powerful of thinkers, a Gilgamesh of the intellect, could subdue!

Experiencing the emptiness of such rhetoric, we are warned that talk of courage should not be in the cause of striking heroic existential postures, but rather serve as the sober observation that discouragement will tempt us at every step. How often it will all seem to be—for nothing. Indeed, if there is any truth at all in Heidegger's account of the fusion of the essence of technology with the life of the contemporary university we may guess at the likelihood that anyone who undertakes such thinking in the context of academic life as presently constituted will not find in it a key to career advancement, but rather to sidelining and rejection. Nevertheless the academy remains an important forum in which to attempt thinking about God if we hold to the conviction as to the necessary publicness of theology/thinking about God. How such thinking might establish a creative dialogue with the technological university *within* the technological university itself is a question to which we shall return in greater detail in Chapter 8.

The very nature of what it is we are attempting to think here does, however, contain a check upon the kind of self-regarding heroism of much of the philosophical literature shaped by the death of God and the privileging of human freedom. Take *Being and Time* itself. Heidegger's concern there was to reopen the question of Being, and to do so precisely without reference to God or any transcendent object but basing himself solely upon what is disclosed in the human being's own way of being. It is quite consistent with this self-limitation (which is also perfectly justifiable in its own terms) that Heidegger's argument comes to depend crucially on the realization of particular human possibilities, such as the possibility of courageous resolve. If it is only human being that is in question or only Being viewed from within the perspective of the human, then maybe human heroism will do the job. In attempting to think about God in an age of technology, we have also taken as a starting point what comes to us simply as a human possibility, namely, the possibility of being able to think about God. But—and here the difference from the Heidegger of *Being and Time* is clear—the realization of this possibility, the fulfilment of the intention to think about God, is *in principle* not something that can be brought about solely by our own will or our own courage. More in the spirit of the later Heidegger such thinking is set in motion not by its own courageous resolve, but by being caught up into the current of what constantly withdraws from it and in this way 'calls for thinking'.

It is clear that there is no way in which the free resolve to think about God can 'make' God exist, any more than thinking about Narnia can make Narnia exist. Even if we assert that once certain thoughts have been thought they become as much a part of the data of science as any 'objective' facts—even though they *never had to be thought*—thinking about God cannot of itself make God 'real' other than in terms of the kind of reality that belongs to thought qua thought. Yet the overwhelming consensus of humanity's many traditions of thinking about God is that whatever God is or may be, God cannot be 'merely' a product of human aspirations or intentions. A God who has been reformulated as the *focus imaginarius* of our deepest or highest longings or values lacks precisely that quality that makes God 'God'. Such a God—as Feuerbach already saw—is one step away from unqualified humanism. If this is all God is, then we may well find it more consistent to reconstruct religion as a religion of Being than of divinity, so that Cupitt has been entirely consistent in his move from 'taking leave of God' to the 'religion of Being'.[32] Even though speaking of 'Being' may be to speak of what surpasses any single act of cognition or volition or any combination of such acts and to orientate ourselves towards what is not merely the product of our active subjectivity, we can still conceive of Being as having an already constituted

---

[32] See D. Cupitt, *The Religion of Being* (London: SCM Press, 1998).

internal relation to our human possibilities, no matter how hidden from our limited day-to-day preoccupations this relation may be. 'Being', in other words, is always there to be discovered, if only we know how to look. With God it is otherwise. Indeed, if it is still possible to speak of Being as, in some sense, a fundamental datum belonging to the bedrock givenness of our lives, we have seen that the outcome of the centuries-long leave-taking of God is that God can no longer be a given of our cultural, intellectual, and personal lives. Although we cannot get behind the sheer fact that we *are*, we can very well (and many do) choose not to think about God at all or to think of God as one of those things that don't exist, like Narnia. If, to put it in technical philosophical terms, some kind of ontology (no matter how profoundly revised and reconceived) remains an intellectual possibility, we can by no means presume that such an ontology will contain the key with which to unlock the problem of theology, i.e. how to think about God. On the contrary, the conditions under which Being can be thought may be precisely the opposite of those under which God would have to be thought, if God could be thought at all.

The thought of God does not compel us to think of God as existing or as 'Being'. Nevertheless, there remains a dividing line between the thought of God and the thought of Narnia or any other imaginary world. The realization that Narnia is a fiction does not diminish its enchantment, since the delight of entering a world where the laws of everyday reality no longer hold is intrinsic to the magic of fantasy. In saying that the thought of God is not quite like this we acknowledge that thinking about God arises out of what concerns us in the midst of our worldly dealings with the world. More importantly, however, we are also making the point that even if God is no longer encountered as a 'given' of or within our world, the thought of God is the thought of one who also remains free in relation to the world, so that God can only be thought as one who gives himself, as a gift—or, as religious writers and philosophers have put it: God is freely transcendent, prevenient, 'wholly other', 'He that hath made us and not we ourselves', the one on whom we are 'absolutely dependent', grace, self-revealing, and self-communicating and only to be known or thought of on the basis of that free self-giving, self-revelation, and self-communicating.[33] Unlike Narnia, the thought of God can only with difficulty co-exist with the realization that we ourselves have invented it and that it is only our imagination that keeps it in being. An extreme possibility of Cupittian-style non-realism is, of course, to try to hold on to the thought of God precisely as a human projection of such a self-bestowing, gracious 'Other', as if it were a matter of a certain kind of special logic. Such a possibility is extremely ambiguous, since it could equally well

---

[33] Although I am treating these terms in the present context as different ways of saying essentially the same thing, a theological approach might—legitimately—wish to distinguish between them in various ways and ponder the respective merits of each within a Christian (or other) theological context. Thus Schleiermacherian 'absolute dependence' would be judged by many twentieth century theologians as *not* saying the same as an insistence on God's 'wholly otherness'.

denote a movement of return from non-realism to another kind of thinking about God or, more simply, the last twist of an unhappy consciousness that, for whatever reasons, wants to keep its non-realism within the boundaries of historic Christianity.[34]

Whichever way we turn the matter round, however, it is of constant concern in the attempt to think about God that we think about God in such a way that God is *not* set up in advance so as to be reducible to a self-projection of our own consciousness. What is being attempted here is not some kind of postmodern rewriting of Anselm's ontological argument, since (as I have insisted) the thought of God is not necessarily accompanied by the Being of God (and what that Being would be must, for us, lie very far beyond any possible thought we are as yet in a position to think, it would be a Being that belonged to 'another reality'). On the contrary, the distinction between thinking about God and ontology, a distinction contextualized in our acceptance of the 'truth' of technology, means that the attempt to think about God remains 'critical' in the Kantian sense of containing an intrinsic reflection (or openness to reflection) on its own limits. If willing to be the beings that we are of itself brings into being the Being that is to be thought, the question of God remains a question whose outcome cannot solely depend on our willing. Instead, thinking about God must wait upon its object. It cannot put that object on the rack and force it to disclose its secret, as Bacon said the scientist should do with nature. Still less can it force that object to *be*, if it does not exist of itself. It remains open to its intended, desired 'Other' in the full sense of 'open': receptive to, ready for but not enclosing, not having, and not possessing. Thus does it wait upon God and its courage is the courage of waiting. In the *Upbuilding Discourses* that also modelled a kind of thinking about God (although within the genre of devotional rather than philosophical writing), Kierkegaard put constant emphasis on just this element of patience and, in doing so, exploiting the etymology of the Danish term for patience, *Taal-mod*, a word that contains within itself a doubling of courage and patience, meaning, literally, 'courage to bear'. Not, in this case the courage 'to bear' the weight of a determinate content (as in Nietzsche's talk of the courage needed to 'bear' the thought of eternal recurrence), but the courage to bear the burden of waiting on a God who, though omnipresent in the world is also concealed by it in such a way that He never is and never will be present in it as a visible or knowable object of thought or action. The discouragement that accompanies the venture of thinking about God will be as likely to take the form of sheer tedium and a sense of utter

---

[34] Something like this seems to be the argument of Theo Hobson's provocative study *The Rhetorical Word: Protestant Theology and the Rhetoric of Authority* (Aldershot: Ashgate, 2002), where Hobson argues that the rhetorical self-assertion of Protestantism is somehow enough to dispel the cobwebs of non-realism. The problem is why anyone who did not already want to be persuaded would subject themselves to the authority of such rhetoric.

pointlessness as that of heroically confronting opposition.[35] In such dully courageous waiting we realize and *in freedom* make our own the sublime 'touch' or
'urge' or 'decreation' that occasions our thinking about God.

There has already been occasion to note several times that talk of the 'end' of
metaphysics and therefore of the age of technology should not be taken to mean
that at some point in the near future we are going to pass out of (or be able to
'overcome') the era of technology and move into some other as yet mysterious
division of history. In thinking about God we are not thinking towards some
realizable intra-historical goal. Thinking about God is thinking that must wait
upon its 'object' and, in terms of the historical timescale, it is likely that it will
have to wait a very long time indeed. In fact (perhaps in principle, if Kierkegaard
is right) it will never be able entirely to complete its task, so that the element of
waiting will remain as a permanent feature of its identity. Such patient endurance
of its own state of incompleteness and lack of fulfilment will naturally bring with
it a modesty and a caution regarding its own right to issue pronouncements or to
force its (provisional) conclusions upon others. Perhaps it will even imbue
thinking itself with a propensity for silence, and an avoidance of a kind of
speaking that does not proceed from the truth of what is being thought
about.[36] If it could win one word of truth, that, at least, would be worth a
hundred volumes of print or a thousand websites. But what that word is or could
be, it does not yet know.

Of course, if the rhetoric of will, courage, and heroism tends to induce a
certain overinflation of the intellectual ego, the rhetoric of patience and waiting
also carries risks. Patience, modesty, and a preference for silence can become an
excuse for not speaking when it is time to speak. If courage needs the restraint of
patience, patience too needs the force of courage if it is to be true to itself and to
be able to bear the strain of its long wait. But is this still not a little bit too
'heroic', even if it is heroism in a minor key? Is it not a little too serious?
Masochistic even? Can we not, should we not, be speaking not only of courage
and patience but also of delight? Can we not, should we not, say that the thought
of God, simply as a thought, merely as pure possibility, has the power to lift and
delight the mind? Are we not already brought into the presence of a paradox that
is not only mysterious but also joyously miraculous that we, creatures of the
primeval slime that we are, all too recognizable descendants of mutually devour-

---

[35] Although this points in a very different direction from the rhetoric of *Being and Time*, it is
worth noting the treatment of boredom and of the sheer tedium of existence in time brought to
expression in boredom as a way into fundamental metaphysical thinking in M. Heidegger, *The
Fundamental Concepts of Metaphysics*, tr. W. McNeill and N. Walker (Bloomington: Indiana
University Press, 1995). Heidegger's later thought is, as has often been noted, marked by a retreat
from and even a reversal of the 'heroism' of *Being and Time*, as in his appeal to the Eckhartian
Gelassenheit.

[36] Heidegger sometimes even talks about 'sigetics' (on analogy with 'dogmatics' or 'systematics')
as a science of silence, although he is chary of using it in such a way as to allow that there could be a
science of significant silence!

ing reptiles (Dostoevsky), could think such thoughts! To think that a world that has only too often and only too plainly displayed itself in the guise of a Kingdom of Death, could be blessed with the thought of God!

Even as mere possibility, the thought of God already comes to us as a joy from beyond our actual present possibilities of being. Shall we not then say that whatever else it may involve, thinking about God must from the beginning take shape as gratitude? Heidegger already suggested that all essential thinking is thanking, that simply thinking at all is, at its heart, to take an attitude of grateful wonder towards what comes to us in thought. The question now is, how far does that gratitude reach? Could it reach all the way to thanking in the strongest sense of the term, i.e. thanking some*one*? But thanking whom? We do not yet know God or even if there is a God. We are only just beginning to think about God, and can scarcely say what it would mean to give our thanks to one who is as unknown as God. And if we were at this point to insist that it is God we have to thank for the thought of God, hasn't a long-running debate in which anthropologists, philosophers, and theologians have all had their say brought into prominence the point that this might immediately have the effect of robbing what has been given of its character as gift and turning our gratitude into payment, reducing the joy of pure possibility to exchange and bringing us back to the interlocking systems of economic, social, and technological calculability to which the thought of God was to have offered a decisive counter-movement?

What is the problem here? Is the problem that we do not know God and therefore cannot pretend to thank [Him]?

Let us ponder the question from another angle, and do so in the light of these words from Hölderlin's poem 'Bread and Wine':

> When we bless the meal, whom may I name, and when we
>   Rest from the livelong day, tell me, how should I give thanks?
> Do I name the exalted one then? A god does not love what's unfitting.
>   To grasp him, our joy is almost too small.
> We must often keep silent; holy names fail,
>   Hearts are beating but speech yet holds back?

Hölderlin's hint—and, since these are poetic words we cannot say more for them than that they speak in the language of hints, metaphors, and enigmas—is that it is not our ignorance of God that reduces us to silence when we wish to express gratitude. It is rather the meanness, the poverty, and the torpor of our first stirrings of joy that make us incapable of giving a fitting holy name to the one towards whom our gratitude flows. It is that we have not yet seen into the sheer joy of our own possibilities overflowingly revealed to us in thinking about God. 'Giving thanks' would then itself be the gift of the joy that wants to be able to give thanks and by no means the payment of a debt. For, if we cannot yet say what it is to name God in such thinking, how could the thought of God be a debt that the act of thanking itself might pay in whole or in part? All we can say is that in the astonishment of the possibility of giving thanks is a revelation of who we ourselves are—*even if the possibility itself is never fulfilled or is unfulfillable*. As such it is a gift of a larger vision of our lives, 'one and whole' and hoping for better.[37] Yet even this, as essentially unknown, cannot be the object of a calculable pay-off. It remains: astonishment.

Thinking about God, then, if it is to be true both to the critical principles that require it to register its non-functionality in terms of any available paradigm of thought as well as to the assumption that God, whatever else God may be, is beyond all conceptualization, representation, and is inherently and irreducibly mysterious, resistant to being thought in a singular degree, will therefore live in a constant tension of arousal and non-fulfilment, seeking what can never be found, open to what never appears. Yet, as we have seen and should not forget, this thoughtful condition is founded upon a free decision to realize the possibility that thought itself gives to us of thinking about God. That this possibility comes to us precisely as—*as if*—given may occasion our thinking to lift itself to thankfulness and, in the mystery of gratitude, seek first to name what God can still be for us, the measure of a fullness of life that is both the measure of who we really are and a life we have not yet realized.

---

[37] In thus reflecting on the essential role played by the moment and movement of gratitude it is important to note that this is not annulling what was emphasized in the conclusion of the first chapter: that the cumulative process of modernity's long farewell to God means that God is no longer a 'given' of our world, no longer an immovable element in the universal *consensus gentium*. But to say that the thought of God comes as if it were a gift is by no means to say that it is a 'given'. On the contrary, it is precisely characteristic of what is truly a gift that it comes as something we haven't been able to count on, something that has an element of utter surprise that overwhelms all expectation even when the gift is at one level expected—whereas a 'given' is something we can indeed incorporate without further comment into our toolbag of working assumptions. (Although it might be that if we were really to probe the structure of such 'givens' we would be brought back by another route to see them too as 'gifted' and, therefore, by no means to be taken for granted.) For the debate about 'the gift' in recent philosophy and theology see, e.g. A. D. Schrift (ed.), *The Logic of the Gift: Towards an Ethic of Generosity* (London: Routledge, 1997); J.-L. Marion, *Reduction and Givenness: Investigations of Husserl, Heidegger, and Phenomenology*, tr. T. A. Coulson (Evanston: Northwestern University Press, 1998); and J. D. Caputo and M. J. Scanlon (eds.), *God, the Gift and Postmodernism* (Bloomington: Indiana University Press, 1999). Apart from the key essay by Marcel Mauss (included in Schrift's collection), Heidegger's lecture 'Time and Being' is also crucial. See M. Heidegger, *Identity and Difference*, tr. Joan Stambaugh Dual language edition (New York: Harper and Row, 1969).

5

Putting it into Words

We have been trying to find a foothold to begin thinking about God, yet virtually everything that has been said up until this point could equally well be said of all serious thinking. Doesn't any effort of thought require the free resolve of the thinking mind, patience, and at least an analogue of gratitude? But is this a problem? Surely we might wish to emphasize that thinking about God shares essential traits with any thinking that both takes seriously the need of the present and that also tries to think beyond that need. Isn't it important to be able to say that in freely choosing to think about God we are not contradicting any principle of essential thinking as such? Let us be glad that in venturing with courage into an open space whose silence we must endure with patience we are thinkers amongst thinkers. Even underlining the need for an element of gratitude in thinking that seeks to raise itself to thinking about God need not entirely separate the thinker who thinks about God from thinking scientists or artists whose work has developed in them a habitual sense for what Umberto Eco called 'a structural grace in things'. What has yet really been said that would give direction to thinking about God other than the subjective choice of the thinker to make this the matter of his thought? Even though talk of patiently and gratefully waiting upon God (taken with allusions along the way to Kierkegaard, Lévinas, and Weil) suggests something very different from existentialist self-affirmation, isn't this a matter more of style than substance? Isn't the thought of God as God, God thought in a godly way, still waiting to be thought? But, even if that is so, it doesn't count against what has been said, since this might be seen as what this thought always does, eluding us, or withdrawing from our grasp, as if at the last minute! And if, inspired by Heidegger, we then claim that this is precisely why this thought of all thoughts most calls for thinking, don't we need something more if we are to take seriously the claim that this is thinking about *God*? Mustn't there be more than a sense that something has been withheld or with-*drawn* from our grasp in a kind of divine hide-and-seek? Mustn't there also be a *drawing*, a calling, a prevenient summons in a specific direction, if we are not to be left floundering in some sort of sheer infinity of possibilities of which each is as good as the other? If God is simply the 'wholly other' of thought, then can't God be anything and everything?

Indeed—but let us imagine that we are called to think about God not because God is presented to us as an intriguing and fascinating possibility for thinking we haven't yet managed to get our heads around but because *God calls us* to such thinking. How, in this case, are we to know, to see or to say what it is in this calling (that must necessarily take a concrete form adapted to our capacities) that is truly godly and not reducible to our own projection or invention? How, in other words, could we distinguish a free decision to think about God from a supernatural calling to think about God? And if our free decision to think about God really were to succeed, that is, if we really did find ourselves thinking about God in such a way that our free decision to try thinking about God turned out to be the mode in which God had been calling us all along—how would we come to *know* this? How could it be that we could ever really know that *God as God* was the matter of our thinking?

The point we are considering is illuminated in a curious way by one of theology's most familiar commonplaces: Anselm's argument for God's existence. God, in Anselm's famous definition, is that-than-which-nothing-greater-can-be-thought, and, if we do not follow Anselm in attempting to use this as the starting point for a proof of God's existence, we may still concede that he pinpointed a crucial element in the way in which God has been thought about in the Western tradition. God, as that-than-which-nothing-greater-can-be-thought, is the limit to all thinking and is therefore both what cannot be thought and what serves as the generative ground of all thought—what Tillich, in his reformulation of Anselm's argument, called 'the depth of reason'.[1] It might seem as if the assertion that in thinking about God we cannot obtain assurance that it is God as God, God in God's own way of existing, that we are thinking about implies that that-than-which-nothing-greater-can-be-thought cannot in fact be thought and that this straightforwardly contradicts Anselm's position. But doesn't Anselm's intellectual need to add 'existence' to the concept of God signal the inadequacy of the concept on its own *without the supplement of existence*, so that Anselm's argument itself suggests, indeed, hinges on just this: that the *concept* of that-than-which-nothing-greater-can-be-thought (i.e. the highest possible *thought* of God) will always fall short of the reality of God? The concept of God is and must be a concept that is *not just* a concept: but what does this mean if not that its intended object (God) cannot itself be conceived? In other words, in thinking about God we are always engaged in pursuing what continually withdraws from thought. Which, if we follow Heidegger, is to say that just this is for that very reason what most calls for thinking.

For all the differences between the various arguments for the existence of God, the ontological argument has a formal structure that is reflected in many other such arguments. God has been repeatedly postulated in terms of the hypothetical conclusion of a trajectory of thought that takes its line of orientation from within

[1] See P. Tillich, *Systematic Theology*, (Welwyn, Herts.: Nisbet, 1968), i. 88–90 and 227–31.

the world (whether this is in terms of causality, design, being, value, etc.) but which never finds its terminus within the world. In this way the concept of God is shown to be a concept that in its various forms (whether as First Cause, Cosmic Designer, Supreme Being, He Who Is, etc.) can never fulfil itself within any possible schematization of intra-worldly discourse. The intra-worldly chain cries out for something 'greater'. For those who proposed the arguments, this was precisely what lay at the heart of the 'proof': that only an absolute 'First' could guarantee the meaningfulness of any series of worldly relations and that the fact of such series (i.e. the fact that there is such a thing as causality, design, etc.) demonstrates the need for the existence of the absolute First. However, since Hume drew attention to the shift in logic from assertions relating to particular events or particular constellations of circumstances within the world (to which some level of probability can always be attached in the light of experience) to assertions concerning what is altogether unique, this transition has been rendered highly problematic. Rather than proving God's existence, the singularity and exclusiveness of God as the first or ultimate term of the relevant series bespeaks a resistance to conceptualization that cannot be broken down. In other words, we would not know what it could mean to say that God was the First Cause other than that he was the ultimate term of all possible chains of causality, but since our knowledge cannot operate without some idea of causality being in play we just wouldn't know how to deal intellectually with such an 'ultimate term'. Precisely in singling it out as the 'first cause' we make it unlike all other cause, so that it becomes a mere 'unknown X'.

Such criticisms, however, are not the prerogative of philosophers alone. Even before Aquinas put his 'five ways' of proving the existence of God to paper, Moses Maimonides had warned against taking the catergories of intra-worldly physics and cosmology and applying them to God. Theologians too have sought to match the movement of argument from worldly states of affairs to God or the defence of doctrinal definitions by the counter-movement of negative theology and apophaticism. In this way whatever is said about God must always also be immediately unsaid. God is good, but not in the way we understand goodness. God exists, but in a mode of being different from that of any other existing being. God is transcendent, mystery, wrapped in darkness. God is to be known in unknowing, in divine ignorance, and adored in silence. When it comes to God, language, image, and symbol are twisted out of their normal meaning and normal usage and redeployed in an eminent but incomprehensible manner.

If theologians point to such currents in the theological tradition as evidence that theology too has resources with which to defend itself against the charge that the conceptualized God of classical theism is necessarily an objectified and de-divinized God, philosophers in the line of linguistic philosophy have worried away at what could be a licence for meaninglessness or, from the side of deconstruction, have suspected theology of merely ratcheting up the dialectic of negation and affirmation in the service of an unstated affirmation. Thus, the super-essentiality of God in negative theology is seen simply as a way of talking about the essentiality of God but, as it were, in a louder and more ponderous voice. As if to say 'My God is not only great, He's so much greater than great that you can't even say how great He is!'[2]

From the side of ecclesiastical theology, too, negative theology and the mystical theology associated with it cannot but be suspect, as they seem to imperil certain key affirmations about God that Christian theologians want to insist on: that God is good as a loving Father is good, that God is able to direct history to a good end, that God exists. (Pseudo-)Dionysius, whose *Mystical Theology* provided negative theologians in the Christian tradition with a certificate of legitimacy, is indeed prepared to say that 'It' (NB!) 'does not live nor is it life... It is not sonship or fatherhood and it is nothing known to us or to any other being. It falls neither within the predicate of nonbeing nor of being. Existing beings do not know it as it actually is and it does not know them as they are... There is no speaking of it, nor name nor knowledge of it.'[3] Such negations, however, even if they are intended as a form of praise, as a way of giving maximum honour to God, could well be read as striking at the very heart of the Church's own claim to speak meaningfully and salvifically of God. If, for example, we take as the criterion of theological correctness Luther's stipulation that God is to be known and believed in as He shows Himself in the Christian experience of the forgiveness of sins, i.e. as sheer grace and love, then to say that there is a deep unknowableness in God would seem to introduce a doubt as to whether the grace and love experienced in forgiveness *really* express the real heart of God. If we don't really *know* who God is in the ultimate depths of His being, how can we be sure that His will concerning human beings is in the final accounting benevolent? Perhaps like the smile of a Stalin, God's show of benevolence may be a mask concealing some terrible malice? Are there not real, urgent and evangelical reasons for Christian theology to set certain limits to negative theology? Surely there are some things that must be said of God and others that must be denied?

The difficult implications of negative theology for religious belief are illustrated from another side in Hume's *Dialogues on Natural Religion,* where Hume uses the figure of Demea, the dogmatist who insists on the transcendence and unknowability of God, to undermine the theistic arguments of Cleanthes, who has sought to give God a human face and a human meaning. Demea's move, however, plays precisely into the hands of the sceptical Philo. From a certain angle of vision radical apophaticism and atheism seem scarcely distinguishable. In this connection, it is not surprising that amongst those attracted to secular and death of God theologies in the 1950s and 1960s were many influenced by the thorough-going emphasis on God's transcendence in the theology of Karl Barth.

---

[2] This is a criticism especially associated with J. Derrida. See J. Derrida, *In the Margins of Philosophy,* tr. A. Bass (Chicago: University of Chicago Press, 1982), 6.

[3] Pseudo-Dionysius, *The Complete Works,* tr. C. Luibheid (New York: Paulist Press), 1987, 141.

Even if Barth himself disowned these, his own insistence on the utter otherness of God seemed, logically, to demand the readiness to abandon even theology itself. After all that Barth had said against the 'merely human' nature of religion in his commentary on Paul's *Letter to the Romans,* and his acceptance that dogmatics itself could not be regarded as a science in anything like the same sense in which other sciences were scientific (since that would be to limit the sovereign freedom of the ultimate 'object' of dogmatics, God in His self-revelation),[4] it seems strangely inconsistent (not to say *parti pris*) to continue to give a unique privilege to Scripture, to the historical events of the life of Jesus Christ or to the doctrine of the Church. Once the claims of transcendence are raised to such heights, isn't everything that can be said equally valid and equally worthless? Might we not just as well speak of God by speaking about something else altogether?

Yet, unsettling as the extreme emphasis on God's transcendence and unnameability may be for the Church's conventional beliefs about God (whether the emphasis is more on the religious need to find assurance that God really *is* love or to defend particular concepts or sources of faith), it would appear impossible to exclude the moment of infinite otherness from constituting a *sine qua non* of God being God and not merely the projection of some human fancy, 'man writ large'. In dealing with God we are in principle dealing with what cannot be conceptualized, what cannot be thought through, what cannot be placed in the service of any project of intellectual or social construction, what cannot be managed. And yet, to repeat, this need not mean that God is simply consigned to the category of 'the unthinkable' but can rather be taken as underlining the urgency of the call for thinking that lies in the question of God—not as doctrine, fact, or concept but precisely as question, possibility, and lure. What, in resisting being thought, calls for thinking.

All of this is a standing challenge to theological or philosophical attempts to articulate a concept of God. But I do not presume that we have yet got as far as actually forming any thinkable concept of God. We are still only thinking *about* thinking about God, about what it would take to think of God, if God could be thought. And it is the very inconceivability, the very resistance of God to being thought that keeps such thinking about God gripped by its essential concern. This alone is suited to arouse what Kierkegaard called the highest passion of thought.

But if we have once removed the discipline laid upon thought to inquire about what *is* and to frame its concepts in the light of their relation to the way in which the object of thought shows itself in existence, does it have any resource other than to follow the way of negation with the utmost rigour, in the manner recommended by Dionysius? Isn't any attempt to construct a positive view of God disqualified from the outset, since even the weakest form of analogy must

---

[4] See K. Barth, *Church Dogmatics*, 1.1, tr. G. W. Bromiley (Edinburgh: T.& T. Clark, 1975), 3–11, also 275–87. We shall return to some of the issues connected with this in Chapter 8 below.

make some claim as to the fittingness of the analogy to its object and therefore assert that we do have some sort of 'knowledge' of the object, something definite to think about?

Should we then choose simply to remain silent, gratefully, mystically, silent? Let us not belittle silence. What conversation was ever without its moments of silence, and do these not also play a role in the processes of communication and understanding? Is it merely an idle figure of speech that we say of those moments when a roomful of people fall silent that the angels—the bearers of messages—have passed overhead? Is there not a wonder in such shared moments of silence that makes for a sudden intimacy that speech so often hinders? Doesn't silence correspond supremely to the sense of grace, and the impossibility of economic calculation in thinking about God? We have no need to deny that thinking about God may have need for its own internal 'sigetics', but if silence itself is once understood as a form of communication, a giving of grace from one to the other, then is it not already close to becoming a kind of speech, something for which we must, in speech, be responsible, for which we must answer, and of which we must give an account?

Language has, of course, been one of the most prominent commonplaces of twentieth-century theology. Much of the debate about religious language that has flowed through such various channels as linguistic philosophy, Thomism, and deconstruction has focused on the relationship between linguistic representation and what, it is claimed, is meant to be 'represented' in language (the thing signified). At this point in the argument we are by no means ready to take up a position concerning whether this or that version of God-talk was justifiable. We do not yet know what it would be to think about God, let alone 'speak' about God. Yet if we are not to be forced into either affirmation or denial, then we must have some way of speaking, some kind of language to think in, that does not commit us to either affirmation or denial, that maintains a reserve concerning the possibility of speaking even in the act of speech itself.

II

In turning to the question of language at this point, it should be emphasized that I am not concerned to find a way of understanding language that would justify a particular doctrine of assertion concerning God. My aim is different from that of the protagonists in the so-called 'University Debate' that so largely moulded the discussion of religious language in British philosophy of religion from the 1950s through to the 1980s. There (from the believers' side, at least) the issue was more a matter of finding a way of understanding language that could help justify the claim that propositions concerning God (i.e. that 'God is a loving father to his children') 'made sense' according to one or other paradigm of making sense. In contrast to this my concern is rather to try to identify purely formal characteristics of language that would make it possible for us to conceive of a thinking-about-God-in-words (assuming that thinking must, sooner or later, enter into words) that would not be assimilable to the kind of 'enframing' of thinking that Heidegger sees as the defining trait of technological thinking or thinking that technology can come to employ as resource.

Language is a central theme of Heidegger's own thought, and we have noted how he sought to think his way through and beyond the wasteland of metaphysics/technology by meditating on the basic words of poets and Presocratic philosophers. Analogously we might presume that Christian theology's attempt to think about God might find matter for its thinking in the basic texts of scripture and tradition. Certainly, our own thinking will inevitably be formed by the way in which we find ourselves within and relate ourselves to a concrete tradition of thinking about God. Yet, as I argued in Chapter 2 with regard to the limitations of the narrativist position, no tradition is hermetically sealed and no tradition can give guarantees as to its own trustworthiness. Least of all can this be the case with any religious tradition whose basic terms, not least the very idea of God itself, have become so exposed to the crossfire of multiple criticisms. Even within the tradition's own terms, however, we face a problem that would seem to be more intractable than anything confronted by Heidegger in his attempt to think the truth of Being. For, as was noted with regard to the question of courage, there is a sense in which Heidegger is justified in presuming that, in some sense, 'Being' is a possibility to which we have access from within our own range of existential possibilities (if, that is, one assumes that, in one way or another, we 'are'). If only we dare do it, if only we are clear-sighted enough, why should we not face up to the meaning of our own Being? But things would seem to be rather different in the case of God. Especially if we orientate ourselves from within the biblical tradition, it would seem to belong to the Godness of God that God is free to evade the clutches of those who seek Him and to conceal Himself within clouds and darkness. The thought of God is a thought that the heart of man has not conceived. Even if we then add that the biblical God is nevertheless a God who has also pledged Himself to us as both Creator and Redeemer, as a God who can therefore be trusted, and whose Word is faithful and sure, we cannot put aside the arguments of the negative theologians, arguments that suggest that there is no direct or unproblematic transition from the language we use of God, or the human language that God is reported as having used, to the truth of God's way of being there for us. It belongs to the idea of God to transcend all human capacities in a way that Being never does. This makes any method of reflection on 'basic words' or whatever else we may find 'within' language deeply questionable as a method for coming to think about God. But, as I have argued, being the language-using beings that we are, we must have some way of speaking, some kind of language to think in, even when thinking about the God whose relation to all our languages is so ambiguous.

Following Wittgenstein there has been a lot of talk about the 'grammar' of religious language in British philosophy of religion, but it was not often entirely clear what this meant, and often the point seemed not particularly grammatical, e.g. that the grammar of talking about the love of God required the talker to be actively engaged in trying to emulate that love. Let me therefore try a rather different 'grammatical' turn, and let us think for a moment about the grammatical *mood* in which we talk about God. In terms of the point at which we have now arrived, can we at least say that if, in setting out on its long and difficult path, thinking about God dare not venture so far as to affirm or to deny or to issue commands to other thinkers, it may nevertheless still say what *may* or what *might be* thought about God? In thus thinking of God *subjunctively* we think of a possibility of which we cannot say that it is or is not, that it must or must not be, but only that it *may* be. This '*may*'-ness reflects the situation that being able to think about God is neither forced upon us ('*Muss es ein? Es muss sein!*') nor refused us and that therefore does not derive from any actual configuration of our own reality. It is a *perhaps* in the deepest and strongest sense of the word: what doesn't *have to* be, but what *may be*. To acknowledge the hypothetical quality of 'perhaps-ness' or 'maybe-ness' with which the subjunctive invests what is said does not mean that we are musing without direction. On the contrary, we are committing ourselves to an extremely demanding discipline of reserve towards, on the one hand, a too easy readiness to make indicative assertions and, on the other, an over-exaggerated cult of negation. But if we consistently hold to understanding our God-talk as purely subjunctive, we are also sparing ourselves the distraction of incessantly 'unsaying' and revoking every assertion, the constant repetition of 'as it were' or 'so to speak' (Plotinus) or other 'apophatic markers', since the indeterminacy of mood of the discourse as a whole already implies a distance from straightforward indicative assertions.[5] To negate what has not actually been asserted is already to slip a gear. What is on the go in such a subjunctive discourse is not what is said or denied but how it is said or denied.

It is interesting in this connection that several modern languages appear not to have a separate form for the subjunctive. In other words, a statement made in the subjunctive mood may well have the form of a simple assertion. Yet it is understood as subjunctive. That it is thus understood, however, is dependent not merely on finding the right linguistic expression but on a thinking act of interpretation. The subjunctivity of the discourse calls for and demands the singular subjective commitment of the thinker (speaker, listener, writer, or

---

[5] For a discussion of 'unsaying' and 'apophatic markers' see M. A. Sells, *Mystical Languages of Unsaying*, (Chicago: University of Chicago Press, 1994). Amongst other texts dealing with questions of apophatic and negative theology in recent philosophy of religion, see (from a very large literature): Kevin Hart, *The Trespass of the Sign: Deconstuction, Theology and Philosophy* (Cambridge: Cambridge University Press, 1989); Harold Coward and Toby Foshay (eds.), *Derrida and Negative Theology*, (Albany: State University of New York Press, 1992); D. Turner, *The Darkness of God. Negativity in Christian Mysticism* (Cambridge: Cambridge University Press, 1995); Orrin F. Summerell (ed.), *The Otherness of God* (Charlottesville: University Press of Virginia, 1998); John D. Caputo, *The Prayers and Tears of Jacques Derrida: Religion without Religion* (Bloomington: Indiana University Press, 1997).

reader) who is attempting to think about what is being said. Thinking about God in this way can only be thought if *I,* whoever *I* may be, courageously stake my own thought on it. It is not a thought that lies ready to hand on the plane of formal statements. Mood cannot be commanded. It is, to echo Lévinas (and also Kierkegaard and Heidegger), a matter of *le Dire,* the manner of a saying, and not of *le Dit,* of what is said.[6] It is a question of interpreting the movement of the breath—*Geist, ånd,* spirit—that is the all-pervasive atmosphere of language though not itself a part of speech. This breath is the movement in which I am present as an actual, living being in what I am saying, what I am hearing, and what I am thinking. In these terms, even my relation to a written text is also a *breathing* relation.

To speak in the mood of subjunctivity is to speak of what *may be,* and therefore to speak of possibility. If, in the beginning, we cannot claim an experience or a revelation as the foundation for what we are setting out to think (i.e. we cannot claim, right out, that we *can* think about God), the mere possibility of such thinking (and if we have established nothing else, *the possibility* of thinking about God has accompanied every step of the enquiry thus far) allows for the idea of God—*as possibility* (I say no more than that). If, then, we stay with this possibility for a while, if we give it time to disclose its many facets to us, what might we find ourselves thinking of?

But wait—isn't this all a little too dreamy? Can thinking about God as pure possibility ever do justice to what religious believers (for example) might want to say about God? Even in terms of the limited characteristics of thinking about God we have thus far identified, one might ask how it would be possible to give thanks or show gratitude to a merely possible God? Isn't it a basic feature of religious language that, as Kierkegaard put it, it is concerned with *actuality*? And isn't 'possibility' by definition always at one remove from reality? Doesn't the subjunctive need to be fulfilled in indicatives or imperatives, such that what might be the case is decided by reference to what is or what should be the case? Is there not a danger that we are talking up the motif of the subjunctive a little too glibly and using it to slip past the difficult questions? As if we could simply repeat everything that historic Christianity has taught, without qualification or correction—only to add, 'But, remember: it's all to be taken in the subjunctive, as pure possibility, a simple thought experiment. Understand it as you will.' When we speak—even when we speak in the subjunctive mood—don't we take on a kind of responsibility (towards ourselves, towards those to whom we speak and towards that about which we speak) for which the free-floating milieu of possibility is too thin, too insubstantial, too dispassionate? We shall return to this question at the end of the next chapter. First, however, I should like to deepen the model of religious language that I am seeking to develop.

[6] Lévinas, *Autrement qu'être,* ch. 2, sections 3 and 4 ('Temps et discours' and 'Le Dire et la subjectivité').

Once more, *The Cloud of Unknowing* offers a preliminary orientation. It is striking that even a 'mystical' text such as *The Cloud* (which, being mystical, might be presumed to have a penchant for silence) does not abandon the realm of language, although it invites us to adopt a very different relation to language from that to which we are accustomed. Rather than setting us to spinning and unravelling a complex net of definitions and negations, the author recommends whittling the language in which we think our way towards God down to a single word—an early example of thinking with a hammer, maybe! Just two words, he suggests, 'sin' and 'God' are enough to do all the work that we have need for in prayer.[7] Such a strategy may seem to reflect the motivation behind negative theology, but it is not in itself negative. Nor, I suggest, is it simply to be read as the reduction of the word to a mere expression of emotion, a kind of voiced sigh. Despite the analogy drawn by the author with a person caught in a fire simply crying 'Help!' he makes clear that in using the words we use in prayer we must *understand* what we mean by them. But in deliberately separating the word/ thought from its/their familiar syntactic context possibilities are opened up that that context itself normally conceals from view. The one who thinks about God will, in other words, be ready to sacrifice syntax itself for the sake of holding to the true thought of God.

At a decisive moment in the argument of *What is Called Thinking?* Heidegger moves to meditate on a fragmentary 'word' or saying of the early Greek thinker Parmenides. The specific content of the word is not immediately relevant to our reflections here, but what is important is that Heidegger lays special emphasis on the paratactic form of the saying. In other words this is not a sentence held together by the synthesizing function of syntax but a sequence of words set out alongside each other. He explicitly rejects the charge that this reflects the fact that Parmenides was a 'primitive' thinker who hadn't yet learned how to think in such a way that subject and object are synthesized in a determinate judgement by the copula. Rather, Heidegger suggests, it means that we, as readers of the saying, must look to the spaces between the words in order not merely to find but to enact *the thinking that makes the saying meaningful*. In other words, Parmenides' saying is or becomes meaningful by virtue of the thinking that thinks its component words in an original way.[8]

I suggest that if we read *The Cloud* not as a guide to having mystical experiences but as an invitation to a certain kind of thinking, then it points in a similar direction. It does not ask us to abandon our capacity for thought, nor simply to negate the linguistic structuring of thought with which we think day after day, but to think otherwise and to use our language otherwise than we are accustomed to. Seeing the sometimes weird perturbations of language within religion in the light of Heidegger's comments about parataxis may help us to

---

[7] See *The Cloud of Unknowing*, ch. 37–40.
[8] M. Heidegger, *Was Heisst Denken?* (Tübingen: Niemeyer, 1997), 111 ff.

understand them in a new light. Importantly, they continue to keep open an alternative to the simple confrontation between 'positive' and 'negative' formulations.

Let us take another example: the document known as Pascal's *Memorial,* generally regarded as the record of a dramatic conversion experience. Here is an extract from it.

> From about half-past ten in the evening till about half-past twelve,
> FIRE.
> God of Abraham, God of Isaac, God of Jacob,
> not of the philosophers and scientists.
> Certainty, certainty. Feeling. Joy. Peace.
> God of Jesus Christ.
> Deum meum et Deum vestrum.
> Thy God shall be my God.
> Forgetfulness of the world and of all, except God.
> He is to be found only by the ways taught in the Gospel.
> Greatness of the human soul.
> O righteous Father, the world hath not known Thee, but I have
> Known Thee.
> Joy, joy, joy, tears of joy.
> I separated myself from Him.
> *Dereliquerunt me fontem aquæ vivæ.*
> My God, wilt Thou forsake me?
> May I never be separated from Him eternally.
> 'This is life eternal, that they might know Thee the only true God, and Jesus
> Christ, whom Thou has sent.'
> Jesus Christ
> Jesus Christ
> I separated myself from Him; I fled Him, renounced Him,
> Crucified Him.
> May I never be separated from Him!
> He is to be kept only by the ways taught in the Gospel:
> Renunciation, entire and sweet.[9]

Whatever is thought of Pascal's contribution to the philosophy of religion in texts like the *Pensées,* the *Memorial* might be dismissed as 'merely' the doomed attempt to express a kind of emotional intensity that resists transcription into language. As such it is to be dealt with in the biographical introduction to Pascal's thought rather than as a part of the thought itself—except, of course, for the repudiation of the God of the philosophers in favour of the 'God of Abraham, God of Isaac, God of Jacob' that is referred to in every textbook on the philosophy of religion. But if we abstract from whatever we imagine Pascal's

---

[9] Quoted in the translation given in D. G. M. Patrick, *Pascal and Kierkegaard: A Study in the Strategy of Evangelism* (London: Lutterworth Press, 1947), 76–7.

emotional turmoil during these two hours of spiritual ecstasy to have been, we are in fact presented with an extraordinarily complex text. That it is not simply an explosion or a sigh from the depths is already indicated by the way in which a sequence of texts from very different parts of the Bible are woven into it, either as direct quotations or as reappropriations by the writer in his own person of biblical words, including words of Christ himself ('O righteous Father, the world hath not known Thee, but I have known Thee.'). We note that there are also shifts between French and Latin, and shifts of person and address: is 'God of Abraham, etc.' addressed to God, or is it a third-person comment on the kind of God the writer wants us to be thinking about? And who is addressed in 'Thy God shall be my God'? In the Bible these are the words of Ruth the Moabitess addressed to her Israelite mother-in-law Naomi. Here they are given added emphasis by being written in both Latin and French (the only such doubling in the text), but to whom are they spoken and what is their import? The grammar of the text is too under-determined for us to say, but perhaps the ambiguity is itself important. There are what look like dogmatic assertions ('He is to be found only by the ways taught in the Gospel') and personal professions ('I separated myself from Him'). The text opens with a date and a time, but it speaks of eternity. And how, in any case, is our relation to it changed by the fact that we read it now in translation?

We do not need to deny the emotional reality of the experience out of which the text was produced to say that over and above that reality it is also a text that calls for and provokes thinking of the most demanding kind about what exactly such hours of religious ecstasy mean. Is religious truth a kind of truth that can only be spoken in the mode of address, as the 'Thou' of our being, as Buber might have put it? At some points in the *Memorial* Pascal seems to speak to God as to a 'Thou' and yet these words of address are themselves citations. So in what way does the certainty, feeling, joy, and peace of the individual depend on the biblical revelation and to what extent does it depend on a unique and experiential 'FIRE'? What is 'the greatness of the human soul'? What is it to be separated from God or from Jesus Christ—is it what 'I' do, or may it be that it is God who forsakes us, as seems at one point to be hinted at? Surely the very power of this testimony is to do with the fact that it does not set out the answers to these or to the other questions it raises in a systematic way but, in its very unfinishedness (even, we could say, brokenness), calls us into the circle of question and reply, of text and experience in which it itself moves.

It is, I have hinted, not enough to categorize the *Memorial* as a kind of amputated chunk of raw experience whose meaning can only be discovered by virtue of a disciplined comparative process of contextualizing it in terms of Pascal's knowledge of the Bible, his relation to the Church, his theological assumptions, his psychological condition, his historical situation, etc. That is certainly the kind of process that anyone engaged in the philosophical interpretation of a historical text needs to do. The problem is that it would be precisely the 'correctness' of such a procedure that would most imperil the provocation of the text in the direction of thinking. If the teaching of the *Memorial* could be translated into a grammatically correct form, if the critical process was a scientific method for supplying the missing syntax, we would scarcely need to *think* about what was going on in the text any more. We would need only to reproduce in our minds a meaning that was already 'there'. The disequilibrium of the text would be absorbed into the stabilizing field of an interpretative method. Even if (as is actually the case) we imagine the interpretative process more in terms of an open-ended and multifaceted debate (rather than as the simple application of an undisputed method), the whole process of the debate would be determined at every point by the possibility of a conclusion, the 'hope' of a correct reading that would tell us what Pascal 'really' meant. If, however, we take seriously the syntactical inadequacy of the text, and if we are not prepared simply to discard it as meaningless, then we are led to recognize the depth of our own responsibility in, so to speak, supplying the missing grammar that makes sense of it. This can, of course, serve as an excuse for a kind of lazy subjectivism, making the text mean whatever we want it to mean. But precisely because we ourselves as readers are thus engaged in constructing the text we cannot take a step towards it without also questioning the impulse that guides our preference to this option rather than to the other. The interpretation of the text becomes self-interrogation, driving us to reflect on what we ourselves really think it would be to experience 'FIRE', if 'experience' is indeed the matter of the *Memorial*. And how would our under-standing at this point be affected if we had not had anything we might think of as remotely analogous to Pascal's experience? How far can the text, simply as text, open up to us a sense of what such an experience might mean? Or do we, perhaps, already have a premonition of what such experiential 'fire' might be in the joy that each of us has access to in the simple possibility of thinking about God?

That this is not just a matter of some romanticizing preference for the immediate and the subjective can be seen if we look at another, very different text, George Herbert's poem 'Prayer': a highly reflective, highly structured literary work but one that also bears testimony to the pressure of its religious content on the syntactical structures of language.

> PRAYER, the Churches banquet, Angels age,
>   Gods breath in man returning to his birth,
>   The soul in paraphrase, heart in pilgrimage,
> The Christian plummet sounding heav'n and earth;
>
> Engine against th'Almightie, sinner's towre,
>   Reversed thunder, Christ-side-piercing-spear,
>   The six daies world-transposing in an houre,
> A kind of tune, which all things heare and fear;
>
> Softnesse and peace, and joy, and love, and blisse,
>   Exalted Manna, gladnesse of the best,

> Heaven in ordinarie, man well drest,
> The milkie way, the bird of Paradise,
>
> Church-bels beyond the stars heard, the souls bloud,
> The land of spices, something understood.[10]

There is no question here of saying that what is said in the poem is not also 'thought', not 'something understood', even though the poem's thought dismantles the expected synthesis of conventional discourse. Although Herbert's poetic *œuvre* is permeated by a sense of experiential religious anguish no less intense than Pascal's, this is a pondered and crafted text that can scarcely be regarded as the instantaneous record of a sudden rapture. It could, of course, be pointed out that although the juxtaposition of images is indeed startling and even self-contradictory (as when the 'Engine', i.e. the siege-engine 'against th'Almightie', is set in apposition to the 'sinner's towre'), the grammatical disruption is, strictly speaking, minimal. Isn't it obvious that in accordance with a not uncommon poetic convention Herbert simply omits 'is' from the first line and that the poem is consequently a simple (if elegantly balanced) list of the various things that prayer 'is'? But is it obvious? *Is* prayer all these things? Or is it simply 'like' them? Are we in the realm of *definition* or *similitude*? And, if the latter, are the likenesses in question necessarily of the same kind? To think of prayer as a siege-engine 'against th'Almightie' or as a tower of refuge for the anxious soul of the sinner would be to think of it in ways that are in clear accord with popular Reformation piety where the religious scenario is that of the guilty soul, condemned by the strict requirement of the Law, seeking the favour of a justly angered God: but how does that relate to a theology that can see prayer in a more unitive, mystical mode as 'Gods breath in man returning to his birth'? And is the tough theological rigour of the 'heart in pilgrimage' an analogy of the same order as the sensuousness of 'The milkie way, the bird of Paradise . . . The land of spices'? And how do these voluptuous images relate to the insistence that what is being spoken of is 'The Christian plummet sounding heav'n and earth', i.e. a process of deliberate and careful weighing and checking, a concern for 'something' that must be 'understood'? Doesn't analogy itself become imperilled in this vertiginous succession of images, since it would seem that a different kind of relation between the image and its subject-matter is in play in each separate case?

In her study *Equivocal Predication*, Heather Asals has argued that what we see in Herbert is the working out of Anglicanism's early acceptance of equivocation as an ineluctable characteristic of human speech about God. She cites Bishop Ussher as explicitly refusing the Thomist recourse to analogy: 'Of the first cause there can be no causes, therefore no words to express them . . . for these over-arching terms of thing, beeing [sic], somewhat, nature, & c. which seem to contain the Word of God as well as all other things created by him, doe not

---

[10] Quoted from *George Herbert's Works in Prose and Verse* (London: William Pickering, 1848), ii. 48.

expresse any materiall cause of God, neither do they contain these words God and creature, as the generall doth his specials or kinds but are spoken of them equivocally, so that the tearm onely, and not the definition of the tearm, doth agree to them.'[11] This is, of course, precisely to accept the state of affairs from which the Thomist doctrine of analogy was trying to escape. This acceptance, Asals claims, not only marked the English Church's repudiation of Catholic scholasticism and the Catholic attempt to exorcise the spectre of equivocation by means of the doctrine of analogy, it also called for a very particular mode of ontological thinking in which the 'being' of God and the reality of God's saving dealings with human beings are never separated from the concrete process of appropriation in repentance and sanctification. Thus, the reader's task in reading 'Prayer' as a religiously thoughtful text is to ponder the nature of the copula connecting the apparent subject with the apparent predicate(s). Where the syntactically finished sentence pre-empts the synthesis that thought must think through, we are here left to wrestle with the question as to what kind of synthesis is being sought. Is it the 'being' of prayer, the kind of thing that prayer *is* or *is like* and thus an act of predicative judgement? Or is it perhaps an invitation to the reader to pray and, in praying, to enter the relationship of which the poem is a sign? Where analogy implies that the primary meaning of the term is already in some sense 'there' and only waiting to be discovered, what Herbert's quiet diction both conceals (by not stating) and brings to the fore (by making us think about it) is the endlessly thought-provoking interdependence of being and interpretation focused by Wittgenstein in the phrase '*seeing-as*'.[12] What is it to see prayer 'as' 'God's breath in man'? Is it to sketch a likeness? Or is it to name the manner of God's presence to us and in us? What did it mean for Herbert to write it? And for me to read it? And what is implied—or given in experience—by the breathing that is a necessary condition of the poem's being read at all? Could this be the point at which God's breath, God's spirit, is closest to us, so close indeed that it is 'in' us, in our own breathing? By leaving open the question as to the meaning of the 'being', the copula, on which the poem turns, Herbert points us once more to the permissiveness of the subjunctive, focused and brought to a point of interrogation and—*it may be*—existential urgency.

It would certainly not be implausible to read a text such as 'Prayer' as exemplifying the figure of pleonasm, a figure of speech that has recently been

---

[11] H. Asals, *Equivocal Predication: George Herbert's Way to God* (Toronto: University of Toronto Press, 1981), 12. Asals also cites Richard Baxter in similar mood: 'I pray you distinguish between Jesuitical dissembling Equivocation, and the laudable yea necessary use of Equivocal words, when either the transcendencies of the matter, the incapacity of men, the paucity of terms, the custom of speech, & c. hath made them *fit or* needful' (ibid.). This acceptance of equivocation complements the emphasis on 'circumstance' in Anglican theology of Herbert's time. See R. Barbour, *Literature and Religious Culture in Seventeenth-Century England* (Cambridge: Cambridge University Press, 2002).

[12] But which was already central to the conception of truth that lay at the heart of Heidegger's early phenomenological work.

singled out as peculiarly characteristic of religious discourse by John Milbank. Milbank points to the sheer self-exceeding fecundity of primary religious language, as in the psalter's endless multiplication of epithets for God, a multiplication sustained by the familiar parallelism of Hebrew poetry. This parallelism enacts a process of poetic representation that gives voice to the desire always to say 'more' about God by repetition (just as Anselm seeks always to think more about God than thought has hitherto thought) or, as Milbank puts it 'to say the same thing in complicatory fashion'.[13] However, despite what is intriguing and illuminating in this suggestion, it would seem that a strategy of pleonasm would be ill-suited to serve as the *primary* medium of a rigorous attempt to think about God, since the more immediate rhetorical effect of pleonastic excess is to disorientate and to confuse thought, to make it harder not easier to think what we are thinking about, and to make it easier not harder for mere verbosity to supplant the quieter discipline of genuine thoughtfulness.

As far as Herbert is concerned, it cannot be denied that he knew how to make use of such a rhetoric of excess, but this cannot be separated from an equal and opposite current in his poetry whereby the inflationary and complicatory cycle is suddenly deflated—as by the final, downbeat 'something understood' that cuts off a sequence of singularly exotic images and, therewith, concludes the poem. Often, such a change of tack is accomplished in a single word in a manner that the author of *The Cloud* would surely have approved. A good example is the poem 'A True Hymn', in which the poet's desire to articulate his love for God is built up in a steady crescendo that is resolved and deflated by God's single, answering word: *Loved*, as if God were saying, 'You do not need to be concerned with how best to express your love of me, just accept that I love you' (only this paraphrase is, of course, not itself what either Herbert or Herbert's God actually *says*: they stay with the one word: *Loved*).

> My joy, my life, my crown!
> My heart was meaning all the day,
>   Somewhat it fain would say:
> And still it runneth muttering up and down
> With only this, *My joy, my life, my crown!*
>   Yet slight not these few words;
> If truly said, they may take part
>   Among the best in art.
> The fineness which a Hymn or Psalm affords,
> Is, when the soul unto the lines accords.
>   He who craves all the mind,
> And all the soul, and strength, and time,

---

[13] J. Milbank, *The Word Made Strange: Theology, Language, Culture* (Oxford: Blackwell, 1997), 71.

> If the words only rhyme,
> Justly complains, that somewhat is behind
> To make his Verse, or write a Hymn in kind.
> Whereas if the heart be moved,
> Although the verse be somewhat scant,
> God doth supply all the want.
> As when the heart says (sighing to be approved)
> *O, could I love!* And stops; God writeth, *Loved.*[14]

If the poem as a whole can be read as a defence of simple, 'heart-felt' religious devotion against poetic excess, the final couplet would seem to focus the counterpoint between these two modes of thinking about God in a dramatically condensed way. We do not have to assume that the poet is insincere: his heart, we may guess, is genuine in its sighing after God and its desire to give expression to this sigh in the beauty of verse: yet it is, after all, perhaps a little too self-regarding, a little too desirous of an elegant phrase in which to give voice to its feeling. It wants, as Herbert says, 'approval'. But it cannot say of itself that it is 'approved'. The most it can say is, 'O, could I love', exhausting itself in the unfulfilled and unfulfillable possibility of its desire. But then, in a sudden dehiscence of this inflated rhetorical passion, God *writes* the whole meaning of the poem and of the poet's religious crisis into one word: *Loved.*

Milbank speaks of pleonasm as marking a break within the continuum of speech, a breathed pause, that fades away, 'not' 'to the benefit of a spiritual, solipsistic, intentional presence' but to make room 'for the arrival *both* of a new sign [i.e.word] and a new speaker, or new speaking-event'.[15] Herbert's line might seem almost to offer a perfect illustration of this, except that the final, written word is not so much a supplement or expansion of the foregoing but rather a correction or reduction. This functions both in terms of theological conception and of poetic execution. As both the religious and the poetic longing find themselves exhausted in the cry 'O, could I love!', they seem to run out of breath, and to find themselves in a kind of vacuum, brought to a 'stop' in which there is nothing left with which to take the matter further. At just this point, however, the advent of a new word ('God writeth, *Loved*'), which could be a quotation from Scripture (John 3: 16), both gives a theological correction of what has gone before (pointing out that the important thing is not that we love God but that God loves us) and effects a sharp reversal of the poetic dynamics. Where the crescendo that culminates in the sigh 'O, could I love' is thus an expression both of the force of the poet's desire and of the exhaustion of his spirit/breath (such that he has nothing more to say and no breath to say it with), the answering, monosyllabically deflationary word: *Loved, written* by another, leaves us with an unvoiced surplus of breath, a space for us to breathe in and, in that breathing, experience 'Gods breath in man returning to his birth' (as it was put in 'Prayer'). The

---

[14] *George Herbert's Works*, 192–3   [15] Milbank, *The Word Made Strange*, 70.

divinely written word is at one and the same time a downbeat counter to the hyperactivity of the poetic word and the opening of a space of free self-transcendence that lets us feel the love that the poet merely declaims. This effect is achieved precisely by a gesture of reduction and not by the accumulation or of restatement in a 'complicatory fashion'. Herbert the ex-Orator knew well enough that human beings have no difficulty in complicating things, not least their relation to God. What they need is not further complication but liberation into the simplicity of what God's love wills for them. Such double movements of excess and deflation (in which, however, 'deflation' is itself the paradoxical consummation of what has been devoutly wished) are amongst the most characteristic technical and intellectual means that give Herbert's poetry its distinctive content, rigour, and force. Everything, it could be said, depends on context and usage, and it is not necessary to condemn all pleonastic excess as merely a kind of baroque encrustation that needs to be stripped away. What matters is whether in each particular case thought is being stirred and sustained or merely being buried in a fog of words.[16]

III

With characteristic hostility, T. W. Adorno saw Heidegger's appeal to parataxis as a typical manifestation of 'the thinker's' mystifying archaism.[17] Adorno offered a very different justification of Hölderlin's paratactic formulations in terms of a historically specific refusal of a premature closure of dialectical movement, holding open the demand for an actual and not merely a theoretical or mental synthesis. According to Adorno, Hölderlin's parataxis has a determinate philosophical value in countering Hegel's endorsement of the new reality of nineteenth-century bourgeois society as the resolution of the conflicts coming to expression in the French Revolution.[18] Might we similarly say that the texts we

---

[16] We could see an analogy to the issues being discussed here in the criticism by some Anglican divines of the excessive metaphoricity of extreme Puritan writing, 'the language of Canaan', as Bunyan called it—a language which he and other Puritans delighted to acknowledge as incomprehensible to Mr. Worldly-Wiseman and his like (see, e.g. M. I. Lowance, Jr., *The Language of Canaan: Metaphor and Symbol in New England from the Puritans to the Transcendentalists* (Cambridge, Mass.: Harvard University Press, 1980)). But, as opposed to those like Wilkins who sought to counter 'the language of Canaan' with a prototype language of quasi-scientific univocity, my aim is not to exclude any particular model or practice of religious language but simply to explore how suited the example under consideration is to assisting us in the laborious attempt to begin thinking about God. Given the difficulty of this task, I do not see it helpful to multiply difficulties by invoking a language or a rhetoric that is more difficult than it needs to be. For the seventeenth-century debate see Isabel Rivers, *Reason, Grace and Sentiment: A Study of the Language of Religion and Ethics in England 1660–1780, i. Whichcote to Wesley* (Cambridge: Cambridge University Press, 1991).

[17] Adorno's remarks are in fact made with specific reference to the latter's Hölderlin interpretation rather than to his comments on Parmenides.

[18] See T. W. Adorno, 'Parataxis' in *Gesammelte Schriften*, ii. *Noten zur Literatur* (Frankfurt am Main: Suhrkamp, 1947), 447–91.

have been examining should primarily be interpreted against the background of the specific historical crises of religion in the early Enlightenment period? Are they primarily to be read as concrete and determinate negations of particular formulations of faith in an age when approved ecclesiastical discourse is beginning to buckle under the impact of religious existence itself, torn between the vividness of religious experience and the reality of the new, scientific world? Certainly we have no reason to object to giving as much historical specificity to the formation of our texts as possible (something that Adorno himself, trapped in generalized and loosely Marxian categories, rarely achieved in practice!), whether with regard to the crisis of representation in the fourteenth century or the onset of confessional divisions and the early scientific revolution in the seventeenth century. However, the very widespread distribution of such examples from the literature of religious devotion might suggest that, even if historical context is always important, something more fundamental than a particular historical crisis of bourgeois thought is going on here, and that what we are dealing with is, at the very least, a long-term issue in religious thought and not something isolable as the product of a non-recurring historical configuration.

Yet, if the appeal to such paratactic formulations is not dismissed as the manifestation of mere emotionality or the resurgence of primitive formlessness, it might be objected that the case being developed here is being too closely tied to the literature of piety adequately to answer the need of a philosophically coherent venture of thinking about God. But whether in the manner of piety or of philosophy, it may seem a considerable step from the kind of willed turning of the mind towards God in which thought dwells patiently on its wanting (both lacking and desiring) God to a thinking about God in which the intention of thought would be fulfilled, in which we *really would be thinking about God*. Given that our starting point is simply that of thinking about the need of our time and that we do not have the resources of metaphysical deductions or authoritatively sanctioned revelations, is there anything more to be said than this: that we *may* allow our thinking to take form as a conscious and willed need of God (that is to say, a 'free need'), but the only content we can give it is the poverty and emptiness of that need itself? God, then, would be only a remote, unachieved, and perhaps unachievable goal, the lure of thought that cannot be thought or, at best, thought and expressed only in the 'primitive' broken discourse of the kind recommended by *The Cloud* and exemplified by Pascal's *Memorial* and Herbert's 'Prayer'? Is this all that is to be had from trying to use such texts as means of learning to think about God? Are we doing more than cobbling words together in an ad hoc and aimless way?

In turning for help to such 'classic' texts that, in differing ways, represent important streams within the Christian tradition, we are by no means finding 'answers'. Rather, we are engaged in what, following John D. Caputo, we might call a disastrous hermeneutic: a hermeneutic that has lost its guiding star, the inner light that redeems its topic from the darkness of the forgotten, the never-known, or the impossible. Schleiermacher, famously, named the decisive moment of the hermeneutic process 'divination', since it is in 'divining' the meaning of the other that I come to understand him or her. In engaging with the tradition in the way we are doing here we are also attempting to 'divine' its meaning, but in a subtly different and more paradoxical way: we are attempting to 'divine' it in the exact sense of seeking that in it which is indeed divine, which speaks thinkingly of God in such a way that, in understanding it, we too can come to think the thought of God. Yet we have acknowledged to ourselves and have discovered in our texts that the thought of God is not so easily thought: that to make our thought truly 'divine' may prove to be a throw of the dice against impossible odds, as if we were being asked to believe that Quixote's windmills were truly giants.[19] A hermeneutical process of this kind will never give us 'answers' as if we could just go back and check what our authoritative sources once said and meant and merely translate that into our own time. It is more a provocation to thought than an answering of thought's leading questions. And does this then mean that we are simply lost in a maze of 'words, words, words', erring with Mark C. Taylor through language's endless self-deconstruction? Can we still hope, with Heidegger, that we might yet come by such a path to what we have never yet managed to think?

Think again of what happened in the final line of 'A True Hymn'. The disjunction between 'O, could I love' and 'loved' was not something that the self, by itself, could overcome. The replenishing of the exhausted spirit came through a word given, written by, and even quoted from another. The movement in Herbert's poem and in our reading of it is not therefore the expression of an internal monologue but the enactment of a dialogue of voices and texts in the common public space of language. So too the hermeneutic task is public and dialogical through-and-through, right from the beginning and all the way down. If the filter of parataxis allows the essential brokenness of religious language to come to expression in, with and under the medium of subjunctivity, dialogue points to the responsibility that we have, in speaking, for what we say, for the one (or for those) to whom we say it and for ourselves in saying it. Dialogue here is not a means subsequent to the articulation and determination of a given content, as if we could say, 'Now we know what to say, but we can only get it across if we are prepared to be dialogical about it.' Rather, dialogue, speech, talk, conversation ('turning things round together'), is the way in which we first learn to speak—about anything, and here, particularly, about God. The words we use are not some kind of personal possession we can take out and spend according to a fixed rate. They change in the moment of utterance, as they are spoken, and as

---

[19] That Quixote's vision is indeed a *true* vision is the argument of Miguel de Unamuno's study, *Our Lord Don Quixote: The Life of Don Quixote and Sancho*, tr. A. Kerrigan (Princeton: Princeton University Press, 1976). Here Unamuno claims Don Quixote as a prototype for a Kierkegaardian faith in the power of the absurd that—according to Unamuno—is nevertheless also a revelation of the truth of the human condition.

they rise, fall, tremble, are interrupted, exhausted, choked on, or jubilantly acclaimed. As a specification of breath, language lives from the sounds that resound when human beings gather. And, conversely, in attending to the respiratory rhythms of speech encoded in writing, we relearn the movements that inflect the otherwise opaque formality of the written sign. We learn to hear what is being said in writing and so become capable of answering in our own turn and of becoming answerable for what we have now said. If, in a certain perspective, the onward course of human conversation, spoken and written, is more a matter of endless errancy and self-unravelling than of purposeful goal-oriented striving or self-discovery, the principle of dialogue and the exigency of attention intrinsic to genuine dialogue, make of it a matter of care and responsibility, of attention not only to what we say but to the breath and spirit of the thing, the real human context in which we say it and in which it first becomes meaningful.

It is with reference to this dialogical dimension that we can also address a suspicion that might have been simmering beneath the surface of the previous pages. This is the suspicion that although we have been setting out to find a way of thinking about God that is not absorbable or reclaimable by the processes of technological enframing, the very forms I have chosen allow my suggestions to be read as a kind of ideology of the hi-tech world. What is a preference for the subjunctive if not a mirroring of a world in which knowledge has become virtual? What is parataxis if not a dignifying of the fragmented speech that emails and texting are making the universal media of hi-tech communication? But the degradation of language in these forms is precisely to do with the fact that they are without breath and without the possibility of embodied dialogue. They are— or are constantly on the edge of becoming—autopoietic systems uninhabited by living speakers.

We have for some time focused the discussion on language, a focus that corresponds to a deep current of modern thought. But are we right to take language in isolation in this way? True, we have insisted on attending to the breath that makes language into speech but which never itself appears in language, and we have even conceded a role to silence, the silence that constantly accompanies language as a wise friend who now and then taps language on the arm and puts a gentle finger to her lips, but is language itself the sole measure of that which we are attempting to think about God in language? In relation to God, or to any other fundamental dimension of our lives, is language not a means of saying something that is indeed *said* in language but that goes beyond or comes from outwith language itself?

Let me put it like this. Can we assume that, in broad outline, the evolutionary view of human origins is in some sense correct and that human beings have evolved from pre-hominid higher apes? Without entering into the specialist debate as to the apes' capacity for language, it is nevertheless clear that we share a wide range of cognitive, emotional, and behavioural characteristics with the language-less or, at any rate, language-poor higher apes. What this means is that our capacity for language is exercised within a biological environment that was largely developed prior to language. Language may articulate our life-world. It did not create it. Language is led not only by itself (*'Die Sprache spricht'*— 'language speaks'—said Heidegger) but by what we apprehend by means of our sensory and motor interaction with the world, by what lies beyond language and, in a sense, precedes or transcends language. But if the body is the all-embracing condition of our coming to think anything at all, might this not be as true of our thoughts about God as it is of our thoughts about food or the warmth of human love? But does it make any kind of sense to talk about *thinking* as being led by what is beyond language? Isn't thinking necessarily a matter of words? Maybe— though we should not be tricked into thinking that because language may be a necessary condition of thinking that it is a sufficient condition for it. Let us at least, for once, suspend our disbelief and think about how things might be if the near-universal consensus amongst both conservative and radical philosophers of religion and theologians that there's nothing outside language were mistaken. What are the words we have struggled to say *about*?

We may not seem to have advanced very far at all in learning to think about God, still less can we claim to have filled our thinking with a rich content that would entitle it to be called 'knowledge of God'. The warning given in the last chapter concerning patience is proving to be justified. Nothing here is going to happen in a hurry. 'We do not want to be beginners. But let us be convinced of the fact that we will never be anything else but beginners, all our life!' wrote Thomas Merton about the life of monastic prayer.[20] Perhaps the same lesson applies to thinkers, and that it is already a sign of lacking the patience necessary for the task to want to be more than a beginner. Yet even the beginner sets out in the power not only of a decision to begin but also of a hunch as to the direction to be taken. What then is to direct our words about God?

[20] Thomas Merton, *Contemplative Prayer* (London: Darton, Longman and Todd, 1969), 43.

6

Seeing the Mystery

I have been seeking an opening for thinking about God in the fundamental freedom of thought to think whatever it chooses to think, although I have also argued that this freedom needs to be critically self-aware of its own limits. Far from being the 'absolute' freedom of idealist philosophy, it is a freedom that accepts that it is always positioned by what Lévinas called a pre-reflective 'passivity before passivity'. Existentially, such a venture of thought may be characterized by courage, patience, and gratitude: the courage of being resolved to think for oneself; the patience that waits upon the self-disclosure of that with which we are, in thinking, concerned; the gratitude that such a matter is given us to ponder. But this is only a beginning, a preliminary sketch, as it were, and, as yet, says little or nothing about *what* is involved in thinking about God in the sense of what such thinking would actually be *about*.

Clearly, we can have many thoughts of many different kinds about God. But in what way can we say that *God* could ever be present to us in our thinking, and what would our thinking then need to become? Surely it would be very different from the summaries of the history of ideas about God that make up the bulk of most theological literature? Certainly no existing body of texts will provide the content of our thinking for us if we have not thought about or are unable to think it for ourselves. But such thinking, as we have seen, can only begin in a sustained, willed openness to the possibility of God being thought about. But can we ever be sure that we are not waiting on *nothing*? To be sure, I have written that we cannot reduce God, whatever God may be, to a *focus imaginarius* without our losing something integral to what makes it worthwhile to think about God at all. Cupitt is right: to understand God as a *focus imaginarius* is to take leave of him. But no matter what heights of ascetic sublimity we may achieve in the kind of patient, all-enduring waiting upon God to which the free decision to think about God commits us, such waiting can never, of itself, deliver God to us. If it did it would thereby cease to be waiting upon God and become instead the construction or deduction of God. Free as we are to think about God, that freedom itself does not guarantee that it will be *God* we think about, or that we are thinking in a truly *godly* way.

At the risk of repeating, let me note again that whether or not God can be thought directly as a concept or as the object of thinking, it is clear that *even if we don't understand what it might mean really to think about God* we can nevertheless be concerned about God in thinking, even if only to ask what 'God' could possibly mean. For to be able to have a clear conception of something and to be able to think about it are by no means one and the same thing. It is one of the motifs of Heidegger's later thought that what chiefly calls for thinking in any matter is what withdraws itself from thinking or what, as yet, remains unthought. The problem that lures us into a field of enquiry is the problem we can't solve. The depth of a great thinker of the tradition is precisely the impossibility of summarizing their essential thought because that thought itself was directed beyond itself to something it had not yet grasped. Conversely, the easier it is to summarize this or that exercise in thinking, the less interesting or important it is likely to be. The predictable intellectual textbooks produced by the kind of Hegel disciples whom Kierkegaard so mercilessly satirized present no difficulty in terms of being understood and we no longer read them. It is, on the contrary, a measure of the greatness of the great thinkers that their thought is inexhaustible, that a Plato can still generate new questions and new interpretations more than two thousand years and libraries of commentary later. In this perspective, then, far from God being disqualified as a topic of thought by the fact that it is so extremely hard even to know that in thoughtfully waiting upon God it is truly God we are thinking about, God may be what most calls for thinking.

Once more, however, the doubt recurs that nothing that has yet been said gives direction to thinking about God other than the subjective choice of the thinker to make this the matter of his thought. The questions that set the previous chapter in motion must therefore be repeated: if the style of patiently waiting upon God is very different from existentialist self-affirmation, isn't it ultimately only a matter of style and not of substance? Isn't what is being proposed here also a self-chosen human option? If, by being withdrawn from the possibility of thinking, the thought of God calls all the more for thinking, mustn't there be more than a withdrawing if we are to take seriously the claim that this is thinking about *God*? Mustn't there also be a drawing, a calling, a summons in a specific direction, if we are not to be left floundering in some sort of sheer infinity of possibilities of which each is as good as the other—what older theologians called God's 'prevenience'?[1]

In the previous chapter we allowed ourselves—as if spontaneously (so deeply are our cultural habits engrained)—to be guided by a selection of classical texts from the tradition, texts that 'everyone knows' are 'about God'. But if in reading them we also found ourselves thinking about God, did we do so merely because

---

[1] See, e.g. Fr. von Hügel, 'The Facts and Truths concerning God and the Soul which are of most Importance in the Life of Prayer', in idem, *Essays and Addresses on the Philosophy of Religion*, (Second series) (London: Dent, 1930).

we somehow recapitulated the intention of the authors, Pascal and Herbert, in our own conscious minds? But could we do that if we did not already know for ourselves what it would mean for a text to be *about God*? Mustn't we 'always already' have some sense of what 'about God' would mean before we can come to the work of interpreting a religious text? Doesn't every act of understanding such a text ultimately presume upon a kind of pre-literate existential encounter, depth, or dimension, something we can only call 'experience'? But, then, isn't to understand thinking about God in the light of 'experience' to limit it to the existing horizons of human cultural and linguistic practices so that the supposedly 'divine' depth of our experience becomes readable as just another textual or anthropological phenomenon? Worse still, as a psychological event, isn't experience necessarily exposed to scientific measurement or explanation and, even, technological manipulation (as in the use of chemicals or electrical charges to stimulate mystical experiences)? It would seem, then, that there is nothing we could possibly experience that would assure us of the godliness of our thinking. We can only wilfully, courageously, patiently, gratefully wait upon God, keeping open the possibility of God in face of the prevailing currents of thought that seek to terminate such a possibility once and for all. How could any kind of experience slip itself into the emptiness of our waiting without undoing its essential openness? Isn't it the collective wisdom of Neo-orthodoxy, Post-Wittgensteinian linguistic philosophy, and Continental post-structuralism that experience is best left out of the picture when it comes to thinking about God?

But is it correct to say that all experience is, simply as such, objectifiable in psychological or cultural terms? Or is this a particular prejudice of our own immediate culture that needs to be challenged? Recent writing on the subject of mysticism has discussed the possibility of 'pure consciousness' of a mental state of entire translucence that is both conscious, yet determined neither by a specific subject nor by a specific object and that is, in that sense, not an 'experience' of the kind that theologians and philosophers of religion are anxious to avoid. It is, some have claimed, just this 'pure consciousness' that comes to expression in the oblique, broken negations and stammerings of mystical writers.[2] Elsewhere, against the background of Kitaro Nishida's account of nothingness as 'the *topos*' or site (Japanese: *Basho*) of mystical experience, I have tried to develop the idea of an 'experience of nothingness' that might set in motion a possible future religious discourse that had fully internalized the problem of modern nihilism.[3] Such an experience would read the relativizing of all existing religious positions and the impossibility of any objective or ontologically grounded knowledge of God as the negative occasion of an openness to a God who inherently overflows all possible human forms of consciousness. Key features of such an experience of nothingness

---

[2] See Robert K. Forman (ed.), *The Problem of Pure Consciousness: Mysticism and Philosophy* (New York: Oxford University Press, 1990).

[3] See G. Pattison, *Agnosis: Theology in the Void* (Basingstoke: Macmillan, 1996), esp. ch. 4.

would include (1) the distinction between nothingness as the *topos*/site of experience and any idea of nothingness as the object of 'an' experience, whether this latter meant the revelation of nothingness as ultimate reality or as a kind of cipher for the divine plenitude (as Schopenhauer sometimes suggests[4]): nothingness, the lack of ground or ultimate 'reason' as the pervading condition of thinking and being we can never get behind; (2) the existential realization of this condition as the anxious awareness of our susceptibility to error and, crucially, of our mortality and finitude; (3) the acceptance that nothingness as the *topos*/site of thinking and being is permanent in such a way that this anxious awareness cannot be 'overcome' or done away with, and does not need to be. Nothingness is not identical with what a later Japanese philosopher, Keiji Nishitani, called the 'nihility' of Western scientific and existential nihilism, since it does not isolate the individual from the world or expose him to the anxiety of meaninglessness but it is precisely an insight into the condition that unites him with all possible beings and phenomenal forms: as Japanese Buddhism regularly insists, insight into the emptiness of all forms of being is the obverse of the compassionate recognition that no forms of being are ultimately alien to each other, resulting in what Nishitani refers to as a 'double exposure' in which nothingness/being, death/life are always simultaneously interdependent.[5]

There is no doubting the appeal of Buddhist metaphysics as a framework for religious language and practice that does not seem to breach the critical limits called for by contemporary criteria of knowledge. Thus Cupitt suggested that in taking leave of God he was turning towards a form of 'Christian Buddhism'. Nor are the links between the kind of thinking we find in Nishida and his school and the West's own mystical tradition (Meister Eckhart, etc.) merely fanciful. There are fruitful possibilities here for the deepening and renewal of theological self-understanding. *But*—and the 'but' is familiar from every introductory textbook on the relationship between Eastern and Western thought (yet no less significant for all that)—there seems to be something missing from such a pure and empty experience that most Christian thinkers at least would claim is essential to what they want to say. Let me make the point in the form of an almost grotesque question: Could the Void love us? Or must it not rather be supremely indifferent to our coming in and our going hence? And, in the end, is it not more worthy simply and stoically to accept this indifference rather than through prayers and supplications and anxiety to attempt to invest it with some kind of personal value?[6] Nishida himself speaks of nothingness as 'personal' but, as

---

[4] See A. Schopenhauer, *The World as Will and Representation*, tr. E. F. J. Payne (New York: Dover, 1966), i. 409–10.

[5] See K. Nishitani, *Religion and Nothingness* (Berkeley and Los Angeles: University of California Press, 1982), 52.

[6] A difference one might see reflected in the differing comportments of the grimly realistic squire and the metaphysically tormented knight in the 'last supper' scene of Ingmar Bergman's *The Seventh Seal*.

with theological radicals such as Tillich and Robinson, the desire to emphasize that the human being is affirmed and sustained in its highest personal endeavours and self-reflection in the experience of nothingness is not quite the same as ascribing a personal character to the pre-objective and pre-subjective ground on which the sense of the personal itself arises.

In *The End of Theology and the Task of Thinking about God* I drew attention to our immediate sense of self as the hinge separating a purely scientific, reductionistic world view from a religiously orientated path of thinking. Such a sense of self is significantly different in character from Descartes' idea of the immediate consciousness of consciousness, however. It is not merely or purely 'consciousness' that matters, but that I am conscious of myself and of the other personal beings I encounter in the world as having an interest, a concern, a passion in relation to existence that cannot be fitted in to the framework of any explanatory system or made into the object of technical manipulation. Or, rather, even though we can very well imagine that sometime in the near future a theory of consciousness *will be found* that can account even for this sense of self—the lived quality of existence—and that machines *will be made* that can replicate this sense, even so, my own feeling that my life, your life, our life *matters* is not diminished or changed. In fact, even if it could be shown, once and for all, that this sense of self was an illusion, an epiphenomenon of electrochemical functions or a sensor for the selfish gene, then, as I put it ' I *am* an illusory being—but this illusion is precisely what matters most of all to me: it is what I am for myself, and in myself.'[7] Or, to put it in cosmic terms, it doesn't actually matter to me all that much that 'consciousness' should continue to be a future feature of the universe:[8] what matters to me is the concrete personal shared world of those I know as human beings in the actual present. They are—or, I can't help thinking, *should be*—worth more than the consciousness of some future post-human entity.

Whilst insisting on the personal in this way registers an interest to which any theological discourse must do justice, it does not of itself seem to move us forward in the attempt to progress from merely wanting to think about God to actually thinking about God, actually having God as the focus and matter of our thinking. I shall return to the requirement of a personal element in the attempt to think about God, but, first, I want to open another line of access to the question which, I think, will enable us to understand better what that personal element might mean.

---

[7] G. Pattison, *The End of Theology and the Task of Thinking about God* (London: SCM Press, 1998), 49.

[8] The Astronomer Royal, Sir Martin Rees, has recently suggested that the 'justification' of human beings in the history of the cosmos is to be found not in tracing the phenomenon of consciousness back to some anthropic principle at work in the heart of the Big Bang but in the chance we now have to make it possible that consciousness continues to be a feature of the universe *even if the future bearers of this consciousness are no longer human.*

II

We have for some time been hovering on a boundary projected by our desire to think about God, looking and waiting for a sign that there is something 'out there' and, in the meantime, wondering how we would know it if it came, how such an *extra nos* would distinguish itself within the seamless flow of our own consciousness. But is this not to misrepresent the situation in a fundamental way? Is our thinking as direction-less as a wind sock, merely waiting for some passing breeze to fill it and lift it in this direction or that? Let us think again of phenomenology's insistence on the intentionality of consciousness, and let us recall that although this embraces the idea that consciousness is always actively intended by the agent of consciousness (which is what was emphasized in Chapter 4), it is also (and many commentators would say *especially*) characteriz-able as intentionality-*towards*. This suggests that there can be no such a thing as 'pure' consciousness, consciousness simply and exclusively 'of nothing', since consciousness is always consciousness *of* this or that. If this is so, then nothing-ness, for example, could never be the *object* or *content* of a thematized act of thought but, as the *topos*/penumbra of thinking about God, would be a boundary or horizon that can never in itself be made into an object or content, a shifting margin that accompanies every movement in thought that we can never outflank. Yet, within the field bounded by this penumbra we are always and ineluctably engaged in concrete acts of thought. In this sense, the desire to think about God is not the desire somehow to penetrate the penumbra of nothingness that encircles and groundlessly grounds all our thinking—to get into thinking's 'outer space', as it were—but it is the desire to think of God *within* the field of illuminable possibilities. Bearing in mind the stipulation that such thinking is also to engage our sense of personal reality and identity, we can then say that what we are seeking to think about is the thought of God as illuminating and illuminated by the concrete possibilities of our concrete and actual life-world, the real world here and now in which we live and move and have our being.

What I am saying, then, is that thinking—always intentionally directed, always thinking-*of*—occurs in the power of some pre-reflective apprehension of that towards which it is drawn (although, of course, we cannot right now say 'what' it is thinking of, since that would be to imply a definite 'object'—but we haven't yet got that far). At this point we might—perhaps we have no alternative but to—resort to analogy and metaphor to articulate what is being said. We could, for example, say that thinking is always guided by a 'hunch', that it 'feels' its way forward, or 'follows its nose'. Instead, I shall say that thinking never occurs without *vision*. What might this mean? 'Vision' might mean, simply, what I see from the window or the painting or the person I'm looking at. But it might also be the vision that is decisive for the fate of an individual or a nation—'without vision, the people perish'. 'Vision' is not necessarily to be understood as some naïve encounter with a primordial fullness, something to which we could appeal as providing the 'answer' to thought's entanglement in language. If vision can illuminate the world that lies 'beyond' the boundaries of language, the world in which we learn the meaning of such visions is one that has 'always already' been flooded by language. Acknowledging both that 'vision' is not necessarily to be taken literally (least of all when we are not talking about what is immediately and empirically visible) and that other metaphors (such as those listed earlier in this paragraph) might have as good a claim to our attention, I nevertheless choose to follow the clue provided by the idea of vision for a number of reasons. Firstly, metaphors of vision appear to have a 'natural affinity' with questions of thinking, knowledge, and truth. 'I see!' we cry when we understand something. 'Don't you see what I'm trying to get at? Just *look* at the evidence before you,' we shout at the uncomprehending interlocutor. Again, however, it must be acknowledged that such expressions are not exclusive. We might equally well say 'Ah! I get it!' or 'I hear what you're saying.' Secondly, and building on the previous point, key words in the philosophical vocabulary of the West have consistently incorporated such metaphors of seeing (in Plato's case at least, self-consciously and deliberately). Many of these are no longer transparent to English speakers who have no knowledge of Greek or Latin, but such terms as 'idea', 'phenomenon', and 'intuition', not to mention the more readily recognizable word 'vision' itself, are fundamentally rooted in seeing. Closely related to such expressions are a further group of terms drawing on a metaphorics of light: we praise a *lucid* or *illuminating* or *transparent* argument, we call for *clarification* but spurn what is *opaque* or *obscure*, we *reflect* on the question under consideration. In many other European languages such connections lie even closer to the surface. The German *Anschauung* (= intuition, but also in such expressions as *Weltanschauung* = world view) means literally 'looking at', while *Erklärung* (= explanation) means 'making clear'. In the theological tradition, the vision of God, though reserved by most theologians for the world to come, is the final measure of all Christian truth claims. Now it may be that the presence of such metaphors is a cause for complaint, that our philosophical language would be better if we could somehow root them out. Hegel argued that the development of knowledge was precisely a development *away from* vision (*Anschauung*) and *towards* 'grasping' (*Begreifen*) its object. Indeed, in his view, it was one of the limitations of religious thinking that it could not go beyond the limits of a certain pictorializing way of representing its object, as in the myths, narratives, and images that typically (he thought) formed the world of religion. Even so, the question of vision remained one of central importance, and without the initial intuition, the path to conceptual knowledge would remain forever closed.

In his remarkable sermon 'Seeing and Hearing', Paul Tillich described seeing in the following terms.

Seeing is the most astonishing of all our natural powers. It receives the light, the first of all that is created, and as the light does it conquers darkness and chaos. It creates for us an ordered world, things distinguished from each other and from us. Seeing shows us their unique countenance and the larger whole to which they belong. Wherever we see, a piece of the original chaos is transformed into creation. We distinguish, we recognize, we give a name, we know. 'I have seen'—that means in Greek 'I know'. From seeing, all science starts, to seeing it must always return. We want to ask those who have seen with their eyes and we ourselves want to see with our eyes. Only the human eye is able to see in this way, to see a world in every small thing and to see a universe *of* all things. Therefore the human eye is infinite in reach and irresistible in power. It is the correlate to the light of creation.[9]

But, as Tillich goes on to emphasize, seeing is not simply to be equated with science's detached vision, our capacity to see *what* something is. 'Where we see,' he says, 'we unite with what we see. Seeing is a kind of union. As poetry has described it, we *drink* colors and forms, forces and expressions.'[10] This, one might say, is all very splendid—but if what we want is to *think* about God rather than to conjure forth ecstatic feelings how then can 'seeing' guide us? Even if, as Tillich later argues, it is possible for us to see more than we see, in the sense that my bodily vision of the lines and features of someone's face enable me to 'see' how they're feeling, vision would seem to need something near at hand, something present, in order to get to work. But it is a presupposition of this whole enquiry that, in the wake of two hundred years of secularizing thinking and under the conditions of an age of technology, 'God' is not available to us in that way. We have lost our guiding star. There is no *visio dei* out there, waiting for us to arrive. Even mainstream Thomism insisted that such a vision was, in any case, not for this life. And, at a simpler level, the millennia-long consensus of Jewish and Christian versions of theism has been that God is *in*visible. 'Clouds and darkness are his dwelling-place.' Or, more sternly, that God is not to be portrayed in 'the likeness of anything in the heavens above, or on the earth below, or in the waters under the earth'. Even with regard to our ordinary human life in the world, St Augustine taught that it is precisely the visual sense, 'the lust of the eye', that is the most dangerous of all the senses, in terms of its power to distract the self from its true and ultimate concern for the things of God. And, still more troubling in terms of our specific aim of exploring thinking about God in a way that cannot be appropriated by technological enframing, wasn't it precisely the fixing of truth in terms of its visualized aspect or 'idea' that paved the way for the emergence of technological enframing (at least on Heidegger's version of the history of ideas)? Isn't 'vision' the prototype of all the forms of representation that underlie the whole project of rationalism? What could it mean, then, to claim that our attempt to think about God is 'always already' set in motion by some vision of that about which it seeks to think? And how could we put our own thinking in service to vision without (at however many removes) bringing it into the orbit of enframing? Doesn't asserting the primacy of vision mean asserting the primacy of

[9] P. Tillich, *The New Being* (New York: Scribner, 1955), 127–8.
[10] Ibid. 128

a subject who stands over against the world and encloses and limits that world in terms of the perspective that he imposes upon it?

And so we return to the question of the subject, to the immediate pre-reflective sense that my life, what I experience, what I do, who I am, matters—and matters infinitely—if only to me. What of this subject who *sees*: what do we see when we really turn to look at *the one seeing*? Any number of more or less journalistic histories of ideas have taught us to believe that the seeing subject of Western thought is exclusively identifiable as the all-dominating male gaze. But what do we actually see when we intro*spect*—when we turn to reflect on this immediate sense of self? Is it in fact this all-dominant male gaze, stamping itself upon everything that falls within its field of vision? Let us reflect on the following remark by Mikhail Bakhtin: 'A person has no internal sovereign territory, he is wholly and always on the boundary; looking into himself he looks into the eyes of another or with the eyes of another.'[11] What is Bakhtin saying here?

We have supposed that 'I' have an immediate sense of self. I feel that it matters that *I* am writing this text here and now and that, although I am using my computer to write it, it is *I* who am writing it and not the computer. But does this immediate sense of self require us to envisage the self as a self-contained monadic entity or a kind of human equivalent of the pure activity of God? Surely not. While the sense of self gives us something to think about it does not come with a definitive and instantly readable interpretation of its own identity in the manner of a lapel badge. The more conscious we are of this sense of self, the more we realize that we are a riddle to ourselves, unfathomably mysterious. It is just this extraordinariness of what, for human beings, is the most ordinary consciousness of all that makes the self such a provocation, such a lure, such a topic for thought. To take the 'sense of self' or the 'I' as a starting point, then, is not immediately to commit oneself to a path that leads ineluctably to some kind of theory of the absolute ego or of the world as the creation or representation of some individual mind. It is, in itself, merely to open a door to reflection.

Let us, then, take Bakhtin's assertion and use it as a question: when we turn to intro*spect*, do we expect to see our true self presenting itself to us in some kind of pure luminous state? And whatever our expectations, is it not more likely that we only ever get to see the self only in the measure that we see it emerging from and relating to the dynamic network of other selves to which, as self, it belongs? As I suggested in *The End of Theology and the Task of Thinking about God*, 'My spontaneous sense that my personal life matters, and matters infinitely, is essentially the inner aspect of a bodily and social exchange. "I" is itself a learned word, and my sense of personal value is brought into focus by my childhood nurture.'[12] The comment is banal, but even in its everydayness decisive. Importantly, it also

---

[11] M. Bakhtin, *Problems of Dostoevsky's Poetics*, tr. C. Emerson (Minneapolis: University of Minneapolis Press, 1984), 287.
[12] Pattison, *The End of Theology*, 50

meshes in with the basically dialogical character of language adduced in the previous chapter.[13] Here, however, I want to retain the focus on its implications for what we *see* in any act of introspection. If we follow Bakhtin, what we see are the eyes of another: that is, we only get to see ourselves to the extent that we find ourselves judged, praised, described, desired, spurned, etc. by others. Our self-identity is not a solid or absolute revelation or fact but a struggle and a dance in which who *I* am emerges as the counterpoint to my vision of you and your vision of me.

Sartre, famously, was deeply repelled by the thought that I could become the object of another's gaze, even though he conceded that it happened all the time. To be conscious of myself as being seen by another is, he claimed, to have an alien limit placed upon my intrinsic freedom. In the eyes of another I am always and only an object. To become who I am—a centre of active freedom—it is therefore necessary for me continually to contest the view of me that others have, to wrest my freedom from their gaze. Such a struggle, according to Sartre, was without end and, ultimately, hopeless. As opposed to Hegel's account of the struggle between Master and Slave, there is no final resolution in which each recognizes the other's humanity and both affirm their mutual freedom. In Sartre's judgement, we will nearly always slide into some sort of imbalance, such that now we masochistically allow ourselves to be dominated and determined by the other's view of us, now we sadistically subject the other to what we would have them be. Lévinas's insistence that the inescapability of my being bound in the deepest roots of my being to the other is to be understood in terms of my being accused, persecuted, held hostage or *obsessed* by the Other might be seen as confirming Sartre's analysis (even if, of course, Lévinas himself evaluates this situation very differently from Sartre[14]).

Bakhtin, however, does not draw attention to the presence of the other's gaze in our very interiority in order (as Sartre might) to rally us to assert our own rights as subjective centres of absolute freedom nor does he speak in terms of hostage-taking or accusation. His point is rather that acceptance of the situation that my self-vision will always be refracted through the eyes of the other is not in itself a limitation or restriction of my freedom (though he shows how this way of understanding the situation shapes Dostoevsky's pathological characters) but constitutes the very possibility of seeing myself as a person at all. Let me try to explore further what this might mean, first with reference to Tillich's sermon on 'Seeing and Hearing', then with two more or less serendipitous examples: the first from the world of icons and the second from a recent Japanese film entitled *After Life*.

---

[13] In another respect, it also points to a link with the kind of emphasis on the role of mimetic behaviour in the construction of human identity, as emphasized in the work of René Girard.

[14] See Lévinas, *Autrement qu'être*, esp. ch. 4, 'La Substitution'.

The excerpts quoted from the sermon on 'Seeing and Hearing' might be understood as treating vision as the outward-looking gaze of the centred subject. However, in addition to all the positive things he says about vision, Tillich also makes clear his view—familiar from his concept of 'ultimate concern'—that if we make the mistake of confusing our finite, partial, and limited view of truth with truth itself, then what we have is an idol and not the true and living God. Visions of God, on this view, are always prone to slip into such idolatry, leaving believers with a mere outer form that has become severed from the fullness it had when it first dawned in intuition. This is, indeed, the typical temptation of religion and Tillich argued forcibly that the justice of the iconoclast's complaint must always be upheld against such diminished images. From a Protestant point of view, this would be a context in which to understand the Reformers' protest against a medieval religious culture that had over-invested in the visualization of Christian worship, life, and doctrine. In such a situation it became important to recall that 'hearing', i.e. the word, also had its rights. But, Tillich reminds his listeners, the New Testament itself tells us that the divine word has given itself to be *seen*. The incarnate word is not a mere visual aid to assist us in rising to a more intellectual understanding of its truth, but it is itself in its earthly visibility divine truth. As such, however, it is also situated in the midst of a world full of many things that are not good to see, things that, perhaps, should not be seen. So, Tillich concludes,

> ... when we are tired of seeing the abundance of the world with all its disorder, its hate and separation, its demonic destruction, and if we are also unable to look into the blinding light of the divine ground, then let us close our eyes. And then it might happen that we see the picture of someone who looks at us with eyes of infinite human depth and therefore of divine power and love. And those eyes say to us 'Come and see.'[15]

If we are familiar with Tillich's habitual caution with regard to ascribing personality to God, this is a remarkable passage, since it suggests that there is a sense, at least in relation to the Incarnation, that God is not merely the unrepresentable ground of our being but that God somehow 'looks at' us with eyes of love. The truth of vision is not, finally, the truth 'enframed' by the vision of the seeing subject but is only disclosed in a kind of reversal or turning of that vision, when seeing means 'being seen'. Both in this sermon and throughout his theology Tillich is centrally concerned with the struggle of the self to find a centre and ground that is constantly threatened by estrangement, disintegration, and even the wild upsurge of the demonic. Christ, for Tillich, is typically the symbol of what we experience as the renewal of our centred being, the possibility of being able to hope and love 'in spite of' the centripetal structures of destruction in which we are historically enmeshed. Yet here, unusually, it is first in the moment when we allow ourselves *to be looked at* that we are invited to 'come and see'. In

---

15 Tillich, *The New Being*, 133–4.

other words, the vision that guides us in our search truly to think about who we are, the 'answer' to our quest for a truly integrated and centred self, is a vision of ourselves received from the eyes of another.

Can we imagine how this might actually occur as a kind of experience within the field of vision, taking the term vision in its ordinary everyday sense? Let us try, even if what such examples can achieve will inevitably be no more than what Heidegger referred to as an 'ontic warrant', i.e. an illustration from experience or culture of a phenomenon that the illustration itself cannot ground or justify, but to which it can, nevertheless, bear witness.

My first example centres on a quite particular personal experience of one well-known Russian icon.

Of all the icons made available to us through books and reproductions, none has perhaps achieved such popularity as the icon often referred to as 'The Old Testament Trinity' in the version of the fifteenth-century Russian icon-painter Andrei Rublev. Rublev's icon illustrates the incident recorded in Genesis Chapter 18 of three mysterious figures who visit Abraham and foretell the birth of Isaac. In Christian tradition these figures came to be widely regarded as the actual personal presence of the Trinity. Rublev depicts them as angelic forms, numinously radiant, deeply tranquil, yet linked in a mutual reciprocity that several commentators have interpreted as a visual representation of the dynamic inner being of God's Trinitarian life.[16] Wouldn't a work such as this arguably have to be the high-point of any attempt to visualize the heavenly world? Can we imagine any more perfect picture before which to give ourselves over to the contemplative rapture engendered by the visual revelation of God's transcendent beauty? Many would say not, but I suggest that there is a dimension of vision that does not come to expression in this icon, or that does so only in a hidden way.

Rublev's icon of the Trinity is to be seen today in Moscow's Tretiakov gallery, where it is exhibited in a free-standing frame within the icon gallery. Whether intentionally or not, this arrangement can give rise to a surprising visual effect. As one approaches the icon, one finds oneself being watched. Not by a museum attendant (though that is also possible), but by the unwavering gaze of a fragmentary icon on the wall to the left, a gaze falling precisely onto the space into which one is even now stepping in order to admire the Old Testament Trinity. The icon from which this gaze originates is also by Rublev and is known as the icon of Christ the Saviour. The original icon was significantly larger than the Old Testament Trinity, being painted on a board equal to a man's height. However, the paint has largely disappeared, leaving only a small area in which we can see—or, I am suggesting, find ourselves *being seen by*—the gaze of a Christ who, in the icon's original form, would have been seated in majesty as Christ,

[16] For a classic account of the icon from an Orthodox point of view see L. Ouspensky and V. Lossky, *The Meaning of Icons* (Crestwood, New York: St. Vladimir's Seminary Press, 1983), 200–4. See also my *Art, Modernity and Faith* (London: SCM Press, 1998), 128–30 and O. Davies, *A Theology of Compassion* (London: SCM Press, 2001), 256–8.

Ruler of All. In its present condition it is as if this theological context has literally fallen away, leaving only a fragile and residual crust of paint formed in the image of a face whose expression is at one and the same time sovereign, reposed, clear, steady, and compassionate. A look of love, we might say, if we can imagine love without sentiment or preference: the look that might have met the unnamed woman who threw herself penitently at the feet of Christ, or, equally (but with very different effect), the rich young man who went away sorrowing because he could not find it in himself to give all he had to the poor and follow where the look of Jesus asked him to go.

A sensitive reader of paintings could easily enough discern all this for herself. However, the particular way in which the two works are juxtaposed, so that we cannot *see* the Trinity without entering the field in which we *are seen* by Christ the Saviour, gives dramatic force to the realization that before we can become contemplators of God, we must allow ourselves to be seen as God, in Christ, sees us: to know ourselves as seen in this way is what it means to be saved. This is a break in continuity, a reversal, that we have already encountered in the final line of George Herbert's 'A True Hymn', where the ardour of the poet reaching out in love towards God is exhausted, checked, and reversed by the given word *Loved* or in Tillich's description of how, having once been blinded by the 'light of the divine ground' we see ourselves being regarded by 'someone who looks at us with eyes of infinite love'. Something similar can be experienced in the impact of the look that meets us from the icon of Christ the Saviour.[17]

No more than Herbert's poem or Tillich's sermon does this meditation on two pictures *prove* anything at all. In a parabolic manner it merely sketches one way in which 'vision' or 'seeing' could guide us in the attempt to think about God. The point is this: that in speaking of vision I am not claiming that we could in anyway elevate ourselves to some kind of direct vision of God and that this could give us the material basis for subsequent reflection on what this vision means, etc. Nor even that God in some way grants us a vision of himself, a kind of first fruits or

[17] This sequence reverses the familiar 'potentiation' of being-seen developed in Kierkegaard's *The Sickness unto Death*, according to which we must first learn to see ourselves as existing 'before God' and then and only then, having been purged by the rigorous gaze of the Father, learning to see ourselves 'before Christ', 'ransomed, healed, restored, forgiven'. The present work is not a dogmatic treatise of the kind in which the theological justification of one or other sequence might be discussed, but I suggest that these approaches are not necessarily opposed: rather, we might imagine a spiralling sequence of deepening and returning patterns of self-transcendence in which now we stand naked before the absolute transcendence of the ineffable deity, now we are clothed in the saving love of the Christ. I may add that throughout this passage and especially the pages from this point onwards, I am conscious both of a significant affinity with but also a significant distance from the theology of David Ford with its emphasis on the interconnected themes of 'the face', love, and eucharistic remembrance. The difficulty in being more precise as to the points of convergence and divergence is perhaps to do with the fact that, as said, even when the present enquiry talks a Christian language it is not, finally, a doctrinal work and I am more concerned with the formal characteristics of thinking about God than with developing their theological content for a specific faith community (though I am happy if what I am doing is taken up in that way). See D. Ford, *Self and Salvation: Being Transformed* (Cambridge: Cambridge University Press, 1998).

promise of more—a Hegelian *Anschauung* that we could then work up into and grasp as a clear and distinct concept. It is rather that as we turn to introspect upon our pre-reflective sense of self we will never find the self waiting for us as the object at the end of the tunnel. What we find first (and, of course, we cannot yet say if this is also what we find *last*) is a *given vision* of what or who we are. The very possibility of introspection is opened up by a view of the self that appears to come from elsewhere.

I shall call this kind of seeing 'vision that flows back upon itself'. I choose this inelegant phrase rather than, say, 'reflective vision' which could too easily be taken to mean vision in which the seer becomes self-reflective in a Cartesian, Hegelian, or other 'subjectivist' way. This latter would point to the kind of scenario in which introspection is understood as the self making itself the object of its own vision. But although I took introspection as a point of departure, the issue at the moment is not whether the object of vision is 'out there' or 'in here'. The example of the encounter with the icon of Christ the Saviour was taken from an encounter with objects (albeit 'art-objects') located in the world 'out there'. What I am attempting to bring into the open, then, is a quality of the kind of seeing that is happening in such moments. It is not vision determined by its subject nor vision determined by its object, each of which would in Heideggerian terms lend themselves to the dynamics of enframing. Nor is it even a kind of interactive model in which vision takes shape as the moment of static tension between two poles, like an object hovering at the point of intersection of two magnetic fields. Vision that flows back upon itself is, precisely, vision that comes to view as a doubling-back of vision upon itself in a movement of mutual enfolding, the concurrence of two distinct tidal flows: seeing as being-seen, being-seen as seeing: *re*cognition in which there is neither a grounding nor a consequent cognition; vision whose inner mobility suspends any possibility of privileging either the subjective or the objective pole. 'Pure vision', we might say, only not 'pure' in the same sense as when we spoke of 'pure experience', since what was important about such experience was that it was empty: here, however, we are speaking of something that is full of all that gives itself to see and be seen as the reflux of vision upon itself. Maurice Merleau-Ponty spoke of a depth of vision—such as he saw revealed in the paintings of Cézanne—that could make for the bestowal, in vision, of the divine.[18] What I am attempting to describe is an analogous phenomenon, only where the metaphor of depth might suggest something 'behind' what is seen, a kind of infinite background that underlies every possible foreground, I prefer to think of every background as gathered and concentrated in the double-flow of vision: it is all here, giving itself, now, in this moment of seeing/being-seen. And it is just his characteristic of giving itself as what-it-shows-itself-as that makes it possible to speak of it not simply as the

[18] See especially M. Merleau-Ponty, 'Eye and Mind', in J. O. Neill (ed.), *Phenomenology, Language and Sociology* (London: Heinemann, 1974).

revelation of what was already there, waiting to be discovered, but the offer of something new. It is the possibility of a paradigm shift, a new gestalt, that we had not anticipated,[19] the opening of a horizon of a hope we believed was always already lost,[20] Eckhart's 'God born in nothingness',[21] a self-relation whose demand is that we remain in the debt of love.[22] If Sartre would always interpret this as enslavement and Lévinas as being under accusation we are under no obligation to accept their powerful but ultimately under-argued accounts. Buber, for example, long ago interpreted the situation that I am always already addressed and claimed by the Other not as an accusation or as being held hostage, but as address, grace, and the possibility of meaningful existence.[23] And for Christian thinking, at least, the kind of view in the self that is bestowed in the gaze of Rublev's icon of Christ the Saviour (for example) is a *saving view*, a view that gives us the possibility of entering into a re-creating God-relationship (if, that is, we are willing to accept the self-vision of the view that is offered to us in such moments).

If the example of Rublev's icon relates specifically to the Christian tradition, I shall take my next example from a culture far removed from that of European Christianity, namely Japan. It is the film *After Life*, directed by Kore-eda Hirokazu and with a screenplay by Shiho Sato and Masayuki Akieda. Like the previous example this also takes its point of departure in vision in a quite literal sense, but it also draws attention of what such visions might require of us, the seers.

The action takes place in an institution to which the newly dead come for processing. Arriving on a Monday they have until Wednesday to select from their lives one single memory of happiness which they will be allowed to take with them into heaven. When they have done this the staff recreate that moment on film and, on the Saturday, the films are shown and the subjects released into the next stage of existence. One of the newly dead is exceptionally difficult. The problem is that he is an utterly boring person who has never been excited by anything in all his long years. Dutiful in everything he lived out his three score years and ten without ever really engaging with life at any deep or passionate level. In a desperate attempt to prod his memory his assigned helpers retrieve a video record of his life from their archives and set him to watching it. We see his wife appearing and now discover that she had, in fact, been engaged to one of the staff members—Mochizuki—before he (Mochizuki) was killed in the last year of

[19] See, e.g. J. Ferreira, *Transforming Vision. Imagination and Will in Kierkegaardian Faith* (Oxford: Clarendon Press, 1991).

[20] See, M. Theunissen, *Der Begriff Verzweifelung. Korrekturen an Kierkegaard* (Frankfurt am Main: Suhrkamp, 1993).

[21] See Meister Eckhart, 'Sermon Nineteen', in *Sermons and Treatises*, tr. and ed. M. O'C. Walshe (Shaftesbury: Element, 1979), i.

[22] See Rom. 8: 8 and S. Kierkegaard, *Kjerlighedens Gerninger* [Works of Love], in *Samlede Værker* (Copenhagen: Gyldendal, 1962), xii. 170 ff.

[23] See, e.g. M. Buber, *I and Thou*, tr. W. Kaufmann (Edinburgh: T. & T. Clark, 1970).

the war (although in the film he, like the others, appears as the age in which he was when he died). We also learn that the staff members themselves are drawn from those who failed to choose and who will thus continue indefinitely in limbo unless or until they are able to do so. Eventually, the old man chooses a 'moment' just sitting on the park bench with his wife. Mochizuki, recalling that he had sat on that same bench with her, is spurred on to find his former fiancée's file and see what scene she chose: it is in fact of the two of them (she and Mochizuki) sitting on the bench, shortly before his death in battle. Now he can make his decision: But the key is not that he has remembered a forgotten happiness, a picture from his own memory album, as it were. It is that it is enough for him to have been the occasion of another's happiness (hers). Consequently, his 'moment' is not of the two of them on the bench, but of himself alone, sitting on the bench and looking out towards his comrades in the afterlife. Only through his experience there and through having learned the value and meaning of others' memories is he finally released to heaven. Appearing-to-himself-as-another's-view-of-himself is liberating, but only because he is willing to learn and move on from the situation of eternal stasis. It is telling that when Mochizuki resolves to make this his 'eternal memory' the screen goes completely dark for several seconds. The darkness lasts so long that the audience begins to grow uneasy and to wonder whether there is a malfunction in the projection room. In this way the director underlines that taking-to-oneself-another's-view-of-oneself is not itself an act that can be represented or managed.

If, then, introspection does not lead us to a reflective vision of pure subjectivity but rather to a defining moment of appearing-to-oneself-as-another's-view-of-oneself, how are we to distinguish—as we surely must—between those views that are to be resisted if we are to claim our own personhood (the condemning views of our internalized judges, or the impoverishing views of those theories of human beings that serve what G. Marcel called 'the denigration of the human person') and the views that, by being accepted, become means of fulfilment and, believers might claim, salvation? Or to put it in another, simpler, way: how can we distinguish between the false and the true views offered by introspection as to who we 'really' are?

III

We have already touched on Heidegger's innovative and distinctive view of truth as *alétheia* or unconcealment. Over against the view that defines truth as the correspondence of thought and reality, Heidegger sees it as a movement from the side of the world that, as it were, opens up out of itself in the unfolding of nature (*phusis*) and radiates forth as the *phainomena* in and through which—or, more precisely, *as which*—Being gives itself to our apprehension. The kind of view of the self that meets us as if from the eyes of another as we begin the movement of introspection is also, in this sense, a moment of unconcealment, the disclosing of a possibility that belongs to our past, present or future. But this might be read as saying that all views are equally true, that, in effect, 'view' = 'true view', so that, in fact, no real distinction between true and false is possible any more. Instead, how we see ourselves comes to depend on some kind of arbitrarily willed choice. 'I willed it thus!' is Nietzsche's Zarathustra's answer to the question concerning the continuity and coherence of the self. Isn't this the logical result of an understanding of the world in which Being becomes true simply in and as its own phenomenalization (i.e. its self-unconcealment in phenomena)? Is Heidegger himself doing more than giving a cloak of philosophical formality to Nietzsche's renowned perspectivism?

Like Heidegger, the Russian Orthodox thinker Pavel Florensky also saw the word *a-létheia* as expressing the negation of the root *-lath*.[24] However, Florensky's interpretation takes a slightly different turn (though not, I think, a turn that is necessarily incompatible with Heidegger's). What Florensky emphasizes is that form of concealment that is encountered in forgetting, in *léthargos*, which he describes as 'a longing for sleep, *Schlafsucht*, as the desire to immerse oneself in a stage of forgetting and unconsciousness, and, further, the name of a pathological sleep, lethargy'.[25] And, he continues, 'The ancient idea of death as a transition to an illusory existence, almost to self-forgetting and unconsciousness, and, in any case, to the forgetting of everything earthly, finds its symbol in the image of the shades' drinking water from the underground river of Forgetfulness, "Lethe".'[26] But forgetting, the obliteration of consciousness that finds its ultimate term in death, was not just some kind of accident in the Greek understanding, Florensky states. It is not a weakness in memory but the active power of 'all-devouring time'.

All is in flux. Time is the form of existence of all that is, and to say 'exists' is to say 'in time', for time is the form of the flux of phenomena. 'All is in flux and moving and nothing abides,' complained Heraclitus. Everything slips away from the consciousness, flows through the consciousness, is forgotten. Time, chronos, produces phenomena, but, like its mythological image, Chronos, it devours its children. The very essence of consciousness, of life, of any reality is in their flux, i.e. in a certain metaphysical forgetting... But despite all the unquestionableness of [this truth], we cannot extinguish the demand for that which is *not* forgotten, for that which is *not* forgettable, for that which 'abides' in the flux of time. It is this unforgettableness which is *a-létheia*... Truth is the eternal memory of some Consciousness. Truth is value worthy and capable of eternal remembrance.[27]

---

[24] The proximity of Florensky's interpretation of truth to that of Heidegger is also commented on in R. Slesinski, *Pavel Florensky: A Metaphysics of Love* (New York: St. Vladimir's Seminary Press, 1984).

[25] P. Florensky, *The Pillar and Ground of the Truth*, tr. B. Jakim (Princeton: Princeton University Press, 1997), 16.

[26] Ibid.   [27] Ibid. 16–17

For Florensky, however, the Greek view (as he interprets it) is still not sufficient to do justice to the full Christian concept of truth. Drawing attention to the etymological connection of the Russian term *Istina* with words denoting being, breathing, and becoming, he insists that, as opposed to the theoretical interests of the Greeks, what is at stake in the Christian idea of truth is not simply the remembrance of a consciousness or a value but the remembrance, the truth, of an existing, living being or person. Nor can such truth be maintained without the actual existential commitment of the being concerned. Although truth is always the truth of what 'abides', of what is *unforgettable*, the truth as to 'who we are' is not something ready-made that we have merely to preserve. It is inseparable from the struggle against time and forgetting, a struggle to keep in remembrance an image of the human person as worthy of truth, i.e. as worthy of remembrance, worthy of not being annihilated in death. Such a struggle cannot take its criteria simply from 'how things are in the world' but orientates itself in the light of a hope that transcends the present possibilities of existence and the laws of rational evidence. Thus Florensky—and can we say that the fact that he died in an unknown place on an unknown date as an anonymous prisoner in Stalin's Gulag falsifies his idea? Of course not. Florensky was well aware that time, history, and death are, in their own terms, insuperable. The question is whether these are the only terms available, whether the judgement of history is the only judgement that matters, whether it is Stalin or his victims who are to define reality.

Let us return to Rublev's icon of Christ the Saviour and to *After Life*. Noting the formal correspondence between the kind of vision that flows back upon itself and the idea of truth as time flowing back upon itself, let us ask the following question: might the view of ourselves that we catch in being regarded by the image of Christ the Saviour (an image that, in its ruined state, itself testifies to the power of time and death) or in the realization of a long-dead other's love for us be such views, views capable of bearing truth? That we will remember such views only if we actively remember them, only if we struggle to keep the memory of them alive in the face of time, only if we actively choose them and accept them as definitive for our vision of ourselves—all this effort is one side of what it would mean to call them 'true'. But there is another side: that such a moment of vision first claims our attention before we 'decide' to remember it. It abides: we remember. That not all visions have such a capacity to abide is suggested by the common experience of memories that fade, often the very memories of what we most want to remember. Some 'unforgettable' memories are, of course, trivial in terms of their content, mere accidents that have stuck in our minds without context or point. But there are other memories which, from the beginning, are constituted by moments of experience in which vision has flowed back upon itself. This power of abiding, then, is not due simply to their aesthetic power but rather to the way in which they figure a personal claim, which we might aptly call the claim of love. A picture, of course, can only do this in the manner of representation: what it discloses is not that I feel bound to reciprocate the love of a picture but that, in its figurative way, it occasions my becoming conscious that 'I am not alone' in the world but bound in love. This is what abides in remembrance.

We shall shortly return to this personal dimension of vision, but first let us stay a while with the issue of its temporality. As both Heidegger's and Florensky's understanding of truth emphasize, then, the question about the truth of the look that meets us in, e.g. Rublev's icon, is a question about the temporality of the image, its power to *abide*. This could be understood in the sense that in remembering our visions we are responding to a quality of perdurance that belongs to the image itself, that the image has a kind of unchangingness, an intrinsic power to remain unmoved and unmoving qua image in the midst of time's stream, an 'eternal' work of art outlasting the relativities of culture. That might be one way of understanding the comments in the preceding paragraph— 'It abides: we remember.' But even if we are to ascribe abidingness to the image itself (apart from our appropriation of it), this need not mean that what we have seen is a kind of solid base undergirding the linguistic articulation of thought about God, as if vision were the unmoving substructure beneath the shifting superstructure of language. On the contrary, the very description of vision flowing back upon itself hinged on the inner mobility of such vision. Its power is not a power to stop time but to create folds and depths of meaning in what would otherwise be the uniform and featureless forward movement of time. Its constancy is not that of the fixed centre of a turning world or of a fragment of time that has to be kept intact through time's forward current but the constancy of that which accompanies us in time's onward movement, repeating in an ever-new time the refolding of time upon itself. Already in this inner mobility of the abiding vision, then, we have an analogy to the inner mobility of language that comes to expression in metaphor and dialogue. The appeal to vision is not the attempt to find some sort of bedrock on which language can come to rest. Vision too is in motion. This realization underlines the inescapability of equivocation by showing that the dynamism and mobility of language go 'all the way down' into the pre-linguistic phenomenalization of the world. Yet vision also reveals this situation as truthful and hopeful. For the truth that has been disclosed is not the truth of an event or fact but a truth about myself as being claimed by the Other in the most intimate moments of my self-consciousness, even, in a sense, before I am capable of self-consciousness (so that: in the moment I loved her I knew that I had always loved her, in the moment I learned to love God I learned that I had always been loved by God). In active remembrance I allow this claim, this vision, this truth to abide and so reveal that which, in time, is more than empty flux.

Active remembrance of this kind is expressed by one of the key words of the Christian understanding of the sacraments. As recorded both in the first three Gospels and in St Paul's first letter to the Corinthians, it was a word that Jesus spoke at a decisive moment in the Last Supper that He shared with His inner circle of disciples. Taking, blessing, and distributing bread and wine He asked them do this in remembrance, *anamnesis*, of His being among them. The words themselves are repeated every time Christian communities re-enact the ritual of the bread and wine in what is variously referred to as the Mass, the Eucharist, the sacred mysteries, the Holy Communion, or the Lord's Supper. As many non-believers and even many believers are likely to look at it, what is happening is that believers 'remember' Jesus's life, death, and resurrection in the sense of attempting to preserve a particular constellation of historical events, a particular historical person, from annihilation at the hand of all-devouring time. His is a memory that must be kept alive, they seem to be saying. But, at this level, it is hard to see how such remembrance could be qualitatively distinguished from what would happen if a group of enthusiasts gathered regularly to 'remember' their favoured historical figure, Henry VIII, let us say, or Captain Cook, or, perhaps, the collective memory of a learned society devoted to a Hegel, a Kierkegaard, or a Kant. Do not all such 'cults', whatever their level of sophistication, have their limited cultural shelf life? Isn't the collective remembrance of Jesus's life as limited as any other in this respect? And does it—can it—really help if we tag on to this particular act of remembrance a set of dogmatic claims as to who this Jesus really was (or even *is*)?

In the context of the argument that has been being developed here, however, the issue is not the memory of a historical personality but a view onto who we ourselves are. What is being remembered is not so much the historical memory of Jesus of Nazareth, AD 1–30, but the view of the human condition made possible by the light his look threw on it. Each act of remembrance is therefore an affirmation of the truth of the self-understanding and self-commitment that just this *look* makes possible. St Paul, famously, spoke of salvation as a light that both shines in the hearts of believers and is 'the knowledge of the glory of God in the face of Jesus Christ' (2 Cor. 4: 6) and, recalling the connection made by Tillich between seeing and creation, it is also interesting that Paul prefaces this verse with the remark that the God who sends this saving knowledge is the God 'who said "Out of darkness light shall shine" ' (2 Cor. 4: 6), thus pointing to a connection between the original work of God in world-creation and the saving work of God in redemption. In the development of liturgy in the Church of the first centuries further dimensions were added or given added emphasis. Already in Jewish prayer, the orientation towards creation and towards the past was complemented by an orientation towards the future and the hope for the coming of the Messiah. Although Christians claimed that the Messiah had, in fact, come in the person of Jesus, they also looked to a future second coming and the consummation of all things in God's kingdom. These future events were also part of what the congregation, here and now, held 'in remembrance'.[28] They too are to be seen as refracted through the eyes of this other.

---

[28] See especially G. Wainwright, *Eucharist and Eschatology* (London: Epworth Press, 1971).

These features of liturgical remembrance confirm that what is in play is something very different from the simple memory of a past event, no matter how important that event is deemed to be. The matter of remembrance is an understanding of human life and, crucially, one in which past, present, and future—time—are no longer envisaged as all-consuming Chronos, but as susceptible of being gathered, in remembrance, into an image of human being that finds its centre in the dynamic tension of thanksgiving and hope. To commit oneself to living with the remembrance of a vision that is not merely my vision of the world but a view of the self that *this* event, *this* face has made possible is to say that this view does not simply satisfy some short-term or private need. It is to affirm that it allows for, encompasses, and actively summons forth all that is truly important for my existence, that it illuminates and brings out from unconceal-ment, forgetfulness, and the effects of *Schlafsucht* (longing for sleep) a new and abiding image of the self that gives itself to be remembered if I gratefully and hopefully engage myself in the struggle to do so (if, that is, I choose to live in its truth). That remembrance is thus embedded in creation, redemption, and eschatology suggests that, as against Lévinas, it is a remembrance which is more about being set free to be than about being held hostage, although the acknowledgement of the need for redemption and of the requirement of judge-ment that this context also contains does set a limit to the mere assertion of the autonomous ego. In disclosing to me that my truth is found in the love borne me by another I am bound, in remembrance, to 'remain in the debt' of that love.

Yet it might seem that we are forgetting everything that was said about the necessary patience of thinking about God. If we are able so quickly to arrive at a vision that we then take as a truth to be upheld against all comers, what has happened to the patience that knows that it does not have God in its grasp and that it must wait on God to bestow whatever of God's truth it is capable of receiving? In what has been said about remembrance, haven't we fashioned a concept that, in spanning the beginning and the end of creation, makes patience redundant? In such remembrance aren't we already claiming to know the end of all things? I suggest not, and that the reason why not is that remembrance itself remains determined by the fact that it is practised *in* history, *in* time, and that it belongs to the very nature of the truth it seeks to maintain that this, *in time*, is what it is only in the struggle with time. The uniting of creation, historical past, and eschatological future that is spoken of in Christian worship's active remem-brance is not itself an act of union absolved from the characteristic tensions and demands of life in time. Its media are gratitude, expectation, and hope, not the assertion that 'this is so'. It too is joyfully, hopefully, stretched out in the burden of the 'not yet' and it too, joyfully, hopefully, must wait upon God. In its joy there is an element of 'despite' that is the trace of a despair from which we are being released (even if, in the moment of worship this 'despite' and this 'despair' is as if forgotten), in its hope a sign that the promised fulfilment is not yet consummated. Although we remember redemption as those who are no longer inhabitants of paradise but not yet incorporated into the Heavenly Jerusalem, and our gratitude is that of those who cannot presume upon any right or claim to the gifts of God, our remembrance is joy and it is worship.

Following Florensky, the focus of the last few pages has been on the relationship between truth and time, a relationship concentrated into the idea of remembrance. But, remembering that what we are considering here is, primarily, the formal characteristics of a thinking about God that would be otherwise than the thinking that finds expression in contemporary technology, it should be added that such thinking will have its place as well as its time. This connection between place and remembrance is already warranted, if only negatively, in the biblical witness: 'The days of man are but as grass, the wind blows over it and it is gone and its place will know it no more' (Ps. 103) or 'Here we have no abiding city'. Here too we might broach the whole thematic of land and promise.[29] The politics of the Middle East today have, inevitably, raised the most troubling of questions about this aspect of biblical theology. Yet if Heidegger is correct in seeing 'planetary homelessness' as one of the marks of the age of technology, may we not expect that a non-technological thinking may look to find a place as well as a memory that has the power of abidingness? Like the rhetoric of a 'Holy Land', Heidegger's own reflections on place, in their proximity to aspects of the Nazi ideology of *Blut und Boden* ('Blood and Earth'), also underline how troubling and, indeed, dangerous the rhetoric of place can be. Where, then, might we find a place to think about God that would not embroil us in one or other form of territorialism? For now, I only mark the question, but I shall offer a tentative answer in the postscript, 'City of the Homeless'.

We have spent some time in territory that seems to be the exclusive territory of those who can claim to be Christian believers. But whether or not we embrace the Christian sacraments as a revelation of the light of God in the face of Jesus Christ, the point here is not primarily to promote or defend the content of a particular example of active remembrance but simply to try to illustrate the phenomenon of active remembrance itself, a phenomenon that may have many parallels in other religious traditions or in the wider, non-religious culture. Whatever its more precise content, the kind of vision that stimulates active remembrance would be the kind of vision that might best give a direction to thinking about God—if we were to choose to travel the path of such thinking. Crucial in my account of this vision is that it is not so much a revelation of how things (God or the world) *are* but a way of continuing to affirm a sense of self subsequent to or in despite of the checking or interruption of an original will to self-affirmation. Such a moment of check was encountered in the exhaustion of the ardent heart in Herbert's 'A True Hymn', in Tillich's blinded vision, in the sudden and alarming awareness of being watched by the eyes of Rublev's icon of Christ the Saviour, in Mochizuki's

[29] See, e.g. W. Brueggemann, *The Land: Place as Gift, Promise and Challenge in Biblical Faith* (Philadelphia: Fortress Press, 1982).

realization of the meaning that another's memory had for his self-understanding. In each case the breach in self-continuity is matched by the gift of a new truth—in the first case by an abiding, written word, in the second by the sense of being seen by eyes of infinite love, in the third and fourth by an actual vision of what being seen in this way might mean in human terms. By urging the obligation of remembrance, the gift that comes from the far side of the breach bestows the time that the self requires in order to become what it is, and its truth is realized precisely by our faithfulness in maintaining this obligation in time. Even if I, as the individual I am, with an individual's need for a specific faith, might wish to claim that it is in the look of Christ that I find a true disclosure of the meaning of a love that is worthy and capable of being upheld in the face of time and relativity, this does not exclude my admitting that other visions, other views, other ways of configuring the sense of self, may not also have their own claim to truth. Such another view might be the disclosure of personal truth in the face of the Buddha or in the revelation of the Law on Sinai. The definition of truth as the reversing of time's voracious forgetfulness allows us to accept that, in time, it will always remain open to debate which view will prove itself to be true or even if, in the end of all things, differing views might not each turn out to have their truth. Truth is precisely what is at issue in the passage of time—not in the sense that history then becomes identical with the Last Judgement and that history's victors are ipso facto to be applauded as 'the righteous ones'. Rather, history is the judgement in the sense that it is only in and through the strife of historically embodied voices that judgement as to truth gets enacted and made into reality—but active remembrance is itself a dimension of this very strife: active remembrance itself decides what is, in time, to count as truth.

At this point we have to pause and ask whether we have really advanced one single step? Have we formulated any criteria that would enable us to know when our thinking had truly begun to be thinking about God and no longer the mere exposition of a certain kind of human self-understanding? If thinking needs to be guided by vision (and, once more, we recall that this is to speak metaphorically), do not our visions themselves need to be argued, justified, proven? Indeed, doesn't the course of this chapter confirm a suspicion that to speak of 'vision' is to speak precisely of what divides, excludes, and limits our freedom of thought? That in the absence of an all-encompassing shared vision, we end up insisting on the vision of one particular religious community over against others? Aren't our visions, precisely as the form in which we individually and collectively acquire a certain definite identity, what lock us into the corral of one or other prejudice? We are the people who have this vision, this promise, this dream, we say, and are proud of it. Even within Christianity itself isn't it the case that, as Blake put it with characteristic pungency, 'The vision of Christ that thou dost see, Is my vision's greatest enemy'? If thinking needs vision, doesn't vision need thought to test, probe, correct, and open it up to common inspection? And doesn't thought require language, in such a way that vision now needs to be folded back into the flow of language? Of course, and nothing else has been claimed. Vision must submit to the discipline of dialogue, to acknowledge that what it shows is only a possibility, something that can never quite be put into words and that can therefore never finally be used as an argument for our choosing one set of words over against another. But, to reformulate a familiar Kantian slogan, if vision without thinking is finally the matter of mere assertion, thinking without vision is empty. Vision does not guide thinking by bringing it to a halt but by opening its depths and offering it a point of entry into the embodied world. Or, to put it another way, it marks the point at which our experience of the embodied world calls for thinking. We may think of this literally in terms of what the eye sees or in terms of the vision that can indwell language itself when language is not reduced to the multiplication of 'complicatory' words but becomes the form in which we think about things that are real, the naming of the miracle of love that reverses the 'always already' fading light of what most of us experience as our too short day under the sun. As such, thinking about God is unassimilable to any project or managed system.[30] Always at the perimeter of knowledge, it claims us in a way that knowledge never can and this claim is the lure to go on thinking about God, even in an age of technology. Whether it is God we come to think about, however, or the thoughtful deepening of a purely human lesson in love is a question that thinking itself cannot finally hope to resolve. But this is not a sufficient reason simply to abandon any effort to think about God, since the humanist no less than the religionist cannot avoid the possibility of absurdity in staking all the passion and faithfulness of thinking on a vision that, precisely because it is what calls for and gives direction to thinking, will never be reducible to what thinking itself can guarantee.

[30] Others will disagree. Philip Clayton, for example, openly embraces the view that an ongoing research programme has the potential to advance the metaphysical resolution of the question of God. See P. Clayton, *The Problem of God in Modern Thought* (Grand Rapids: Eerdmans, 2000), 43.

PART III

CONTEXTS

7

From Thinking about God to Acting in the World

I

If we have been able to take some few, hesitant steps towards thinking about God in a manner that would be resistant to absorption by technological enframing, and if we have discovered as a part of this that it involves us 'remaining in the debt of love' to the other who is closer to us than we are to ourselves, we may still be left with the question as to how any of this might bear upon the actuality of humanity's contemporary efforts to deal with the very real and very urgent exigencies of living with technology. A scattering of thinkers may choose to let their thoughts dwell, subjunctively, joyously, gratefully, and dialogically on the thought of God and may do so to such an extent that they come to see such thoughts as the *most important thing of all*—but how does this help them and others confront the actual complexities of evaluating new technologies and deciding what to do about them? Heidegger, after all, did speak about fundamental thinking as preparing the way for some kind of decision concerning planetary technology, but both his own quasi-poetic 'piety of thinking' and the thinking about God we have been exploring seem to be so far removed from the hard places where bold decisions and painful compromises have to be worked out and put into effect as to render them practically useless. Seen from the point of view of 'managerial action' (Ellul) it is all just daydreaming, castles in the air, and—despite what I have claimed—essentially of a kind with fantasy fiction. All very enjoyable for the individual concerned, no doubt, but irrelevant to the rest of the world.

Of course, there is a certain kind of practical person who would direct a similar charge against virtually any theology or ethics, even if it came with much more flesh-and-blood than the mere outline that has been offered here. Such a one would say that anything that stands in the way of or distracts us from the forward rush of innovation and success is to be brushed aside. But when they are not the expression of mere thoughtlessness of this kind, the demands of 'real life' merit at least some attention. However, I should emphasize (again) that my experiment in thinking about God was not offered as an immediately practical solution to the concrete problems of technology. It is simply impossible to suppose that the kind of meditation I have been developing could lead either to the 'solution' of some particular technical problem or to a revised view of technology as a whole, or provide an 'answer' to the question concerning technology. How then does it relate to the demanding conditions of life in the technological world?

Tillich liked to speak of his theological method as a 'method of correlation'. This meant that the theologian takes the best and deepest formulations of the questions posed by contemporary society and shows how the Christian doctrines can be correlated with them so as to 'answer' them. It might seem as if something like this is what is being attempted here. After setting the stage with a survey of secular theologies, we looked at a number of interpretations of the technological world that rendered the assumptions and goals of that world highly questionable. Then, I attempted a sketch of a kind of thinking about God that might constitute a counter-movement to these assumptions and goals. Is it now a question of 'correlating' our theological perspective to the reality of the technological world so that we can give a Christian 'answer' to the question concerning technology? By no means. The thinking about God with which we have been experimenting neither claims nor aims to be the demonstration or construction of a position from which practical directives could be deduced, nor even to be a kind of contemplative wisdom that would unerringly give direction and purpose to practical wisdom in its struggles with life-as-lived. It does not advertise itself as being 'higher' than technology nor as having 'overcome' technology nor as setting parameters or directives for technology. All it seeks in its own terms is to make clear that it understands itself to be something very different from the kind of thinking appropriate to the thinking involved in technology itself and in the management of technology. There it can agree with the practical man that it doesn't really help him, because it doesn't intend to *or not in that way.*

I have, admittedly, spoken at several points of thinking about God and, implicitly, of all essential thinking as in some sense instantiating a counter-movement to technology. However, this counter-movement by no means presumes to determine where technology should, so to speak, begin or end. Are we then left with some kind of dualistic antithesis, with science and technology on the one side and thinking about God on the other, two opposing currents that never meet? Of course, if (following Heidegger and Ellul) we say that the problem with technology is precisely its tendency to swallow up all competing discourses and to make itself the sole arbiter of what is to count as true and worthwhile in the public domain, then the assertion that there *is* an alternative is at the very least a check to technolog*ism*. It is to say that there are human aspirations, values and possibilities that lie outside the scope of the technologist's world view and that these aspirations therefore need to be taken into account in any definitive assessment of what it is that makes us human. Thinking about God may, in this scenario, be one way of holding open a more diversified view of the world than technologism would offer us, if it were left to itself. This holding-open need not be understood as hostile to either science or technology. It does not need much imagination to conjecture that a one-sided and exclusive pursuit of technological goals and the exclusive cultivation of technological values may lead to technological disaster or to the downgrading of humanity to the status of a mere adjunct to technology. The realization in the late 1960s that there were limits to growth, followed by a string of disasters and near-disasters (Bhopal, Three-Mile Island, Chernobyl) and the prospect opened up by genetic engineering of a 'post-human future' has suggested even to friends of science and technology that these are not activities that should be left alone to run the world. Of course, it can be argued that many of these disasters—Chernobyl, for example—were the result of faulty technology or of the bad management of technology and that it has been science itself that alerted us to many of the dangers of current technology, such as the damage to the ozone layer. That is entirely correct, and I indicated in the Introduction that the world we are in now is one in which we could not suddenly be without technology even if we wanted to be. Precisely because of the high level of our current technologization we need to understand, to develop, and to manage technology in its own terms to the highest possible technical standards. I am not saying that 'thinking about God' could do the kind of job that was done by the scientists who discovered the hole in the ozone layer or who are developing models for predicting the transgenerational effects of genetic intervention in plants or animals. All I am saying for now is that a mental culture in which a maximum degree of diversification flourishes is more likely than a conformist monoculture to be productive of independent and critical-minded scientific interventions, not to mention it being a culture that is humanly richer and therefore contributing more to a life worth living. I shall return to further aspects of this question later in this chapter as well as in connection with the role of thinking about God in the life of the contemporary university,[1] and for now merely flag the point that if thinking about God seems to be placing itself on the side of the opposition, this can perfectly well be construed as a 'loyal opposition', that is, an opposition that does not merely oppose for the sake of opposing but for the sake of the balance of the whole, in order that what is opposed is driven to refine and redefine itself and thus come to do its job better in its own terms.

But isn't this still a little too dualistic? If, after all, the same human subject can both be active in the world of technology and in thinking about God, mustn't there be a point where the two meet? Mustn't there be an area of encounter or overlap and therefore of interaction? Doesn't the picture we have presented of two mutually balancing extremes leave a gaping hole in the middle? Yet isn't this middle precisely where most of us *are* most of the time in life as it is lived? Where are the concrete forms in which thinking about God might influence or be

---

[1] See Chapter 9 below.

related to our actual lives as makers, maintainers, and users of the technological system?

There are good reasons for being cautious at this point. If there is a certain anxiety about contaminating the purity of thinking by too close a contact with the realities of the world, there is a no lesser fear from the side of science and technology that some kind of unmediated religious fundamentalism might attempt to impose itself on the domains of research, development, and application in which its lack of competence is matched only by the inflexibility of its utterances. If the concerns about technology of the person who finds his or her joy in thinking about God are to mesh with the reality of a technologized world, then surely there has to be something more to thinking about God than has yet been said, or else we must avail ourselves of other possibilities of thinking that can relate both to thinking about God and to the world of technology. There must, after all, be a kind of correlation, although it is not a correlation constructed in order that the theologian can communicate his answer to the question posed by the world. It is instead a correlation of questions, practices, procedures, and ways. As such it is not so much a matter of directly correlating the *content* of thinking about God with the truths or realities of science and technology, but of identifying and interpreting those milieus in which the two sides find themselves sharing a common space and common concerns. In this and the following chapters I shall focus on three such places. The first is the complex of issues that have arisen as a result of the impact of technology on traditional topics of ethics (most sensationally but by no means solely in bioethics), the second is the life of the contemporary university, and the third the field of art and culture.

I note that these could be seen as contemporary versions of the great idealist trinity of the good, the true, and the beautiful. Of course, we no longer think in these idealistic terms: much modern ethics makes no particular appeal to any sort of objective or ultimate 'good', much modern art has little direct concern for beauty and may, indeed, reject it outright, whilst the question as to the true is precisely what is at issue between those who find truth in thinking about God and those who find it in whatever makes for technical efficiency. Yet such configurations of ideas as that of the good, the true, and the beautiful have not held so influential a position in the history of thought accidentally but because of their innate power to articulate fundamental structures of spiritual life (taking the world 'spiritual' here in its Germanic sense of embracing all the great forms of the life of the mind). However, in drawing attention to this parallel, I do not place any greater weight on it than to let it serve as a mild caution against imagining our contemporary situation to be totally without precedent. In the following chapters, then, we shall see how thinking about God and the world of science and technology meet, conflict, and co-exist in a variety of ways in these three areas. My method will be exemplary rather than descriptive, i.e. I shall attempt to take particular questions and examples which, I believe, bring the key issues into focus. Finally, I shall return to a larger canvas and pick up the interwoven threads of the city and planetary homelessness as the larger context within which these three domains belong.

II

It is widely acknowledged that one of the effects of technological innovation has been to provoke a new interest in ethics.[2] Some have noted that the present phase of technological development has in fact given ethics, arguably a rather moribund philosophical discipline in the mid-twentieth century, a new *raison d'être*. Certainly, the unsettling nature and speed of some areas of technological innovation have led to both governments and corporations investing heavily in setting up 'ethics committees' or promoting ethics symposia. It is becoming almost routine for any major public or private body to institutionalize some form of reflection on its 'values' as an integral part of its self-definition. Yet if technology has breathed fresh life into ethics it has posed a challenge to dominant ethical systems that goes far beyond providing ethical reflection with a succession of new topics or problems. Some might argue that technology simply changes the basic rules of ethical reflection. A generation ago Hans Jonas argued that the tradition of ethics derived from the classical world had never previously been confronted with the need to make nature and our responsibility for nature the matter of ethical thinking. For the Greeks, as in the great chorus on the greatness and finitude of humanity in Sophocles' *Antigone*: 'man's inroads into nature . . . were essentially superficial, and powerless to upset its appointed balance.'[3] Right through to the twentieth century the corresponding assumption that nature lay outside the area of ethical concern and that ethics was, therefore, properly and strictly anthropocentric has been one of the most pervasive and unchallenged of all our (Western) assumptions. This limitation was reflected in and reinforced by the no less general assumption that ethics and morality had what Jonas calls a 'proximate range of action',[4] i.e. that when I act morally I can readily envisage the likely or possible outcomes of my action and spontaneously include the implications of these outcomes for myself in any moral calculation I make. What technology has done is to revolutionize these assumptions by putting us in a

[2] In what follows I do not attempt to maintain any firm technical distinction between 'ethics' and 'morality' or 'the ethical' and 'the moral'. Attempts both to establish some kind of consistent usage in English have repeatedly floundered on the fact of the variety of actual usage. When we then attempt to maintain some kind of correlation with the leading European languages the situation becomes hopeless. Bearing in mind the classical distinction between the German *Sitte*, the ethos of the tribe, and *Moralität*, the individual's free judgement concerning what is right, and noting that not only have 'ethics' and 'the ethical' been used to cover both but so have 'morals' and 'morality', I nevertheless think that English usage is flexible enough and contextual enough usually to make clear what is being meant.

[3] H. Jonas, *Philosophical Essays: From Ancient Creed to Technological Man* (Chicago: University of Chicago Press, 1974), 5.

[4] Ibid. 7.

situation in which our action towards and responsibility for each other is indissociable from our action towards and our responsibility towards nature whilst at the same time almost unimaginably extending the time-lag between action and its outcomes. We can no longer pretend to have more than the roughest of guesses as to the long-term implications for humanity or for its environment of many technological actions, although (in many cases) we can be sure that we ourselves as agents (and perhaps even our grandchildren) won't be around to reap whatever we have sown. The phenomenon of technology, then, requires and provokes a whole new agenda for ethical thinking—and ethics has responded to the challenge with massively renewed energies.

The area where this sudden boom in ethics is most apparent is 'bioethics', which, however defined, is a striking by-product of the new biology and its potential to transform humanity in hitherto unimaginable ways. What the rise of bioethics means in practical terms for the social or political 'management' of technology remains open. Some commentators, like Francis Fukuyama, tend to see the sociology of bioethics as pointing to the institutional 'capture' of ethics itself by technology (and thus, we might say, yet one more example of technology's constant expansion of its pervasive monoculture). As Fukuyama remarks 'In any discussion of cloning, stem-cell research, germ-line engineering, and the like, it is usually the professional bioethicist who can be relied on to take the most permissive position of anyone in the room.' Fukuyama comments, perhaps somewhat cynically, that

This happens for many reasons, including the dependence of the regulators on the regulated for money and information. In addition, there are the career incentives that most professional bioethicists face. Scientists do not usually have to worry about winning the respect of ethicists, particularly if they are Nobel Prize winners in molecular biology or physiology. On the other hand, ethicists face an uphill struggle winning the respect of the scientists they must deal with, and are hardly likely to do so if they tell them they are morally wrong or if they depart significantly from the materialist worldview that the scientists hold dear.[5]

Whilst acknowledging that the kinds of factors adduced by Fukuyama probably have a real effect on the overall disposition of the debate, it would be over-cynical to say that this is the only way in which ethics functions in relation to technology. In many contexts, and in many of its representatives, the ethical debate reveals genuine criticism of technology, as well as genuine respect for and appreciation of technology's achievements and possibilities.

In attempting to relate contemporary ethical thinking to the venture of thinking about God, on the one hand, and the question concerning technology on the other, I shall focus in this chapter on Jürgen Habermas. I choose Habermas rather than an ethical theorist more exclusively concerned with scientific or technical issues (such as a representative of the new bioethics) for a

---

[5] F. Fukuyama, *Our Posthuman Future* (London: Profile Books, 2002), 204.

number of reasons. The first is that although Habermas is highly critical of what he sees as Heidegger's negative position vis-à-vis modernity and of the political judgements likely to flow from such a negative position (sometimes expressing his objections with quite extreme sarcasm), his own intellectual horizons share enough common ground with Heidegger's to make him an appropriate partner-in-dialogue for extending an enquiry that has taken a decisive orientation from Heidegger.[6] Not the least important element in Habermas's proximity to Heidegger is a certain reserve towards science and technology.

Although, *contra* Heidegger, Habermas basically sees the story of technical progress as a story of human liberation, he does not go along with those forms of Marxism that identify technical progress with progress as such and that deplore only its distortion at the hands of, for example, the capitalistic system of deploying technology in production and distribution. Once capitalism has been consigned to the dustbins of history (or so this kind of Marxism taught), technology will be free to do its work in eliminating 'the idiocy of rural life' and the opiate illusions of religion. Habermas's view, however, is more nuanced. From the 1950s onwards Habermas linked himself to critical theorists such as Horkheimer, Adorno, and Marcuse (the latter especially influenced by Heidegger at an early point in his development) in resisting the excessive dominance of instrumental reason over the aspiration to inaugurate a social order in which both freedom but also justice played a decisive role. Instrumental reason, it should be emphasized, is not immediately the same as the reason underpinning science and technology. It exists already in pre-scientific and pre-modern societies in the ensemble of practices by which human beings secure their physical survival and social cohesion. Even within the modern situation it is not science and technology as such that are the problem but more a kind of ideology of science and technology that, on the basis of their effectiveness in securing the material basis of human existence grounds, endows technocratic thinking with authority over the definition and determination of all possible human experiences and practices. In contrast to some of the other critical theorists, however (and explicitly in contrast to Marcuse), Habermas refuses to see the complex of science and technology itself as in some sense culpable for, e.g. the destructive workings of the military-industrial complex and of capitalist economics on twentieth-century Europe and across the world. Habermas argues that if science and technology have now become linked in such a way that it is increasingly difficult to separate pure scientific research from technical applications (with the result that pure science is pursued only in the context of what serves the interest of governments or corporations), this conjunction is only a relatively recent historical fact. Up until the late nineteenth century, science still preserved something of its

---

[6] A particularly vocal case for seeing Habermas's problematic in continuity with that of Heidegger—and not least as regards the question concerning technology—is to be found, if overstated, in J. Keulartz, *Die Verkehrte Welt des Jürgen Habermas*, tr. I. van der Art (Hamburg: Junius, 1995).

'philosophical' character, i.e. the pursuit of a knowledge of 'how things are' that was not immediately dictated by the demands of instrumental reason.[7] Neither is technology itself to be regarded as the perversion of pure science since it is what it is as essentially as an extension of the human body and of a relation to the world that is limited by the natural parameters of the body. In words from 1969 that will be prophetic of some of the concerns about technology that have recently engaged him, Habermas wrote 'it is impossible to see how we can renounce technology, i.e. the technology *we now have* so long as the organisation of human nature does not alter...'[8]

If Habermas thus takes up a critical position in relation to some of his fellow critical theorists, there are, of course, important differences from Heidegger. Not the least of these is that not only does Heidegger (like Marcuse) see technology as such as inherently likely to endanger human fulfilment, but he also focuses exclusively on thinking and poetry as a way out of the darkness of a technicized world. In contrast to this Habermas looks to the kind of ethics that he calls communicative action as the counter-pole to one-dimensional instrumentality. But it is just this that points to a second reason for turning to Habermas at this point: that his thought is permeated by a concern for the ethical. Moreover, even if he does not speak for any clear consensus (since, in any case, there probably is none), he does give expression to a widespread and deeply held view as to how ethical discourse might serve to humanize the technical possibilities of the present age.[9]

Thirdly, although Habermas by no means regards himself as a religious thinker, his view of the ethical raises important questions for the relationship between thinking about God and ethical life, not least in relation to the question concerning technology. Although I shall not venture to judge whether one can speak of a hidden or latent theology in Habermas,[10] I shall suggest that his

---

[7] J. Habermas, *Technik und Wissenschaft als 'Ideologie'* (Frankfurt am Main: Suhrkamp, 1969), 72 ff

[8] Ibid. 56–7.

[9] This, incidentally, also invites the reanimation of the political as a counter to the purely technological and managerial ordering of society. However, the assumptions of such a politics are, I suggest, very far from the kind of heteronomy implicit in, e.g. Heidegger's embrace of the will of the Führer as something capable of giving direction to social institutions such as the university. A Habermasian politics will have thoroughly internalized the modern institutional requirement of autonomy and rationality. That is to say, it will not be the assertion of the power of the polis *over* technology, but the debate within the polis as to the scope and limits of technology—a debate in which the managers of technology must also have a voice.

[10] The Danish theologian Jens Glebe-Møller has argued that Habermas is an essentially 'Protestant' philosopher in that his emphasis on the transformation of the sacred into language mirrors Protestantism's emphasis on the word (as opposed to Catholic sacramentality) and that his idea of a perfectly consensual society without distorting power relations corresponds to the Protestant idea of the priesthood of all believers. Moreover, he argues, Habermas leaves open a sphere for religious activity in the 'pastoral' provision of comfort and hope in the face of ultimate issues in life (such as the individual's confrontation with death) that will never be adequately dealt with on the basis of mere reason. Glebe-Møller also notes Habermas's own testimony, in an interview from the 1980s, that behind his philosophy lies an intuition that is found also in Protestant and Jewish mysticism. See J. Glebe-Møller, *Jürgen Habermas: En Protestantisk Filosof* (Copenhagen: Gyldendal, 1996).

thought, defined by a parabola encompassing both the unquantifiable infinity of Kantian freedom and the publicness of rational discourse, might offer a model for mediating between thinking about God and the world of contemporary technology. On the other hand, I shall also suggest that this 'mediation' is itself highly problematic: from the side of an ideology of science and technology, for example, it might seem to invoke almost as many unjustifiable postulates as religious thinking itself.

I shall not argue that an ethical response to technology (such as that of Habermas) 'needs' a religious basis. It is not a question of constructing some kind of hierarchy running from the religious through the ethical to the hard-nosed practicalities of managing the golem, as would be the case if we were to return (for example) to Maritain's model of the degrees of wisdom descending from the religious/contemplative through practical wisdom to mechanical func-tionality. Rather it is a question of marking affinities or, to use an image often invoked by Heidegger, to map a kind of fugal articulation in which the parts, though ceaselessly interactive, are irreducible. What Habermas is pre-eminently able to do, then, is to help us to identify such affinities and to see how the freedom that belongs both to thinking about God and to ethical thinking might be brought into relation to the concrete tasks of technological decisions.

Even a cursory glance at Habermas's thought shows that it is exceptionally capacious in its references and applications, and I cannot pretend here to do more than to focus on one or two elements that are especially pertinent to the present discussion. As noted, a key factor, taken over via critical theory from Max Weber, is the concern for the aporia of rationalization: that when the Enlightenment consciously adopted a strategy of rationalization it did so as part of a programme of liberating human beings from servitude both to the inhumanity of nature (bad harvests, disease, premature death) and from the mystificatory forces of social authority (crown, church, and, later, capital); however, this process of rational-ization leads to a bureaucratization and standardization of life such that the fulfilment postulated as a goal by the early Enlightenment is itself undermined, and the individual comes to enjoy a freedom that is merely that of the consumer of standardized goods and services of the citizen of a bureaucratized state. This may be a freer and more rational world than that inhabited by the medievals— but it is a 'desacralized' and 'disenchanted' world, a world without love, pity, meaning, or magic. In the words of Matthew Arnold's poem 'On Dover Beach' (a poem often quoted by British philosophers of religion), a world 'which seems/To lie before us like a land of dreams,/So various, so beautiful, so new' but that 'Hath really neither joy, nor love, nor light,/Nor certitude, nor peace, nor help for pain.' Failure to recognize the importance of this sense of disenchantment as a problem for theories that placed too great a confidence in the process of rationalization as the main or even sole bearer of all-round human progress led Marxism into a number of problems. To use the expression put into circulation by George Lukacs, reification was the inevitable concomitant of rationalization in the context of advanced industrial society. Liberated from the impersonal realm of nature, modern humanity found itself sold back again into a kind of enslavement to the new, man-made impersonal realm of reified social relations. In the Soviet Union the contradiction at the heart of this dilemma is crystallized in the title of Andrzej Walicki's study *Marxism and the Leap into the Kingdom of Freedom: The Rise and Fall of the Communist Utopia*.[11] In other words, one more five-year plan, one more hurdle of technical progress to overcome—and then the apparatus of State and terror will fall away and we will all leap into the 'Kingdom of Freedom'. Only—of course—the moment of transition was constantly deferred, as technical and economic progress never seemed to reach the point at which the great leap could occur (something a Kierkegaard or a Dostoevsky could have predicted in advance of the 'great experiment').

Habermas's way out of this quandary is to distinguish between different forms and levels of rationalization and communication. There is one form of rationality that belongs to the practice of science and technology and, for example, to pure economics. The other is the no less rationalized discourse of modern ethics. To these Habermas adds a third: the human need for self-expression. These forms of rationality have their correspondingly different forms of communication: firstly, there is what Habermas calls 'constative' speech-acts, that is, speech-acts directed towards truth, cognition, and correctness; secondly, there are expressive or dramaturgic speech-acts, i.e. those acts in which the person gives expression to how they feel in a given situation and that are governed not so much by the imperatives of objective truth but by those of truthfulness ('this is how I really feel, even if it is absurd'); thirdly, there are regulative speech-acts aimed at the rightness of what is under discussion, asking the question '*should* it be done?' and seeking to establish some kind of normative evaluation of the matter at issue. Importantly, however, society as we know it does not present these various forms of rationality and communication in their pure forms. So, for example, the kind of rationality that is rooted in scientific research is not limited to the laboratory. It may also be applied in the context of social relations and used in the service of the 'strategic' goals of social planners, who, indeed, see society's problems merely as technical problems to be managed or solved. A very different approach would be one that was directed towards acting only on the basis of a shared, consensual understanding that embraces not only what we take to be the case or technically possible but also how those affected feel about it and whether they think that it is right that it be done. Thus, in the context of a debate that has recently come to be of great concern to Habermas, namely, the implications of genetic technology, the first form of rationality asks only whether the science underpinning the technology is correct and whether the technology is doable. At the second level different individuals will express their personal enthusiasm or alarm at the

---

[11] A. Walicki, *Marxism and the Leap into the Kingdom of Freedom: The Rise and Fall of the Communist Utopia* (Stanford: Stanford University Press, 1995).

prospect of such 'brave new worlds' and write their utopian or dystopian novels in the light of these personal feelings. These feelings, however, are not enough to decide whether permission should in fact be given by legislative or judicial bodies for the development of such technologies, either in general or in respect of any particular case. This can only occur if we are able to discuss the relevant criteria of normativity in a fully rational way. In practice, however, powerful institutions (multinational companies and governments, for example) proceed on the basis of strategies that presuppose particular answers to such ethical, political, and legal questions.[12]

It is characteristic for the current phase of social development that the first form of rationality has come to dominate the landscape of human discourse. For the most part aided and abetted by the philosophy of science in the West (and by the official ideology of the old Eastern Bloc), this way of approaching problems has come to set the standard for all other forms of discourse. If Ayer's version of logical positivism went to an extreme in simply dismissing as meaningless any propositions that failed to answer to the requirements of verifiability or falsifiability, it is Habermas's conviction that the actual dominance of science-based industry in modern society has given the speech-acts most characteristic of science and technology a de facto hegemony over the other forms. Yet these survive. Even within Marxist theory, in which any attempt to establish an autonomous moral discourse was slapped down as 'bourgeois', revisionists such as Marcuse and Adorno could in their different ways look to art and to the expressive function of language as a way of preserving aspects of the human and which, they believed, could not or should not be reduced to the mere functionality of serving industry, the state or the economy, i.e. 'being useful'. Art was especially well suited to this function within the horizons of secular thought because it neither invoked the transcendent claims of religion (except perhaps in a purely rhetorical way) nor the trans-historical claims of morality. For Habermas, however, it is primarily through the communicative action of a rational discourse about norms—a discourse he has articulated in increasingly Kantian terms—that humanity is going to be best able to defend itself against reification, dehumanization, and becoming a mere cog in the machine of technology (even if this no longer means functioning as a drone in some 'paleotechnic' factory but 'freely' availing oneself of the market choices of electronic communication and genetic self-improvement).

What, in Habermas's perspective, is the role of religion in this? Aware that his closest predecessors in critical theory retained a curiously ambiguous sense for the pathos of religious messianism and even a kind of belief in God that co-existed with the denial of God's existence (not so very far, it would seem, from some

---

[12] For the most succinct summary of his position concerning the differing kinds of speech-acts see J. Habermas, 'Erste Zwischenbetrachtung', in *Theorie des kommunikativen Handelns* (Frankfurt am Main: Suhrkamp, 1981), 367 ff.

forms of negative theology or the radical Kantianism of Don Cupitt's non-realist theology),[13] Habermas has consistently sought to downplay any idea of a 'hidden theology' in his own work.[14] In the perspective of *A Theory of Communicative Action*, religion is more or less identified with a mythical stage of social development, in which the different forms of communicative action are essentially confused. 'We do this,' the religious person says, 'because it is right, and it is right because it is in accordance with the way God made the world in the beginning, and because the joy of the liturgical promulgation of the doctrine and the misery of disobedience show that this is indeed God's way'. Thus, even if Habermas's own views concerning genetic engineering coincide on some points with the teaching of the Catholic Church, he would see this coincidence as deriving from very different assumptions. Whatever the reasons for being opposed to any particular technical application, they cannot include appealing to some supposed pre-human law of nature or of God. This would, once more, be to fail to establish any common discourse about what is right on a proper rational basis, where different alternatives can be weighed and evaluated in accordance with criteria that are equally available to all members of the ethical community. A culture can only discipline itself in such rational normative discourse if it is willing to accept the differentiation of the differing spheres or forms of communicative action, if it allows the criticism of its own premises, and if it allows for the institutionalization of learning processes directed towards the differentiation of cognitive and value-oriented elements.[15] But this is just what religious institutions and traditions—according to Habermas—*cannot* do. If the religions are to contribute to the moral discourse of modern society they can only do so by submitting their claims (e.g. about the sacredness of the individual foetus) to the 'common sense' of a public debate in which no one side has any special privileges over against any of the others. At the most, it seems, the appeal to God as the only being endowed with the right to create life might have a powerful symbolic effect (and thus be understood, perhaps, as a kind of dramaturgic expression of how a believer *feels* in the face of genetic engineering) but it cannot of itself decide the rights or wrongs of the case.[16]

---

[13] See J. Habermas, *Glauben und Wissen* (Frankfurt am Main: Suhrkamp, 2001), esp. 27–8.
[14] See n. 10 above.
[15] See ch. 5 and 6 of *Theorie des kommunikativen Handelns*.
[16] This plainly invites the response from the side of a theology that values the sacred that the sacred cannot in fact be transmuted into language without remainder as Habermas seems to imply, that there is an ambivalence in the sacred that resists rationalization and a corresponding residue of subjectivity that cannot be absorbed entirely into inter-subjectivity (i.e. social 'common sense' reason). Both these elements can, for example, be seen in Kierkegaard. See H. C. Wind, *Religion og Kommunikation: Teologisk hermeneutik* (Århus: Århus University Press, 1987). On the other hand, one could argue (with Tillich—cf. his idea of 'the Protestant principle') that Protestantism offers an example of a Church that has fully internalized the principle of self-criticism. One might also imagine a more 'Catholic' notion of tradition that, rather than being a straitjacket for thought, provides a community of remembered experiences that nurture and support individual ethical development rather than restraining it in the name of some primal or archaic power.

Habermas finds in Kierkegaard a limit case with regards to the possibilities of a religiously based ethics. Why is this? As he understands Kierkegaard, the latter construes the ethical task of the individual as being the appropriation of a character and destiny bestowed upon him by another, or, rather, an Other. In the language of *The Sickness unto Death* the self only becomes a self by choosing itself as the particular configuration of relationships that it uniquely is and, in doing so (and as a condition of doing so) becoming transparent to itself in 'the power that grounds it', i.e. God. Human existence, in other words, is not a matter of arbitrary self-invention. Life is given to us with a certain determinate shape, with such-and-such possibilities, and such-and-such responsibilities; *and*, according to Kierkegaard, it is so given to us not merely as human beings, as participants in the characteristics, possibilities, and responsibilities of the species (such was explicitly the case for Feuerbach's materialistic humanism) but as the particular individual that each of us is individually created and called to be. This view is *ethical* in the sense that I cannot be the person I am simply by virtue of my natural, familial, or social endowments. I am given my life, but I have to make it my own through free acceptance and the free assumption of the responsibilities that come with it. I am thus free and responsible for being what or, better, who I am, albeit under God, before God and to God, the ground and giver of the whole. To attempt to invent ourselves, without reference to the original donation of being by virtue of which we are what we are (or, at least, have the possibility of becoming whatever we might become), is to embark upon a path that leads to despair, whether we are motivated by anxiety at the prospect of assuming such a responsibility or by the defiance that simply wants its own will at all cost (which, however, may—if Michael Theunissen is correct—simply be two sides of the same coin[17]). Habermas accepts the outline of this Kierkegaardian plan, but rejects a key element of it: that the dependence we owe is first and foremost a dependence on God. It is right, he says, that we recognize limits to our autonomy and that these limits are not merely to be identified with the limits imposed by nature but have a personal character. However, the 'Other' who is our limit and term, in relation to whom alone we are able to become who we are, is not God but the linguistically formed symbolic universe of social being.

We are already met by a power that transcends us in the forms of communication in which we reach an understanding with one another concerning some occurrence in the world or concerning ourselves. Language is nobody's private property. Nobody possesses exclusive rights over the common medium of understanding that we intersubjectively share ... [Speakers and listeners] are only free thanks to the binding power of the claims they make on one another, claims that come with the obligation to give grounds [i.e.

---

[17] See M. Theunissen, *Der Begriff Verzweifelung: Korrekturen an Kierkegaard* (Frankfurt am Main: Suhrkamp, 1993).

reasons]. An intersubjective power is embodied in the logos of language which precedes the subjectivity of the speaker and is its basis.[18]

At this point, however, the prospect of genetic engineering intervenes by offering a completely new way of configuring this basic human interdependence. For Habermas, it seems, it is a basic condition of our being able to participate in an ethical community, i.e. to regard one another as free individuals with equal rights to contribute to any possible moral debate, that the 'givenness' of our lives is something we all, equally, share. It is a basic presupposition of being able to talk about 'the human condition' at all, a sense that at the deepest level we are all in the same boat. But what happens with genetic engineering? According to Habermas this puts into effect an 'irreversible' disruption of the basic reciprocity within which alone moral discourse is possible. That we owe what we are to God, or to nature, or to the happenstance of being born into this particular linguistic community at just this stage of history—these, though coloured by individual differences, all constitute a deep commonality. Each of us represents a particular variation on the general theme, but we are all, equally, marked by the same burden of contingent givenness, what Heidegger called 'thrownness' and Sartre 'facticity'. But this bedrock of commonality cannot survive the transformation introduced when this facticity itself becomes the matter of human choice. That I choose blue eyes, or delete the gay gene, or enhance intelligence on behalf of my offspring (or, for that matter, somebody else's offspring), makes me the agent of another's destiny in a way that has never happened before (Habermas says). The new person 'produced' in this way is no longer 'thrown' but planned and can no longer experience the contingencies of their existence as simple facticity but as a programme to be followed. I cannot therefore make such a choice without reducing the other (the person to be produced) to the status of a means to my ends, i.e. treating him without regard to his freedom. His very existence as the particular person he is comes to depend on a kind of violation of freedom that is without precedent in history. He no longer participates in the same way as he did previously in the common lot, since his very biological existence is itself the product of another's freedom.

One may argue as to whether or how far Habermas is correct in discerning some sort of radical novelty in the situation we are now entering. Proponents of critical theory are, of course, well known for being contemptuous of anecdotal references to farmers,[19] but is the kind of predetermination of a child's inherited capacities aimed at by genetic engineering really all that different from what old-fashioned farming families still look for in weighing up the merits of this or that candidate for marriage to the heir to the estate? Clearly there is an enormous

---

[18] J. Habermas, *Die Zukunft der Menschlichen Natur* (Frankfurt am Main: Suhrkamp, 2001), 25–6.

[19] See Adorno's comments on Heidegger's chats with farmers in T. W. Adorno, *The Jargon of Authenticity*, tr. K. Tarnowski and F. Will (London: Routledge and Kegan Paul, 1986), 55–6.

difference in terms of precision, but is the principle all that different? Onora O'Neill, for example, limits herself to speak of 'ambiguous' and 'confused' family relations rather than of an irreversible disruption.[20] From another angle N. Katharine Hayles suggests that although the idea of a subject possessed of 'an agency, desire, or will belonging to the self and clearly distinguished from the "wills of others" is undercut in the posthuman' and thus far agrees with Habermas regarding a certain loss of possible moral autonomy, she goes on to state that 'even a biologically unaltered *homo sapiens* counts as posthuman' in the accumulative perspectives of a liberal market society, cognitive science, and artificial life research.[21] Habermas would, however, find (theological) support from Oliver O'Donovan, whose title *Begotten or Made?* points precisely to what he sees as the inability of a technological society to distinguish between the two—begetting and making—and the ethical confusion that results from becoming consequently incapable of acting and reacting appropriately to what is not made but, simply, begotten.[22] John Harris provides a very different—some might say almost cavalier—perspective, seeing no real qualitative difference in the questions posed by genetic engineering from those posed by previous crises in human development. Welcoming 'the possibility of a new breed of persons with life chances not available to us now',[23] Harris sees the problems, challenges, advantages, and benefits of biotechnology as not requiring anything more than human beings doing their best to make the most of the situation, maximizing the advantages and minimizing the disadvantages and not being put off by alarmists—as (he believes) they always have done.

Habermas's view of the novelty of our present situation is, therefore, challengeable on a number of fronts. However, the point in his argument that I wish to stress here is that it does not involve appealing to some kind of timeless human nature. Although in 1969 he could still speak of the factual 'organization of human nature' as dictating the necessity of keeping the technology we have, when technology puts human nature itself in question, he no longer finds such an appeal to 'human nature' convincing. In any case, Habermas has, in the meantime, made his point more precise purely in terms of his own philosophical development. Both the reductionist view of science and certain religious or philosophical views of the person that ascribe dignity and worth to the human being on the basis of its biological identity are, he says, mistaken. Moral freedom cannot be derived from ontology in this way, but is what it is as and by virtue of free participation in a moral community. Here, Habermas is at his most Kantian:

[20] See O. O'Neill, *Autonomy and Trust in Bioethics* (Cambridge: Cambridge University Press, 2002).

[21] N. Katherine Hayles, *How We Became Posthuman: Virtual Bodies in Cybernetics, Literature and Informatics* (Chicago: Chicago University Press, 1999), 3–4.

[22] See O. O'Donovan, *Begotten or Made?* (Oxford: Clarendon Press, 1984).

[23] J. Harris, *Wonderwoman and Superman: The Ethics of Human Biotechnology* (Oxford: Oxford University Press, 1992), 201–2.

'Only when they are neutral as regards any particular world view can assertions concerning what is equally good for each individual claim to have good grounds for being acceptable to all.'[24] The decisive imperatives are thus that the other must be treated as an end and not as a means and that any decision I take concerning the other must, in principle, be universalizable. That such-and-such a decision answers these requirements is not a matter of tracing it back to some universal assumptions about human nature.

This latter approach is that taken by Francis Fukuyama, who shares Habermas's profound unease at what the latter, in a moment of sarcasm, calls a future created by 'science-fiction-inspired engineers'. Fukuyama, whilst maintaining a reserve towards religious belief, asserts that there has been a kind of 'qualitative, if not ontological, leap' in the process of human evolution, such that the final whole is irreducible to any of its parts.[25] It is in the name of this 'whole', closely identified with consciousness, that Fukuyama asserts the principle of human dignity that, in his view, the proponents of genetic engineering are simply riding roughshod over. If the full-scale impact of gene technology is as yet some way off, we are already experiencing a kind of foretaste of some of the issues (and a warning as to the likelihood that such technology will indeed be used as and when it becomes available in ways that the scientists may or may not anticipate) in the popularity of drugs such as Ritalin and Prozac. This, he says, 'demonstrates just how eager we are to make use of technology to alter ourselves. If one of the key constituents of our nature, something on which we base our notions of dignity, has to do with the gamut of normal emotions shared by human beings, then we are *already* trying to narrow the range for the utilitarian ends of health and convenience.'[26] Habermas's view, however, is not dependent on any particular version of human nature, but simply on the possibility of mutual moral accountability.[27] This has important implications for their respective views as to the relationship between human dignity and religion. Fukuyama does not explicitly embrace a religious grounding for the principle of human nature he espouses, but he keeps the option open. For Habermas, however, it is essentially irrelevant, because the question of *human nature* is itself irrelevant.

How does this help us with regard to opening a field of interaction between thinking about God and the ethical dilemmas raised by technology? The key point, I suggest, has to do precisely with the role of the ethical (as opposed to the natural or

---

[24] J. Habermas, *Die Zukunft der menschlichen Natur*, 61.

[25] Fukuyama, *Our Post-Human Future*, 170.   [26] Ibid. 173.

[27] A kind of middle position seems to be that of Peter Kemp who, like Habermas, argues from an essentially Kantian perspective. Here, however, it is not so much the postulate of moral freedom that is the issue but the irreplaceability of the individual. This, Kemp argues, goes much deeper than external relations between individuals and is something more in the spirit of Jesus's question 'What does it profit a man if he gains the whole world but loses his soul?' See P. Kemp, *Det Uerstattelige: En Teknologi-Etik* (Viborg: Spektrum, 1991), 32–6. Also available in German translation as *Das Unersetzliche: Eine teknologie-etik* (Berlin: Wichern, 1992).

biological) in Habermas's discussion of genetic engineering. For Habermas provides a model for combining an ethical discourse grounded in a non-technological reason with the concrete engagement with tasks set by new technologies. This is not necessarily to say that I believe Habermas to be correct in the specific judgements he makes about, let us say, human genetic engineering—and I have just indicated some of the ways in which one might reasonably differ from him on this point. Nor, on the other hand, am I saying that there is not a radical difference in our contemporary situation, compared with that of previous ages, but simply that it is extremely difficult to pinpoint just where the decisive difference lies. The point is simply this: that Habermas, like Fukuyama, ultimately posits some kind of qualitative 'leap' in all ethical decisions, something that can never be adequately analysed in terms of pure theoretical rationality. For Habermas's argument depends on the possibility of a kind of thinking that cannot be grounded in nature, in ontology, in 'how things are', in science or technology. It is rational, he claims, yet it has a rationality that is of a different kind, with different roots, different criteria and different aims from the rationality of science and technology.

In these terms, we might say that where Marxism, including previous versions of critical theory, remained bound to the myth of a future leap into the Kingdom of Freedom (even if official Marxism never dwelt on the miraculous or voluntaristic aspect of this), Habermas's leap is not projected into some possible future. Rather it is the constant accompaniment of our existence in the present. To this extent we can say that where Soviet Marxism and critical theory retained a kind of future-oriented eschatology, Habermas holds to what theologians used to call 'eschatology-in-the-process-of-being-realized'. In a critical dialogue with Marcuse he himself almost says as much—precisely with regard to the question concerning technology. Marcuse, he says, envisages a future age in which a different technology will be required in order to give effect to the different relation to nature that will be enjoyed by a fully liberated humanity, a relationship in which nature is no longer the mere object (*Gegenstand*) of human activity but a fellow player (*Gegenspieler*) and when the human dominion over nature is not longer repressive but liberative. However, Habermas, says, not only is this utopian possibility (that Marcuse shares with Schelling and Ernst Bloch and with concealed elements in Marx, Horkheimer, and Adorno) ultimately derived from Jewish and Protestant mysticism, but what Marcuse describes in the form of successive historical stages is a misdescription of what are in fact two different forms of concrete action: the one being that of purposive technical intervention, the other being that of symbolic communication. What Marcuse projects into an improbable and even fantastic future is, in fact, a present possibility as communicative action, i.e. the common pursuit of the question concerning meaning and validity in the context of socially significant action.[28] The very process of bringing a moral critique to bear on one or other economic policy or one or

[28] Habermas, *Technik und Wissenschaft als 'Ideologie'*, 54–8.

other form of technological innovation is already to be engaged in the activity in which freedom becomes what it is: it is already to experience a foretaste of the Kingdom of Freedom even in the midst of the Kingdom of This World.

If Marcuse's utopian fantasies needed to be demythologized, ethical communication can and must also be differentiated from the machinations of technical reason itself. For, precisely on Habermas's account, moral perspectives cannot be a part of the furniture of the world that we somehow or other discover, perhaps by analogy to the way we discover hitherto hidden properties of the physical universe. If they were, then they too would become material for some kind of instrumental reason, 'goals' and 'targets' rather than 'values'.[29] They exist in and as a part of the process of building up the moral community, i.e. by virtue of the occurrence of a free and open discourse about norms that is equally accessible to all members of the relevant community. It is this process itself that gives such values or norms 'existence'. But if this is not a 'Kingdom of Freedom' waiting for us to leap into at the end of history, as the present practice of freedom here-and-now (in the midst of the Kingdom of This World) it is available to us only on the basis of a kind of 'leap'. Even if we add that, as a matter of fact (and to put the whole matter in more pedestrian terms), we are always already practitioners of such freedom in some form or another (as when a group of employees discuss whether it was 'fair' that such-and-such a colleague was dismissed and do so, of course, without recourse to formal philosophical reflection), it remains the case that normative discourse of this kind cannot be justified within the horizons of objective knowledge or instrumental reason. There is a point at which the discourses that end 'But this is not how the world is' or 'But this is inefficient' may simply be incompatible with or essentially different from the discourse that ends 'But it's not fair'. No matter how closely they may be correlated (and it is important for Habermas that we do strive to correlate them, both so that moral discourse retains a responsible relation to the realities of science and of the technological society and so that moral discourse is able to act upon the shaping of that society), they are not, finally, discourses of the same kind.

Again, we must resist too easily seeing in this proof that Habermas is on the same side of the 'qualitative leap' that Kierkegaard talks about in connection with faith. That his perspective is not immediately reducible to that of science or technology does not mean that it is religious and, as we have seen, Habermas himself is keen strictly to keep the boundaries of common human discourse in place. The matter of moral reflection is more a matter of common sense than transcendent reality. Yet it is, after all, a kind of leap. At the same time, Habermas wants to hold on to the idea that moral or practical reason is, nevertheless, reason. Kant, of course, was similarly concerned to distinguish his idea of moral or

---

[29] Although one might need to comment that in contemporary management parlance the term 'values' is coming to be used in an instrumental manner and is being assimilated to goals and targets as part of a complex of functional criteria for measuring the success of an individual or an institution.

practical reason from anything that could become the objective of theoretical reflection, whether empirical or metaphysical. Freedom, in other words, could neither be deduced from metaphysical principles nor from social or biological realities. Freedom is freedom only in and as it is exercised. Yet though this falls short of what many theologians have wanted to say about the basis of faith, Kant himself finds in this the germ of a kind of faith that is able to survive the 'shipwreck of metaphysics'. Whether either Kant or Habermas are finally justified in calling moral reflection or ethical action 'reasonable' or 'rational', and whether the reasons that drive Habermas to hold on to the idea that thinking that is other than the thinking of science and technology is still 'rational' are, in the last resort, philosophical, political, or rhetorical questions I do not wish to pursue here. The point is simply this: that Habermas's whole project depends on the postulation of a realm of discourse that is irreducible to and thus essentially other than the discourse of science and technology. This is not for the sake of refuting these, but of making sure that they serve human ends by being contextualized within humanity's collective and ongoing moral reflection about norms. This has a number of implications for the question as to how a non-technological thinking about God may be related to the concrete questions of technology.

To start with, it offers one way of showing how a discourse that is not itself constructed within or for the sake of the paradigm of science and technology may nevertheless be defended and promoted as offering a reasonable response to the issues with which science and technology confront us. Thus, the fact that thinking about God does not originate in science and has no technical outcome or spin-off does not of itself mean that it has to be irrelevant to the experience of what it is to be human in an age of technology. For, clearly, simply to indulge in such non-cognitive and non-productive thinking is already to put into effect a judgement concerning the right of science and technology to legislate for the whole field of human thinking and acting. Even if it does not do so in the same way as Habermas's communicative action, thinking about God prizes open a breathing space within what might otherwise come to be experienced as an all-consuming 'infernal machine'. As such (although this does not follow necessarily) it may serve a larger project of humanizing the technicized world. Moreover, if Habermas is justified in claiming that the kind of discourse about freedom that he seeks to further is no less rational, no less a matter of common, public reason than the instrumental rationality it seeks to curb or balance, then it is clear that the fact that thinking about God is not thinking of the same kind as that involved in scientific or technical work does not mean that it is irrational. Of course, as I have indicated, there would be many from within the ideology of technologism who would turn this analogy another way and argue that the kind of moral thinking being proposed by Habermas is itself as unscientific (= irrational) as anything found in religion. However, as far as the general state of play in contemporary society goes, there would perhaps be more within the liberal-humanist mainstream of Western society who would accept the rationality of collective moral reasoning whilst drawing a line at admitting religion into the discussion. Yet, ultimately, both ethics and religion involve some kind of leap away from a purely scientific-technical rationality into another kind of thinking and that even if these leaps (the leap of ethics and the leap of religion) are not identical they reveal an analogy that makes—or that should make—it possible for ethicists to acknowledge possibilities of dialogue with religionists that do not need to be inhibited by anxieties about now traditional conundrums such as the opposition of autonomy and authority.

But we can also look at this from the other side, as it were, i.e. from the point of view of thinking about God needing the supplement of ethical thinking, perhaps in the shape of the practice of communicative action recommended by Habermas. I sought to stress that thinking about God is thinking that in its deepest roots knows itself as not alone in the world, but bound in the debt of love, yet it does not obviously offer imperatives for dealing with actual issues of technological intervention in which our mutual responsibility is at stake. At the same time, there does seem to be a kind of analogy or even proximity between thinking about God and communicative action, in so far as both of them are forms of discourse that operate within a realm of irreducible freedom. To put it at its simplest: thinking about God (theology, if one likes) and communicative action (ethics) are well-placed to talk to one another—but only so long as they do so on the basis of a recognition of the other's freedom to be what it is. It is in and through such dialogue—and not by issuing mandates from on high—that thinking about God will come to bear upon the hard place of real-life decisions.

If we are asked to specify more precisely the ground on which thinking about God and communicative action might possibly meet, one might do so by reflecting on one of the striking but often unnoticed features of the rhetoric of sermonic speech, namely that the imperatives of preaching are typically 'optative impera-tives'. The sermon that stands under the sign of grace does not simply instruct in supernatural facts or issue a list of 'shalts' and 'shalt nots', but rather calls to and summons the listener by appealing to his or her own thought and judgement: 'may we...' 'let us...' (or, 'may we not...' 'let us not ...'). These are the decisive formulations of sermonic address, formulations in which the listener is not pre-sented with an assertion or a command but a possibility, yet—and this is the point—a possibility oriented towards some form of actual transformation in the listener's life. The Church's proclamation cannot make directly ethical demands, yet it can offer to ethical reflection possibilities that, through ethical reflection itself, may be made into the stuff of normative discourse.

One may argue as to whether the view that thinking about God *should* involve itself with the real problems of the real world is a demand that thinking about God places on itself or whether it is a demand placed upon it by the circumstance that the one who is engaged in such thinking is also an ethical subject. Either way, the actual configuration of what it means for thinking about God to engage with such questions—cell-stem research, let us say—will only emerge in and as it deepens its dialogue with the ethical. And for the outcome of such deliberations we are thrown back on a key concept of early Anglican moral theology: circumstance—a concept that can be closely correlated with the acceptance of equivocity at the level of linguistic articulation.[30] In other words, each new situation will place its own singular demands on our religious and moral reflection, and, just as in thinking about God itself, we will find ourselves always having to become beginners and to think through the issue in question from the ground up.

When thinking about God engages itself in ethical questions in this way, the ethical itself will never be deducible from or subordinate to thinking about God, just as the latter will never be reducible to 'mere' ethics. Human beings can be concerned about the good and perhaps can even be good or be in the way of pursuing the good without necessarily having to think about God, whilst even if thinking about God may often seem to incline us towards particular ethical judgements, it can only assure itself of the viability of those judgements by virtue of its participation in ethical debate as such. In other words, the deep gratitude for life that I have adduced as one of the basic traits of thinking about God may well incline us towards some general ethical concept about the sacredness of life. However, to say what follows from this in some specific context cannot be reached merely by straightforward deduction. In such cases it is, finally, the ethical judgement that counts, not the religious background that might have impelled us to involve ourselves with the question at all. It is only if the judgement really makes sense ethically that it will deserve to be taken as the basis for action. This does not necessarily mean that everything that is practised under the rubric 'theological ethics' is a mistake, merely that the expression itself condenses at least two distinct mental functions that must both be undertaken with due regard for their respective rigour if thinking about God is truly to work for the concrete liberation of human beings, and not least for human beings whose destiny is to inhabit a technological society.

This brief discussion of a large, growing and fiercely argued set of issues scarcely scratches the surface of the range of questions relating to encounters of ethics and religion in a technological society. Technology is inextricably entangled in many other issues that press in upon us today, not least questions of social justice raised by the management of technological innovation in the context of a globalized liberal market economy and the resultant disturbances and distortions in economies and in the lives of those human beings dependent on them. However, what has been argued here may be taken as offering a generalizable pattern for such questions: that there is no simple or direct route from a purely theological 'thinking about God' to concrete decisions in ethics, and that human ethical reasoning has a legitimacy that cannot be overruled by theology: equally, and no less importantly, thinking about God cannot absolve itself from the claim of the ethical, a claim that in its qualitative infinity is potentially present to every human activity, theoretical, practical and technical.

---

[30] See Ch. 5, n. 11 above.

8

Cyberversity or University?

I

In choosing Heidegger as a point of reference for developing the question of thinking about God in an age of technology, I laid particular emphasis on the way in which he relates the question concerning technology to the transformation of the university in the contemporary world. Let me quote again the words in which he summed up this transformation, as condensed into the figure of the person he calls 'the research man'.

[T]he decisive development of the modern character of science as ongoing activity also forms men of a different stamp. The scholar disappears. He is succeeded by the research man who is engaged in research projects. These, rather than the cultivating of erudition, lend to his work its atmosphere of incisiveness. The research man no longer needs a library at home. Moreover, he is constantly on the move. He negotiates at meetings and collects information at congresses. He contracts for commissions with publishers. The latter now determine along with him which books must be written. The research worker necessarily presses forward of himself into the sphere characteristic of the technologist in the essential sense. Only in this way is he capable of acting effectively, and only thus, after the manner of his age, is he real.[1]

This description will surely resonate with anyone who has extensive experience of modern academic life. Take the annual meeting of the American Academy of Religion, which welcomes 8,000 or more delegates. Under the umbrella of this massive event a myriad of ongoing research programmes and working-groups go about their business, young scholars and old network at seminars, dinners, and receptions, pre-approved papers are presented at hundreds of parallel sessions, thrusting young research students throng the interview hall in which scores of universities hire the up-and-coming talent, while older colleagues negotiate with publishers in the Book Hall.[2]

---

[1] Heidegger, *The Question Concerning Technology*, 125.
[2] The last time I attended this event was when it took place in Disneyworld, Florida, where card-carrying delegates filled the vast hotels adorned with crude buildings that were reminiscent of the colossal monuments of Stalinist architecture—except that they were painted in benign pastel tones

About relations with publishers Heidegger had these further words to say in an appendix to his essay:

[The publishers'] peculiar work takes the form of a procedure that plans and that establishes itself with a view to the way in which, through the prearranged and limited publication of books and periodicals, they are to bring the world into the picture for the public and confirm it publicly. The preponderance of collections, of sets of books, of series and pocket editions, is already a consequence of this work on the part of the publishers, which in turn coincides with the aims of researchers, since the latter not only are acknowledged and given consideration more easily and more rapidly through collections and sets, but, reaching a wider public, they immediately achieve their intended effect.[3]

These words might seem more accurate today than they did at the time when Heidegger wrote them, a time to which many now look back with a kind of nostalgia as the idyllic age before higher education succumbed to large-scale expansion and commercialization. With these latter developments the construction of public knowledge is assimilated into a larger project that is not inappropriately described as the knowledge industry (in the same way that what was once 'the sport of Kings' has become 'the racing industry', etc.). Within this industry the research man is, first and foremost, the manager of the knowledge that the industry exists to produce, certify and disseminate.

And of course it is not only publishers who are involved. Governments too are important stakeholders in the knowledge industry. The terms in which they understand this are themselves instructive. University departments in England and Wales have in recent years had to produce statements of aims and objectives for the government's Quality Assurance Assessment for Higher Education (and similar exercises have been conducted in many other countries). What sort of

and prettified by huge statues of 'friendly' marine animals instead of Party symbols and statues of heroic workers and peasants. On a more serious note, George Grant, a Canadian Christian philosopher whose critique of technology was largely influenced by Heidegger (although he remained critical of Heidegger's assumptions concerning religion and his general lack of concern with issues of justice), would not have regarded it as fortuitous that my example at this point is precisely that of the *American* Academy of Religion. For Grant, the United States of America was the technological society *par excellence* and its higher education structures (which Grant called the Multiversity, as opposed to the University) were both an example of what this entails and a vehicle for expanding its power. (Grant is particularly concerned with the way in which Canadian universities in the post-war period came to redefine themselves according to the pattern of the Americans. A specific example of this was the increasing focus on research as opposed to teaching and what Grant called dialectic, which, he said 'just means conversation—sustained and disciplined conversation'. G. Grant, *The George Grant Reader*, W. Christensen and S. Grant (eds.) (Toronto: University of Toronto Press, 1998), 202. As Grant saw it there were fundamental questions with which university teachers and students should be concerned but which could not be 'solved' by the methods of research. Such questions include 'What is justice? How do we come to know what is truly beautiful? Where do we stand towards the divine? One just has to formulate these questions,' he continued, 'to see that they cannot be answered by research. Yet thinking people need to be clear about such questions and therefore they cannot be excluded from the university' (ibid.).

[3] Ibid. 139.

documents are these? Inevitably they are documents couched in the terminology of governmental bureaucracy and PR, reflecting both the university's acceptance of the government's own aims and objectives and its readiness to 'compete' in the marketization of knowledge (which is also, of course, one of the government's own aims and objectives). Here, as elsewhere, the market/business model emerges as the decisive factor in the whole equation, with governments regulating and resourcing but never (as in old-time socialism) commanding. The resulting model of what universities should be doing therefore produces much talk about 'scholarship', 'research', 'excellence', 'resources', 'integrated structures', 'learning skills', 'transferable skills', and even (in the context of theology and religious studies) the 'intellectual potential of the faith traditions and communities' (whatever that means)—but not about 'truth'. But why should we expect to learn about truth from such documents? The university qua public institution is no longer 'about' truth, but about the management of learning and research, about the validation, dissemination, and commercial exploitation of knowledge as much as knowledge itself. This is not to say that there is no longer any commitment anywhere in the university to the pursuit of truth, whether that is understood as hard-nosed secular scientists tracking down the fundamental facts of how things are, or as confessional theologians expounding the truths of scripture or tradition within the parameters of a particular faith tradition. But though truth may still be pursued within the university it is no longer particularly significant for the business of the university qua public body to pursue or to promote any particular understanding of truth. In an important sense the contemporary university is essentially value-free in the sense that it operates across all ideological and cultural boundaries, absorbing local traditions but stripping them of their authority in the process. Its business is to manage the projects gathered under its umbrella, to ensure fair access to its resources and facilities for students, appropriate career development for its employees, and, by balancing its budgets, to ensure its survival so as to resource the next generation. In the spirit of one of the most common of all contemporary English catch-phrases, used alike by surgeons, soldiers, and criminals, it has a job to do and it gets on with it. This is what constitutes both its professionalism and its essential amorality. Amorality, however, is not immorality, and to say that the main task of the contemporary university qua institution has become knowledge management is not necessarily to register a complaint. There has never been so much knowledge available as there is today. I am sitting at a computer which, in 0.9 seconds, opens access to 2,990,000 web sites mentioning Jesus Christ and, of course, if I wanted, to all manner of scientific, scholarly, governmental, political, recreational, and news information. The sheer quantity of knowledge makes knowledge management a necessary and vital task for us today.

Many of those working in universities regard the combined impact of new technologies and the demands of market forces as destructive of what universities should be about. Heidegger's depiction of the research man seems to reflect this kind of reaction (though, as we shall see, his attitude is not simply that of rejection). But there are others for whom this new situation is experienced as essentially liberative. Mark C. Taylor, having arrived at the end of the road of a particular line of modern theology, came to view the new virtual reality of the internet as a cornucopia of pedagogical liberation. Taylor celebrates the transition from the old-style nineteenth-century university modelled, he claims, on the paradigm of the factory to the 'postmodern cyberversity' in which the campus is replaced by a 'multi-user-simulated-environment'.[4] Taylor chronicles his own initiation into this environment in connection with his use of teleconferencing to run a joint global seminar with a colleague in the University of Helsinki. Subsequently he developed a sequence of projects to develop the new paradigm further.

In one of my most successful courses, *Cyberscapes*, I have developed a media lab in which students learn to create multimedia hypertexts to probe philosophical questions and analyze cultural developments. With the growth of the web, I also created a CyberCollege for Alumni/ae in which my courses for undergraduates at Williams College were webcast synchronously and asynchronously to alumni/ae throughout the world. Students and graduates met in virtual environments to discuss issues raised in the course. To help faculty colleges explore new technologies, I established a Center for Technology in the Arts and Humanities and secured funding to support research... In 1999, I founded the Global Education Network with Herbert A. Allen, who is the president of the leading New York investment firm, Allen & Co. In my work with the Global Education Network (GEN), I am attempting to extend the experiments begun in the Helsinki seminar and the CyberCollege by putting the theory of network culture... into practice. GEN brings together educators, educational institutions, investors, and businesses to provide high quality on-line education in the liberal arts for people of all ages throughout the world.[5]

Utopia—or dystopia? Whatever one makes of Taylor's experiments, it is scarcely surprising (although he himself admits to having been surprised) that many of his colleagues resisted the innovations he was making. Quoting an article by James Perley and Denise Marie Tanguay, Taylor acknowledges the view that on-line institutions 'raise the spectre of a higher-education system that is nothing more than a collection of marketable commodities—a system that could turn out to be all but unrecognizable to the scholarly communities that invent and reinvent higher education on a daily basis.'[6] However, he himself hears the claim that cultural critique and political resistance 'can be preserved only if institutional autonomy remains inviolable' as a cover for a situation that 'presupposes full-time lifelong employment and the protection of separate departments in the university' and, while using the rhetoric of academic freedom, such e-sceptics 'are actually

---

[4] See Mark C. Taylor, 'Unsettling Issues', in *Journal of the American Academy of Religion*, 62/4 (Winter 1994), 949–63.

[5] Idem, *The Moment of Complexity: Emerging Network Culture* (Chicago: University of Chicago Press, 2001), 10.

[6] Ibid. 239.

more interested in protecting job security, that is tenure'.[7] Strangely, the tone of
Taylor's remarks concerning the recalcitrance of such hypocritical colleagues
echoes that of Heidegger in 1933. But whereas Heidegger's scorn for conservative
faculty members' whingeing about academic freedom was uttered in the context of
his bid to rescue the university from succumbing to the technologizing of knowledge, Taylor's project is precisely aimed at furthering such technologization
Opposed as they are in this respect, both highlight what has become the ineluctable interface between the university and technology, in Taylor's case the technology of the current information revolution. For, despite the unmistakable hostility
of Heidegger's policy in 1933 and the continuing tone of reserve in his post-war
portrayal of the research man, he too recognized that the old fashioned scholar in
his library, toiling for decades on a definitive article about some detail of Cicero-
nian grammar, has become a thing of the past. The cyberversity of the present and
future has surpassed the scholarly ideals of the nineteenth century by as great a
distance as that differed from the academy of Plato. This may send shivers down
the spines of those whose aspirations are symbolized in the figure of the scholar
closeted with some ancient 'volume of forgotten lore', but their reservations will be
dismissed by others as merely the self-interested and faint-hearted hesitations of
reactionaries who are too idle or too unimaginative to ride the wave of change and
transmute their 'scholarship' into the practices of the cyberversity.

As has just been noted, and even if their alternatives lie in virtually opposite
directions,[8] Taylor's brusque dismissal of old-fashioned notions of academic
independence eerily echoes Heidegger's own contemptuous comments about
academic freedom in the fateful moment when he became Rector of Freiburg
University and declared himself in favour of the Nazis' programme of *Gleichschaltung*, a co-ordination of university teaching and research with the aims and
objectives of the Third Reich. In his subsequently notorious Rectoral address of
May 1933 'The Self-Assertion of the German University', Heidegger declared
that 'The much-lauded "academic freedom" will be expelled from the German
university. For because it was purely negative, this freedom was false. What it
chiefly meant was lack of concern, an attachment to arbitrary views and opinions,
and no commitment either in action or in refraining from action.'[9] Heidegger
returned to the theme a number of times in speeches and addresses from 1933
and 1934. In November 1933, for example, he wrote that 'We have said goodbye

---

[7] Idem, *The Moment of Complexity*, 255.

[8] Where Heidegger sought to hand this freedom over to the state, Taylor offers it away from the
heavy hand of the state to the market (although one might add that in a situation in which the state
chooses to cede many of its historical responsibilities to the market this difference is by no means
absolute).

[9] M. Heidegger, *Reden und Andere Zeugnisse eines Lebensweges, Gesamtausgabe*, 16 (Frankfurt am
Main: Vittorio Klostermann, 2000), 113.

to the idolization of a form of thinking that is without a relation to its ground or to power. We anticipate the end of the philosophy that supported it.'[10]

In a summer-school course from 1934 Heidegger made clear just what it was that had, in his view, gone wrong with such 'groundless' academic freedom and, in doing so, already anticipates his post-war description of 'the research man'. The problem is, in effect, a repetition, within the circle of academic studies, of the general crisis of complexification and resultant fragmentation that afflicts modern society as a whole. Whereas—as we shall see—the original idea of the university reformers of the nineteenth century was that philosophy should provide the living bond of all university studies, in practice 'the individual sciences became incapable of mutual understanding. Secondary literature became more important than the matter at issue. And this literature then becomes a matter for publishers and their business priorities... The individual sciences now sought their unity in international specialist conferences and the even greater widening of their scope that these produced. Each strove to come away from the original unity of knowledge.'[11] The 'unity' of the university is now merely a formal and bureaucratic unity. What Nazism offered, Heidegger believed, was an opportunity to reconnect the university to the social reality of a common national purpose, in which 'scholarly workers' would be essentially engaged in a common effort for the self-definition of the nation. Academic freedom, in other words, is to be sacrificed in the cause of national unity. This is not a great sacrifice, in Heidegger's view, since this freedom is in any case vacuous and the new conditions of academic life will, in fact, prove more advantageous for a genuine commitment to science than the mere pursuit of individual interest.

It is widely recognized that extreme examples are likely to make for bad arguments, and the relationship between the university and the Nazi state is, obviously, an extreme example. It is also, of course, one that (in most eyes) throws Heidegger himself in a pretty poor light. Nevertheless the whole saga is grimly instructive. In order to learn from it, however, it is important to be clear about the issues. These are not simply that trying to subordinate the university to a regime that was to turn out to be as wicked as that of Hitler was a moral and political failure. The more general issue—which this extreme example throws into sharp relief—is that of the relationship of the university to the larger society, and to values and strategies that are not derived from the university's self-chosen aims of scholarship and science (however we understand these). These issues have been central to debates about the nature of university life that have had nothing

---

[10] Ibid. 192. Note that the word I have translated 'ground' is the German *Boden*—a key word in Nazi propaganda, referring to the soil or ground that belongs uniquely to a particular people or *Volk*. Thinking that is without a ground in this sense is thinking that lacks connection to the historic soil of the people, thinking that is cosmopolitan and rootless or, as we have heard Heidegger put it elsewhere, 'not German'.

[11] Ibid. 298.

to do with Nazism and they are central to the questions concerning the place of theology and religion and the role of technology and its commercial or governmental applications in the university. In this context the difference between Heidegger and Taylor becomes slightly more confused, since *if* one made the assumption that our contemporary society was correctly described as a 'technological society' and as determined by the demands of a globalized market, then the 'co-ordination' of university education with 'for profit E-ed' would seem to be far more closely analogous with the subordination of the university to the totalitarian state than might at first seem to be the case.

In a study of Heidegger's politics, Miguel de Beistegui has pointed out that the whole debate about the university and society that blew up in 1933 was not without precedent. In fact, the demands of the incoming government resurrected a discussion that lay at the heart of the modern university system in Germany and that found its classical formulation in the debates about the foundation of the University of Berlin in the first two decades of the nineteenth century. As de Beistegui argues, the issue was focused in the two contrasting views of J. G. Fichte and F. D. E. Schleiermacher. Fichte's vision, set out in his *Deductive Plan for an Establishment of Higher Learning to be Founded in Berlin* was of a university that both reflected the authoritarian structures of the Prussian state and that was itself essentially subordinate to the state. Schleiermacher's response to Fichte's plans, in his *Occasional Thoughts on Universities in the German Sense*, insists on a manifold freedom in university study: the freedom of the university as a whole from the state, the freedom of the professors in research and teaching, the mutual freedom of teaching (the university) and research (the academy), and the freedom of teaching from the requirements of other, i.e. technical, schools. Von Humboldt, charged with making the final recommendation regarding the University's constitution, opted for Schleiermacher's proposals. As de Beistegui comments 'The modern foundations of the German university were thus laid by the theses of Schleiermacher. It is that very university which was to be annihilated by the Nazis in 1933, that very university which Heidegger offers to revolutionize in the name of "the essence of the German university".'[12]

Schleiermacher's conception of the university was also, of course, one that included a very clear reflection on the place of theology in university life. Inevitably, this conception was formulated within a context in which most European states gave special privileges to one particular denomination. The place of theology within the university was therefore developed with an eye to

---

[12] M. de Beistegui, *Heidegger and the Political Dystopias* (London: Routledge, 1998), 37. It would not be hard to argue that the whole question of the nature of university studies as one of the defining commonplaces of German idealism and that many of the theoretical discussions as to the nature of science and knowledge were, in fact, inseparable from the concrete implications of these discussions in university life. It is in this respect surprising that the recent and generally excellent K. Ameriks (ed.), *Cambridge Companion to German Idealism* (Cambridge: Cambridge University Press, 2000) has no indexed entry to the topic 'university' or 'University of Berlin'.

the overall role of the Church in national life. Clearly we are now in a situation where many of Schleiermacher's assumptions about the nature of 'science' and the nature of the relationship between Church and State are no longer self-evident. However, precisely because our own situation is characterized by such uncertainty and controversy on these matters, it will be helpful to revisit a debate in which the issues were thought through with extraordinary penetration and clarity—even if it is a clarity one must work to find in the slow-moving and painstaking periods of the Schleiermacherian style.

From the beginning of the discussion of the new university a central issue was the meaning of the term 'science' and the nature of the university as a 'scientific' institution. Von Humboldt stated the ideal with the succinctness of an accomplished administrator and scholar.

The concept of higher scientific institutions as the summit where everything that occurs in the moral life of the nation is brought together is determined by whether these institutions are fitted to work scientifically, taking this term in its deepest and broadest sense, not treating the materials made ready for them by cultural and moral education as needing to be subordinated to imposed goals but as themselves intrinsically purposeful.[13]

At one level this was something to which nearly every contributor to the debate could sign up. Fichte, Schelling, Hegel, and Schleiermacher all agreed on the decisive value of 'science' in the sense not of natural science (with which it has become broadly identified in English usage) but *Wissenschaft* as a form of knowing that reflects upon itself and understands its own principles and methods and, as such, is equally characteristic of natural, humanistic, and practical 'science'.[14] Nevertheless, within this broad consensus there were differences of emphasis, not least as concerns the relationship between theology and philosophy and, inseparably from this, between confessional faith and university studies.

Schleiermacher's *Occasional Thoughts on University Studies in the German Sense* begins by emphasizing the limitations of the state with respect to the quest for knowledge. This quest, Schleiermacher believes, is both natural and naturally self-communicating, so that it is almost inevitable that associations for study will spring up without the state's intervention. The only situation in which the state would need to be pro-active would be one in which there was in fact no interest in the pursuit of knowledge in a given society. However, though the state does not initiate or set the direction of the pursuit of knowledge, it is in its own interests to support this and, therefore, in its own interests not to interfere with it. However, it is important to note that it is specifically the question of the 'German'

---

[13] W. von Humboldt, 'Ueber die innere und äussere Organisation der höheren wissenschaftlichen Anstalten in Berlin', in *Werk in Fünf Bänden* (Stuttgart: Cotta, 1964), iv. 255.

[14] In the following I shall stick to 'science' and 'scientific' as translations of the German *Wissenschaft* and *wissenschaftlich*. This may lead to formulations that seem a bit odd in English, but it is crucial to an understanding of the German debate that, e.g. literary criticism and history no less than chemistry or physics aim at being 'scientific'. To say 'scholarly' or 'academic' already carries connotations of the 'mere erudition' that the research man shows up for what it is.

university that Schleiermacher is addressing, and Schleiermacher's aim is to promote a university that can serve all of the German-speaking people and not simply those who are citizens of the Prussian state. That the state as such should be limited with respect to the university does not mean that the university is not to be responsive to the wider society of which it is a part. In this respect de Beistegui's sharp distinction between the Heideggerian model and the Schleiermacherian model is perhaps overdrawn. The difference in 1933 is precisely that the state now believes itself entitled to speak to and for all of the German-speaking peoples. Heidegger's option is not so much the rejection of the Schleiermacherian model as one way of interpreting this model in new and radically changed circumstances.

The educational situation in which the shaping of a new university occurs is one in which three kinds of institutions are potential stakeholders—the schools, the academies, and the university itself. As Schleiermacher sees it, these should have an interdependence that finds its mid-point in the university. If schools are aimed at developing the intellectual talents of the young, and if the academies are devoted to specialized research, the university is the place where the students are able to submit their talents to the discipline of 'science' and so make themselves fit for research or, it may be, for one or other of the professions, medicine, law, the Church, or schoolteaching. With regard to the last, Schleiermacher believed it to be important that those who taught in schools should themselves be persons of scientific competence and therefore very much a part of the community of higher education, rejecting the aspersions of those who looked down on schoolteachers as a kind of practical tutor. If schools instruct in knowledge (*Kentnissen als solche*) and the academies pursue 'insight into the nature of knowing in general', the university is the mid-point in which the general principles of knowledge are, so to speak, meshed in with the detailed stuff of practical, professional, and empirical life. The academician's ability to pursue knowledge, the scientific spirit, does not appear out of nothing, but emerges out of a process. 'The university is primarily concerned with beginning a process that looks beyond its first developments. But this is nothing less than a completely new spiritual life-process.'[15] What is set in motion is the pursuit of knowledge as a whole, a totality, above all through the 'learning of learning'.

This 'learning of learning' is chiefly the business of philosophy, which is thus reckoned as the basis of university studies as a whole. However, philosophy is 'never given as something actually completed, but only as a constantly progressing [movement of] approximation and growing in understanding'.[16] In this connection, Schleiermacher throws out a polemical aside against those who believe that the scientific spirit is something that can be developed in abstraction from life's concrete circumstances 'in pure transcendental philosophy, ghost-like, something which many have, alas, sought after and thus found themselves pursuing spooks and uncanny beings'.[17] Rather than going down the path of this kind of abstraction, the university must remember that it is both 'post-school' (*Nachschule*) and 'pre-academic'. It is in this context that its intimate relationship with professional training finds its justification.

Over against systems in which private tuition is the primary focus of teaching and learning, Schleiermacher also insists on the lecture as the 'holy of holies' (*das Heiligthum*) of university life. This is not because he is unaware of the importance of dialogue in education (he was himself the leading translator of Plato's dialogues) or imagines that the scientific spirit can be imparted by top-down instruction. On the contrary, the lecturer must seek to internalize the spirit of the Greek dialogues in his lectures, he must not simply read a prepared text or 'tell what he knows, but reproduce his own way of knowing, the act [of knowing] itself'.[18] The importance of the lecture to the university is that it exemplifies the living process of thought. That this is to be done in a *lecture*, in a *public* environment is crucial, because this publicness enacts the essentially communicative and essentially communal nature of university life.

That teaching does not stop with lectures, however, is made clear when Schleiermacher goes on to adumbrate the manifold ways in which teachers and students both do and should interact. Beyond the lecture hall the teacher will arrange more personal periods of group supervision and discussion which, in turn, may be the occasion for personal relationships to form, through which the teacher will come to understand the needs and aspirations of the students. Thus, says Schleiermacher, 'Only in so far as he gradually forms and makes use of such relationships will the teacher be able to combine the masterly confidence of the ancients, whose discourses always hit the mark, with the noble modesty of the moderns, who have to presuppose that a process of spiritual development (*Bildung*) will have already begun and be independently underway.'[19]

The place of theology in the university, Schleiermacher states, is justified by the role of religion in society as a whole, specifically in the fact that the state has chosen to treat one particular religious confession as normative. From our pluralistic or multireligious perspective this comment clearly begs the question as to whether, in our circumstances, theology does indeed have any right to participate in the life of the academy. This is a question to which we must and shall return.

However, even if theology is chiefly justified in terms of its serving as a professional qualification, rather than as the pursuit of some form of pure and disinterested knowledge, theological knowledge in and for itself, an interesting and important element in Schleiermacher's conception of the scientific or philosophical underpinning of university studies as a whole means that all university

[17] Ibid. 37.   [18] Ibid. 48   [19] Ibid. 50

teachers, including theologians, must have a level of competence in philosophy—i.e. in knowing what knowing is as such—that gives him the freedom to research and teach outside his own specialization (i.e. theology). This, Schleiermacher believes, will outflank any tendency to a conflict between the faculties, since all will be mutually assured as to the proper competence of the others. It also underlines the point that even if the need for a faculty of theology is ultimately derived from the religious arrangements of the state, it can only function as a university discipline if it is capable of being taught and studied as a science.

The general institutional picture given in these *Occasional Thoughts* is reflected in Schleiermacher's more narrowly theological reflections on the relationship between theology and philosophy. In his *Short Description of Theological Study* he makes clear that the philosophical treatment of Christian doctrines is limited by the fact that the original essence of Christianity is not something that could ever be 'constructed' in accordance with a pure science. Philosophy has to take the individual and communal piety of Christianity as something already given, prior to reflection. This means that the chief form in which philosophy will be present in theology is as an historically oriented critique, i.e. a testing of the way in which the actual configuration of Christian experience approximate to universal principles and criteria of reason. This is not so much a matter of finding a rational justification for given credal or institutional forms as of projecting a horizon within which they are to be interpreted and understood. Remembering that, according to Schleiermacher, even philosophy is inseparable from its own specific historical stage of development and is never present in the form of absolute knowledge as such, it means that the critical, philosophical examination of religion will only ever be a matter of approximation, never of final judgement. There is no neutral view from on high, since the philosopher himself is also a participant in and limited by the historical process.

An important strand in Schleiermacher's thought is the aspiration, shared with other German idealists, to provide a model for combining the universality or absoluteness of ideas with the stuff of life as it is lived. From what has been said here, it is clear that, in Schleiermacher's version, this combination existed only as a process of unification, not as an achieved state. It was something to be worked out in the personal life of the devout person and in the historical and textual or natural studies of the scholar. In this regard there is a clear and interesting difference between Schleiermacher and Hegel, and the distinctiveness of Schleiermacher's position is well brought out by contrasting it with that of his contemporary and (in many respects) rival. There are, it is clear, many similarities between them and probably more than either of them cared to acknowledge: both are concerned with the unification of such polarities as ideal and real, infinite and finite, absolute and relative; both see this unification in terms of a historical process; both assign to philosophy the decisive role in determining the shape of knowledge, in theory as well as in the actual processes of university education. However, Hegel seems to hold that we can establish assured criteria of truth that are, in some sense, prior to experience. Although actual scholarly work must strive to show how any given phenomenon in fact manifests the idea, that it does so, and the general form in which it does so, are determined in advance by the logical schema within which the phenomenon is to be located. In some ways this makes Hegel appear at times almost more theological than Schleiermacher. Thus, for Hegel, the idea of God as Trinity has a pre-eminence over all other ideas of God because it answers most closely to the inner structuring of thought as such in terms of the triadic principle of thesis-antithesis-synthesis. Schleiermacher, however, seems to incline finally to the view that the doctrine of the Trinity can only be justified as an approximate rendering of the experience of God in the lives of believers and communities. Finally, he suggests, God must be affirmed as essentially One. Putting it simplistically, one might say that whereas for Schleiermacher philosophy is able to play a prescriptive role, it does so by virtue of its descriptive adequacy, whereas for Hegel its descriptive adequacy is guaranteed in advance by virtue of its internal logical self-consistency. Schleiermacher's readiness to stay within sight of lived experience makes his thought rather more shapeless than that of Hegel, but it is, of course, a question as to whether Hegel's beautiful systematic clarity is won at the cost of reality. Hegel wrote that 'the Truth is the whole', but whereas he seemed to believe that the philosopher did indeed finally have a view onto that whole, Schleiermacher, whilst agreeing with the need to pursue a holistic vision, would concede that 'the whole' itself remained unattainable. In the meantime, however, we can, we should, we must engage in the clarification and interpretation of what we have, thus far, attained. This process is in principle open-ended and never-ending. It is therefore by no means coincidental that Schleiermacher was to be a powerful influence on the emergence of the history of religions school of the nineteenth century, one of the intellectual ancestors of contemporary religious studies. Precisely because he saw Christian faith as inseparable from the universal development of humanity's religious consciousness, the whole field of historical forms of religion became suddenly relevant to theology itself in a way that had never occurred before. At the same time, historical and comparative study is not itself, qua intellectual practice, final, since it calls for further reflection on the truth of what we have understood, reflection that seeks to clarify what, in the yield offered by hermeneutical investigation, stands firm under the critical duress of dialectical scrutiny: what, in short, can be known.

II

So what does Schleiermacher's thought mean for the place of religion in university studies in a context in which the state does not in fact endorse the privilege of any one religious tradition, or in which—in those European countries where Christian theology of one or other confessional church still has a statutory pre-eminence in faculties of theology—the legitimacy of this privilege in the eyes of the wider society can by no means be taken for granted? In particular, what does it mean for the contemporary debate between theology and religious studies and for the relationship between these and the task of thinking about God as I have adumbrated it here?

It seems that whether we follow the Schleiermacherian or the Hegelian model, there are no 'scientific' grounds for giving a privilege to any one confessional form of faith. In the Schleiermacherian perspective, the special role of Christianity is always at risk of being subsumed into a more general category of 'religion'— something that such theological critics of Schleiermacher as Karl Barth have forcefully pointed out. On the other hand, whilst Hegel does seem to give a clear ranking between different forms of religious life, according to which Protestant Christianity emerges as the highest possible form of religion, this 'superior' role is itself subsumed into the higher level reflections of philosophy. Philosophy has the same content as religion, Hegel says, only it presents this content and understands it in a higher and purer form than that of religion itself. Philosophy 'knows' religion with respect to its ideal content, not to its ever-variable power of edifying this or that individual. If, in the one case, the faith-perspective of the student is dissolved into the detail of philological and historical comparison, in the other it is subordinated to a kind of intellectualism that, from Kierkegaard onwards, believers have experienced as essentially alien to faith. Yet if the first movement of a Schleiermacherian pedagogy is to relativize the religious starting point of the believer, this does not mean that university study has no concern for the truth of what religion is 'about'. But it is only at the point where the yield of comparative study is subjected to critical reflection that the question as to what can be *known* (in the strong sense of the word) leads on to the further question as to the fundamental principles, values, beliefs, and goals that shape our estimation of knowing, i.e. that explain why we regard knowing as a worthwhile activity. If history means the relativization of faith, philosophy creates an environment in which, once more, the truth of faith can become an issue. Once we begin to think about the meaning of thinking itself, what thinking is *for*, we are, therefore, entering the intellectual domain in which thinking about God not only belongs but is also, in certain cases, called for. Only it is vital to remember that on the Schleiermacherian model (as opposed to its Hegelian counterpart), such reflection is not conceived so much as the truth that faith merely adumbrates but as the process in which it becomes possible to argue for or against the truth of one or other version of faith. It is philosophy as the medium but not the arbiter of university study and of truth.

Already in the first half of the nineteenth century, then, the place of confessional belief as the matter of academic reflection was under discussion and, in the kind of university established in Berlin, it would only require a shift in external circumstances for that place to be drastically weakened. If the models of knowledge in play in those forms of religious studies that wish to exclude faith perspectives from the study of religion are in many respects different from those of Schleiermacher and Hegel, they can be seen as taking the radical implications of their thought through to its logical conclusion. Once 'science' has been made the governing criterion of university life as a whole, the historical privileges of what were then referred to as 'positive' religion will, it seems, inevitably fall away. If today there are still ancient universities that retain some echo of their religious foundation (as in Oxford and Cambridge), private confessional universities (as in Catholic and Protestant universities in the USA), and public universities in which the theology of an established religion has a legal privilege (as in Germany and Scandinavia) these are increasingly under pressure both from more value-free models of the scientific study of religion and from the declining support for religion in the population at large.

One significant result of this is that even where confessional theology has managed to preserve its place in university studies, it is obliged to conform itself to the general requirements and standards of teaching, research, and examination. Students will not be disadvantaged or 'failed' because, let us say, they defend the doctrine of transubstantiation or argue against the divinity of Christ in the context of a Protestant faculty of theology. What matters is whether they show themselves to be competent in understanding the relevant literature and arguments and whether they are able to think through the implications of their position with regard to other areas of the discipline and even Church practice. Even in confessional contexts, university theology cannot be simply an extension of catechesis. That there have been few if any 'scandals' in this area (i.e. students 'failing' on account of some form of unorthodoxy) is largely due to the intuitive sense of the vast majority of university teachers as to the way the land lies; or, putting it less cynically, most university teachers' own commitment to the best scientific standards. As was noted in connection with Quality Assurance Assessments, the issue is not the truth of what is being put forward, least of all its personal or subjective truth, but the ability to meet specified criteria, aims and objectives; to fit the frame of enframing. In this situation the difference between theology and religious studies may, in fact, be much less than it seems to protagonists of one or other extreme view. Both equally have to conform to the requirements of academic standards. Theology practised in these circumstances is not essentially different from religious studies. The difference is simply in the choice of particular fields or practical applications within the field of religious thought and action.

In an article entitled 'The Academic Study of Religion', Sam Gill succinctly articulates what he sees as the key elements in our contemporary situation. These include

1. The academic study of religion must not depend upon or require of its researchers, teachers, or students any specific religious belief or affiliation, race, culture, or gender...

3. The term 'religion' must be understood as designating an academically constructed

rubric that identifies the arena for common discourse inclusive of all religions as historically and culturally manifest...4...Religion is a category whose subdivisions are categories [i.e. specific 'religions'—GP] that demand comparison.[20]

Or, as Mieke Bal has put it even more incisively 'Theology, then, is the name for a specialization within the domain of cultural analysis that focuses...on those areas of present-day culture where the religious elements from the past survive and hence "live".'[21]

Neither of these views is exclusive in the sense of barring practising members of one or other faith community from studying, researching, or teaching. The point is simply that whatever they do in these areas must be altogether abstracted from their private lives as religious believers. However, in such a perspective— whether it understands itself as 'theology' or 'religious studies'—the question of thinking about God, that is, the question as to whether we can hope, ever, to think about God in a godly way or whether our thinking about God is prede-termined in advance by one or other projection of cultural enframing, is simply excluded. This question, the question of thinking about God, is not, of course, identical with that of defending one or other form of confessional theology, which is usually assumed to comprise more or less all of the possibilities for a religious concern for God within the university. But is this assumption justified? Do the faith perspectives of actual religious communities define the possibilities for whatever kind of thinking about God might lie beyond the purely descriptive phenomenological or social constructivist perspectives of religious studies? Is it not rather the case that the question of thinking about God in the sense that this enquiry has been pursuing is a question that first arises precisely at the point where the scientific element of confessional theology and/or the study of religion as cultural analysis reach their limit? Then the question is: is this limit itself and its transcendence, its 'more', an appropriate topic for thinking? Is this not precisely the point at which, according to Schleiermacher, we move to an interpretative and critical evaluation of the *truth* of what we have come to know? And is this not the same point where, with Heidegger, we move towards what withdraws itself from thinking and thus what most calls for thinking—the point, that is, where what is to be thought is subject to the rigour of a philo-sophical interrogation?

A positive answer to these questions might be suggested by noting the implications of a negative answer: that if the question as to the meaning of the limits of academic enquiry into theology and religion were to be excluded from that enquiry itself, then we would have to accept that although we might have gathered vast amounts of resources and provided ourselves with enough material

---

[20] S. Gill, 'The Academic Study of Religion', in *Journal of the American Academy of Religion*, 62/4 (1994), Special issue: *Settled Issues and Neglected Questions in the Study of Religion*, 965.
[21] M. Bal, 'Postmodern Theology as Cultural Analysis', in G. Ward (ed.), *The Blackwell Companion to Postmodern Theology* (Oxford: Blackwell, 2001), 6.

for outputting an infinite number of research projects, conferences, journals, monographs, etc., we would not have begun to think what importance, what claim, what meaning any of this could have for our own attempts thinkingly to know our own responsibility for what we must say or do as religiously engaged persons in this singular moment of time and space.

But isn't the proponent of academic theology or the scientific study of religion at that point entitled to turn round and say: that's true; I agree; but that is not the matter of my scholarly work; that is a matter for me as a private individual? Yes, but surely there must be a point at which the scholar and the individual are aspects of a single actual living human being and surely that point itself cannot be put out of the way of philosophical scrutiny? Moreover, even if it is the case that there is a strong current of contemporary thought that calls for religion to be made into an exclusively 'private matter', that point has scarcely been reached in most Western societies and the question of religion and its place in public life remains very much a matter of continuing debate. The issue of actual 'belief' is rarely if ever a simple matter of private opinions but exists in an interlocking network of personal, moral, social, and political beliefs and commitments. If it is now the exception rather than the rule that a given society requires a particular form of religion to be incorporated into university studies, it may nevertheless still be the case that it would be of greater value to society to raise the debate as to the conflicting truth claims of religious communities into the disciplined environment of university studies rather than restricting the academic study of religion to the 'neutral' horizons of religious studies as understood by, for example, Gill and Bal.

We shall return to this last point, but we shall first go back to the relationship between the individual and his or her own religious commitments. It is, I suggest, deeply unsatisfying to encourage and even to institutionalize a situation in humanistic studies in which the personal commitments of the practitioner are in principle excluded. However, it is clear that a certain understanding of the scientific nature of academic study would seem to rule out such personal involvement. The question then is whether this model of scientific work is, in fact, desirable or practicable. One could, for example, point out that quite outside the field of religion there are many humanistic subjects where much of the best work of the last couple of hundred years has unashamedly reflected the aesthetic, moral, and political orientations of the students and teachers concerned. Advocacy of the view that Milton was the pre-eminent poet of the English language would by no means be grounds for excluding a scholar from the academy if the view that was being advanced contributed to raising the general understanding and appreciation of Milton, even amongst those who, finally, disagreed with the core proposition. It would, indeed, be hard to imagine the modern academic landscape without the contributions of those whose work has both been inspired by and has reflected their commitments to particular world views: Marxism, Freudianism, libertarianism, pacifism, feminism, etc. If some of these (e.g. Marxism and Freudianism) are now generally agreed to contain key claims that are plainly false, this does not mean that the contributions of those influenced by them have been worthless. But the key question is not what happens to have been the case up until now. More fundamental is the question as to the conception of university life underlying any particular practice. That such commitments should be excluded in principle is a reflection of the dominance of technocratic models of knowledge, but why should we accept such models as normative for the humanities? Is it not a profound and fundamental categorical error to assume that all forms of academic life must conform to that of natural science, with its claim to disinterested and value-free enquiry? However, if we once accept that the actual practice of science as we know it today is inseparable for the most part from its technological application, then it becomes clear that this claim to disinterestedness is disingenuous. Modern science is very much in the service of what Habermas would call 'strategic' interests. Which is not to say that these interests are necessarily malign, but is precisely to register the need for an appraisal of their implicit claims to short-circuit scrutiny of their claims to normativity. Such an appraisal might also involve noting that there are other interests in play in the world of the university that may have no less important a claim to our attention. If, for example, we accept that the modern university has its roots in those medieval institutions that grew up to serve medicine, law, and the Church, and if it remains the case that universities continue to be an integral element in the education both of such traditional professions (and, indeed, of other, newer forms of professional life), isn't it in the nature of the professions to require more of their members than simple specialist competence; that they require a kind of 'practical wisdom' that involves the ability to synthesize and to judge complex and often seemingly incommensurable domains of experience and action?[22] My argument, then, is that there is a legitimate place for humanistic study (including theology) that does not exclude the existential commitments of its practitioners from their professional work and that even, perhaps, depends upon such commitments being in play.

But where might we look for an alternative model of university education? Am I not feeding a covert demand for the subordination of academic freedom to external social forces—not, in this case, the state, the market, or technology, but the Church? Is it not to open a door to the kind of heteronomy that Heidegger proclaimed in 1933? I think not. We have already noted that, for Schleiermacher himself, a recognition of the larger social context of university study went along with a definite limitation of the claims of the state. But the actual practice of

---

[22] I do not know if the practice still continues, but when I was teaching in Cambridge, the medical school gave students the option of spending one year on a non-medical subject. I had the good fortune to teach several medical students who had decided to take theology for a year. Whatever else might be said for or against this, it indicated a sense that being a doctor must mean more than simply being a technologist, that the medical service of the community was enhanced if this service could, through its practitioners, also participate in the wider cultural life.

academic life itself already provides us with the elements of an alternative model. It was Schleiermacher who pointed to the 'natural' process whereby a lecturer will interact with students on a number of levels, from the more formal through to personal friendship. This living bond, he suggested, is in fact the key to his ability to do his job as a lecturer. Schleiermacher's own conception of the university did not perhaps make this element of personal relationships central. However, there were other nineteenth-century visions of university life that did.

The most elegantly articulated of these was John Henry Newman's *The Idea of a University*. This is not now the moment to begin a full exposition of Newman's 'idea', but it will prove useful to focus on one element that is characteristic for his conception, though easily overlooked in the more extensive deliberations on, e.g. the relationship between theology and philosophy. Perhaps even more than was the case with Schleiermacher it is necessary for us to come to Newman with a certain historical charity. The kind of university life that both shaped Newman and that he himself did so much to influence is, in many respects, altogether alien to all but the most conservative elements of the ancient universities (not least regarding the assumption that universities should be all-male institutions). Yet we must recall that Newman is describing his idea of a university from a Catholic point of view that is already far removed from his own Oxford experience, and he now views the Oxford system as deeply corrupted by its essentially Protestant character. He is nevertheless still able to discern certain key virtues in it. Principle amongst these is precisely the element of personal association. This concerns, firstly, the relationship between teachers and students. 'A university's great instrument, or rather organ,' he says, 'has ever been that which nature prescribes in all education, the personal presence of a teacher, or, in theological language Oral Tradition. It is the living voice, the breathing form, the expressive countenance, which preaches, which catechises. Truth, a subtle, invisible, manifold spirit, is poured into the mind of the scholar by his eyes and ears, through his affections, imagination and reason ... '[23] In this connection it is worth noting Yves Congar's observation (commenting on the same point in Aquinas) that the supremely personal nature of the teacher-pupil relationship is nowhere better demonstrated than in the fact that the three founders of the West's dominant traditions of science, ethics, and religion—Pythagoras, Socrates, and Jesus—left no written record of their thoughts but transmitted them through their unwritten influence on their pupils.[24]

Yet for Newman there is something possibly even more important than the relationship between teachers and students, namely, the relationships between students themselves:

---

[23] J. H. Newman, *The Office and Work of Universities* (London, 1859), 22.
[24] Y. Congar, *Tradition and Traditions: An Historical and a Theological Essay* (London: Burns and Oates, 1966), 372.

[I]f I had to choose between a so-called university, which dispensed with residence and tutorial superintendence, and gave its degrees to any person who passed an examination in a wide range of subjects, and a university which had no professors or examinations at all, but merely brought a number of young men together for three or four years, and then sent them away as the University of Oxford is said to have done some sixty years since, if I were asked which of these two methods was the better discipline of the intellect—mind, I do not say which is *morally* the better, for it is plain that compulsory study must be a good and idleness an intolerable mischief—but if I must determine which of the two courses was the more successful in training, moulding, enlarging the mind, which sent out men the more fitted for their secular duties, which produced better public men, men of the world, men whose names would descend to posterity, I have no hesitation in giving the preference to that university which did nothing over that which exacted of its members an acquaintance with every science under the sun... How is this to be explained? I suppose as follows: When a multitude of young men, keen, open-hearted, sympathetic and observant, as young men are, come together and freely mix with each other, they are sure to learn one from another, even if there be no one to teach them; the conversation of all is a series of lectures to each, and they gain for themselves new ideas and views, fresh matter of thought, and distinct principles for judging and acting, day by day.[25]

Newman himself would scarcely have advocated a course-less and teacher-less university as the best available model, nor is his point to promote such a thing. Rather, in the manner of a thought-experiment, it is to draw attention to an element that he regards as essential in all university education, namely the quality of the personal relationships which exist in it, that those who are learning and teaching do so as the real human beings that they actually are. For, as Newman understands it, the university is not training future researchers or specialists, but equipping its students for life. As he goes on to say:

[A] university training is the great ordinary means to a great but ordinary end; it aims at raising the intellectual tone of society, at cultivating the public mind, at purifying the national taste, at supplying true principles to popular enthusiasm and fixed aim to popular aspiration, at giving enlargement and sobriety to the ideas of the age, at facilitating the exercise of political power, and refining the intercourse of private life. It is the education which gives a man a clear conscious view of his own opinions and judgements, a truth in developing them, an eloquence in expressing them, and a force in urging them. It teaches him to see things as they are, to go right to the point, to disentangle a skein of thought, to detect what is sophistical, and to discard what is irrelevant. It prepares him to fill any post with credit, and to master any subject with facility.[26]

Again, it should be stressed that in reading such a passage today we need a more than usual charity in hermeneutical imagination. Most universities today would not see their task as aiming to raise the tone of society or to produce future

---

[25] J. H. Newman, *The Idea of a University* (New York: Image Books, 1959 [1853]), 165–6.
[26] Ibid. 191–2.

leaders in the sense that that might have had in nineteenth-century Oxford. Yet Newman is surely right in this, that even today the career patterns of graduates, especially in the humanities, do not necessarily bear any direct relation to their academic specialization and will probably only rarely do so over the whole course of their careers. As in Schleiermacher's emphasis on philosophy as the 'learning of learning' what is more directly relevant are habits of critical reflection, interpretative imagination, intellectual flexibility and openness, a sense for the complexity of situations, and a readiness both to make judgements concerning these situations and to take responsibility for the consequences of those judgements. These 'virtues' *may* be relevant to future research careers, but they may be no less relevant to future careers as teachers, clergy, civil servants, aid workers, journalists, or whatever. If the state of the University of Oxford in the late 1840s seemed to some to exemplify the worst possible results of the kind of 'personal association' model implied by Newman, the reformers did not seek to do away with this in favour of professorial chairs and academic specialization, but to regularize and incorporate it into a more 'scientific' model.[27]

And Newman is surely also right in this: that whatever the formal arrangements for teaching and examining, the university is a 'complex space' that cannot be understood entirely in terms of its formal regulations. Alongside the official academic business of the university the social dynamics of bringing a large number of mostly young, mostly intelligent people together will of itself generate a multiplicity of what might be called 'para-academic' environments and activities. These reflect the cultural, political, religious, and social interests of the university's members. They may include political pressure-groups, prayer circles, sports clubs, drama societies, drinking clubs. Many of these have themselves become institutionalized in more or less formal ways, such as university chaplaincies, endowed extra-curricular lecture series, or inter-varsity sporting events. Others will have the formal approval of the university and others may be actively discouraged. Even if the project of creating a completely value-free working academic environment were to be realizable, the existence of these para-academic activities reflects the reality that the total experience of university life normally involves all who participate in it being in one way or another engaged in relating their study to the larger horizons of their life in the world. I suggest it is congruent with most people's experience of university that these para-academic environments and the learning processes associated with them are integral to the overall impact, effect, and benefit of a university education.

Putting to one side for the moment the question concerning the place of thinking about God in the academic study of religion, it would only be in the

[27] Mark Pattison, for example. As a liberal Protestant tending towards a kind of post-Christian evolutionary optimism and with a particular interest in encouraging the participation of women in the life of the university, Pattison occupied a very different ideological position from that of Newman. See J. Sparrow, *Mark Pattison and the Idea of a University* (Cambridge: Cambridge University Press, 1967).

most totalitarian of contexts that such thinking was excluded from the university in the larger sense that includes what I have called the para-academic dimensions of university life. It may well be that such contexts are, in fact, the best place for a kind of thinking that seeks to suspend the framework of any given system of subject areas and methodologies, thinking that seeks only to be guided by the thought of God. In the para-academic environment (which might well include worship) such thinking is free to relate itself to any possible area of life and not simply to what theology in the narrower sense prescribes as its current canon of privileged texts and questions. In this environment it finds a natural link to an encompassing practical-theoretical exploration of the best life to which a human being might commit him- or herself. And it also allows for a range of resources very different from those to which the cyberversity limits itself.

But can this kind of reflection be carried over into the context of academic study itself—or must it be restricted to the realm of extra-curricular activities? The more technical model of university education would, of course, seek to ensure clear boundaries between the academic and the para-academic, but the recent history of academic development gives many examples of how issues that have originally found a place in the para-academic environment have been taken up into the mainstream of academic discourse. In the 1960s one might find a 'Gay Soc', a 'Women's Soc', or a 'Film Soc' on the more adventurous campuses, but by the 1990s Gay Studies, Women's Studies, and Film Studies had become a regular part of academic study. Theology, of course, might be said to be moving in the other direction, as it moves from being a core academic discipline ('Queen', even, of the sciences!) to the status of a merely free-time activity, something one does in the chaplaincy centre. That is as maybe. My point here, however, is merely to indicate how, under certain conditions, the boundaries between the academic and the para-academic are permeable and changeable. Additionally, it is also important that at least the first two of my three examples are likely to allow for their practitioners taking a strong advocacy line, i.e. that they are not ashamed of asserting that there are certain values or social practices associated with being gay or female that should be positively promoted and not simply described from a standpoint of scientific neutrality. Of course, there will be those who see these examples as illustrating precisely what is wrong with contemporary academic life, i.e. the proliferation of subject areas overbidding their real status in order to claim the rank (and funding) of 'disciplines'. Different views will, of course, be held, but again the point is relevant to the study of religion: precisely when 'religion' itself is described (as by Gill) as simply an academic construct, it raises the question as to whether, in fact, 'religion' *can* function as the unifying centre of a distinct academic discipline with a distinct methodology. Nor is it only theology that might contest the claims of religious studies to be the discipline best suited to study the phenomenon of religion. For traditional humanistic disciplines such as history and the study of literature are very frequently concerned with texts or events that have a religious nature and they too might claim a certain competence in dealing with the religious aspects of these texts or events in accordance with their own characteristic ways of working. Once the question of thinking about God as a possible horizon of my existential truth has been removed from the equation, it is far from clear whether something called 'religion' (a 'something' that will inevitably be defined in a variety of ways) is a sufficiently powerful or coherent object to justify institutionalizing a whole discipline around it. Why not simply allow it to find its place as a theme within more secure disciplines such as history, literary studies, sociology, or philosophy? Is religion even sufficiently *interesting* to function on its own without a defining context?

Self-evidently, religious studies as it is practised is by no means a uniform academic discipline and different institutions have different traditions concerning their understanding of the subject and the extent of its divergence from theology. In some situations students can freely choose from both subject areas as part of a common degree, in others they are strictly separated; in some, religious studies is conceived in terms of a 'science of religion', in others it is more a matter of supplementing traditional Christian theology with the faith-perspectives of other traditions. Rather than being the 'science of religion' it is then something more like multireligious theology. Given what has been said about the personal dimension both of teachers' and students' relation to their academic study, it seems far from obvious that one model is going to be 'better' than the other in terms of students' learning experience, in terms of intellectual excitement and the possibility for demanding and provoking debate and clarification of the matter at issue. Moreover, the larger social environment may well have greater benefit from multireligious theology than from a putative science whose basic terms are as contestable as those of religious studies! Such multireligious theology might at least hold out the promise of advancing the prospects of peaceful and creative cohabitation between the varieties of religion currently represented in society, a prospect in which society itself (if not the religions) have a significant interest. That, I should add, is not what is chiefly being advocated here. For, simply as an academic discipline, even such a multireligious theology would not guarantee that God was really put to the test of thought in a thinking way.

I began this book with a survey of a particular tradition of radical theology that called for theology to secularize itself, to throw off its churchy presuppositions and Gothic idioms and stand with 'modern man' ('come of age') on the ground of his thoroughly secular worldliness. In the context of university studies, I am suggesting, theology—even when officially confessional—already is essentially secular. It is a discipline amongst disciplines that will advance or retreat in the light of pressures and counter-pressures analogous to those faced by all other disciplines. It is not as if theology is secular science's conscience, a kind of backdoor to transcendence. Rather, the question of transcendence, or of a God who would be more than anything that ear could hear, eye see, or the human heart conceive, arises at a boundary that is equally compelling for any academic discipline, including theology. But the existence of this boundary by no means implies that the question of such a God is alien to the life of the university as a whole, if that is conceived as a complex environment of human and not merely of 'scientific' education.

Let us attempt a thought experiment that might clarify some of these issues. Let us say that an imaginary student has fallen under the spell of George Herbert's poetry and has reached a stage in her development at which she is considering pursuing study at postgraduate level. Coming from an undefined humanities background, she finds herself with a choice. In the university to which she is considering applying there is Professor Church, a theologian renowned for his encyclopaedic knowledge of Anglican theology and spirituality, and whose output includes a defining monograph on Herbert's view of faith. Over in the English department of the same university is Professor Form, a world expert on seventeenth-century poetry who has likewise written a defining mono-graph, this time on rhythm and metaphor in Herbert's poetry. On going into the website of the history faculty, our already confused student discovers that Professor Old is Britain's leading authority on aristocratic culture and rural life in the reign of Charles the First and has written a fascinating study of the mirroring of just this relationship in the life and work of George Herbert. One more click of the mouse and she finds herself in the religious studies department, where a spicy young reader, Dr Pixel, is in the midst of developing a computer programme for modelling the semiotic dynamics of religious texts as manifested in aberrant frequency vocabulary. Amongst the primary examples of this ongoing project (accessible on the department's website) is, of course, the poetry of George Herbert. Finally, and quite by chance, she discovers that the new junior lecturer in Queer Studies is about to publish a book on *Christ as the Sublimated Penis of Herbert's Desire*. As our by now somewhat bewildered student discusses the situation with her friends, she also discovers that none of these distinguished or up-and-coming scholars are, in fact, on speaking terms, none of them regards any of the others as even remotely scholarly, and that there is no way she can practically have the best of all worlds by receiving teaching from all of the above (which, in a rational university system, she could). She must choose, and we leave her to agonize over her choice. My questions are simply these: Is it at all clear that one or other of these perspectives has any a priori legitimacy over any of the others? And is it necessarily the case that any of them must or should exclude the attempt to read Herbert in the light of what he can show us of the possibility of thinking about God? I suggest that it is clear that we cannot, in fact, expect any discipline to put us in the position of being able to adjudicate over the truth of Herbert's vision but, equally, that a concern for this truth can legitimately co-exist with the practice of any of them and, indeed, be fruitful for any of them. Not even a theological account of Herbert's faith can satisfy the requirement of a religious reading of the text if it overlooks the qualities of his verse, the social and political contexts of his life and work, its formal characteristics, or its complex eroticizing of the divine-human relationship. For Herbert's faith, whatever it was, was the faith of a living, fully incarnated human being who therefore participated in all of these dimensions (and more). But—and this is equally important—we will only ever be able to find in Herbert's words an occasion to think about God if we venture beyond the intellectual space projected by any particular disciplinary enframing or by any combination of such enframings. To think once more in Heideggerian terms, it is what remains unsaid and unsayable in the poem, its spirit/breath/life that most calls for thinking.

All examples necessarily have their limitations, and it might be that a highly reflective poet from a high literary culture is precisely not going to provide the sort of religious 'text' that the more typical anthropological or sociological approaches of the more scientific kind of religious studies are going to prioritize. It would probably be impossible to come to a text such as this without some historical or literary aptitude. The same might be said of my example of Rublev's icon. The poem and the icon alike will also generate a personal response that involves both a response of taste and, for some, a sense of being directly addressed by God in their personal life. But this again suggests that the task of thinking about God is precisely not a task that will be accessible along the path of a reductionist methodology that typically seeks out the more elementary forms of religious life and behaviour. Yet, for us, the question of religion and of the claim of religion as a truth to live by will be most decisively articulated in texts such as these that resist easy reduction. The truth of God is most likely to be real for us in and as we discover it in relation to the fullest incarnation of human life in the reality of a world in whose culture we participate and through which we are ourselves defined. To think about God at a level that is less complex than that of the cultural time and space we actually inhabit will be precisely not to think about a God whose truth could actually be truth 'for us'.

9

The Religion of Art in an Age of Technology

I

That thinking about God must return to earth and that thinking about God in an age of technology must return to the concrete interfacing of thinking and reality not only relates to the exigencies of confronting the ethical challenges posed by technology and to the technological society's public discourse concerning knowledge, but also to many other spheres, amongst which art has a particularly important place. In fact, since the dawn of the industrial revolution, the question of art has been marked by a profound ambivalence as regards both religion and technology. Already in Schiller's *Lectures on the Aesthetic Education of Mankind* art and poetry were recommended as the pre-eminent way in which the fragmentation and alienation of modern life was to be overcome and healed. This idea was to be taken up and reworked in manifold ways in romanticism and romanticism's various heirs in a wide range of artistic and theoretical movements. As far as religion was concerned, the redemptive role now being given to art could cut both ways. On the one hand art could come to function as a kind of substitute religion, a realm of revelations, eternal values, and sublime experiences that did not require what, at the end of the nineteenth century, William James would call 'over-belief'. Nor did it require submitting one's moral freedom to any external authority. The only prerequisite for seeking salvation in art was the experience of art itself as a source of meaning and illumination. Art, unlike ecclesiastical religion, was presumed to be self-authenticating. 'Art, nothing but art!' proclaimed Nietzsche. For art required neither rational justification nor institutional coercion to be convincing. If it took up one or other form of theorization or came under the aegis of one or other 'academy' it was also the case that, throughout the period of romanticism and modernity, art had a penchant for iconoclasm and for revolutionary innovators who gained accreditation as 'artists' precisely by virtue of their readiness to overturn established canons and conventions. Yet if art could in this way take over key functions previously associated with religion, art and religion have also often sought mutual support, not least in relation to a common opposition to the world of industry and technology. Through art—especially music, visual art, and poetry—religion has given drama, warmth, and colour to its 'message', whilst art has found in religion a kind of guarantor for its claims to ultimate significance. Within

Christianity this has been notably the case in various currents of Catholicism and Anglo-Catholicism, though it has also been an element both in Lutheranism (where Tillich's theological engagement with modern art was an outstanding example[1]) and in the rising interest in Orthodoxy, although the 'aesthetic' view of Orthodoxy may reflect more of the conceptual problematic of modernity than of traditional Orthodoxy itself.[2] Nor is it accidental that at key points in the present enquiry I have appealed to what are generally taken to be 'works of art'— Herbert's poetry and Rublev's icon-painting[3]—as focusing the meaning of thinking about God.

As with religion, so with technology. A broad current of romanticism and post-romanticism has chosen to define itself by virtue of its opposition to the world of technology. Art expresses the feelings of the heart and not the abstractions of the mind. It is the realm where we find ourselves close to the living pulse of nature and matter, where we encounter things in the light of their individual uniqueness and 'inscape', and not as they are made serviceable for the projects of technological manipulation. Of course, art and the aesthetic sensibility cannot simply avoid technology, but they have repeatedly experienced it as essentially threatening. A classic example of this is John Ruskin's meditation on the meaning of the colour purple amongst the ancient Greeks. Ruskin argued that purple originally and essentially meant 'fire-colour' and, especially, 'the scarlet, and orange, of dawn'. When Homer called the sea purple, Ruskin claimed, he did not mean 'the colour of cloud shadows on green sea' but 'the gleaming blaze of the waves under wide light'. By a sequence of associations with the sun and fire the word also comes to acquire the connotations of the Latinate 'purple'. 'So,' Ruskin remarks, 'the word is really a liquid prism and stream of opal.' But that is not the end of the story:

And then, last of all, to keep the whole history of it in the fantastic course of a dream, warped here and there into wild grotesque, we moderns, who have preferred to rule over coal-mines instead of the sea (and so have turned the everlasting lamp of Athena into a Davy's safety-lamp in the hand of Britannia, and Athenian heavenly lightning into British subterranean 'damp'), have actually got our purple out of coal instead of the sea! And thus, grotesquely, we have had enforced on us the doubt that held the old word between blackness and fire, and the fear of it, by giving it a name from battle, 'Magenta'.[4]

---

[1] See my *Art, Modernity and Faith: Restoring the Image,* especially ch. 6, 'Into the Abyss'.

[2] Ibid. ch. 7, 'Icons of Glory'.

[3] Both in the examples I have used and more generally in Herbert's poetry there is, of course, a highly self-conscious reflection on the tension between the 'artistry' of the work and its religious intention. Rublev is a slightly different case and although we must go to an 'art gallery' to see both icons discussed here, there is a case for seeing them under Hans Belting's rubric of 'the image before art', i.e. works that were not produced as 'works of art' but as serving a sacred and liturgical function in which they are not the 'objects' of aesthetic contemplation qua compositions of line and colour.

[4] J. Ruskin, *The Queen of the Air* (London: George Allen, 1904), 123–5 (numbered paragraphs 91 and 92). Mining has served many commentators as the epitome of the dehumanizing and

Thus Ruskin embellished his point that the industrial production of a paint colour both expressed and gave effect to an almost complete reversal both of aesthetic sensibility and of humanity's whole experience and view of life. This reversal is, indeed, so complete that most people simply do not notice it. We read Homer's colours through the lens of a modern industrialized and technologized colour palette instead of through the natural spectrum of colours made available by sea, sky, and sun.

However, the example invites the comment that the situation is by no means as simple as Ruskin portrays it. For how would the achievements of nineteenth-century painting have been possible without key innovations in paint production, innovations that had an essentially technological character? We have only to step back from the rhetoric of the romantic's complaints against technology to see that there is virtually no art that has not gladly taken into itself the benefits of technical progress. Whether we think of books of poetry (products of printing technology), the pianoforte, or the instruments of the modern orchestra, painting or, not least, architecture, it is almost impossible to think of an art-form that was not already in some measure 'technologized' even before the advent of photography, film, sound-recording and the computer. And, of course, this is not simply a matter of art slipping, unnoticed, under the hegemony of technology. Many artists have been amongst the loudest advocates of technology and of its potential role in creating an art that is genuinely 'modern'. In contrast to Ruskin's preference for the purity of the Greek vision over the dark and corrupt vision of an industrial society we could cite the Italian futurist F. T. Marinetti, who declared that 'a racing car whose hood is adorned with great pipes, like serpents of explosive breath—a roaring car that seems to ride on grapeshot is more beautiful than the *Victory of Samothrace*.'[5] And where Ruskin saw the darkness and corruption of industrialization as reaching its pinnacle in modern warfare,[6] Marinetti could write that 'War is beautiful, because thanks to the gasmask, the fear-inducing megaphone, the flame-thrower and the little tanks it establishes the dominion of man over the machine subordinated to his will, and it inaugurates the dream of the metallization of the human body.'[7] Naturally, whilst other futurists and ultramodernists (Mayakovsky, for example) shared Marinetti's extreme enthusiasm for all things technological, including techno-war, there have been many others whose embrace of technology took less violent forms. To take a

denaturalizing effects of technology. See, for example Lewis Mumford's discussion in his *Technics and Civilization* (London: Routledge, 1934), 65–77, a discussion summed up in his comment that 'The mine . . . is the first completely inorganic environment to be created and lived in by man: far more inorganic than the giant city that Spengler has used as a symbol of the last stages of mechanical dessication' (p. 69).

[5] Quoted in U. Apollonio (ed.), *Futurist Manifestos* (London: Thames and Hudson, 1973), 25.

[6] See the last essay of *The Queen of the Air*, 'Athena of the Heart', especially paragraphs 114–19.

[7] Translated from the German version cited by W. Benjamin, 'Das Kunstwerk im Zeitalter seiner technischen Reproduzierbarkeit' (Zweite Fassung) in idem, *Gesammelte Schriften*, 1.2 (Frankfurt am Main: Suhrkamp, 1978), 507.

more or less random example, the sculptures of Anish Kapoor use the best available technical means for rendering the possibilities of their materials, but their impact on the viewer is very different from anything intended by a Marinetti: though often destabilizing the viewer's conventional sense of space, sometimes disturbing and sometimes provoking laughter, their final effect is one of deep tranquillity, if that word can be kept free of its unfortunate sentimental associations.

Recognition of this situation does not necessarily deal a terminal blow to romanticism. Acknowledging the ineluctability of the conditions of modern industrial society for all artistic production and reception, a critical theorist such as Marcuse can nevertheless claim that art remains a repository for instinctual forces that keeps open the utopistic horizons of erotic desire in, with, and under the repressive conditions of capitalism's technological society (and again one might remark that the function ascribed to art by Marcuse very much suggests that it is serving as a kind of substitute messianism).[8] It is characteristic of the grip of romanticism on the popular view of art, however, that commentators often express surprise at the fact that (for example) Leonardo da Vinci was an engineer and a designer of helicopters as well as an 'artist'.

Heidegger, as was briefly noted in Chapter 3, was extensively preoccupied with the possibilities inherent in art (above all the poetry of Hölderlin) for providing a counter-movement to technology. If 'the thinker' has a privileged place in relation to the hope of revealing a new truth other than the truth brought to expression in science and technology, the thinker would have nothing to go on were it not for the word bestowed by the poet or the silent presence of the world of 'things'. Importantly, these themes are closely interconnected in Heidegger's own thought with the question as to the absence of God (or 'the gods') from a world shaped by the imperatives of technology. That a major theme of Hölderlin's poetry is the flight of the ancient gods and the disenchantment of the modern, godless world is therefore crucially important for Heidegger's reflections on Hölderlin. In terms of the present enquiry, it is also worth noting that Hölderlin not only had important personal and intellectual links with Hegel, but also with Schiller—in other words, that he stood close to those who, just at this time, were defining many of the key concepts of the philosophical and artistic response to the alienating effects of modernity.

As Heidegger reads Hölderlin, the poet assimilates the world of the South German landscape, a landscape defined primarily by its great rivers, the Rhine and the Danube, to that of the Greek gods. The rivers themselves are depicted as 'demigods', descending to earth from the Alps, the realm of immortals and of the divine thunder, and, in their courses, shaping a landscape that thus comes to provide a dwelling place for mortals, 'preparing the ground for the hearth of the

---

[8] See H. Marcuse, *The Aesthetic Dimension: Toward a Critique of Marxist Aesthetic* (Boston: Beacon Press, 1978).

house of history', as Heidegger puts it.[9] The Danube (which, as Heidegger notes, Hölderlin refers to by its classical name, the Ister) is especially significant as an actual and symbolic link between East and West, Germany and Greece and even, beyond Greece, the Indus. Not the least important element in this link is that the East is literally, in German, 'the morning land' and the West 'the evening land'. These meanings lend themselves to the idea that the East (Greece) was the land in which European civilization had its dawn, a time of dreams and enchantment, a time when gods and mortals communicated almost naturally, whereas the West, 'the evening land', is the land from which the light and innocence of dawn have long since faded leaving us with only a memory of the gods who once moved among us.[10] Both the deep meaning of the rivers in their demigodlike work of providing an historical home for mortals and the memory of the gods are, on Heidegger's reading of Hölderlin, pre-eminently made available to us in and as the poetic word, above all the poetic word of this particular poet. In both cases the poet and his word come to operate as mediators between gods and mortals, i.e. between the gods who are active in nature and the gods who were once familiar amongst mortals.

Under the conditions of a disenchanted world, the poetic word is a re-enactment of the sacred festival in which the union of the gods and mortals was consummated and celebrated.[11] But even the poet can only 'remember' such a consummation, for the poet himself stands within the destiny of 'the evening land', far from the original luminosity of the dawn. As a poet, he too (like the rivers) is a kind of demi-god, gifted with the task of transposing the divine speech into human language, but as a human being he shares the fate of his contemporaries—a tension compacted into the question 'why poets in a destitute time?' (from Hölderlin's 'Bread and Wine'). This means that although the poetic word both preserves and, by preserving, keeps open for the future the possibility of renewing the union of gods and mortals it does not and cannot make the divine actually present, here and now, amongst mortals. Against at least some versions of romanticism, where poets and artists become virtual plenipotentiaries of the divine, Heidegger's Hölderlin bears witness to the historically ineluctable experience of alienation, abandonment, and homelessness. Consequently, the poetic word itself is a riddle and hinting sign, only interpretable under the rubrics of

---

[9] M. Heidegger, *Hölderlins Hymne 'Der Ister'*, in *Gesamtausgabe*, 53 (Frankfurt am Main: Vittorio Klostermann, 1984), 183. For a fuller discussion of Heidegger's interpretation of Hölderlin, see my *Routledge GuideBook to the Later Heidegger*, ch. 7.

[10] Although it lies outside the purpose and scope of this enquiry, there is much here that invites a comparison with Ruskin. Despite the latter's suspicion of German philosophy, and despite the very different intellectual and political orientation of his thought, there are striking similarities to Heidegger in his depiction of the relationship between early Greek sensibility and the modern world.

[11] See especially his comments on Hölderlin's poem *Andenken* ('Remembrance') in M. Heidegger, *Hölderlins Hymne 'Andenken'*, *Gesamtausgabe*, 52 (Frankfurt am Main: Vittorio Klostermann, 1982).

paradox, risk, and the leap. 'We are a sign, uninterpreted/Without pain are we and have almost/Lost language in a strange land,' as Hölderlin himself put it in the poem 'Mnemosyne'. Yet, as just mentioned, this uninterpreted sign *may* signal the enigmatic possibility of a future God, 'the last God', as Heidegger sometimes puts it. We recall that Nietzsche was seen by Heidegger as 'the last thinker of metaphysics', as the one who, in his idea of eternal recurrence (i.e. the infinite repeatability of technology's procedures and products), brought to expression the essence of technology. But Hölderlin is given an even more significant role in Heidegger's 'history of Being': for he is the one who even in the era of metaphysics/technology articulated the idea of a future 'beyond' its infinitely recurring orbit. This future is identical with the advent or revelation of 'the last God', an event enigmatically hinted at in the poetic word and in this way becoming a possible focus for reflection or thinking that also seeks to think otherwise than in the mode of metaphysics/technology. And, Heidegger seems to be saying, this—for now—is all we are getting. There will be no breach in the wall of ambiguity that guards this enigmatic sign.

What Heidegger says concerning the poet also holds true of the other mode in which, under the spell of art, the world may come to appear to us in a different light from the measured and artificial light of technological enframing—the revelation of 'the thing' in its essential simplicity.

In his essay 'On the Origin of the Work of Art' Heidegger speaks of the very different ways in which matter—the world of things—is treated in technology and in art. In the former, the material element is strictly subordinated to the specific use or purpose for which the instrument or tool is designed. What matters is that the jug is capacious enough, that the axe is sharp enough, or that the shoe fits and is hard-wearing. As Heidegger puts it, 'Because it is determined by usefulness and serviceability, equipment takes into its service that of which it consists: the matter. In fabricating equipment—e.g. an axe—stone is used, and used up. It disappears into usefulness' (*PLT*, 46). The corollary of this is that once such a thing, the thing as mere equipment, has served its purpose, it becomes mere junk—cracked, broken, rusty, rotten stuff to be cast aside. Paradoxically, then, although modern industrial society is often described as 'materialistic', there is a sense in which it is actually far, far removed from the simple reality of things. In another essay, 'The Thing', Heidegger remarks on the familiar phenomenon that 'all distances in time and space are shrinking' (*PLT*, 165). The technologies of travel and information mean that the ordinary citizen has more immediate access to anything, anywhere in the world than at any previous time. Yet, Heidegger asks, 'the frantic abolition of all distances brings no nearness' (*PLT*, 165). We have, in other words, lost the capacity for really experiencing the world in its concrete and immediate uniqueness. It is no problem for me to buy a ticket to Thailand or Australia and to accomplish in a single day a journey that even a couple of generations ago would have taken weeks if not months. But what do I 'experience' when I get there? Many would say that even if it is not a hotel-life more or less identical with the hotel-life of London or Paris it is an 'experience' of nature or of an exotic culture that is pre-packaged and managed in such a way that actually makes it impossible for me to have anything like real insight into the life of Thai hill-tribes or the fauna of the Australian outback. The same is true—perhaps even more true—if my 'experience' of these phenomena is limited to what I see on television or the internet or read about in a newspaper supplement. Materialistic as we are, we are curiously distant from the real materiality of the world.

Art, Heidegger suggests, relates to its material element in quite another way. Let us once again read the description of the Greek temple from 'The Origin of the Work of Art':

Standing there, the building rests on the rocky ground. This resting of the work draws up out of the rock the mystery of the rock's clumsy yet spontaneous support. Standing there, the building holds its ground against the storm raging above it and so first makes the storm itself manifest in its violence. The luster and gleam of the stone, though itself apparently glowing only by the grace of the sun, yet first brings to light the light of the day, the breadth of the sky, the darkness of the night. The temple's firm towering makes visible the invisible space of air. (*PLT,* 42)

The temple does not merely *use* things in order to instrumentalize them in the cause of (in this case) the 'work' of a religious cult. As *art*-work the temple brings to birth a world, an ordered and connected whole, in which each element can become and be seen for what it is. As Heidegger will put it several pages later, 'the temple-work, in setting up a world, does not cause the material to disappear, but rather causes it to come forth for the very first time... The rock comes to bear and rest and so first becomes rock; metals come to glitter and shimmer, colors to glow, tones to sing, the word to speak' (*PLT,* 46).

If a work such as this may seem too sublime, too distant from our everyday experience, Heidegger makes an essentially similar point in a no less celebrated meditation on what the reader is led to picture as an ordinary, everyday clay jug. Here he combines two different strands in his reflections. The first is focused on the way in which the jug is used for pouring, the second on the material quality of what is poured. The way in which the jug is used for pouring, Heidegger suggests, is very different from that of a purely functional 'thing', a tool or an instrument. When the jug is 'used' for pouring a glass of water or of wine what is poured is given and experienced as a gift. Even when a drink is poured out to satisfy a thirst, there is an element in the act of pouring that is more than the functional and quantifiable process of alleviating a physical need. The drinker does not simply *use* the jug, he receives from it. This, Heidegger says, makes the jug very different from a scythe or a hammer, tools that exist only to be used. Moreover, he continues, the water and wine preserve within themselves the natural sources from which they are taken, 'The spring stays on in the water of the gift. In the spring the rock dwells, and in the rock dwells the dark slumber of the earth, which receives the rain and dew of the sky... In the gift of water, in the gift of wine, sky and earth dwell' (*PLT*, 172). In giving this water and wine to mortals, the jug also helps preserve mortals themselves in being, whilst in pouring a libation for the gods it creates a possibility—perhaps within the occasion of a feast that such a ritual act both 'stills and elevates'—for mortals and gods to be brought together. Thus, Heidegger introduces one of the characteristic ideas of his later authorship—the 'fourfold' of earth, sky, mortals, and gods: the dimensions of a world that has a very different mode of being and of presence than anything that could become the object of technical manipulation. 'When and in what way do things appear as things?' asks Heidegger. 'They do not appear *by means of* human making. But neither do they appear without the vigilance of mortals. The first step toward such vigilance is the step back from the thinking that merely represents—that is, explains—to the thinking that responds and recalls' (*PLT*, 181). That is to say, the thinking characteristic of science and technology, representational and explanatory thinking, will never be able to bring us into the nearness or presence of things, because it will always overlook that nearness for the sake of the purpose or use which the thing is to serve.

In the essay on 'The Thing', Heidegger seems almost to be saying that, yes, the encounter with the thing itself can occasion a disclosure of the fourfold such as he describes. Might he, then, be offering something similar to the aesthetic philosophy of the Japanese potter and aesthetician Yanagi Soétso? Yanagi argued for a view in which quite humble craft-made tea-bowls are seen as fulfilling the highest demands of aesthetic theory. These are not tea-bowls or porcelain produced with ideals of beauty or art in mind or 'works of art' expressing the consciousness of some genial artist. They are what they are as the result of 'the overall environment, the received traditions, the selfless work, the simple way of life, the natural materials and unsophisticated techniques'.[12] Testimony to the power of such simple artefacts is Yanagi's description of how 'As I lie in bed, I have had pots and pictures brought into my room for me to look at. I have got into the habit during long sleepless nights of allowing my thoughts to ponder over the strange miracle of the quiet beauty of each object.'[13] I suggest that this description of 'the strange miracle of the quiet beauty of each object' corresponds closely to what Heidegger more discursively unfolds as the fourfold meeting of mortals, gods, earth, and sky in the experience of the nearness and presence of the 'thing'.

The sense of a certain proximity in the relationship between the German thinker and the Japanese potter is almost palpable, but Heidegger's aim is not to argue for a handicraft aesthetic, though there is every reason to suppose he might have found much pleasure in the products of handicrafts. Rather, although he

---

[12] S. Yanagi, 'The Dharma Gate of Beauty', in *The Eastern Buddhist*, 9/2 Oct. 1979), 15–16.

[13] S. Yanagi, 'The Pure Land of Beauty', in *The Eastern Buddhist*, 9/1 (May 1976), 18. It is worth mentioning that Yanagi's thinking had a considerable influence on Western potters, not least the British potter Bernard Leach, who played a pivotal role in the revival of hand-crafted pottery and whose own work reveals a strong East Asian influence.

does not emphasize this at all in 'The Thing', I think it more likely that he sees the experience of nearness in the encounter with the thing as primarily made available for us in the mediation of the same poetic word that, for example, mediates the semi-divine being of the German rivers. The chief argument in favour of this view would be the simple accumulative force of his many essays on or references to poetry in which the key terms of the essay on 'The Thing' are invoked. In our 'destitute time' we do not actually and cannot actually experience such immediate nearness or presence. We know it only in the memory, the remembrance, the word that names the thing for and as what it is for us. In this respect it is entirely irrelevant that, at the time when Heidegger wrote his description of the Greek temple, he himself had never actually *seen* one. Where Ruskin will often make his case by insisting on his personal experience of what it is like to stand in such and such a place and see the way in which a particular quality of light is transformed in a certain passage of time, Heidegger is not offering anything as subjective or as psychological as this. For it is first in the word, the poem, that 'things' become what they are and, in the light of this refraction, co-reveal the elements of the world with which they belong together. That is to say that Heidegger never deliberately lets slip the note of caution that is integral to his whole grand narrative about the 'forgetting of being' that is the encompassing condition of the modern world. Only as poetry, only as 'a sign that is not read', a riddle and a hint can we experience the advent of 'the last God' or (which I take to be essentially the same) the present gathering of the fourfold.[14]

This is a bold and, in many respects, provocative vision. There is much in it that might seem to feed the view that Heidegger's is an essentially reactive position, to be understood purely in terms of its opposition to the world of science and technology. However, I suggest that it can consistently be read in terms of the model of a counter-movement that is not aimed at destroying technology but at providing a balance, a larger view of truth that gives a context of meaning that technology itself cannot supply. It is precisely this tension that shapes the characteristic tension and ambiguity of the poet's own destiny. Thus, it is not inconsistent that Heidegger recorded a number of his own talks and even a reading of Hölderlin's poetry for radio and for release as gramophone records (available today as CDs and purchasable on the internet), since he never sought to deny the reality of the technologized world in which we live. One might nevertheless comment that precisely the focus on the poet obscures or even

[14] The point I am making here has been well put by Gerald L. Bruns, when he writes that 'it is a caricature' to picture Heidegger as asserting that there is some sort of poetic word which will 'make Being show itself at last after the whole history of metaphysics has failed to flush it out of hiding. I think,' Bruns continues, 'that it is Heidegger's point (as it is also Derrida's) that if there is such a word (and it is not clear what it means for this to be the case), that word is just what withholds itself, refuses itself, remains unspeakable and strange—the word as absolutely other, which explodes every order of signification that we construct in order to subdue it . . . I see the later Heidegger as being closer to Derrida, or Derrida closer to the later Heidegger, than perhaps Derrida does, certainly closer than many of Derrida's readers see him.' G. L. Bruns, *Heidegger's Estrangements: Language, Truth and Poetry in the Later Writings* (Newhaven: Yale University Press, 1981), 198–9.

mystifies the real significance of technology for the production and experience of art. Though poetry is usually known through printed words and, as we have just noted, can be propagated through radio, recording, and other media, it retains a connotation of personal expression and immediacy which, even if deceptive, somehow suggests a simpler process than that under which a great work of architecture (the Sydney Opera House, let us say) or a film is produced. The technological element is sensed as exterior to the poetic work in a manner that cannot possibly be the case with the Opera House or the film where the work is inconceivable except as a technological product. Thus the very choice to focus on poetry may already suggest a kind of distancing or non-engagement on Heidegger's part in relation to the very question he is seeking to illuminate. If Yanagi's 'strange miracle of the quiet beauty of each object' is a plausible description of how we might feel in coming to understand a poem of Hölderlin (read in a suitably Heideggerian manner), how could such a deliberately naïve embrace of the nearness of things be replicated within the technologized art-forms that are characteristic of the modern world? Surely it could only be 'replicated' by itself being brought into the orbit of technological reproducibility and, therefore, losing those very qualities that made it a focus—however vulnerable, however ambiguous, however temporary—for resistance to the omnivorousness of the technological system.

We shall return to this question shortly. First, however, there is another aspect to Heidegger's treatment of the poet that requires comment in the context of an enquiry concerned with 'thinking about God'. As was already noted in Chapter 3, Heidegger's talk of 'the gods' or 'the last God' cannot immediately be conflated with the 'God-talk' of Christian theology. On the contrary it may seem to represent a kind of paganizing theology that Christian thinking about God might need to resist, perhaps in alliance with Jewish and Islamic theologies that similarly seem to appeal to qualities of transcendence and personality that Heidegger simply does not allow for. Heidegger himself often attempted to put a clear distance between his own thinking and that of mainstream theology, not least because, as we also saw in Chapter 3, he believed this theology to be irretrievably implicated in the kind of objectification and instrumentalization of thinking that was part of the millennium-long ideological preparation for the advent of a strictly modern science and technology. In the lectures on Hölderlin's poem 'Remembrance' he castigates Protestant liberal theology, Neo-Orthodoxy, and Catholic theology collectively, since, despite their obvious disagreement with each other, they are all trapped within the paradigm of nineteenth-century intellectualism. All theology, he asserts, 'posits in advance the *Theos*, the God, and does so in such a confident way that wherever theology arrives, the God has already begun his flight.'[15]

---

[15] Heidegger, *Gesamtausgabe*, 52, 132–3. Rather embarrassingly (the lectures were given in 1941–2), he goes on to add that whoever thinks in the manner of theology denigrates the essential being of the Fatherland 'and, if he thinks at all, is not thinking in the German way [*denkt nicht Deutsch*]' (ibid. 133).

Yet there is a problem here for Heidegger. Not only does his reading of Hölderlin reflect a pattern of fall-redemption-second coming that has clear roots in Jewish and Christian faith and theology[16] but Hölderlin himself pointed to a unique role for Christ which Heidegger assiduously avoids. This seriously imperils his interpretation of Hölderlin in general and especially a poem such as 'The Only One' (*Der Einzige*), which deals explicitly with Christ—who is, indeed, 'the Only One' (or, perhaps, the Unique One, the One-and-Only) of the title. In the poem Hölderlin writes: 'Always there stands something between men and Him. And as on a stairway the Heavenly One descends.'[17] Heidegger identifies this 'stairway' as the place where the poetic disclosure of humans' dwelling place occurs. It is poetic production that builds the stairway on which the Heavenly One is to descend, he says.[18] However, the poem itself allows and arguably requires a more directly 'Christian' reading. On such a reading the 'stairway' can be interpreted as the succession of former gods who are seen by Hölderlin as preparing the way for the coming of 'the Only One' who both fulfils the economy of mythology and brings it to an end. This does not exclude the extension of its meaning to encompass the poets in whose words these gods are celebrated. The role of both gods and poets, however, is no more than prepara-tory. The 'stairway' is, in a special sense, the mode of revelation of 'the Only One' and, as such, also a providential dispensation of the one who sent him, 'the Father', as he is named in the poem.

This is not to ascribe to Hölderlin the kind of theologizing of which Heidegger says that it is so confident of its ability to name 'the God' that it is in fact the surest sign that the God has already removed Himself. On the contrary, Hölder-lin's poem underlines how it is precisely the coming of the Only One and his ascension back to the Father that have, at a stroke, secularized the world of both gods and poets. He (the Only One) summons forth a love that goes beyond any possible poetic articulation ('This time my song has been too much from my own heart'), provoking the reflection that the poet can never 'find, as I want to, the right measure'. He adds 'But a God knows when that which I wish for will come, the Best' and the poem concludes that 'The poets, even the spiritual ones, must also be worldly.' Which is to say that precisely the love the poet has for Christ, as the One who would uniquely fulfil his poetic striving, sets a limit to the possibilities of the poetic word. On the one hand, Christ has been returned to Heaven, to a realm whose plenitude and joy cannot be expressed in human

[16] See, e.g. V. M. Fóti, *Heidegger and the Poets: Poiésis. Sophia. Techné* (Atlantic Highlands, NJ: Humanities Press, 1992), 65–6. See also, K. Löwith, *Heidegger: Denker in dürftiger Zeit* in *Sämtliche Schriften* (Stuttgart: J. B. Metzger, 1984), vol. 8; H. Jonas, 'Heidegger and Theology', in idem, *The Phenomenon of Life: Toward a Philosophical Biology* (Chicago: Chicago University Press, 1966); J. D. Caputo, *Demythologizing Heidegger* (Bloomington: Indiana University Press, 1993).
[17] Though these words are found only in later fragmentary reworkings of the first published version of the poem.
[18] Heidegger, *Gesamtausgabe*, 53, 195.

words. On the other hand, the words with which the poet has been left are revealed as essentially 'worldly'—they are broken and unfinished, fragments and enigmatic riddles. Hölderlin, then (and, it seems, against Heidegger), holds open the paradoxical possibility of the Christian God as the term—the goal, the limit, the elusively unthinkable and unsayable telos—that both motivates the poetic art and makes its task eternally unfulfillable.

But even if there are moments in which a poem might breathe the atmosphere of Yanagi's 'quiet miracle' and somehow, paradoxically and almost impossibly, make us aware of the nearness of 'the Only One'—whether it is a poem of Hölderlin or of anyone else—could we imagine such a thing in the context of any art form that had fully internalized the 'enframing' instrumentality of the technological system? Whatever Heidegger says about Hölderlin being in some way already 'beyond' the aeon of technology, isn't it rather the case that Hölderlin might—to follow Heidegger's manner of putting things—be more plausibly seen as the 'last poet of metaphysics', as the poet of a nostalgic remembrance whose allusions to some future Second Coming are merely the reflection of a past that is irretrievably lost? These questions constitute a challenge that must be addressed if we are to argue for a congruence between art and thinking about God of such a kind that it both keeps open possibilities that are irreducible to the technological and also resists casting itself in the figure of the romantic retreat from the technologically managed world. In other words, is it possible to argue for or to find an example of the kind of role Heidegger ascribes uniquely to the poet in a context in which the means of artistic production have been assimilated to the paradigm of technology?

II

The question invites a reference to one of the most influential twentieth-century contributions to the discussion of the relationship between art and technology— Walter Benjamin's 'The Work of Art in the Age of Technical Reproducibility'. Like many of his friends on the German left in the 1920s and 1930s who were interested in questions of art, Benjamin found himself caught in an uncomfortable dilemma. On the one hand, the official Communist Party line was increasingly hostile to the kinds of artistic experimentation and theorizing which they found attractive. On the other hand, as Benjamin states in the opening paragraphs of the essay, the rhetoric of traditional aesthetics, in which art and artist are hailed in terms of creativity, geniality, eternity, and mystery, was all too easily appropriated by Fascism, and, indeed, absorbed into its political self-presentation in rallies and parades in which ritual and myth were used to create a sense of participating in some more-than-political and profoundly mysterious national awakening. Heidegger is never mentioned in the essay but, from the standpoint of critical theory, his emphasis on the privileged role of the poet in shaping the destiny of the nation was of a piece with his involvement in Nazism.[19] This is a piece of mystification that obscures the real nature of artistic production and reception in an age of technology.

What is Benjamin's alternative? Acknowledging that art has always been essentially reproducible (one cave-painter could always, in principle, have copied the work of another), Benjamin claims that around the middle of the nineteenth century there occurred a paradigm shift, which he identifies with the discoveries of lithography and photography. This shift finds its most complete expression in film, especially once film has incorporated sound-reproduction into its own technical apparatus. With these changes, art is thoroughly technicized, and this means (amongst other things) that it is in principle and in an entirely new way infinitely reproducible, indeed that it is made precisely in order to be reproduced. An oil painting was made to be an unique work of art, something that could only exist in one form and in one place, inseparable from the hand of the master, as it were. An illustration in a magazine, a record, or a film are, by way of contrast, made to be reproduced. In an important sense, there is no original any more. As Benjamin puts it, the work of art loses 'its once-off existence', its quality of 'genuineness' or, in what is perhaps the essay's most cited expression, its 'aura'.[20] When I listen to a recording of, say, a Mozart mass-setting, 'The Cathedral leaves its place to be received into the apartment of the art-lover...'[21] But this transformation is not to be understood as if it were simply taking place in a relatively autonomous zone of human activity labelled 'culture'. It is rather the reflection and expression of a change in the very way in which human beings experience and perceive the world, a change for which the 'loss of aura' is the most decisive epitome but which could also be described in terms of 'bringing things closer' and 'repeatability'.

All of this has important implications for human beings' relation to history as well as to their experience of the present. The aura, the once-offness of a work of art, was essentially connected with its embeddedness in a particular tradition. Torn from this context it becomes something quite different—the way in which the Greeks 'experienced' a statue of Apollo in the environment of temple and cult is incommensurable with the way in which we experience it in a museum of art or antiquities or as an illustration in a book, television programme or website. It is even going to be different for us if we avail ourselves of the resources of modern tourism to 'see' the statue in its 'original' location or to attend a Mozart mass in Salzburg. The Renaissance's 'religion of art' and the nineteenth-century's slogan of 'art for art's sake' were attempts to prolong something of art's original aura, its ritual quality, as it were. But technical reproducibility is inherently corrosive of

---

[19] Some of the issues here are discussed—with reference to Benjamin—in P. Lacoue-Labarthe, *Heidegger, Art and Politics*, tr. C. Turner (Oxford: Blackwell, 1990).

[20] The terms in quotation marks translate Benjamin's 'einmaliges Dasein', 'Echtheit', and 'Aura': Benjamin, *Gesammelte Schriften*, 1.2, 475, 476, 477.

[21] Ibid. 477.

ritual. If ritual demands its special time and place (a mass for the nativity can *only* be held in a sacred space in the season of the nativity), technical reproducibility means that the work can be transported anywhere at any time. I can look at a reproduction of the statue or listen to the mass on the toilet if I want to (or on a plane, or in the office . . .).

It is clear that such an analysis can lend itself to the kind of complaints about the levelling tendencies of modern society that are characteristic of much conservative rhetoric. However, the analysis is not necessarily tied to some kind of nostalgia for the ages when art came clad in the aura of tradition, ritual, myth. Theologians, at least, might think kindly of Tillich's 'discovery' of visual art through poor quality illustrations which he studied in the trenches of the Western Front or of Karl Barth's daily habit of listening to recordings of Mozart. Benjamin, for his part, is not to be understood as if he is merely bewailing a loss. The aim of his essay is rather to record and to identify an existing state of affairs without regard to its moral or religious value. Moreover, recognition of this state of affairs is important if we are to avoid the inappropriate use of another age's aesthetic concepts and categories. Such misuse can only mystify our own present reality and make us vulnerable to fascism's aestheticization of politics.

But if a Mozart mass-setting or a statue of Apollo are material for incorporation into the technics of reproducibility, exhibits in what Malraux called the global 'museum without walls', art-forms such as film—indeed, especially and supremely film, according to Benjamin—are determined through-and-through by the exigencies of such reproducibility. In this being-determined-as-reproducible film represents the most extreme possibility for giving effect to the project of the museum without walls, as the whole heritage of past art becomes material for film treatment, whether in terms of filmed versions of Sophocles, Shakespeare, or Ibsen or in film biographies of actual or fictional artists, Michelangelo, Mahler, or Shelley, for example. Even sacred texts and rituals themselves become material for film, as in the many film portrayals of Christ. Film has the potential to remake the entire cultural heritage.

Every frame of a film is a carefully constructed technical product. Stop at any of the twenty-four frames a second and you will see a coherent and planned effect. No longer do actors act for an audience or lose themselves in a role but, instead, they act for the camera. The artist is never in any real way 'present' to the public, except on the basis of technical mediation. Even the effect of the film on the public is managed, in the sense that the requirements of marketing are built into the very processes of production, casting, and direction. The mediation of the market-place is already a part of every film and not merely a by-product of some kind of accidental 'success' or 'failure'. The personality of the star is the nearest substitute in the world of cinema for the lost aura of ritual art. Ultimately, the dynamics of reproducibility mean that the public will more and more require to see itself in film, something Benjamin sees already happening in Soviet films of everyday proletarian life. In the near future, he guessed, everyone would at some time or another appear on film. The advent of video and the television talk-show has fulfilled his prediction in ways he perhaps scarcely envisaged.

Much of Benjamin's analysis remains true even after a further seventy years of developing cinema. Although it might be objected that video, hand-held cameras, the improvization of dialogue, and other innovations open up possibilities for spontaneity and the 'presence' of the artist (whether this means the director, the cameraman or the actor) in the work, this can also be seen in terms of a further refinement of technical mediation. To believe that the Danish 'Dogme' film movement, with its elimination of the traditional artifices of Hollywood cinema, really reinstates some kind of naïve or unmediated relationship between artist and viewer is itself extremely naïve. There is all the difference in the world between the way in which a director such as Lars von Trier uses a hand-held camera and the products of amateur video-making. Just as it was a mistake to believe that quantum mechanics and the principle of uncertainty meant that physics had abandoned the attempt to construct the most accurate possible picture of reality (whereas the new concepts actually reflected the fact that the net of description and prediction had been drawn even tighter), so too these new techniques actually represent a technicization of new layers of experience and perception left untouched by the studio film art of the previous decades. In a faux-naïve film such as *The Blair Witch Project* the repeated switching between film and video is itself integral to the slow build-up of tension for which the film was so renowned.

Let us recall the question that led us to Benjamin and these reflections on film art. It was whether it was possible to envisage anything like the 'strange miracle of the quiet beauty of each object' in art once art has become subjected to the dynamics of technical reproducibility. Film, on Benjamin's account, offers us an example of an art that has not simply been taken up by the technologies of reproducibility but that is in its inception and inception determined by these technologies. In this respect it has (or seems to have) a quite different relation to technology than that of poetry, the poetry of a Hölderlin, for example. Could anything like the preservation of the possibility of the sacred be experienced in relation to film?

Of course, film has often taken up religious themes and motifs. European and American cinema-goers are familiar with film versions of the life of Christ and other biblical epics, with tales of the Early Church, and with depictions of martyrs, missionaries, religious fanatics, and impostors in just about every conceivable historical situation. Doubtless Bollywood can offer plentiful parallels in relation to the religious traditions of India. It is tempting to say that the failure of the vast majority of 'religious' films to treat their subject matter in anything other than a painful and embarrassing way might be taken as an indirect proof of Benjamin's thesis. But not all religious films are simply 'bad'. There have been film lives of Jesus (I'd say Pasolini's 1964 *The Gospel According to Saint Matthew*) or films dealing in a direct way with the religious life (e.g. Bresson's 1952 adaptation of Bernanos' novel *Journal d'un Curé de Campagne*) that not only treat their subject matter thoughtfully and sensitively but are also great works of film art. Yet even a positive evaluation of such films does not mean that they are endowed with any sense of miracle or aura. And if we subjectively experience them as having some kind of mystery or magic, is this not simply a sign of our own naïvety as viewers, our susceptibility to manipulation by the planned experience of the film-makers? Remember Kafka's caution that film put 'the eye in uniform'. If Hollywood is 'the dream factory', don't we always have to remember that the 'factory'-element decisively qualifies the 'dream'?[22] And whatever we make of the film itself, isn't the last glimmer of any crepuscular aura irrevocably dispelled by the unashamed marketing that accompanies the release of a major motion picture?

As is the case with any aesthetic judgement, we can never finally *know* such things. That is precisely why evaluations of this kind are, finally, a matter of judgement or of a kind of experimentation whereby we try out whether such and such a work can indeed be seen in the way that is being suggested. And so we need a worked example. Nowhere, of course, is such a tactic more perilous than in relation to a work of art where tastes famously differ and can scarcely be argued for. But not only is it unavoidable, it is also a test of the possibility of there being forms of thinking that cannot be reduced to clear, distinct, and manageable knowledge but that are, nevertheless, forms of *thinking,* involving both disciplined attention to reality and discrimination in thinkingly appraising what such attention yields.

My example is that of the 1983 film *Nostalgia,* directed by the Russian director Andrei Tarkovsky. The film was a co-production between Soviet and Italian production companies and was Tarkovsky's last film for a Russian state company before being exiled by the Soviet government. It was also his penultimate film before his death in 1986 at the age of fifty-four. Just about every discussion of Tarkovsky refers to the 'religious' or 'spiritual' dimensions of his work, as indeed he does himself. Amongst his previous films were a (highly fictionalized) dramatization of the life of the icon-painter Andrei Rublev and the metaphysical science-fiction allegory *Solaris.* One website describes his last film, *The Sacrifice,* as a 'profoundly spiritual masterpiece about the end of the world'. However, it should be emphasized that our question is not about whether such and such a film artist was a religious person who attempted to express something of their spirituality in film. Recall again Yanagi's comments about the ordinary and now unknown potters who produced the 'strange miracles' of everyday tea-bowls that gave him such solace in sleepless nights. The point is not 'Tarkovksy', but the film

---

[22] However, I should stress that I don't want these remarks to be taken as implying some sort of contempt for Hollywood. Even the best of Hollywood is, inevitably, inseparable from the *realpolitik* of studios, stars and the box-office, but the best of Hollywood is, for all that, wonderfully good film-making, even if it is not Hölderlin or Rembrandt.

itself and, in this case, whether the film, as a piece of technically saturated film-art can also give presence to such a 'strange miracle'.

Nostalgia is probably over-long for most viewers, its plot too lacking in drama or character development (even, for that matter, characterization) to sustain the kind of attention that the products of 'the dream factory' aim to address. We are clearly in the realm of the art-house film, and far from Hollywood. Like other Tarkovsky films, *Nostalgia* is laced with strongly allegorical and literary elements that could be seen as extraneous to what is essentially filmic in it. However, although these allegorical elements are important in directing our attention to the film's 'religious' aspect, I do not see them as decisive for an interpretation that opens out into the domain of thinking about God. What is?

The central character, Gorchakov, is a Russian poet, pursuing research in Italy on a seventeenth-century Russian composer. Both Gorchakov and his subject are thus identified as exiles and strangers, and the theme of the difference between Russia and the West is also frequently touched on. In the course of his travels he encounters a strange character called Domenico ('the Lord'?) who may be a holy fool of the type often alluded to in Russian literature. We learn that Domenico had for seven years locked up his wife and children in their home to protect them from the evil world (Yahweh's jealousy for Israel?). When Gorchakov visits Domenico, the latter gives him bread and wine, and also a candle. Neither the bread, nor the wine, nor the candle has the appearance of an item from a Church repository. The candle is just a stump of a cheap commercial candle, the bread just a torn off chunk. But the symbolism is impossible to escape. Mysteriously, Domenico writes an equation on the wall: $1 + 1 = 1$, which also seems charged with theological significance, though whether it denotes the inability of God as Yahweh to break out of his isolation, or whether it hints at the Trinitarian fulfilment of what is begun in Yahweh is unclear (perhaps necessarily so). And there is more. Gorchakov is given a task by Domenico. 'I thought it was enough to save my family,' Domenico says, 'but salvation cannot be for me alone; it must be for all, and it can only be won for all if this candle is lit and carried—without the flame going out—from one end to the other of St Catherine's Pool.' Gorchakov is to go to this ancient thermal pool and perform the seemingly simple task. Why can't Domenico do it himself? Because, as he says, the people all think he's mad, and every time he goes down into the pool they drag him out. Which, being interpreted, seems to mean that the Lord's will is to become incarnate and in and by the incarnation to bring salvation to all, but human beings cannot easily accept such a paradox and for every movement of incarnation from God's side respond by reinstating God as a non-incarnate, 'transcendent' deity. Is Gorchakov then himself to become a Christ, realizing the movement of incarnation that the Father cannot? Or is he the human helper who, in the mode of synergy shares with God in the work of redemption? However, we answer this question—and there is some ambiguity—the limits of Domenico's own powers are powerfully and painfully revealed when he mounts the plinth of a giant equestrian statue of the Emperor Marcus Aurelius in the very centre of Rome itself and urges a silent crowd of more or less indifferent onlookers to seek the spirit they have lost. As his words fall on deaf ears, he douses himself in petrol and then sets fire to it, falling from the plinth in a living fireball. The sound-track—ironically—plays the 'Song of Joy' from the last movement of Beethoven's Ninth Symphony.[23]

If, once, there was a chance that Domenico might have saved the world, he cannot do so any more. God has died, and the task is bequeathed to one who is a poet and an exile, a rootless stranger, cut off both from his own Russian past and from the heritage of the civilization of the West. Finally, having first forgotten the task (or, at least, pushed it into his subconscious), Gorchakov cancels his flight back to Russia and goes to the pool, scarcely believing in or comprehending the task he has undertaken, and wracked by ever more severe heart pains. Located in an ancient cloister, the pool is empty of water, though a few puddles linger here and there, and a couple of workers are clearing rubbish from it. There is a sense of dankness and dereliction. Except for the candle-flame, the colours are all shades of grey. Rather self-consciously (even though the workers pay no attention to him), Gorchakov climbs down into the pool, lights the candle and, sheltering it in his hand, begins to walk from one end of the pool to the other. What follows is eleven minutes of a single tracking shot. The extraordinary length of this shot effects a steady and, finally, almost unendurable build-up of tension as we wait for a resolution that is postponed beyond every expectation. It is virtually silent and, until the final moments, there is no background music. We hear only the scraping of Gorchakov's feet on the ancient stone and his breathing, which becomes increasingly painful and irregular. Half-way across the candle goes out. He turns and looks at the viewers. Whose lack of faith is making the work of salvation impossible, his uncomprehending look seems to ask? He returns to the beginning. Can the task be performed? The candle is, after all, only a stump, and it can only be lit so many times. He starts out once more, protecting the weak flame with his coat. He moves slowly, uncertainly, shuffling his way forward. Again the candle goes out. We see that he is troubled, uncertain whether to try again or just to give up and go. He appears physically afflicted. Finally he decides to try again, though we sense that this will be the last time. Everything depends on this last attempt. The minutes drag by—we are still on the same shot—and we begin to sense that he might, just might, do it. Yet his laboured breathing betrays not only the intense concentration he now commits to the task but the impend-ing possibility of heart failure. Very gradually the camera zooms in on the hand holding the candle, cradled as if it were something of great preciousness and value. The edge of the pool comes in sight and, as the candle is finally lowered

---

[23] Recalling that the words are taken from Schiller and that Dostoevsky is an important part of Tarkovsky's artistic background, it might be noted that Dostoevsky, though often using themes from Schiller, was also frequently sarcastic over what he saw as Schiller's naïve hopes for the realization of an earthly kingdom of universal brotherly love.

into place, the opening chords of Verdi's Requiem begin to well up. Gorchakov collapses and, in a final, dream-like shot, we see him sitting once more outside the wooden house of his childhood memories, now enclosed by the giant piles of a ruined Gothic cathedral: his self-sacrificial act of obedience has reconciled Russia and the West; childhood and the present, nature and the sacred are revealed in breathtaking final unity.

Crucial to the effect of this whole astonishing sequence is that although its 'meaning' has been advertised in advance by the allegorical elements associated with Domenico it has a ritual quality that is *sui generis*, that does not require us to know or to understand the allegory before we can be gripped by what we see happening. That is to say, there is a decisive shift from the allegorical and literary levels of the film to something that is purely and irreducibly filmic, something that can only be articulated in this medium. And what is that? There are, I suggest, three elements that are integral to what is happening here. The first is time. The English title of one selection of Tarkovsky's writings has the title *Sculpting in Time*. This pinpoints one of Tarkovsky's defining ideas about his art: that it is an art whose material is time. As we have just seen, Tarkovsky treats time in a rare and extraordinary way in this scene and it is just through this rare and extraordinary time quality that its emotional power is heightened to an extreme pitch of tension. But it is time represented in the form of image and vision. Which suggests the second element: light, the *sine qua non* of all visual representation and also, in this case, explicitly at the centre of the scene's symbolic meaning. In Gorchakov's slow passage across the empty pool the eye is drawn relentlessly to the one point of illumination, which, in film terms, is the far from dramatic light of an ordinary, everyday candle. But light is not functioning here merely as a focus or as a milieu within which things happen. Light itself is in motion, moving in space and in time. What we *see* is not simply a man walking thirty metres or so holding a candle, but the movement of light through darkness. Thirdly, and in close connection with both of the previous points, there is sound, no less an integral element in film than time or vision. And here too there is a gradual movement, from silence, through Gorchakov's shuffling footsteps and laboured breathing, and on to the still triumph of the final chords.

What is happening here is a kind of ritualization of the materials of film art in which time, light, and sound are incorporated into a dramatic movement that, for the moment of vision, induces us to suspend our disbelief and accept that, maybe, what we are seeing is indeed the salvation of the world. What Tarkovsky works on us then, is a kind of transformation akin to that of liturgy, a transformation in which the materials, the everyday, the earthly things, remain just what they are from the point of view of unbelief or of scientific investigation. But, at the same time, a horizon of meaning is opened up by the specific conjunction of relations into which these things are brought that says 'more' than they say in their non-ritual being. In the monologue declaimed by Alexander, the central character of *The Sacrifice*, Tarkovksy's next and final film, it is not the content of a ritual that matters, but the fact that it is performed *as a ritual, or with a ritual intention.*

It seems, then, that I am arguing that Tarkovsky provides a decisive counter-argument to Benjamin: that even the through-and-through technicized medium of film can recreate the aura of ritual in the midst of a technological society and, in doing so, offer matter and occasion for thinking about God. As has already been acknowledged, such a claim cannot be put beyond the reach of the criticism that we have simply been duped by the technical magic of the film-maker, that our sense of ritual and of the performance of a 'strange miracle' is itself something manufactured, a technical product. Am I not guilty of overlooking the whole technological mediation of the image by the camera lens, sound reproduction, film colour, cutting, and editing? Of course, these things belong to the making of any film, even a mediocre one. But does the craft element, the technical know-how, that was so essential to the building of, say, a medieval cathedral mean that that too is without the power to work 'strange miracles' and to raise thought to thinking about God? Yet, surely, whereas a cathedral creates a space that we can inhabit liturgically, housing rituals in which we can participate, doesn't the specific 'craft' aspect of a film mean that, however much we are moved to admire the vision of the director, we are inevitably reduced to being spectators, looking on at the ritual enacted in the film from the outside? This is always a possibility—but recall what was said previously about *alétheia* and *anamnesis*. Truth, as mediated in active remembrance, is not a matter of some fact 'out there' directly mirrored in our subjective pictures or words. Truth *is* in and as remembrance. But a film is always in a certain sense an act of remembrance, it is always completed before ever it is shown. Whereas a theatrical production, no matter how well rehearsed, has a dimension of present-ness, a film presents what—even as a performance—belongs, strictly speaking, in the past. And, in this case, the very title—*Nostalgia*—reminds us that memory is at issue in the course of the action. First and foremost, the issue of memory centres on Gorchakov's child-hood 'memories' of Russia—but also the memory of a truth, a plenitude of life, a wholeness, for which even childhood memories are only a symbol. As the ritual of the candle enacts the opening of a way back to these memories and their unification with Gorchakov's present adult existence, so we—whilst remaining in one sense spectators—are also invited to think, reflectingly, rememberingly, ritually, on our own possibilities for such a return. Tarkovsky does not give us a liturgical experience, but nor does Christian liturgy. He invites us through ritual action to active remembrance—as liturgy itself does.[24]

---

[24] It might also be objected that watching a film involves an essentially spectator-like attitude that is alien to the participatory mode of genuine liturgy. However, in a discussion of this point in a conference in Russia, one of the Russian contributors suggested that, for a Russian, the distance between spectating and participation is narrowed by virtue of the nature of Russian Orthodox liturgy. Formally, virtually everything is said, sung, or done by the clergy and choir, yet emotionally the congregation participate if anything more intensely than in a typical Western service.

I acknowledged at the outset that an example such as this will, inevitably, be exposed to criticism on account of the inescapable differences in individual and even cultural taste. I know many people who simply find Tarkovsky's films overlong and just a bit too self-consciously meaningful. Any other example, however, would have been liable to these or other objections. It is a part of our cultural situation that there is no contemporary canon that commands universal assent. Every work will be open to conflicting evaluations and interpretations. No reputation is beyond revision. Ultimately, however, the point is not about Tarkovksy but about the possibility of a medium as technologically defined as that of film awakening horizons that are not reducible to those of its own technical production. If this example fails, it does not follow that some other example might, nevertheless, show analogous possibilities.

Nor need our examples be limited to film. Although film was, for Benjamin, the epitome of a technically reproducible art there are other media in which we could also seek openings for a dialogue between art and thinking about God. At the beginning of this chapter I mentioned the sculpture of Anish Kapoor, but one might also think of a video artist such as Bill Viola, whose work has also moved in the sphere of the sacral (even if, as is almost inevitable, not uncontroversially[25]), or, indeed, almost countless other artists working in a wide range of media. Indeed, if we have once allowed that one technicized medium may nevertheless be a site of 'strange miracles' there can be no limit in principle to the ways in which the art of an age of technology might set in motion possibilities for thinking about God.

Heidegger commented with regard to poetry (even the poetry of *the* poet, Hölderlin), that thinking is not the same as poetry, and the artistic lure or provocation to thinking about God does not and cannot exhaust the possibilities of such thinking. Nor, from the other side, can art deliver a final, non-enigmatic, non-equivocal illumination as to the meaning of what is given us in thinking about God. Every work, like every thought, remains open to reinterpretation, misunderstanding, and misrepresentation. 'We are a sign that is not read.' Whether we start with the production of art or its reception or with the thoughts to which art moves us, it is only in the committed activity of thinking poetically (where 'poetically' might include 'cinematically') that what poetry offers to thought will be able to be thought. Idealist aesthetics conceived of poetry and thought as being calibrated on a common scale, such that where poetry expresses thought in figurative form, thought thinks this content 'purely'. But whereas, on Heidegger's understanding, they are thought of as being both in proximity to and yet irreducible to each other, then there can be no question of trying to establish any sort of hierarchy. If each feels a need for the other, this need not be

---

[25] See the discussion in my *Art, Modernity and Faith* (ch. 10) of Viola's installation 'The Messenger' in Durham Cathedral in 1996.

understood as the attempt to reduce the other to its mouthpiece or its guarantor, but as different movements around a common riddle. Thinking about God does not give the answer to the question that art unconsciously articulates, nor can art give life to a thinking that is non-actual and irrelevant. But where each is what it is then—maybe—there can be friendship between them.

10

Conclusion

This enquiry has trod and continues to tread a long, uneven, and circuitous path, marked by many irregularities and unpredictable encounters. That, we may say, is what thinking is always like—at least when it is engaging humanly and historically important issues. Thinking about something as important as the relationship between our contemporary self-understanding and technology cannot be reduced to a sequence of bullet points or an action plan. In the last resort a work such as this can only be a provocation, a lure, a question to thinking—not the delivery of a ready-made answer that the reader merely has to download and apply. Attempting to pull the many and variegated threads of the discussion together into some sort of 'conclusion' would, therefore, seem counterproductive. Yet one or two tings merit being said or said again at this point.

The first is simply to reiterate that, in attempting to find a thinking about God that is other than, resistant to, and certainly irreducible to technological enframing I am not committing myself to the rejection of technology. Technology has literally and metaphorically got nder our skin, it accompanies our every move and mood, it permeates and is the milieu of daily living and global political and economic decision-making. We have heard Guardini's judgement that in the encounter with technology as the reality of our age we are in fact encountering ourselves, and that the decision concerning technology is therefore a decision concerning ourselves. Putting it like this, it seems to me that there is a fundamental sense in which we cannot be 'against' technology since we cannot be 'against' ourselves and continue to be accepting of the gift of life. We might go further, and say with Hefner that the encounter with technology is not merely an encounter with ourselves, but that it is also an encounter in which we discover that we are, in an important sense, co-creators, transformers of the biological materials that we have hitherto equated with being human. As such, he argues, technology is an important site of contemporary religious life. There is a sense in which I agree and have to agree with that, if I have once accepted the omnipresence of technology in contemporary reality.

Nevertheless, there is room here for a difference of emphasis that has significant consequences. For when Hefner and others speak of us as already being *cyborgs*, beings whose existence is inseparable from technology, this covers over a distinction that, I believe, remains fundamental in our relation to technology. Take the example of a man equipped with a rapid-fire assault rifle. If such a man takes it into his head to go on what the tabloids refer to as a killing spree he will, obviously, be capable of inflicting far more damage than he would if he had only his bare hands. His mastery of the machine makes him something else and, to that extent, it is true to say that he has become a cyborg of sorts. He has acquired powers that are not part of human beings' biological endowment. Yet, when he is apprehended, we hold the man and not the cyborg accountable. We require the man to be imprisoned. We do not necessarily require the gun to be destroyed. Something similar holds in many other—less catastrophic—technological relationships. Like the killer's gun, my car too gives me powers of speed and load-bearing that go well beyond my natural capacities. If I crash at speed (or, for that matter at 10 mph) I inflict damage on others, on myself, and on the environment that I could never do alone. Yet even if I am not criminally responsible for the crash, I remain accountable for having been the driver. The same situation holds with regard to the volume at which I play my radio and whether I use my computer for writing books about God or accessing pornography. That a child is born with the assistance of technological intervention does not absolve the community from duties of love and care, nor would those who oppose such technologies seek such absolution. The omnipresence of technology does not do away with human accountability. On the contrary, there is a real sense in which it heightens rather than diminishes it.

Nor is this solely a matter of opening up an ethical dimension that technology cannot of itself encompass. Something similar may be said with regard to what could be regarded as matters of aesthetics or sensibility. The 2004 exhibition 'Future Face' at the London Science Museum invited visitors to ponder the extent to which our idea of what a human face is or should be like is already being influenced by technology, not only as a result of the impact of cosmetic surgery but also in terms of the influence of computer-generated images of faces that are, it seems, already affecting both how we see ourselves and how we want to see ourselves.[1] In this regard, we might pause to picture to ourselves the kinds of faces captured by early photographers amongst pre-modern peoples. Compare their individuality and dignity with the faces of those of our contemporaries who resist natural ageing with every weapon that technology provides. Of course, the pre-modern peoples were lucky to live to see old age and doubtless suffered many debilitating or disfiguring illnesses that we are able to avoid—but is it a foregone conclusion that the new cyborg face is to be preferred?

It is, then, in relation to a broad range of issues that technology remains contextualized in a larger human reality. The many aspects of that reality (including, not least, political and economic life as well as law-making and

---

[1] See S. Kemp, *Future Face: Image, Identity, Innovation* (London: Profile Books, 2004).

law-enforcing) extend far beyond the range of topics dealt with in this enquiry. Here, I have largely limited myself to one quantitatively small segment of cultural life: human beings' concern for God. Even within this selective focus, I have only been able to draw on a limited horizon from the whole range of humanity's religious concern. I have, in particular, occupied myself with that point in our culture at which the language we use about God relates to the discourse of the contemporary academy in philosophy and theology. I have done so, in part, because the academy is one of the crucial institutions in our society where technological ways of thinking and technological values meet under the same roof as artistic, ethical, and religious ways of thinking. Philosophy and theology are particularly sensitive points at which this meeting can be registered, examined and—since we are participants and not merely spectators of it—transformed, if only in some small measure.

At this point, I have been suggesting, neither philosophy nor theology nor any other form of fundamental thinking is obliged merely to accept the seigniorial rights of technology. Here, in the disciplined conversation we conduct amongst ourselves concerning what our religion, our art, and our ethics mean to us, we can allow hesitancies, stumblings, suspensions of judgement, and the questioning acceptance of there being insoluble dilemmas in a manner for which Heidegger's 'research man' would have neither time nor inclination. We don't have to come up with answers or applications and we can and should think as long and as slow as we need. Probably we'll have to think very long and very slow even to get started.

In these terms, 'thinking' does not provide the answer to technology. Not even 'thinking about God' will do that. But the point is not to provide an 'answer'. The point is no more than to open up or to strive to keep open the multi-dimensionality of discourse and to resist the creeping monoculture of a certain kind of bureaucratic technologism. In these terms, I would not venture to say that 'thinking' alone is inadequate for the task, but I would say that thinking about God must draw on levels of commitment and traditions of insight that pure thinking (i.e. philosophizing) *may* do, but isn't fundamentally committed to doing in the same way. In doing so, thinking *about God* has to have an existential sharpness that, in the case of philosophy, may be regarded as an optional extra. However, in the absence of a more sustained evaluation of the relative merits of pure thinking (philosophy) and thinking about God (theology) as forms of such well-intentioned resistance, I would not wish to insist on any stereotyping of philosophy as 'abstract' or 'without passion'. And, in case it is inferred that I wish to exclude philosophy from this task, it should be clear that the manner in which this enquiry as a whole has taken its bearings from the contributions of Martin Heidegger reflects my view that, however we define it more closely, this relationship is rarely one of a simple either/or. In relation to the question concerning technology, neither philosophy nor theology has a ready-made arsenal of resources that can simply be applied: both of them live and achieve whatever they do achieve only in the effort of thinking itself. That the thinking characteristic of theology may take a different shape from that which is characteristic of philosophy (that it might, for example, incorporate gratitude and love) does not absolve it from the constant return to this effort to think against the stream of prevalent cultural assumptions and expectations. No answers, then, but only a call, a provocation, an invitation to think about God in an age of technology. But there is something more to be said.

II

It was never the aim of the central part of this book (Chapters 4, 5, and 6) to produce anything resembling an idea or concept of God that could hold its own on the theoretical level against the deliverances of science or a philosophical perspective oriented towards the justification of contemporary scientific theory. It was not as if an idea of God was developed that could then be brought to bear on the problems of ethics, academic life, and art that were addressed in Chapters 7, 8, and 9. Yet it will seem clear to many readers that there has been an implicit idea of God in play throughout my discussion. And whilst I stressed that I was seeking only to identify the formal traits of a non-technological thinking about God, this form/content distinction can only really be sustained up to a certain point. Form itself is necessarily determined or, at the very least, influenced by what it is that is being examined, represented, or thought about. The forms of thought appropriate to discussing the respective qualities of a Rothko and a Constable are not those appropriate to solving a mathematical puzzle or debating a matter of foreign policy that requires an urgent decision. However indirectly, some kind of idea as to *what* it is that is being thought *about* will colour even the most formal discussion. This idea may not lie on the surface, and, certainly with regard to God, it may never be separable from the indeterminacy of an eschatological not-yet and an apophatic unknowing. Yet I have spoken constantly of thinking *about* God, an expression implying that, in some way or other, thinking is directed towards a specific matter, it is thinking about *God*. This still allows for and even insists on a certain inbuilt imprecision, since thinking about God is not, simply, thinking God, that is to say, it is not a mental event that can be imagined as simply and unproblematically transparent to its object. It is not a straightforward cognitive act. 'Thinking about' is thinking that circles its subject matter, always retaining a distance from it even in the moment when it thinks of nothing else. Conversely, and to repeat, even in keeping its distance it is thinking directed towards and taken up with whatever it is that is to be thought about.

What idea of God, then, is thinkable within the parameters of the formal traits that I attempted to outline? Clearly, it is an idea that falls significantly short of what a philosophical theist would regard as the fullness of the concept of God as found, e.g. in Thomism or more recent versions of Christian theism or even in such variant conceptualizations as post-Whiteheadian process theology. Nothing has been said that would require us to take up a position on such divine attributes as omniscience, omnipotence, impassibility, or existence. The philosophical *concept* of God, in other words, would need a very different kind of justification from what is being attempted here. But it does not follow that the idea of God that emerges from between the lines of my argument is totally content-free. As was made clear in Chapter 4, 'God' is not simply the name for any mere negation of technological rationality and what is being thought about in thinking about God is very different from fantasy fiction or futurological alternatives to technology. What, then, can we say about God that does not breach the suspension of ontological claims required by the self-limitation of our formal guidelines? The answer, I think, can best be developed from those guidelines themselves.

I began, it will be recalled, by noting the freedom of thought to think about God if it freely chose so to do. The corollary of this is that God is a God who allows humans to relate to Godself in freedom. We touch here on the boundaries of what, in the Christian West, has been one of the longest and, sometimes, bitterest of theological and philosophical controversies about the God-relationship, with such eminent representatives of the Christian tradition as Augustine, Luther, and Calvin denying the essential freedom of human beings in relation to God. Whatever position one might take in this debate, one can, I think, nevertheless acknowledge the principle of freedom as an original dimension of the God-relationship. Even where a Luther speaks of the bondage of the will, he acknowledges that, in principle, in the beginning—and again in the end—God's intention in creation and redemption was and will be to endow the human being with the ultimate freedom consistently to choose the good and to respond to God's own gifts and gracious act in freedom, as a free and responsible creature. Whether or not we are free to choose faith, we are, even in Lutheranism (perhaps especially in Lutheranism), free *in* faith. If our choice to think about God is marked by an inalienable and original freedom, then, it follows that whatever else God may be, God is a God who allows us to think about God, even to think about God mistakenly. God lets us be in our own way, free to choose to turn Godwards or not, a point clearly—even beautifully— articulated by Kierkegaard when he wrote that

Yet there is one limitation on God, though he is infinitely stronger [than you]: he has placed a self over against himself, yes, lovingly, with indescribable love, he has placed a self over against himself. For he placed this self there, and he places a self there, every time a human being comes into existence, one whom, in his love, he puts on an equal level with himself. O, wondrous power and love! A human being cannot bear that what he 'creates' might be on an equal level with himself; they should be as nothing in relation to him, and that is why, contemptuously, he calls them his 'creatures'. But God, who creates out of nothing, all-powerfully takes something out of nothing and says 'Be', lovingly adding, 'Be something, even though it be something over against me'. Wondrous love, when even his all-powerfulness is in the power of love!²

But if the possibility of thinking about God was thus rooted in the freedom of the creature to rise above itself and think about God, it was also noted that this did not mean that God could simply be conjured up by an act of thinking. Although thinking about God calls for the active and committed engagement of the 'I' and for a courageous determination to see the choice of such a thought through to the end, in freely choosing to think about God we also place ourselves under the discipline of waiting upon God. In connection with this I remarked on such topics as Kierkegaardian patience, Simone Weil's notion of 'decreation', and Lévinas's idea of a 'passivity before passivity'. The theme of apophatic or negative theology is also relevant here. The cumulative force of these traits of thinking about God can be then taken as correlative to the transcendence of the God who is to be thought about. The God who allows human beings the freedom to think about Godself is a God who cannot simply be thought into being or created as a product of human thought itself. As many commentators have remarked, it belongs to the logic or grammar of the term 'God' that God will always have a certain prevenience or inconvertible priority over the human being who is thinking about God. Merely saying this is not, of course, to have proved that there is actually a God who is actually transcendent. As was mentioned earlier, even some forms of Cupittian non-realism might allow for a kind of humanly produced idea known as 'God' whose unique property is that, in being thought, has to be thought as not humanly produced. Perhaps the kind of formal analysis offered here cannot, finally, contribute more than this. Perhaps even some of the most vociferous forms of contemporary neo-orthodoxy often do little more than declare the rhetorical necessity of asserting God's transcendence, even when nothing is really done (since, perhaps, nothing really can be done) to make good the epistemological or ontological claims implied in such an assertion. Yet the fact remains that if we see thinking about God as a thinking that waits on what it itself has not and cannot produce or determine, then not only is thinking free in relation to God—God is also free in relation to thinking. It is this logic that, similarly, leads Heidegger to speak of what calls for thinking as doing so by withdrawing itself from thinking and bestowing itself precisely in the mode of self-concealment.

---

² S. Kierkegaard, *Christelige Taler* [Christian Discourses] in *Samlede Værker*, (Copenhagen: Gyldendal, 1962), xiii. 124. Similar thoughts are to be found in Simone Weil, e.g. 'In a sense God renounces being everything. We should renounce being something.' S. Weil, *Gravity and Grace* tr. E. Craufurd (London: Ark, 1987), 29. A full treatment of the similarities and differences between Kierkegaard and Weil would be matter enough for an extended study. It is striking that a number of contemporary philosophers of religion have published extensively on both, e.g. Martin Andic, Richard Bell, and D. Z. Phillips. Speculatively, one might find a common source for the idea of creation as a ceding of omnipotence in medieval Jewish mysticism, mediated for Kierkegaard via Protestant mysticism of the seventeenth and eighteenth centuries.

It does not, however, follow that God should be pictured as arbitrarily concealing or revealing Godself, now here, now there, now to this person, but not to that. In speaking of the gratitude that is intrinsic to thinking about God, we also, implicitly, speak of the relation to God as a relation to one who gives, the giver of 'every good and perfect gift'. Although we think about God on the basis of a free decision, that free decision itself, the very freedom that underlies the possibility of deciding, is experienced as a gift, an occasion, an opportunity, a chance, that we did not give ourselves. And within this basic phenomenon of gratitude, we can discern a sequence of further, deepening thoughts about God. Firstly, the idea of God as the one to whom we owe thanks for all our most fundamental capacities and possibilities, and therefore as the one whom we thank as our creator, maker, source, ground of being. Secondly, to the extent that the God-relation is experienced as liberation from a situation of incapacity, non-relationship, and fundamental hopelessness, then our thanks will point to the further idea of God as redeemer and saviour. But this, in turn and thirdly, opens up to why God is to be thought of not merely as a transcendent 'x' but as one to whom we may relate as a God who is in some sense personal since to thank is always to thank some*one*. What 'personal' means more precisely in this context is, perhaps, mysterious—but so is all talk of 'the personal' finally mysterious. In the further extension of this mystery of the personal may also be the root (and, in any case, a necessary condition) of coming to think of God as threefold.[3] Minimally, however, it is in this personal quality that the trustworthiness of the thought of God is grounded, and it is this that is our chief assurance against any kind of arbitrary hide-and-seek view of revelation.

Further dimensions of the experience of God as liberating, saving, and redeeming are implicit in the suggestion that the language in which we best think about God is subjunctive or hypothetical. For a God who can be thus thought about is a God who may be known in, as, and through an open field of possibilities that reach beyond the immediacy or givenness of whatever can be gathered into the determinacy of indicative discourse. To the 'perhaps' of subjunctive discourse corresponds the idea of God as the God for whom all things are possible or, as Kierkegaard put it, 'God is that all things are possible'.[4] Again, this thought can be thought either in terms of creation, as an original endowment of possibility that is a precondition of our existing at all, or in terms of redemption, as the renewal or re-donation of possibility when possibility seemed

---

[3] For an exploration of the interconnection of these themes in the context of a modern Protestant dogmatics see Heinrich Ott, *Wirklichkeit und Glaube, (ii). Der persönliche Gott* (Göttingen and Zürich: Vandenhoeck and Ruprecht, 1969); also idem, *Gott* (Stuttgart: Kreuz Verlag, 1971), especially ch. 5. For a modern Orthodox approach see J. Zizioulas, *Being as Communion* (London: Darton, Longman and Todd, 1985). Of course, the theme of the Trinity has become one of the most widely written-on topics of contemporary theology.

[4] See S. Kierkegaard, *The Sickness unto Death*, tr. H. V. and E. H. Hong (Princeton: Princeton University Press, 1980), 40.

exhausted. In this latter case God appears as the one who breaks through experiences of impossibility, necessity, and the sheer denial of futurity. Something like this would seem to be captured in Ernst Bloch's interpretation of the 'signs and wonders' of the New Testament, in terms of the miraculous event that 'bursts the accustomed status of things'—to which he adds that 'it is only against the world lacking in possibilities of well-being that the interruption brought about by the wonder is directed.'[5] The miracle, in other words, is the 'lightning-flash' of utopistic hope, a moment that transforms our relation to a world where possibilities of well-being, flourishing, and hope have been foreclosed and shut down. The miracle is not merely a sign of God's power over the causal relations of the physical universe, but, in the New Testament at least, is far more a sign of the future, of a messianic kingdom in which we will be what we have it in us to become. The miracle is thus primarily to be interpreted in the light of the divine word 'Behold, I make all things new'. If, then, a discourse that limits itself to the parameters of the subjunctive must appear 'weak' and ineffective in relation to the real and pressing questions and demands imposed on us by the world, it may also be a way of articulating a faith in God as the one for whom all things are possible.

Something analogous to what has been said about subjunctivity may be said regarding parataxis: that even in such 'imperfect' discourse, and perhaps *precisely* in such imperfect discourse, God is shown to be the one who, when structures of meaningfulness become indeterminable, when the tower of grammar is shaken and language fails, can still bestow meaning as language's unobjectifiable spirit, breath, or word.[6] This may seem to reduce speaking about God to 'sighs and groans too deep for words' (Rom. 8: 26). Maybe—but that this does not confine us to some kind of private hermetic world is indicated by noting that the decisive form of Christian communication, the sermon, is a form of communication which, even when at its most urgent and demanding, is not a word of simple statement, nor even of imperious command, but of the open and permissive forms of the question, the hypothetical, or the optative. Such phrases as 'Do we

---

[5] E. Bloch, *Das Prinzip Hoffnung, Gesamtausgabe* (Frankfurt am Main: Suhrkamp, 1959), v. 1544.

[6] Something of what this could mean is explored by Richard Kearney in his *The God Who May Be: A Hermeneutics of Religion* (Bloomington: Indiana University Press, 2001). Kearney lays particular emphasis on the shift in understanding God's word to Moses from the Burning Bush (Exodus 3): where the metaphysical tradition consistently translated God's reply to Moses's request to hear God's name as 'I am that I am', alternative translations point to the futural or eschatological possibilities of the name, as in 'I shall be what I shall be' (already found in Jewish sources of a thousand years ago) or 'I-am-who-I-may-be' (Kearney's own proposal). 'This God,' he writes, 'is the coming God who may-be... This Exodic God obviates the extremes of atheistic and theistic dogmatism in the name of a still small voice that whispers and cries in the wilderness; *perhaps.* Yes, perhaps if we remain faithful to the promise, one day, some day, we know not when, I-am-who-I-may-be will at last be. Be what? We ask. Be what is promised as it is promised. And what is that? We ask. A kingdom of justice and love. There and then, to the human "Here I am," God may in turn respond, "Here I am". But not yet.' (Kearney, *The God Who May Be*, 38.)

not see?' 'Is it not so . . . ?' 'So let us . . . ' or 'May we . . . ' are not merely accidental
or rhetorical flourishes: they reveal something of the heart of what is going on in
all genuine sermonical address. Nor is preaching a form of communication that is
ashamed to enact the breakdown of syntax, to make public the struggle for
meaning when no available words will do. And nor, finally, is it ashamed, *as a
public word*, to fall into the silence of reflection and prayer.

The discussion of vision led to a meditation on active remembrance as truth's
way of being in the world. In relation to this discussion, we may say of God that
God is what is most worthy of remembrance. At the same time, the vision of God
that we call to mind in active remembrance was said to be inseparable from a
vision of ourselves as we might, in the light of God's way of beholding us, be or
become. In saying this, however, two further points are to be stressed. Firstly, that
our choices concerning what we regard as worth remembering are free choices,
choices for which we are answerable, since they are the choices that define us as
bearing responsibility for the form and power of the truth that is in us. To use the
older theological language, the God thus remembered is a God who judges or, in
less heteronomous terms, the God who cares for the truth and the justice to
which our thoughts bear witness. But, secondly, that God can be the theme of
active remembrance implies that God exists for us in a manner that is, simply,
memorizable. That God can be remembered in time, means that God consents to
be known in and through, in and as, in, with, and under the actuality of historical
flux and the forms of common life. This God may be the God whose look meets
us in the gaze of Jesus Christ. At the same time, what has been said here formally
could be interpreted in terms of the concrete historical revelations and traditions
of other traditions: the Law given at Sinai, the Koran revealed to Mohammed,
the pattern of the Buddha's path to enlightenment, the reincarnated divinity of
the supreme Lamas—these too could, arguably, be examples of God becoming in
some way memorizable in the flux of historical time and being-there for human
beings in their social being. The question as to the respective adequacy of such
differing and potentially conflicting memories of God is, of course, a question
pointing far beyond the scope of the present study.

When we think of God in terms of the formal characteristics of non-
technological thinking, we are thus able to do so as of a power 'not ourselves'
who bestows an original gift of freedom that is renewed in the face of many and
(to us) irretrievable failures, holding open possibilities foreclosed by our 'enframing' of our given world and breathing spiritual meaning into the emptiness of our
stuttering attempts to articulate our ultimate concerns. This God is also to be
thought of as one who holds us answerable for the manner in which we care for
truth and justice in real historical time, bestowing signs of being with us and
amongst us that not only allow us to commit ourselves to one or other concrete
form of active remembrance but that call on us to do so.

Postscript: City of the Homeless

In a celebrated passage, now heavy with unintended pathos, Michel de Certeau wrote of the experience of looking down on Manhattan from the 107th floor of the World Trade Center. He described how, from this elevation, the seething chaotic turbulence of the city 'freezes under our gaze'. The viewer's 'altitude transforms him into a voyeur. It places him at a distance. It changes an enchanting world into a text. It allows him to read it, to become a solar Eye, a god's regard. The exaltation of a scopic or a Gnostic drive. Just to be this seeing point creates the fiction of knowledge.'[1] Such vision does not—did not—give the voyeur real insight into the multitudinous activities and relationships that constitute the 'truth' of New York, however. His 'god's regard' was, as de Certeau clearly implies, a self-deception, a 'fiction of knowledge'. Nevertheless, just this view was a consummate epitome of a centuries' long development in the direction of what, in the expression of the Danish urbanologist Martin Zerlang, can be called 'the city spectacular'. From an amalgam of social and architectural relationships built around trade and power, the modern city has emerged as a complex of constantly shifting spectacles. The mazes of winding streets and impenetrable, almost subterranean labyrinths of the overcrowded conglomerations of Europe's medieval cities were, from the seventeenth century onwards, systematically cleared and replaced with the avenues, boulevards, squares, palaces, parks, museums, and malls that enabled the imperial powers to celebrate their military triumphs, display their wealth, and entertain their peoples.

It is not hard to see in this process a repetition in modern terms of the transformation of the Hellenic polis into the Hellenistic city, as described by Lewis Mumford:

The Hellenistic city perfected its busy, orderly, but inwardly anxious and unbalanced life, with its intellectual branches proliferating in every direction, its arts flowering in many vivid colors—and its deeper human roots drying up. In quantitative terms, all these improvements were immense, indeed staggering. The new scale applied alike to political power, to intellectual ability, to superficial esthetic attractiveness: but it framed a social and personal emptiness that mere numbers could not fill . . . perhaps its greatest function was to serve as an arena for massive shows: a container for spectacles. This emphasis on

---

[1] M. de Certeau, 'Walking in the City', in G. Ward (ed.), *The Certeau Reader* (Oxford: Blackwell, 2000), 101–2. See also C. Prendergast, *Paris and the Nineteenth Century* (Oxford: Blackwell, 1995), ch. 3, 'The High View: Three Cityscapes'.

the spectator, this treatment of life itself as a spectacle . . . was uppermost: rich and poor, noble and low, were now united in that role.[2]

This city of spectacles is also, as we learned from Harvey Cox, both the 'secular city' and 'technopolis'. It is secular, not because its citizens are godless—they may or may not be—but because it is no longer organized around the shrines, rituals, and calendars of religion. It is not—as in the vision of Catholic romanticism—centred visually, socially, and culturally as well as religiously on the life of the Cathedral rising literally and metaphorically above its hovels, nor does it attempt to realize on earth some heavenly prototype of the eternal city. If it allows for religious practice and even allows the religious form of the spectacle to take its turn in the cycle of great public events (think of the funeral of Diana, Princess of Wales), this is only one stopping point in a sequence of spectacular events that span every form of human interest and imagination capable of claiming the right to public representation.

To say that the city is in its most basic rhythms a 'technopolis' is no less important and arguably more informative than simply to say that it is secular. And here there seems to be a clear difference between the modern city and its Hellenistic predecessor. For the spectacles of the modern city are not just the great crowd events in which flag-waving multitudes line the streets or fill the stadiums, they are also the spectacles made possible by the transformations of visual experience itself through modern technology. We have already heard from Benjamin concerning what he regarded as the epochal shift in aesthetic sensibility brought about by the advent of photography and, above all, the cinema, but these phenomena themselves are best seen as particular developments within a long-term process of changing modes of visual representation and culture and of the emergence of a culture of spectatorship or voyeurism. From the *camera obscura* of the Renaissance, through the panoramas of the Age of Enlightenment, and on into the magic lanterns, dioramas, 'dissolving views', cosmoramas, stereoscopes, daguerreotypes, zoetropes of the nineteenth century, the cultural ground for the advent of photography, cinema, and virtual reality was well-prepared. In this new visual environment it was not only God who gave up his dwelling place 'out there'. For the one whom Jonathan Crary has called 'the new kind of observer' and who appeared in the early modern period, the world itself ceased to be an objective and stable point of reference for visual representation but, instead, became dependent on the perspective, point of view, or angle of vision of the observer.[3] This observer was supremely at home in the new urban environments

[2] L. Mumford, *The City in History: Its Origins, its Transformations, and its Prospects* (London: Secker and Warburg, 1961), 199–201. Of course, one might conjecture that Mumford is consciously or unconsciously rewriting the story of the ancient city in the light of his interpretation of its modern relative.

[3] See J. Crary, *Techniques of the Observer: On Vision and Modernity in the Nineteenth Century* (Cambridge, Mass.: MIT Press, 1990).

that hosted the new technologies of vision—pleasure gardens and resorts, zoos, museums and galleries, shopping arcades and, of course, theatres and entertainments of various kinds. No less important were travel and tourism, as the cities of the whole world became accessible for the multiplication of spectacular experiences once one had tired of one's own, and as the Alps and other wildernesses ceased to be regarded with dread or horror (or, in the case of Hegel, simple boredom) and became the providers of sublime experiences. If, for us, so much of the nineteenth-century's urban culture has become tame (what is the Eiffel Tower alongside Chicago's Sears Tower or Seattle's Space Needle?), we need to remember just how startling the novelty of these multiple revelations was—when shops first began to experiment with window displays in Copenhagen the police had to be called to control the over-excited crowds!

Despite London having pioneered the modern idea of a world-city in the eighteenth century, it was Paris that, as 'the capital of the nineteenth century', became the laboratory, meeting place and breeding ground for the virtuosi of the new vision, the flâneurs, showmen and showgirls, poets, writers, and artists who created and recorded its *tableaux*, labyrinths, 'impressions', and crowds—as well as its *ennuis*, absinthe drinkers, and prostitutes. A new way of urban being had come into existence that the twentieth century was to extend and to exploit to the full by means of the new media of mass communication bequeathed to it by the nineteenth century and, finally, through its own inventions of television, the internet, and the mobile phone. Now, as Benjamin prophesied, everyone can instantly project their own image into the universal medium of common communication. Everyone can be a star for a night or, at least, for fifteen minutes.

Nothing would seem easier than to interpret a society thus devoted to the spectacular image in terms of the Heideggerian category of 'enframing', a self-presentation that always takes care to package the required image in such a way that only what falls within the designated frame gets to appear in the finished message or experience. Nor is Heidegger's own aversion to the city (best documented in connection with his declining a chair in Berlin in favour of continuing to live and work amongst the farmers of the Todtnauberg) irrelevant in this respect. However, as his comments in 1961 about the way in which even a sleepy little Black Forest town like his native Meßkirch was being drawn inevitably into the global communications network indicated, he recognized that one of the most significant achievements of technopolis is precisely to eliminate the difference between town and country. Today everywhere is potentially a part of the one pulsating technopolitan web. Even the wildernesses, so popular with television film-makers and tourists, are a part of the scene.

In connection with this, it is also possible to see the city as the gravitational centre of the movement Heidegger describes as 'planetary homelessness'. It is not simply that the economic power concentrated in the great urban centres makes them the destinations of choice for the legal and illegal immigrants, the refugees and the economic migrants whose ceaseless and turbulent flow is one of the most striking phenomena of contemporary life. The wealth of the cities is, indeed, a powerful agent in uprooting established communities and linking the remotest provinces to the relentless economic activity of a world underway to globalization. But no less important in this respect is the situation that the city is no longer defined merely by its geographical boundaries, as if at such and such a point on the road one entered the city. Not only does the fact that the travellers are on the road at all indicate that they are already in one way or another involved in the dynamics of cosmotechnopolis, but they had probably fallen under its spell long before they got into the bus, car, train, or plane at the beginning of their journey. Recall that the focus for Heidegger's remarks about planetary homelessness in the Meßkirch address was his observation that every roof in the little town now sported its own television antenna. As he saw it this meant that even when we are at home, we are no longer really at home. A family sitting around the fireplace is something very different from a family sitting around the television. Of course, the former will talk about things they have seen or done or imagined that have happened or that will happen elsewhere, whether down the street or across the ocean, but, Heidegger implies, there is a qualitative shift between this kind of conversation and what happens in the moment when the television is switched on. Then we ourselves are in a very tangible sense elsewhere—in the television studio, in the sports arena, in the front line of the war, or in the past, present, or future imaginary world of drama, film, and soap opera. Suddenly and for a few weeks we are more conscious of the names of a few towns in central Iraq than of those in the neighbouring county—before the focus of televisual interest moves on and we immediately forget them again. No longer rooted to the rounds and rhythms of our actual place in the world, we move backwards and forwards across the surface of the planet, into its depths and out into space, in a constantly expanding virtual universe that lives and has its being only as and by grace of its sustaining technology. Although it would verge on the obscene to compare the mobility of the rich and the middle classes with the enforced migrations of the dispossessed and persecuted, it is no coincidence that in recent years theologians have rediscovered such categories as 'God's pilgrim people' and 'wilderness wandering', whilst other theorists have spoken of nomads, outlaws, or 'Indians';[4] nor should we forget Heidegger's description of the great thinkers of Western philosophy as fugitives from the tempestuous current that was let loose in Socratic thinking. This is indeed a situation of total mobilization, the city of the homeless.

It is not difficult to take this kind of analysis as the basis for a moral or religious condemnation of the contemporary city as 'mere' appearance, as a collective addiction to a world of images that are more and more superficial, making us ever

---

[4] Unfortunately, the kind of place that members of the academy hold in the overall structure of geopolitics suggests that it would be more realistic if they saw themselves as gunslingers and pirates rather than as the 'victims' of rootlessness. However, for all the popularity of Nietzsche amongst contemporary theorists, most would seem to prefer the role of victim to that of warrior.

more incapable of grasping and taking responsibility for the real and pressing contradictions pulsing beneath the glittering surface of the urban spectacle: poverty, crime, drugs, porno, and, with dreadful regularity, war. Was it not a sign of the times when, in 1991, Baudrillard declared the First Gulf War to be a mere simulacrum, an event on TV, as if it was not really the case that thousands of Iraqi soldiers and civilians had died in the most horrible of circumstances?[5] Some commentators have similarly implied that even the city itself is no longer 'real', that it is becoming a mere simulacrum of itself, a process culminating in Las Vegas, a city that is nothing but sign and image.[6] Are we any longer capable of even distinguishing fact from fiction, of separating the spectacular image of the city from its truth? If being in New York feels like stumbling into a film set, even historic cities seem to be caught up into the same self-fictionalizing process. In this spirit, a BBC World 'Just a Minute' feature about Rome described it as 'the ultimate film set', going on to refer to the Gardens of the Villa Borghese as 'Rome's answer to Central Park'—as if even 'the eternal city' needed to be experienced as a simulacrum of the movies and the ultimate urban movie spectacle of New York. A suspicion that something like this was the case, and the symbolic potency of the World Trade Center as the supreme monument of this culture of spectacles (by no means accidentally chosen by de Certeau for his meditation on the fictional god's eye view of contemporary humanity) has doubtless influenced those who interpret the destruction of the twin towers as some kind of divine judgement, a repetition in the world of postmodernity of the fate of presumptuous Babel, impenitent Jerusalem, and Imperial Rome.[7]

This kind of typological reading of the modern city has a long history. The Lisbon earthquake of 1755 was already interpreted in such terms by some contemporary commentators. The popular historical painting of the nineteenth century openly invited parallels to be drawn between one or other more or less fantastical ancient city and the present day, whilst D. W. Griffith's 1916 film *Intolerance* made powerful typological links between modern capitalism, Jerusalem in the time of Christ, and Babylon. Such links have become almost routine at all levels of cultural production and in all art-forms. In theology—and quite apart from what we might find by trawling through the works of popular preachers—we find hints of such an analysis at many places in Kierkegaard's

---

[5] For a discussion of this assertion see, e.g. C. Norris, *Uncritical Theory: Postmodernism, Intellectuals and the Gulf War* (London: Lawrence and Wishart, 1992). I am personally entirely unclear as to whether Baudrillard's comment was meant to be taken literally or whether it was more in the way of an ironic comment on those for whom the reality was masked by the TV images.

[6] See Mark C. Taylor and José Márquez, *The Réal: Las Vegas, Nevada* (Williamstown, Mass.: Williams College Museum of Art and Massachusetts Museum of Contemporary Art, 1977). Whether Vegas is really as novel in this respect as Taylor and others maintain is a moot point. For the opposite view see my article 'Defending the City' in *Cultural Values*, 4/3 (July 2000), 339–51. Here I argue that already in, e.g. Pugin's account of contemporary architecture and Dostoevsky's Petersburg feuilletons, we can see a city designed as 'image'.

[7] One might think also of the close of Martin Scorsese's film, *Casino*, in which—to music from a Bach passion—the absurd and empty façades of Las Vegas crumble and fall.

writings,[8] but the most consistent development of the idea is, once more, in Ellul, in his study *The Meaning of the City*. According to Ellul the biblical typology of the city, condensed into the earthly 'Babylon' and God's own 'Jerusalem' provide a key to the meaning of the city that is superior to anything offered by history or the social sciences. In the history that binds these two cities we see Jerusalem itself becoming Babylon, a city that puts to death the prophets, that does not know the hour of its visitation, and that, finally, rejects the very Christ and hands him over into the hands of sinful men. This role is then, according to Ellul, taken over by Imperial Rome before being brought to systematic completion in the modern technopolis.[9] But let's not be rushed into judgement. These kinds of typologies may be effective in the pulpit or the feuilleton and they may from time to time bring to the fore issues in cultural analysis that merit attention, but they are no more than an interpretative judgement, not a statement of fact. Before we consign technopolis to the fires of destruction along with its ancestral 'types'—Babylon, Jerusalem, and Rome— let us be sure we have given some space to the other side of the case.

In the first place, it is important to hold on to the fact that the description of the modern city as technopolis, as a 'container of spectacles' is not in itself religiously or morally evaluative. If there are forms of voyeurism that do indeed lead to a diminution of the personality, and if there are also potential links between the culture of spectatorship and violence,[10] the multi-media interplay of images that defines our urban 'reality' can itself be the occasion for visions of very different kinds. De Certeau, for example, recommends coming down from the 107th floor and taking to the streets, becoming urban strollers and, in so doing, learning a very different way of seeing the city. At street level the walker escapes the illusion of the fictional overview and 'creates in the planned city a "metaphorical" city or a city in movement'.[11] But aren't such metaphorical strolls very much a part of the meaning of the city spectacular? De Certeau is clearly not thinking here of the gentleman flâneur of the nineteenth century, his lorgnette held at an elegant distance from his eyes as he squints quizzically at one or other urban 'sight', but of a far more empathetic, listening, narrative-oriented kind of urban stroller, the kind who sits down on a bench and listens to the stories of the old men and the children. But isn't this too, in its way, a gift of the visual pluralism of the city, that we can get to see it so many different ways? Kierkegaard—one of modernity's great urban strollers, who combined something both of the flâneur and of the empathetic wanderer—nicely described the imaginative freedom of this condition in his own characteristically self-mocking way:

[8] See my *'Poor Paris!' Kierkegaard's Critique of the Spectacular City* (Berlin: De Gruyter 1999).
[9] J. Ellul, *The Meaning of the City* (Grand Rapids: Eerdmans, 1970).
[10] Pattison, *'Poor Paris!'*, 39–40, 138–9.
[11] de Certeau, 'Walking in the City', 116.

My pleasures especially divide themselves up by variation. Here are two of the main variations. I regard the whole of Copenhagen as a great party. But on one day I regard myself as the host who goes and talks to all the many invitees, my dear guests; on the next day I imagine that it is some great man who is giving the party, and I am a guest. In relation to these variations I am differently dressed, greet people differently, etc. Those who know me have certainly remarked more than once that I can be fairly changeable in the way I am; but they haven't an inkling that this is the reason. If a splendid coach drives past on the day when I am imagining myself to be the host, then I greet it in a friendly manner, and imagine that it is I who have lent them the fine coach.[12]

In other words, the view from the 107th floor and the view of the backstreet stroller are so far from being incompatible that they can be seen as two sides of the same visual mobility that lies at the heart of modern urban experience. Moreover, just as soldiers and civilians really did die in the First Gulf War (as, more recently, they did in operation 'Iraq Freedom'), so too even a fantasy city such as Las Vegas will have its more ordinary 'reality' behind the façade. No city can function without its utility providers, its cleansing department, its fire brigade, its police force, its public housing, its educational institutions, and hospitals. In other words, even a city that is given over to being the image of itself is also a political entity requiring governance, with some kind of public institutions for articulating and resolving (or, it may be, failing to resolve) the issues that confront it qua polis.

Where, then, might we find places and opportunities for thinking about God within the modern city? We have already indicated some of these by implication: we could not even have spoken of Rublev's icons, for example, if these were not preserved in a public museum, requiring heating and lighting provision, plumbing and drainage, general maintenance, appropriate staffing, security, and transport access, not to mention the specialist skills of conservators and art historians and, therewith, the academy.[13] In so far as the infrastructure of urban life is also necessarily governed by the imperatives of technological management, this too has to be counted as a part of the objective context within which any intellectual, cultural, or spiritual formation can occur. In this minimal sense, then, those who would think about God have an obligation to the political life of the city and to accept the need for the kinds of skills and the kinds of structures required for the management of its sustaining technology.

That is a minimum, but not, of course, everything. Technology, as we have repeatedly seen, is not merely the external condition of contemporary life. It is under our skin, it shapes the way we see and experience both the world and ourselves. This makes it possible for us simply to be absorbed into the system of

---

[12] S. Kierkegaard, *Søren Kierkegaards Papirer*, ed. P. A. Heiberg, V. Kuhr, and E. Torsting (Copenhagen: Gyldendal, 1909–48), VI B, 225.

[13] I am, of course, avoiding the question as to whether works such as this should be in a museum at all or whether they should be returned to the churches from which they were taken during Stalin's suppression of religion.

shifting representations in such a way that we are swept along on the current and become incapable of exercising discernment concerning what we see. The images are too powerful and their changeover too rapid for us to ever really take a position in relation to them. Even in academic life, once seen in terms of a kind of seclusion from the world that enabled the scholar to puzzle over a single problem, text, or phenomenon throughout a lifetime of study, last year's project is old news and secondary literature that is more than ten years old is dropped from the reading list. We heard Benjamin's case that cinema represents the ultimate expression of technology's power thus to shape our very perceptions of what we see. The argument could very easily be extended to newer information technologies. However, I argued that we should not be seduced by Benjamin's own opinion that this entails the obliteration of the 'aura' that attached to the art of the past. Even works of film art, I suggested, can create opportunities for us to experience something at least analogous to that aura.

But if an almost infinite mobility of vision is one of the most striking phenomena of the contemporary city, this is not simply a matter of the almost infinite variety of possible points of view for the spectator qua voyeur. In writing about what it might be to 'see' the mystery that gives a needed depth to talking, speaking, and writing about God, I indicated that this vision was not a matter of some kind of static extraterrestrial point of reference but was itself a living, moving, and experiential truth. Furthermore, I suggested that it is characteristic for those visions that break open the surface continuum of perception and reveal the mystery that they involve a kind of shift or reversal, such that I begin—not yet to see as I am seen (we are most of us still far from that) but—to see myself as seen, as being more or other than what I took myself to be, someone who has been ambushed by grace, taken hostage by the Other, decentred, and relocated. This might be understood as implying that the vision involved in thinking about God is of a diametrically opposite kind to that of the visual experiences offered by the city spectacular. Isn't the latter—as epitomized in the god's eye view from the 107th floor of the World Trade Center—always defined by the fact that the human subject is the central radiant point of the perspective within which alone whatever is to show itself must appear? I think not. We do not in fact need to assume that in some way the mobility of vision nurtured by the modern city is necessarily subjectivist, more or less a mere shifting standpoint from which the same relentlessly dominating male gaze looks out over the world as a god might look out upon his creation. Instead, as I suggested with reference to Kierkegaard's not entirely frivolous experiments in perspective change, that mobility may be capable of shifts and reversals that could even go so far as to unsettle our flâneur by bringing him up close to the broken dreams and confused hopes of life at street level. There is no causal law in play here, only a matter of possibilities, of what may (subjunctively!) befall us here and there and now and then. It may—just may—happen that such shifts and reversals become the occasion for thinking about something more than how full life is of all manner of strange things (though that is not a bad thought to have); that in the moment when the continuum of visual expectation fractures or dissolves, we are moved not only to think about the immediate occasion of this disruption but about something that lies deeper... And let us note that such occasions are as almost infinite as the mobility of vision itself, and almost certainly more than we are likely to imagine. There is no available a priori taxonomy of such visions and in principle no limit to them. These occasions may come to us in reading a book, or in visiting an art gallery, or in watching a film, but they may equally come to us in hearing a child's laughter or seeing its tears, in the complaint of a fellow passenger or while drinking a beer at a pavement café, with a lover or a friend or alone, from the 107th floor of the World Trade Center or in a chance encounter on the street, in a glimpse of the sea or in a shaft of spring light. The world may really be always more than we take it to be, every moment may be heavy with possibilities we habitually neglect.

Are there nevertheless special places, special moments where we might be more likely to find such promptings to thoughts of more ultimate things? Does thinking about God not have some abiding place in which to enact its abiding remembrances? We have already spoken of the art gallery, of literature, and the cinema and, by implication of the whole range of cultural forms and activities as possible sites of such moments of awakening and self-questioning, and we have also seen in the university a place where the meaning of these questions may become the matter both of para-academic exploration and discussion and even, under certain conditions, of academic discourse itself. Yet both culture and the academy are themselves permeated by the ambiguity of their being also inseparable from the dynamics of technology in its many and varied forms. If Benjamin is correct in seeing film and, by extension, the internet as the most developed form in which even aesthetic experience is technically mediated, isn't it true of cultural life in general that it is increasingly pre-packaged, as galleries and museums (for example), funded by leading financial and industrial institutions, decide for us whether it is to be 'Sensations' or 'The Image of Christ' that define the cultural agenda of the current season, with their penumbra of publications, t-shirts and chocolate boxes, educational events, television programmes, websites, tourist deals, etc? If, despite all this, there are moments of dislocation that make even these over-determined (and usually overcrowded) events possible occasions of epiphany, can these epiphanies be more than a momentary flaring up of a light that is all too quickly reabsorbed by the relentless enframing of the city spectacle?

The question, then, is whether there are places, significant sites, that have within themselves a power to resist the transformation of our experience of them into the stuff of spectacle and mere image. What of the churches, temples, or shrines of the past, of other cultures beyond the reach of or at the very outer limit of the Western image-makers? Do we not find in such places a quality of liminality, a border that hints at something unfathomable, or, perhaps, a sense of sempiternal presence, an atmosphere that here is somewhere where 'prayer has been valid' and that thus moves us to become aware of possibilities other than those of the modern tourist's pre-packaged experience? Is there not something in the journeys we take to these holy places that separates us from the eternal recurrence of the same—whether it is simply a matter of stepping out of the noise and turmoil of the city into the stillness of a church or a journey over seas and deserts to some still 'undiscovered' monastery? Indeed, it may be like this—I have already stated that I see no a priori restriction on what may or may not be the occasion of such moments. At the same time it has to be said that the power of traditional holy places to be in some way exceptionally significant sites is being rapidly eroded by the whole complex of forces that we have focused in the concept of technology. As Malraux noted, a couple of generations ago, where the nineteenth century gathered what it could of the cultures of other times and other places into its great metropolitan museums, the twentieth century simply made the whole world over into a museum without walls in which every time and every culture became a potential exhibit. Now even the most remote holy places are accessible to the museum-goer, whether this is via the net, television, publications, or tourism. There may still be some places that refuse visitors of one or other sex or sites such as Mecca that are closed to those not of the faith or that in one way or another limit the autonomy of visitors, perhaps requiring them not to take photographs or to observe a certain dress code. But the frontiers are being rolled back inexorably. Observation suggests that visitors are more and more resistant to respecting such local requirements, whilst financial pressures more or less subtly transform the daily lives of the holy places themselves. Governments and other public bodies are increasingly taking an interventionist role in their management (which are often major sources of tourist revenue or symbols of cultural identity), further limiting their ability to be what they are. The difficulty of attempting to maintain an 'authentic tradition' when one is subject to such pressures is further compounded by the way in which the very attempt to 'prove' one's authenticity can itself become a kind of theatrical stance, an act of defiance in which living tradition, with its silent flow of change and adaptation, hardens into an empty image or is hollowed out into mere semblance, a simulacrum of itself. Yet, remember, even the most heavily packaged blockbuster exhibition *may*, for a moment, slip the bonds of its 'economy' and 'marketing strategy' and, for a moment, prove an epiphany. If the holy places of living religions are now as much a part of the museum without walls as any statue of Herakles or Zeus, the spectacularization of religion is not yet a determinate state of affairs but a process—and it is a process in which there are sufficient eddies still to allow for much that is unplanned and uninterpreted.

Am I not perhaps undervaluing the powers of resistance of the holy places? Are there not, even today, ritual activities and functions associated with them that touch the kinds of human feelings and responses that cannot become the mere stuff of the city spectacle. Are these not still, sometimes, places where our lives are marked by the limits of birth and death? Having evoked the *Heimweh* that afflicts the modern world as it is drawn relentlessly into the state of planetary homelessness, and having hinted at how, even in an idyllic out-of-the-way Black Forest town, this homelessness is making itself felt everywhere, Heidegger directed the listeners to his 1961 address in Meßkirch to a very particular place: the graveyard, or, as he put it (self-consciously using the archaic term) 'God's field'. Amongst the many things this term might suggest, he says, is the following:

> What is forever being newly sown in this field is the memory of what has been. So it is that in this field grows the remembrance of the parental house, of youth and therewith the remembrance of all the strength and energy with which its wholesome life was expended, fruitfully and abidingly, sometimes also meaningfully. We must go to meet the unhomely state that is coming upon us from our origins. Thus we confront its noise and fury with silence and reserve . . . In the midst of the unhomely we stage a return to what is homely. Such a homecoming may—if we carefully and without hurrying abide in its way—such a homecoming may ever renew itself in overtaking the powers that are snatching us into the unhomely. Through meditating upon tomorrow we awaken the wholesome power of a yesterday that has been properly understood and genuinely made our own. On such paths we first arrive at the today, which we must endure in the tension between the past and the future. Such endurance helps us to take our place in that which abides in the face of all change.[14]

Very much, perhaps, the reflections of an old man. But even in the most developed countries of the West, alongside whatever of their formal religion remains and more or less officially blessed by the churches, there is a kind of informal religion of the graveyard. With or without any clearly formed beliefs as to the state of the self 'after' death, thousands of families and individuals regularly go to tend and care for the grave of a parent, a lover or a child, perhaps at a birthday or other anniversary, to remember, and, in that remembrance find a kind of continuity with the past for which there seems to be no place in the public life of the modern world, where grief is something to be forgotten in the cause of getting on with life. But even here we can see the corrosive force of planetary homelessness at work. As families migrate, there is no one left to tend the grave. As cremation replaces burial, there is no 'place' to visit, or only one in which there is only the most minimal sense of continuity with the once living body of the loved one. Local authorities and churches are increasingly restrictive in terms of the kinds of memorials that families can erect and financial considerations inevitably limit choices. Uniform rows of standardized gravestones replace the doubtless sub-Christian but nevertheless individualized profusion of the Victorian cemetery. The ritualization of mourning is being steadily pushed back, even in the places dedicated to it. From another angle, funerary rites themselves may be falling under the spell of the spectacular, with the funeral of Diana, Princess of Wales being a striking sign of the times. This was no public 'solemnity', although—to be fair—it had its solemn moments, but a global television

---

[14] Heidegger, *Reden und Andere Zeugnisse*, 580–1.

event, graced by a one-off performance by an international mega-star. But even in the suburban crematorium, a recording of Elvis or Bowie is increasingly likely to replace an organ postlude by Bach or Elgar, or a video of the deceased may supplement the spoken words of the eulogy or sermon. These comments are not intended to be cynical, least of all to suggest that those who choose such things are less sincere than those who opt for traditional liturgies of the dead. It is simply to point out that the 'other space' of mourning is progressively being deprived of its otherness and integrated, like everything else, into the irresistible dynamics of the city spectacular. But if the Victorian necropolises can already be understood as very much a part of the great spectacle (and in such cases as the Glasgow necropolis, Highgate Cemetery, or Paris's subterranean ossuaries have become important elements in the tourist map of the city[15]), the contemporary extension of this is in the direction of its integration into an internationalized, media-defined and 'reproducible' spectacle. If the Victorian cemetery achieved a kind of monumentality, the contemporary sites of mourning betray the featurelessness of our planetary homelessness. It should once more be stressed that this does not exclude such sites from becoming a kind of holy ground on which thoughts of God are engendered—it simply means that they no longer have the distinctiveness that comes from the prioritizing of such thoughts. But this once more underlines the paradoxical outcome of the dialectics of the city spectacular: that difference, variety, and otherness are inexorably subsumed into the same and therefore less and less distinctive, even as spectacle.

In Hans Christian Andersen's novel *Only a Fiddler*, an old Jewish resident on the Danish island of Fyn dies, and his body is taken by boat to Copenhagen for burial in the Jewish cemetery. As two neighbours watch the boat departing, one of them—with reference to the legend of the Wandering Jew—pityingly remarks that these poor people are fated to be wanderers even in death. What could at that time be said of a minority is now the general condition, that even in death we have no permanent place, no ancestral shrine to link the generations in common memory. Our remains are dust to be scattered, and we leave not a trace in the world. Perhaps at this outermost point of the annihilation of the singular, however, it is also possible to detect the ripple of a counter-current, a homeward turn in the midst of homelessness: that if we are now finally to be uprooted from the historic national or familial myths of sacred land, then we have only one home left. This home is defined on the one hand by the totality of the planet itself, in its whole inorganic and organic life into which our ashes are to be absorbed, we know not where, and, on the other, by those who still, within the limits of their own mortality, remember us. It is little enough, but might not the reflection that we are nothing but a handful of elements, the dust of dead stars, and a memory that lives only as long as love, provide some kind of measure

---

[15] See, e.g. P. Ariès, tr. H. Weaver, *The Hour of Our Death* (London: Allen Lane, 1981); see also Prendergast, *Paris and the Nineteenth Century*, ch. 4, 'Paris Underground'.

against which to evaluate some of technology's wilder fantasies? No matter where we might journey in space, no matter how successfully we might upload our brain programmes or reproduce ourselves in genetically identical offprints (clones), we cannot realistically expect to come further than this: to be mortals, moving across the face of the cosmos, encompassed by an infinite space and only so capable, if indeed we are at all capable, of epiphanies that move us to think of God.

This is no great mystical secret, merely a view of ourselves from an angle other than that of technological speculation and planning. It is a vision of ourselves not as beings endowed with an endless capacity for self-transcendence but as limited and vulnerable, yet still capable of wonder, questioning, thinking. And how would it be to take such a vision of ourselves back with us into the city spectacle? In some ways it seems so much less than the flattering pictures with which that spectacle enhances our self-image, but I do not see that it makes us incapable of enjoying the city spectacle for what it's worth, conceding a relative value to every relative pleasure. Knowing that this is no abiding city but a temporary construction of mobile images exchanged between travellers always on the move, ceaselessly migrating across the surface of the planet as we also, simultaneously, journey through time, as beings of time—if this lends a certain irony to our enjoyment and our pleasures, it must surely also make us readier to accept the claims of compassion for all who share this common lot, for all who, whatever their technical power or competence, remain, after all, mortals crawling between heaven and earth.

Buddhist iconography portrays a Buddha-figure (the rotund and jocular Buddha with his sack of bountiful gifts), said to be 'entering the city with bliss-bestowing hands'. To enter the city with such thoughts on mortality and love as these may seem scarcely to qualify us for bestowing bliss. Many might say that commitment to such a *memento mori* makes us better suited to play the part of Banquo's ghost than that of a bliss-bestowing Buddha. Yet, I suggest, knowing ourselves to be but dust is a kind of release both from the compulsions of a certain way of pursuing technological projects that almost seem to promise a kind of immortality and from a certain kind of fear of these same technological projects. If, in such moments of detachment we find ourselves thinking about God, doesn't that thought fall upon us as a kind of bliss? No grand re-enchantment of the world, but a dappled pattern of enchantment on the path we travel through it. And if we are in this way far more in the way of being bliss-receivers than bliss-bestowers, the way of our receiving may also be for others an occasion of questioning and, in the space of questioning, another receiving. For us too, the first step may be not so much a vision of ourselves as other, but of others as other than we had thought, when they voluntarily or involuntarily give themselves to be seen in their finitude, fallibility and humanity. To realize the mortality of fathers, lovers, and friends breaks open the continuum of enframing to allow a kind of view of ourselves from the outside, a moment of decompression within which we might choose to resign ourselves to a world without pity, hope or fear, or, alternatively, give ourselves over to the sheer terror of the thing, or, yet again, to get a new measure of our actual possibilities and limits, think thoughts of heaven. This does not mean to fantasize about an 'other city', a City of God, perhaps, built mirror-image fashion in the catacombs of the faithful dead. There is, realistically, only the secular city, but within it are unpredictable times and spaces that have possibilities of friendship, love, hope, and dreams. From the city of the homeless there is no homecoming other than in the remembrance of the love of those we have met and loved and been loved by on the way. And love, and will love.

> And when we went into the town, he with us,
> The lurkers under doorways, murderers,
> With rags tied round their feet for silence, came
> Out of themselves to us and were with us,
> And those who hide within the labyrinth
> Of their own loneliness and greatness came,
> And those entangled in their own devices,
> The silent and the garrulous, all
> Stepped out of their own dungeons and were free.
> Reality or vision, this we have seen.
> If it had lasted but another moment
> It might have held for ever! But the world
> Rolled back into its place, and we are here,
> And all that radiant kingdom lies forlorn,
> As if it had never stirred; no human voice
> Is heard among its meadows, but it speaks
> To itself alone, alone it flowers and shines
> And blossoms for itself while time rolls on.
>
> (From *The Transfiguration*, by Edwin Muir)

Bibliography

WORKS DEALING WITH ISSUES OF SCIENCE AND TECHNOLOGY

Andersen, S., Andreasen, T. E., Niekerk, K. van K., *Bioetik som Teknologivurdering* (Århus: Center for Bioetik, Århus Universitet, 1997).

Barbour, I., *Ethics in an Age of Technology* (London: SCM Press, 1992).

Barbour, I. G., *Religion and Science: Historical and Contemporary Issues* (London: SCM Press, 1998).

Benjamin, W., 'Das Kunstwerk im Zeitalter seiner technischen Reproduzierbarkeit' (Zweite Fassung), in idem, *Gesammelte Schriften*, 1.2 (Frankfurt am Main: Suhrkamp, 1978).

Birch, C. *et al.* (eds.), *Faith, Science and the Future: Preparatory Readings for the 1979 Conference of the WCC* (Geneva: World Council of Churches, 1978).

Chardin, P. Teilhard de, *The Phenomenon of Man* (London: Collins, 1959).

—— *The Future of Man*, tr. N. Denny (London: Collins, 1964).

Clarke, W. Norris, 'Technology and Man: A Christian View', in C. Mitcham and R. Mackey (eds.), *Philosophy and Technology: Readings in the Philosophical Problems of Technology* (New York: The Free Press, 1983).

Collins, H., and Pinch, T., *The Golem at Large or What you Should Know about Technology* (Cambridge: Cambridge University Press, 1998).

Crary, J., *Techniques of the Observer: On Vision and Modernity in the Nineteenth Century* (Cambridge, Mass.: MIT Press, 1990).

Davis, E., *Techgnosis: Myth, Magic and Mysticism in an Age of Information* (New York: Harmony, 1998).

Dreyfus, H. L., *On the Internet* (London: Routledge, 2001).

Ellul, J., *The Technological Society*, tr. J. Wilkinson (London: Jonathan Cape, 1965).

—— *The Technological System*, tr. J. Neugroschel (New York: Continuum, 1980).

—— *Living Faith: Belief and Doubt in a Perilous World*, tr. P. Heinegg (New York: Harper and Row, 1983).

—— *The Technological Bluff*, tr. G. W. Bromiley (Grand Rapids: Eerdmans, 1990).

Fasching, D. J., 'The Dialectic of Apocalypse and Utopia in the Theological Ethics of Jacques Ellul', in F. Ferré (ed.), *Technology and Religion: Research in Philosophy and Technology*, vol. 10 (Greenwich, Conn.: JAI Press, 1990).

Ferguson, F., *Technology at the Crossroads: The Story of the Society, Religion and Technology Project* (Edinburgh: St. Andrew's Press, 1994).

Feyerabend, P., *Against Method* (London: Verso, 1988).

Fukuyama, F., *Our Posthuman Future* (London: Profile Books, 2002).

Grant, G., *The George Grant Reader*, ed. W. Christensen and S. Grant (Toronto: University of Toronto Press, 1998).

Guardini, R., *Letters from Lake Como: Explorations in Technology and the Human Race*, tr. G. W. Bromiley (Grand Rapids: Eerdmans, 1994).

Habermas, J., *Technik und Wissenschaft als 'Ideologie'* (Frankfurt am Main: Suhrkamp, 1969).

—— *Die Zukunft der Menschlichen Natur* (Frankfurt am Main: Suhrkamp, 2001).

Haraway, Donna J., *Simians, Cyborgs and Women: The Reinvention of Nature* (London: Free Association Press, 1991).

Harris, J., *Wonderwoman and Superman: The Ethics of Human Biotechnology* (Oxford: Oxford University Press, 1992).

Hawkin, David J., *Christ and Modernity: Christian Self-Understanding in a Technological Age, SR Supplements*, vol. 17 (Ontario: Wilfred Laurier University Press, 1985).

Hayles, N. Katherine, *How We became Posthuman: Virtual Bodies in Cybernetics, Literature and Informatics* (Chicago: Chicago University Press, 1999).

Hefner, P., *The Human Factor: Evolution, Culture, and Religion* (Minneapolis: Fortress Press, 1993).

—— *Technology and Human Becoming* (Minneapolis: Fortress Press, 2003).

Heidegger, M., *Poetry, Language, Thought*, tr. A. Hofstadter (New York: Harper and Row, 1971).

—— *The Question Concerning Technology*, tr. W. Lovitt (New York: Harper and Row, 1977).

Jonas, H., 'The Seventeenth Century and After: The Meaning of the Scientific and Technological Revolution', in idem, *Philosophical Essays: From Ancient Creed to Technological Man* (Chicago: University of Chicago Press, 1974).

Kemp, P., *Det Uerstattelige: En Teknologi-Etik* (Viborg: Spektrum, 1991), German translation: *Das Unersetzliche: Eine teknologie-etik* (Berlin: Wichern, 1992).

Kemp. S., *Future Face: Image, Identity, Innovation* (London: Profile Books, 2004).

Marcuse, H., *Technology, War and Fascism*, in D. Kellner (ed.), *Collected Papers of Herbert Marcuse*, vol 1 (London: Routledge, 1998).

Moltmann, J., *Science and Wisdom*, tr. M. Kohl (London: SCM Press, 2003).

Mumford, L., *Technics and Civilization* (London: Routledge, 1934).

—— *The Myth of the Machine: Technics and Human Development* (New York: Harcourt, Brace and World, 1966, 1967).

Myerson, G., *Heidegger, Habermas and the Mobile Phone* (London: Icon Books, 2000).

Newbury, A., D'Aquili, E., and Rause, V., *Why God Won't Go Away: Brain Science and the Biology of Belief* (New York: Ballantine Books, 2001, 2002).

O'Donovan, O., *Begotten or Made?* (Oxford: Clarendon Press, 1984).

O'Neill, O., *Autonomy and Trust in Bioethics* (Cambridge: Cambridge University Press, 2002).

Ong, W., *Orality and Literacy: The Technologizing of the Word* (London: Methuen, 1982).

Pattison, G., *The Routledge GuideBook to The Later Heidegger* (London: Routledge, 2000).

Peacocke, A., *Theology for a Scientific Age: Being and Becoming—Natural, Divine and Human* (Oxford: Basil Blackwell, 1990).

Persinger, M. A., *The Neuropsychological Bases of God Beliefs* (New York: Praeger, 1987).

—— 'Experimental Stimulation of the God Experience', in R. Joseph (ed.), *NeuroTheology: Brain, Science, Spirituality, Religious Experiences* (Berkeley: California University Press, 2002), 279–93.

Polkinghorne, J., *Science and Creation: The Search for Understanding* (London: SPCK, 1988).

Roy, R., *Experimenting with Truth: The Fusion of Religion with Technology, Needed for Humanity's Survival* (Oxford: Pergamon Press, 1981).

Schulze, Q. J., *Habits of the Hi-Tech Heart: Living Virtuously in an Information Age* (Grand Rapids: Baker Academic Press, 2002).

Taylor, Mark C., *The Moment of Complexity: Emerging Network Culture* (Chicago: University of Chicago Press, 2001).

Tillich, P., ed. M. J. Thomas, *The Spiritual Situation in our Technical Society* (Macon, Ga.: Mercer University Press, 1988).

Virilio, P., *The Information Bomb* (London: Verso, 2000).

White, L., 'The Historical Roots of Our Ecologic Crisis', *Science*, 155(10 March 1967).

OTHER WORKS CITED

Adorno, T. W., 'Parataxis', in *Gesammelte Schriften*, ii. *Noten zur Literatur* (Frankfurt am Main: Suhrkamp, 1947).

—— *The Jargon of Authenticity*, tr. K. Tarnowski and F. Will (London: Routledge and Kegan Paul, 1986).

Altizer, T. J. J., and Hamilton, W., *Radical Theology and the Death of God* (Harmondsworth: Penguin, 1968).

Alves, R. M., *A Theology of Human Hope* (Washington: Corpus, 1969).

Ameriks, K. (ed.), *Cambridge Companion to German Idealism* (Cambridge: Cambridge University Press, 2000).

Anon., *The Cloud of Unknowing*, tr. C. Wolters (Harmondsworth: Penguin, 1961).

Apollonio, U. (ed.), *Futurist Manifestos* (London: Thames and Hudson, 1973).

Ariès, P., *The Hour of our Death*, tr. H. Weaver (London: Allen Lane, 1981).

Asals, H., *Equivocal Predication: George Herbert's Way to God* (Toronto: University of Toronto Press, 1981).

Bakhtin, M., *Problems of Dostoevsky's Poetics* (Minneapolis: University of Minneapolis Press, 1984).

Bal, M., 'Postmodern Theology as Cultural Analysis', in G. Ward (ed.), *The Blackwell Companion to Postmodern Theology* (Oxford: Blackwell, 2001).

Barbour, R., *Literature and Religious Culture in Seventeenth-Century England* (Cambridge: Cambridge University Press, 2002).

Barth, K., *Church Dogmatics*, 1.1, tr. G. W. Bromiley (Edinburgh: T.& T. Clark, 1975).

Beistegui, M. de, *Heidegger and the Political Dystopias* (London: Routledge, 1998).

Berdyaev, N., *The Fate of Man in the Modern Age*, tr. D. Lowrie (London: SCM Press, 1935).

—— *The Destiny of Man*, tr. N. Duddington (London: Geoffrey Bles, 1937).

—— *The Meaning of the Creative Act*, tr. D. Lowrie (London: Gollancz, 1955 [1912]).

Bloch, E., *Das Prinzip Hoffnung, Gesamtausgabe*, vol. 5 (Frankfurt am Main: Suhrkamp, 1959).

Blond, P., *Post-Secular Philosophy: Between Philosophy and Theology* (London: Routledge, 1998).

Brueggemann, W., *The Land: Place as Gift, Promise and Challenge in Biblical Faith* (Philadelphia: Fortress Press, 1982).

Bruns, G. L., *Heidegger's Estrangements: Language, Truth and Poetry in the Later Writings* (Newhaven: Yale University Press, 1981).

Buber, M., 'Religion and Modern Thinking', in idem, *The Eclipse of God: Studies in the Relation between Religion and Philosophy* (London: Victor Gollancz, 1953).

—— *I and Thou*, tr. W. Kaufmann (Edinburgh: T. & T. Clark, 1970).

—— *The Tales of Rabbi Nachman*, tr. M. Friedman (New York: Humanity Books, 1974).

Caputo, J. D., *Demythologizing Heidegger* (Bloomington: Indiana University Press, 1993).

—— *The Prayers and Tears of Jacques Derrida: Religion without Religion* (Bloomington: Indiana University Press, 1997).

—— *On Religion* (London: Routledge, 2001).

—— and Scanlon, M. J. (eds.), *God, the Gift and Postmodernism* (Bloomington: Indiana University Press, 1999).

Certeau, M. de, 'Walking in the City', in G. Ward (ed.), *The Certeau Reader* (Oxford: Blackwell, 2000).

Chestov, L., *Kierkegaard et la philosophie existentielle* (Paris: Vrin, 1972 [1936]).

Clayton, P., *The Problem of God in Modern Thought* (Grand Rapids: Eerdmans, 2000).

Congar, Y., *Tradition and Traditions: An Historical and a Theological Essay* (London: Burns and Oates, 1966).

Coward H., and Foshay, T. (eds.), *Derrida and Negative Theology,* (Albany: State University of New York Press, 1992).

Cox, H., *The Secular City. A Celebration of its Liberties and an Invitation to its Discipline* (New York, Macmillan, 1965).

—— *The Seduction of Spirit: The Use and Misuse of People's Religion* (New York: Simon and Schuster, 1973).

Cupitt, D., *Taking Leave of God* (London: SCM Press, 1980).

—— *Life-Lines* (London: SCM Press, 1986).

—— *The Long-Legged Fly: A Theology of Language and Desire* (London: SCM Press, 1987).

—— *The Religion of Being* (London: SCM Press, 1998).

—— *Emptiness and Brightness* (Santa Rosa, Calif.: Polebridge Press, 2001).

Daly, M., *Gyn/Ecology: The Metaethics of Radical Feminism* (Boston: Beacon Press, 1978).

Davies, O., *A Theology of Compassion* (London: SCM Press, 2001).

Derrida, J., *In the Margins of Philosophy,* tr. A. Bass (Chicago: University of Chicago Press, 1982).

—— *Acts of Religion* (London: Routledge, 2001).

—— and Vattimo, G. (eds), *Religion* (Cambridge: Polity Press, 1998).

Dionysius, Pseudo-, *The Complete Works*, tr. C. Luibheid (New York: Paulist Press, 1987).

Dostoevsky, F., *Notes from Underground*, tr. R. Pevear and L. Volkhonsky (London: Vintage, 1993).

Eckhart, Meister, *Sermons and Treatises*, vol. 1, tr. and ed. M. O'C. Walshe (Shaftesbury: Element, 1979).

Ellul, J., *The Meaning of the City* (Grand Rapids: Eerdmans, 1970).

—— *Hope in Time of Abandonment*, tr. C. E. Hopkins (New York: Seabury Press, 1973).

Ferreira, J., *Transforming Vision: Imagination and Will in Kierkegaardian Faith* (Oxford: Clarendon Press, 1991).

Florensky, P., *The Pillar and Ground of the Truth*, tr. B. Jakim (Princeton: Princeton University Press, 1997).

Ford, D., *Self and Salvation: Being Transformed* (Cambridge: Cambridge University Press, 1998).

Forman, Robert K. (ed.), *The Problem of Pure Consciousness: Mysticism and Philosophy* (New York: Oxford University Press, 1990).

Fóti, V. M., *Heidegger and the Poets: Poiésis: Sophia: Techné* (Atlantic Highlands, NJ: Humanities Press, 1992).

Fox, M., *Original Blessing: A Primer in Creation Spirituality* (Santa Fe: Bear, 1983).

—— *The Coming of the Cosmic Christ: The Healing of Mother Earth and the Birth of a Global Renaissance* (San Francisco: Harper and Row, 1989).

Gill, S., 'The Academic Study of Religion', in *Journal of the American Academy of Religion*, 62/4 (1994), Special issue: *Settled Issues and Neglected Questions in the Study of Religion*, 965–75.

Glebe-Møller, J., *Jürgen Habermas: En Protestantisk Filosof* (Copenhagen: Gyldendal 1996).

Grønkjær (ed.), *The Return of God: Theological Perspectives in Contemporary Philosophy* (Odense: Odense University Press, 1998).

Habermas, J., *Theorie des kommunikativen Handelns* (Frankfurt am Main: Suhrkamp, 1981).

—— *Glauben und Wissen* (Frankfurt am Main: Suhrkamp, 2001).

Hardy, F., *Viraha-Bhakti: The Early History of Kṛṣṇa Devotion in South India* (New Delhi: Oxford University Press, 1983).

Hart, K., *The Trespass of the Sign: Deconstruction, Theology and Philosophy* (Cambridge: Cambridge University Press, 1989).

Hegel, G. W. F., *Vorlesungen über die Geschichte der Philosophie II*, xix. (Frankfurt am Main: Suhrkamp, 1971).

—— *Frühe Schriften*, i. (Frankfurt am Main: Suhrkamp, 1971).

Heidegger, M., *Vorträge und Aufsätze* (Pfullingen: Neske, 1954).

—— *What is a Thing?*, tr. W. B. Barton and V. Deutsch (Chicago: Henry Regnery, 1967).

—— *What is Called Thinking?*, tr. F. D. Wieck and J. Glenn Gray (New York: Harper and Row, 1968).

—— *Identity and Difference*, tr. J. Stambaugh, Dual language edition (New York: Harper and Row, 1969).

—— 'Einige Hinweise auf Hauptgesichtspunkte für das theologische Gespräch: Das Problem eines nichtobjektivierenden Denken und Sprechen in der heutigen Theologie', in idem, *Phänomenologie und Theologie* (Frankfurt am Main: Vittorio Klostermann, 1970).

—— *The Question of Being*, tr. W. Kluback and J. T. Wilde, Dual language edition (London: Vision, 1974).

—— *Hölderlins Hymne 'Andenken', Gesamtausgabe*, 52 (Frankfurt am Main: Vittorio Klostermann, 1982).

—— *Hölderlins Hymne 'Der Ister', Gesamtausgabe*, 53 (Frankfurt am Main: Vittorio Klostermann, 1984).

Heidegger, M., *Nietzsche: The Will to Power as Knowledge and as Metaphysics*, ed. D. F. Krell, various translators (New York: Harper & Row, 1987).

—— *The Fundamental Concepts of Metaphysics*, tr. J. McNeill and N. Walker (Bloomington: Indiana University Press, 1995).

—— *Was Heisst Denken?* (Tübingen: Niemeyer, 1997).

—— *Reden und Andere Zeugnisse eines Lebensweges, Gesamtausgabe*, 16 (Frankfurt am Main: Vittorio Klostermann, 2000).

Herbert, G., *George Herbert's Works in Prose and Verse*, vol. 2 (London: William Pickering, 1848).

Hick, J. (ed.), *The Myth of God Incarnate* (London: SCM Press, 1977).

Hobson, T., *The Rhetorical Word: Protestant Theology and the Rhetoric of Authority* (Aldershot: Ashgate, 2002).

Hügel, Fr. von, 'The Facts and Truths concerning God and the Soul which are of Most Importance in the Life of Prayer', in idem, *Essays and Addresses on the Philosophy of Religion*, (Second series) (London: Dent, 1930).

Humboldt, W. von, 'Ueber die innere und äussere Organisation der höheren wissenschaftlichen Anstalten in Berlin', in *Werke in Fünf Bänden*, vol. 4 (Stuttgart: Cotta, 1964).

Husserl, E., *Logische Untersuchungen* (Tübingen: Max Niemeyer, 1993).

Hyman, G., *Journal of Literature and Theology*, 12 (1998).

—— *The Predicament of Postmodern Theology: Radical Orthodoxy or Textual Nihilism?* (Louisville: Westminster John Knox Press, 2002).

Jonas, H., 'Heidegger and Theology', in idem, *The Phenomenon of Life: Toward a Philosophical Biology* (Chicago: Chicago University Press, 1966).

Kearney, R., *The God Who May Be: A Hermeneutics of Religion* (Bloomington: Indiana University Press, 2001).

Kee, A., *The Way of Transcendence: Christian Faith without Belief in God* (Harmondsworth: Penguin, 1971).

Kent, J., *The End of the Line: The Development of Christian Theology in the Last Two Centuries* (London: SCM Press, 1982).

Keulartz, J., *Die Verkehrte Welt des Jürgen Habermas*, tr. I. van der Art (Hamburg: Junius, 1995).

Kierkegaard, S., *Søren Kierkegaards Papirer*, ed. P. A. Heiberg, V. Kuhr, and E. Torsting (Copenhagen: Gyldendal, 1909–48).

—— *Samlede Værker* (Copenhagen: Gyldendal, 1962).

—— *The Sickness unto Death*, tr. H. V. and E. H. Hong (Princeton: Princeton University Press, 1980).

—— *Eighteen Upbuilding Discourses*, tr. H. V. and E. H. Hong (Princeton: Princeton University Press, 1990 [1844]).

Lacoue-Labarthe, P., *Heidegger, Art and Politics*, tr. C. Turner (Oxford: Blackwell, 1990).

Lévinas, E., *Autrement qu'être ou au-delà de l'essence* (Paris: Livre de Poche/Kluwer Academic, 2001).

Lewis, C. S., *The Abolition of Man, or, Reflections on Education with Special Reference to the Teaching of English in the Upper Forms of Schools* (London: G. Bles, 1947).

—— *That Hideous Strength: A Modern Fairy-Tale for Grown-ups* (London: Pan, 1955).

Little, J. P., 'Simone Weil's Concept of Decreation', in R. Bell (ed.), *Simone Weil's Philosophy of Culture: Readings Towards a Divine Humanity* (Cambridge: Cambridge University Press, 1993).

Lowance, M. I., Jr., *The Language of Canaan: Metaphor and Symbol in New England from the Puritans to the Transcendentalists* (Cambridge, Mass.: Harvard University Press, 1980).

Löwith, K., *Heidegger: Denker in dürftiger Zeit* in *Sämtliche Schriften*, vol. 8, (Stuttgart: J. B. Metzger, 1984).

Marcel, G., *Men Against Humanity*, tr. G. S. Fraser (London: Harvill Press, 1952).

Marcuse, H., *Eros and Civilization: A Philosophical Enquiry into Freud* (London: Routledge and Kegan Paul, 1956).

—— *The Aesthetic Dimension: Toward a Critique of Marxist Aesthetic* (Boston: Beacon Press, 1978).

Marion, J.-L.,*God without Being: Hors-texte*, tr. T. A. Carlson (Chicago: University of Chicago Press, 1991).

—— *Reduction and Givenness: Investigations of Husserl, Heidegger, and Phenomenology*, tr. T. A. Coulson (Evanston: Northwestern University Press, 1998).

Maritain, J., *The Degrees of Knowledge*, tr. B. Wall and M. Anderson (London: G. Bles, 1937).

McFague, S., *The Body of God: An Ecological Theology* (London: SCM Press, 1993).

Merleau-Ponty, M., 'Eye and Mind', in J. O. Neill (ed.), *Phenomenology, Language and Sociology* (London: Heinemann, 1974).

Merton, T., *Contemplative Prayer* (London: Darton, Longman and Todd, 1969).

Milbank, J., *The Word Made Strange: Theology, Language, Culture* (Oxford: Blackwell, 1997).

Moltmann, J., *God in Creation. An Ecological Doctrine of Creation*, tr. M. Kohl (London: SCM Press, 1985).

Mumford, L., *The City in History: Its Origins, its Transformations, and its Prospects* (London: Secker and Warburg, 1961).

Naipaul, V. S., *Among the Believers: An Islamic Journey* (London: Deutsch, 1981).

Newman, J. H., *The Office and Work of Universities* (London, 1859).

—— *The Idea of a University* (New York: Image Books, 1959 [1853]).

Nishitani, K., *Religion and Nothingness* (Berkeley and Los Angeles: University of California Press, 1982).

Norris, C., *Uncritical Theory: Postmodernism, Intellectuals and the Gulf War* (London: Lawrence and Wishart, 1992).

Ott, H., *Denken und Sein: Der Weg Martin Heideggers und der Weg der Theologie* (Basel: Zollikon, 1959).

—— *Wirklichkeit und Glaube* (Göttingen and Zürich: Vandenhoeck and Ruprecht, 1969).

—— *Gott* (Stuttgart: Kreuz, 1971).

Ouspensky, L. and Lossky, V., *The Meaning of Icons*, tr. G. E. H. Palmer and E. Kadloubovsky (Crestwood New York: St. Vladimir's Seminary Press, 1983).

Patrick, D. G. M., *Pascal and Kierkegaard: A Study in the Strategy of Evangelism* (London: Lutterworth Press, 1947).

Pattison, G., *Agnosis: Theology in the Void* (Basingstoke: Macmillan, 1996).

Pattison, G., *Art, Modernity and Faith* (London: SCM Press, 1998).

—— *The End of Theology—And the Task of Thinking about God* (London: SCM Press, 1998).

—— *'Poor Paris!' Kierkegaard's Critique of the Spectacular City* (Berlin: De Gruyter 1999).

—— 'Defending the City', in *Cultural Values*, 4/3 (July 2000), 339–51.

—— *Short Course in the Philosophy of Religion* (London: SCM Press, 2001).

Pattison, S., *The Faith of the Managers* (London: Cassell, 1997).

Phillips, D. Z., *Religion Without Explanation* (Oxford: Basil Blackwell, 1976).

Pohier, J., *God—in Fragments*, tr. J. Bowden (New York: Crossroad, 1986).

Prendergast, C., *Paris and the Nineteenth Century* (Oxford: Blackwell, 1995).

Rivers, I., *Reason, Grace and Sentiment: A Study of the Language of Religion and Ethics in England 1660–1780*, i. *Whichcote to Wesley* (Cambridge: Cambridge University Press, 1991).

Robinson, J. A. T., *Honest to God* (London: SCM Press, 1963).

—— and Edwards, D. L. (eds.), *The Honest to God Debate* (London: SCM Press, 1963).

Rudd, A., *Expressing the World: Skepticisim, Wittgenstein, and Heidegger* (Chicago: Open Court, 2003).

Ruether, R. R., *Gaia and God: An Ecofeminist Theology of Earth Healing* (London: SCM Press, 1992).

Ruskin, J., *The Queen of the Air* (London: George Allen, 1904).

Samtire, H. Paul, *brother earth: nature, God and ecology in the time of crisis* (New York: Camden, 1979).

Schelling, F. W. J., *Philosophische Untersuchungen über das Wesen der menschlichen Freiheit und die damit zusammenhängenden Gegenstände* (Frankfurt am Main: Suhrkamp, 1975 [1809]).

Schleiermacher, F. D. E., 'Universitätsschriften', in *Kritische Gesamtausgabe*, 6/1 (Berlin: De Gruyter, 1998).

Schopenhauer, A., *The World as Will and Representation*, vol 7, tr. E. F. J. Payne (New York: Dover, 1966).

Schrift, A. D. (ed.), *The Logic of the Gift: Towards an Ethic of Generosity* (London: Routledge, 1997).

Sells, M. A., *Mystical Languages of Unsaying* (Chicago: University of Chicago Press, 1994).

Slesinski, R., *Pavel Florensky: A Metaphysics of Love* (New York: St. Vladimir's Seminary Press, 1984).

Smith, R. G., *Secular Christianity* (London: Collins, 1966).

Sparrow, J., *Mark Pattison and the Idea of a University* (Cambridge: Cambridge University Press, 1967).

Spengler, O., *The Decline of the West*, tr. C. F. Atkinson (London: Allen and Unwin, 1922).

Summerell, Orrin F. (ed.), *The Otherness of God* (Charlottesville: University Press of Virginia, 1998).

Taylor, Mark C., *Journeys to Selfhood: Hegel and Kierkegaard* (Berkeley: University of California Press, 1980),

—— *Erring: A Postmodern A/theology* (Chicago: University of Chicago Press, 1984),

—— 'Unsettling Issues', in *Journal of the American Academy of Religion*, 62/4 (Winter 1994), Special issue: *Settled Issues and Neglected Questions in the Study of Religion*, 949–63.

Taylor, Mark C., and Márquez, José, *The Réal: Las Vegas, Nevada* (Williamstown, Mass.: Williams College Museum of Art and Massachusetts Museum of Contemporary Art, 1977).

Theunissen, M., *Der Begriff Verzweifelung. Korrekturen an Kierkegaard* (Frankfurt am Main: Suhrkamp, 1993).

Tillich, P., *The New Being* (New York: Charles Scribner, 1955).

—— *Systematic Theology* (Welwyn: Nisbet, 1968).

—— *The Courage to Be* (London: Fontana, 1971).

Tracy, D., *The Analogical Imagination: Christian Theology and the Culture of Pluralism* (London: SCM Press, 1981).

Turner, D., *The Darkness of God: Negativity in Christian Mysticism* (Cambridge: Cambridge University Press, 1995).

Unamuno, M. de, *Our Lord Don Quixote: The Life of Don Quixote and Sancho*, tr. A. Kerrigan (Princeton: Princeton University Press, 1976).

Underhill, E., *Mysticism* (London: Methuen, 1967).

van Buren, P., *The Secular Meaning of the Gospel* (Harmondsworth: Penguin, 1968).

van Leeuwen, A. Th., *Christianity in World History* (London: Edinburgh House, 1964).

Wainwright, G., *Eucharist and Eschatology* (London: Epworth Press, 1971).

Walicki, A., *Marxism and the Leap into the Kingdom of Freedom: The Rise and Fall of the Communist Utopia* (Stanford: Stanford University Press, 1995).

Ward, G. (ed.), *The Postmodern God: A Theological Reader* (Oxford: Blackwell, 1997).

Weil, S., *La Pesanteur et la Grâce* (Paris: Plon, 1948), English translation by E. Craufurd, *Gravity and Grace* (London: Ark, 1987).

Wind, H. C., *Religion og Kommunikation: Teologisk hermeneutik* (Århus: Århus University Press, 1987).

Wolin, R., *The Heidegger Controversy: A Critical Reader* (Cambridge, Mass.: MIT Press, 1993).

Yanagi, S., 'The Pure Land of Beauty', in *The Eastern Buddhist*, 9/1 (May 1976), 18–41.

—— 'The Dharma Gate of Beauty', in *The Eastern Buddhist*, 9/2 (October 1979), 18–21.

Zerlang, M., *The City Spectacular of the Nineteenth Century* (Copenhagen: Center for Urbanitet og Æstetik, Arbejdspair 9, 1995).

Zizioulas, J., *Being as Communion* (London: Darton, Longman and Todd, 1985).

Index

The topics 'thinking', 'God', and 'technology' are, in some sense, present on every page of this book and the entries under these headings can give only an external orientation concerning their place in the book as a whole.